DATE DUE

4.22		
5-10		

SCIENCE IN THE MULTICULTURAL CLASSROOM

SCIENCE IN THE MULTICULTURAL CLASSROOM

A GUIDE TO TEACHING AND LEARNING

Robertta H. Barba

University of New Mexico

Allyn and Bacon

Boston   London   Toronto   Sydney   Tokyo   Singapore

Vice President and Publisher, Education: *Nancy Forsyth*
Editorial Assistant: *Christine Nelson*
Cover Administrator: *Linda Knowles*
Composition Buyer: *Linda Cox*
Manufacturing Buyer: *Louise Richardson*
Marketing Representative: *Ellen Mann*
Production Coordinator: *Deborah Brown*
Editorial-Production Service: *P.M. Gordon Associates*
Text Designer: *Glenna Collett*
Photo Researcher: *Susan Duane*
Cover Designer: *Susan Paradise*

© 1995 by Allyn and Bacon
A Simon & Schuster Company
Needham Heights, MA 02194

Library of Congress Cataloging-in-Publication Data

Barba, Robertta H.
    Science in the multicultural classroom : a guide to teaching
and learning / Robertta H. Barba.
        p.   cm.
    Includes bibliographical references and index.
    ISBN 0–205–15105–1
    1. Science—Study and teaching (Elementary)   2. Multicultural
education.   I. Title
LB1585.B27   1995   94–14852
372.3—dc20   CIP

Printed in the United States of America
10 9 8 7 6 5 4 3 2   00 99 98 97 96 95

CONTENTS

3 | THE HISTORY OF SCIENCE: A CULTURALLY AFFIRMING PERSPECTIVE 52

PART II CONSTRUCTING A KNOWLEDGE OF SCIENCE

4 | WAYS OF KNOWING SCIENCE 70

5 GROUPS IN THE SCIENCE CLASSROOM 98

6 ASSESSING KNOWLEDGE IN THE SCIENCE CLASSROOM 122

PART III DEVELOPING PEDAGOGICAL CONTENT KNOWLEDGE

7 INSTRUCTIONAL STRATEGIES FOR CULTURALLY DIVERSE LEARNERS 154

13 SCIENCE/TECHNOLOGY/SOCIETY IN THE MULTICULTURAL CLASSROOM 320

14 GUIDING LEARNING IN THE MULTICULTURAL CLASSROOM 344

APPENDIXES

GLOSSARY

BIBLIOGRAPHY

INDEX

ACTIVITIES

PREFACE

If you are reading this book, it is highly likely that you are engaged in science-teacher preparation or enhancement activities. *Science in the Multicultural Classroom* was designed to assist you to become a reflective practitioner in the multicultural classroom. The ideas presented are grounded in constructivist theories of learning on the sociocultural construction of knowledge in the science classroom. This book emphasizes the multicultural approach to science education, a culturally affirming view of teaching and learning. In each chapter, you are encouraged to interact with the ideas of science-education researchers on strategies for addressing the needs of all children. The ideas presented will help you to become a reflective practitioner. As you read this book, you are encouraged to translate information that you are reading into classroom practice.

GETTING THE BIG PICTURE

Newly formulated national standards in science education call for involving all students in science education. Among the disciplines currently taught in our schools, science perhaps has remained the most resistant to change over the years. There exists a widespread belief among some science educators and teachers that problems of diversity pertain to other content areas, not to science education. We somehow hold the belief that science education and multiculturalism are unrelated topics. Indeed, this is not the case. The ways in which we view learners and teaching in the science classroom determine the quality of the instructional program afforded children and eventually determine the level of involvement of culturally diverse children in mainstream science activities.

The purpose of this book is to present ways for science educators to meet the needs of all children. This text is divided into four main parts:

- Addressing Diversity
- Constructing a Knowledge of Science
- Developing Pedagogical Content Knowledge
- Teaching through Thematic Units

Addressing Diversity deals with issues germane to the science education needs of culturally diverse learners. This part contains discussions of equity issues, the nature of science, motivational strategies, and the history of science from the viewpoint of culturally diverse learners. Constructing a Knowledge of Science contains a discussion of ways in which children learn and means for facilitating the academic growth of all children. Developing Pedagogical Content Knowledge deals with content-area specific knowledge necessary for effective science teaching. Finally, Teaching through Thematic Units presents models for integrating content areas and for presenting science as part of a unified whole.

REFLECTIVE PRACTICE

Each chapter is designed to assist you in reflecting on your teaching practice. Chapters begin with a **Graphic Organizer,** a visual representation of the knowledge structure of the chapter. The graphic organizers help you get the "big picture," an overview of the information contained in the chapter. Next, a series of questions, called **Points to Ponder,** cue you as to topics for reflective practice. These questions serve as a framework for learning, as guideposts to direct your construction of knowledge. The **Background** section of each chapter presents vignettes, case studies of classroom practice, field-based examples, and/or a summary of the science education research literature designed to provide an overview of each topic. It introduces you to authors who have contributed to our knowledge of the needs of culturally diverse learners and ways to address those needs. The **Classroom Practice** section presents practical, field-tested ways of applying the information in the chapter. Each of the activities in this section is appropriate for use with children and may be used in microteaching situations in adult education settings. This section serves as a bridge between the theoretical and classroom practice; it serves to assist you in translating research into a plan of action for addressing the needs of the children with whom you will interact. Each chapter ends with a **Chapter Summary,** which reviews the concepts that were presented; a **Topics to Review** section, which lists the concepts that were presented and encourages you to check your own understanding; and a **Reflective Practice** section, which serves as springboards for reflection and guideposts on your path toward becoming a reflective practitioner.

ACKNOWLEDGMENTS

Professionally, I am deeply grateful to my colleagues who have counseled, encouraged, coached, supported, and mentored me during the writing of this book, including: Dr. Karen E. Reynolds (San Jose State University), Dr. Peter A. Rubba (The Pennsylvania State University), Dr. Robert Stahl (Arizona State University), Dr. Sandra Marshall (Center for Research in Mathematics and Science Education at San Diego State University), Dr. Margie Kitano (Associate Dean of the College of Education at San Diego State University), Dr. Judith T. Sowder (Center for Research in Mathematics and Science Education at San Diego State University),

Dr. Patricia Grinager (retired and now living in Palo Alto, California), Dr. Ann I. Morey (Dean of the College of Education at San Diego State University), Dr. Patricia Keig (California State University, Fullerton), and Dr. Peggy Blackwell (Dean of the College of Education at The University of New Mexico). Additionally, I am deeply appreciative of Nancy Forsyth, my editor at Allyn and Bacon, for her counsel, encouragement, and patience during the writing of this manuscript.

Additionally, I am deeply grateful to my former graduate students, the teachers of the San Diego City, Poway, Chula Vista, La Mesa, and San Ysidro school districts in California for assisting me in field testing the activities mentioned in this book. Specifically, I would like to thank: Mary Anne Arabia, Deborah Ballard, Kerri Ballard, Stephanie Dahlstrom, Yvette Davis, Florence Decker, Carmen Enjambre, Leslee Fisziewicz, Kathleen Garcia-Horlor, Gay Goodenough-Campbell, Penelope Goya-Cherry, Blanca Hernandez-Stingl, Linda Hotchinson, Judith Inskeep, Coralie Larsen, Dolores Lizarraga, Socorro Martinez-Garcia, Gina Modelo, Rosalia Muhlbach-Brown, Pam Olson, Margo Peters, Sharon Quinn, Angela Rose, Jill Roth, Timothy Shaw, Whitney Smith, Kristine Shoopack, Ernest Stephenson, Michelle Whitaker, René Wilson, and Mary Woods. Thank you one and all for the hours of work that you spent trying out activities and for the wonderful feedback that you provided me.

My thanks go to the reviewers of my book: Professor Joseph Peters (The University of West Florida), Professor Frances H. Squires (Indiana University, Southeast), Professor Randall C. Stom (Shippensburg University), Professor Thomas E. Thompson (Northern Illinois University), and Professor Shirley Key (University of Houston, Missouri City).

I am deeply indebted to my husband Phillip; and to my sons, P. Javier, Aáron Miguel, and Ray, for their support and patience during the writing of this manuscript. Thank you, gentlemen, for being so understanding and so considerate; and for making do a thousand times in the past few years in order to allow me time to write and reflect.

Javie: Hopefully, for your children, science will indeed be for all Americans, not for "snowflakes." Please know that your comments, quoted in the first chapter of this book, caused your mother many a sleepless night. Thank you for telling me in a way that no one else could that science education in this Nation needs to change in order to meet the needs of all of our children.

Gracias para toda, con mucho amor.

Su madre,

R.H.B.

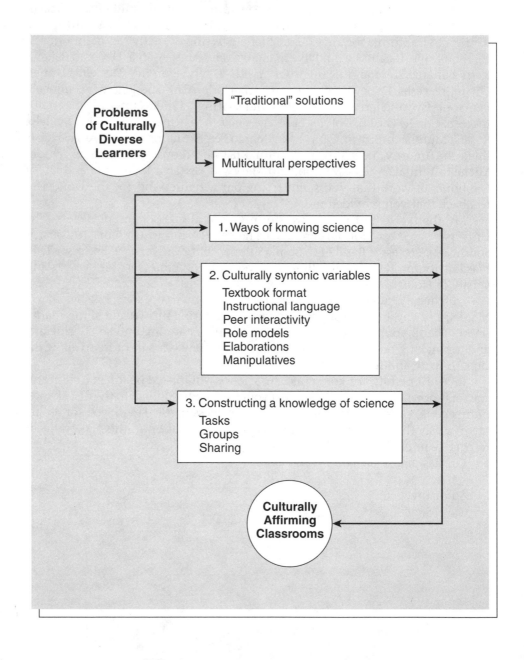

SCIENCE IN THE MULTICULTURAL CLASSROOM: AN INTRODUCTION

 POINTS TO PONDER

1. What is your personal image of science? Of scientists?
2. What factors have influenced the way(s) that you perceive science and scientists?
3. Why are some children reluctant to participate in science-related careers?
4. What can you do as a classroom teacher to make science "user friendly" for all children?

T he evening that I returned home from teaching a university class in science methods and found Javier, my number two son, preparing for high school registration will remain fixed in my memory for many years. According to Javier, he and his father had spent several hours poring over the high school course brochure and discussing his future aspirations. The two had diligently completed filling out the schedule request forms, which were to be taken back to the high school guidance counselor the next morning. Being more than a little curious about the product of their labors, I picked up one of the completed forms and began to read. "Javier, you forgot to take a science class," I yelled. Like many parents I sometimes have to compete with music videos. "Mom," responded Javier, "I don't haf' ta take science next year."

"What do you mean you don't HAVE to take science next year?" I said in my growling, motherly voice. "We only have to take two years of science in high school, and *so I'll take it my sophomore and junior years," answered Javier. For a mother who has spent her entire professional career in science education, this was not the preferred pronouncement. "But, Javier," I protested, "I thought you'd WANT to take science every year in high school." "Oh, Mom, get real!" answered Javier. "I don't like science." "Why don't you like science?" I queried. "Science is dull and boring and besides, Mom, everyone knows science is for 'snowflakes'," Javier answered.*

Javier's words have haunted me every day since that conversation. They haunt me as a parent and as a professional science educator. Certainly, I found Javier's reference to Anglos as "snowflakes" (an expression commonly used in the West Coast inner-city schools that Javier attended at that time) an intolerable racial remark, worthy of a parental tongue lashing. But while Javier's Anglo teachers would have found his remark highly offensive, to the Hispanic/Latino community of this nation, a 40% to 50% dropout rate among Hispanic teenagers is equally offensive. I have come to realize both as a parent and as a science educator that his remarks reflect the feelings of many children of color and of Anglo females who perceive the study of science and pursuit of science-related careers to be available only to members of some sort of exclusive club, one that they may view but not enter. For too long, our children have come to regard science as being a white male domain.

The purpose of this book is to present ways of teaching science that will help you as a science educator meet the needs of all of our culturally diverse learners. This text is divided into four main sections:

- *Addressing Diversity*
- *Constructing a Knowledge of Science*
- *Developing Pedagogical Content Knowledge*
- *Teaching through Thematic Units*

The first section, Addressing Diversity, deals with issues germane to the science education needs of culturally diverse learners. Contained within it are discussions of equity issues, the nature of science, motivational strategies, and the history of science from the viewpoint of culturally diverse children. The second section, Constructing a Knowledge of Science, contains a discussion of ways in which children learn and means for facilitating the academic growth of children of color and of white females. Developing Pedagogical Content Knowledge deals with content-area-specific knowledge necessary for effective science teaching. Finally, the section on Teaching through Thematic Units presents models for integrating content areas and presenting science as part of a unified whole.

SCIENCE EDUCATION AND DIVERSE LEARNERS

Perhaps it is best to begin our discussion of science education and culturally diverse children by looking first at national trends in science education. Hart (1977) states that "despite the faith of under-represented minorities in the American educational system as a means for social and economic advancement, equal education has not assured culturally diverse individuals equal access to opportunity" (p. 2), especially in science, mathematics, and related computer technology fields. African American, Hispanic/Latino, Native American, and other culturally diverse individuals comprise approximately 18% of our American population but only 2.2% of our technical work force. The numbers of culturally diverse students enrolled in mathematics, science, computer science, and computer engineering courses remains low, despite the removal of many social and legal barriers to the full participation of these students in science careers. Colleges and universities in our country are still experiencing an underrepresentation of culturally diverse applicants capable of meeting entry standards in science and mathematics majors. Many high ability or high potential culturally and/or linguistically diverse students face not only educational but also economic barriers to their pursuit of training for highly technological jobs. The gap between low socioeconomic status and higher socioeconomic levels is widening as the upward mobility rate remains less than 3% per generation in this country. It is important to realize that the problem of underrepresentation of culturally diverse students in science careers does not begin at the university level but rather at the elementary school level.

As Table 1.1 clearly illustrates, socioeconomic status is strongly related to educational level. In addition, race or ethnic origin are also strongly related to educational level.

Equity in Science Education

Culturally diverse students, especially those who speak a first language other than English, consistently perform less well on standard measures of academic achievement (e.g., SAT, GRE, MAT) than do their English-speaking peers. High school attrition (drop-out) rates at all socioeconomic levels in this nation are higher for culturally diverse students than for Anglo students (see Table 1.1). Since the passage of the Civil Rights Act in 1965, the high school graduation rate for African-American students in this nation has gradually improved, but the graduation rate for Hispanic/Latino students has actually declined (see Figure 1.1).

The African-American drop-out rate, shown in Figure 1.1, is rapidly approaching the Anglo drop-out rate. The attrition rate for Hispanic/Latino students, although declining a decade ago, has risen rapidly in recent years. The reason(s) for these phenomena are not clearly understood.

Proportionally, few culturally diverse students choose to attend and graduate from four-year degree-granting institutions, a finding that limits the potential of these students, their communities and society in general. University participation rates among culturally diverse and low-income students provide good indicators of progress in educational equity. In 1988, only 27.1% of African-American high school graduates and 21.1% of Hispanic/Latino high school graduates enrolled in colleges or universities (Statistical Abstract of the United States,

TABLE 1.1   Highest Level of Education Attained by 1980 High School Seniors by Socioeconomic Status and Race/Ethnicity (Spring 1986)

Socioeconomic Status & Ethnicity	No High School	High School Diploma	License	Associate Degree	Bachelor's Degree	Graduate Degree
Lower 25%						
White	0.9 %	75.1%	12.2%	5.0%	6.6%	0.3 %
Black	1.4 %	73.0%	12.7%	5.1%	7.7%	0.1 %
Hispanic	1.6 %	73.9%	11.8%	7.8%	4.9%	< 0.05%
Asian	< 0.05%	53.4%	17.3%	15.7%	12.0%	1.6 %
Middle 50%						
White	0.3 %	62.0%	13.0%	8.0%	16.3%	0.4 %
Black	0.3 %	67.5%	14.7%	6.5%	10.7%	0.3 %
Hispanic	1.0 %	67.0%	14.7%	6.5%	10.7%	0.2 %
Asian	< 0.05%	51.1%	11.7%	11.1%	26.1%	< 0.05%
Upper 25%						
White	< 0.05%	44.9%	8.6%	6.2%	38.2%	2.2 %
Black	< 0.05%	56.3%	12.4%	5.4%	30.5%	0.4 %
Hispanic	0.3 %	60.0%	11.4%	9.6%	18.0%	0.7 %
Asian	< 0.05%	42.9%	6.5%	4.8%	40.0%	5.9 %

Source: National Center for Education Statistics. *Digest of Education Statistics, 1989,* U.S. Department of Education, Office of Educational Research and Improvement

1990). Historically, most culturally diverse students have enrolled in two-year community colleges rather than in four-year degree granting institutions. Although many states have made efforts to improve the participation, persistence, and graduation rates of their culturally diverse students, the number of these students enrolled in mathematics and science-related careers lags far behind Anglo student enrollments. Statistics from states such as California (home of the nation's largest population of culturally diverse students) project an image of a nation in which culturally diverse individuals are not preparing for future jobs in mathematics, sciences, or related computer technology fields (see Table 1.2). Within a decade, nearly every state in this nation will face a situation similar to that of California. We are becoming a nation of racial and ethnic "unmeltables," a nation in which "minorities" are becoming the majority population.

Table 1.2 shows the number of degrees awarded in California according to race or ethnic origin. From these data it is apparent that few mathematics, science, and related technology degrees are awarded to culturally diverse individuals, a problem not only in California but in our entire nation.

Factors of race, gender, and socioeconomic status continue to play a major role in the education of culturally diverse students, especially in science, mathematics, and related technology careers that require high levels of specialized or technical training.While race, class, and gender have tremendous impact on the education of Anglo females and culturally diverse individuals in all disciplines,

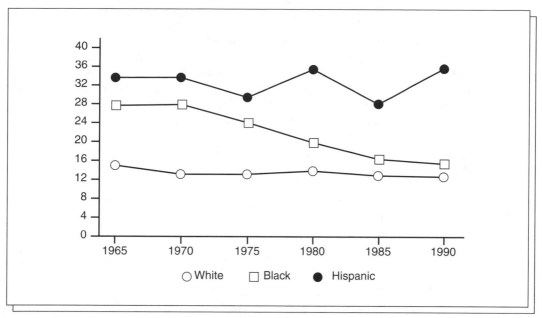

FIGURE 1.1   High School Attrition Rates by Race and Ethnicity

participation rates of culturally diverse individuals in science fields do not seem to follow the patterns of other disciplines. Culturally diverse individuals have made significant gains in their participation rates in business and industry sectors during the past three decades in this nation but have not made gains in science and related technology fields. Why have white females and culturally diverse individuals failed to increase significantly their participation rates in science disciplines?

TABLE 1.2   Distribution of Bachelor's Degrees by Race and Ethnicity in Selected Math and Science Fields of Study

Field	White	African American	Hispanic/ Latino	Asian American	Native American	Total
Computer Science	685	35	72	471	1	1,263
Engineering	2,056	68	274	1,096	23	3,517
Mathematics	368	8	38	82	8	504
Physics	423	15	30	63	2	533
Total Degrees	3,532	126	414	1,712	34	5,818

Source: "Undergraduate and Graduate Degrees Granted, *1988–1990 Statistical Report.* CSU Office of the Chancellor, Division of Analytical Studies, June 1990.

Elementary Science Instruction

Numerous studies have shown that many elementary teachers rely heavily on expository teaching methods and textbooks as the primary means for instructing children in science. On average, across the United States, elementary students spend less than 20 minutes a day studying science (Weiss, 1987). When science is taught in the elementary school, it is taught from textbooks rather than as a hands-on, inquiry-based learning experience. Surveys indicate that 75% of lower elementary (K–3) and 90% of upper elementary (4–6) science instruction involves lecture and discussion teaching methods. Elementary science is taught by many teachers as if science learning consisted of memorizing facts, definitions, and rules. In most elementary classrooms, children are expected to assume a passive role when science is taught. It is little wonder that many children find science dull.

THE NATURE OF SCIENCE

Too often, science is not taught as a way of knowing, as a way of responding to curious questions about the natural world, but as a body of facts and vocabulary words to be memorized and recited. "School science," or science as it is practiced in many American elementary school classrooms, has little to do with real science. In writing on the nature of science, Rubba and Anderson (1978) identified six **characteristics of scientific knowledge:**

- *Amoral:* scientific knowledge itself cannot be judged as morally good or bad;
- *Creative:* scientific knowledge is the product of human creativity;
- *Developmental:* scientific knowledge is tentative, that is, it is the best possible explanation of phenomena, based on what is currently known;
- *Parsimonious:* scientists explain phenomena in terms of simplicity rather than complexity;
- *Testable:* scientific knowledge is capable of being tested; and
- *Unified:* scientific laws, theories, and concepts are interrelated.

Scientific knowledge in and of itself is neither good nor bad; rather, it is our use of scientific knowledge which causes moral dilemmas. Technology is the application of science. Contrary to popular belief, scientific knowledge of the structure of the atom is neither harmful nor helpful. It is simply knowledge. Weapons of war, military technology, or application of the knowledge of atomic structure represent humankind's misapplication of scientific knowledge. Likewise, a knowledge of the mechanism of mammalian reproduction is neither benevolent nor injurious. It is simply knowledge. Technological applications of that knowledge have been developed in many different arenas. As a child growing up on the farm, I remember the visits of the agent from the artificial breeder's association. He appeared periodically and artificially inseminated our dairy herd. My father and mother thought that artificial insemination of the herd was a good idea; it saved us the expense and trouble of keeping a bull on the farm. When this same technology is applied to humans, the result is a plethora of lawsuits regarding surrogate parents, children's rights, and parental rights. *Knowledge is amoral: without inherent value.*

Science is a creative enterprise. Science is not a discipline which urges us to read, memorize, and recite; rather, it is an enterprise which encourages us to use our intellect to solve real-world problems: to create, invent, build, and develop new ideas and ways of thinking. Children who are actively engaged in learning science should be engaged in problem solving. Our society needs creative thinkers: those who look at natural phenomena for new solutions to recognized problems. How will we get to work in the future when our petroleum resources are used up? What is the cure for the current Hantavirus epidemic? A multitude of real-world problems await a new generation of creative thinkers: the children who are in your classroom today.

Scientific knowledge is developmental. It is in process, never fully completed. Each new generation adds to the knowledge of the previous generations. Einstein, in developing his theory of relativity, said that he was "standing on the shoulders of giants." His "new" scientific knowledge was built on the knowledge of previous scientists. As a young child, I remember noticing that, as our neighbor Claude plowed, he would periodically stop his tractor and pick up field stones. He would carry the newly unearthed stones to one of the walls surrounding his fields and add them to the top of the walls. One day I asked him about the practice: he told me that generations of farmers in his family had been adding stones to those walls, that the walls were works in progress, built but not completed. Thus it is with science; science is like a wall of knowledge in progress. Each new generation of scientists adds to the knowledge of previous women and men of science, but there is still more knowledge to add.

Science is parsimonious. Scientists seek simple, comprehensible explanations for natural phenomena; not complicated, complex, contorted explanations. As a child, I remember walking through the woods with my father. On a particularly beautiful autumn day, I asked him why the leaves changed color in the fall. In his usual quiet and gentle manner, he said, "They don't." When pressed for an explanation, my father said simply that the reds, oranges, yellows, and browns had been there all along. I couldn't see them because they were masked by the green chlorophyll. As the chlorophyll was destroyed by the lower autumn temperatures, the other colors became visible to my eye. Good scientific explanations are simple explanations; they are comprehensible explanations for real-world phenomena.

Scientific knowledge is testable. When scientific discoveries are made, other scientists throughout the world are able to duplicate the experiment and achieve the same results. Recently, a friend gave me a recipe for banana bread. No matter how carefully I followed his instructions, I could not duplicate the flavor and texture of his bread. When I asked him about this, he remembered that he had forgotten to list several key ingredients in the recipe that he had provided. Scientific knowledge is testable; folk practice is not. Replicability is a cornerstone of science. This ability to verify new discoveries through experimental replication differentiates scientific knowledge from folklore and quackery.

Scientific knowledge is unified in that scientific laws, theories, and concepts are interrelated. The transfer of energy from potential (stored energy) into kinetic (energy of motion) energy illustrates this concept. In the physical sciences we learn that a rock sitting atop a cliff is an illustration of potential or stored energy. When the rock falls from the cliff, it exhibits kinetic energy. In the human body, as food is burned in the process of respiration, potential energy (stored in the food) is converted into kinetic energy (muscle movement). In the geological sciences, earthquakes are an example of the conversion of potential energy into kinetic energy. The concept of energy transfer is used in physical, life, and earth and space sciences. Laws, theories, and concepts associated with energy are interrelated and apply to all sciences. Scientific knowledge and methods are gender and ethnicity free. All members of our society ought to be encouraged to pursue the study of science.

Ways of Knowing Science

The study of science and related technology often requires students to adapt to a white male culture, to an **Eurocentric/androcentric** world view. The basic assumptions of science, as it is taught to American children in textbooks, focus on male as opposed to female and on European as opposed to Eastern or African or South American ways of viewing the world. The axiological and epistemological beliefs of textbook science are tied to a European or white male way of viewing the world. This culture values competitiveness and individual achievement. Most modern science instruction is based on principles of realism. This value system holds that there is an ultimate truth and that humans can discover this truth in the natural world. The Eurocentric foundation of science focuses on European (and on those of European descent) values, attitudes and ways of knowing.

Androcentric instructional models are those which focus on male or individual ways of knowing and doing things. We emphasize famous "men of science" to children, while ignoring contributions by women and groups to the history of science. Our public schools typically teach mathematics, science, and computer technologies from this Eurocentric/androcentric perspective. In order for the educational process to be successful in these content areas, children must assimilate to this instructional model (i.e., accept an Anglo/European male-dominated instructional model and value system).

Culturally diverse children, that is, those who are **bilingual/bicultural and bidialectic** (i.e., speak a dialect of English other than that used in mainstream middle class America) often do not share many of the values, beliefs, and attitudes inherent in Eurocentric/androcentric science instruction. In addition, white females, although they are linguistically assimilated in mainstream American culture, are often not culturally assimilated to male ways of learning science. The use of Eurocentric/androcentric instructional models excludes the participation of culturally diverse individuals and white females (see Figure 1.2).

White male students find it relatively easy to become engaged in science activities since science is presented in a familiar language and in a culturally familiar manner. While Anglo females may be fully assimilated linguistically into mainstream American culture, they may not be assimilated into male ways of knowing and doing things. Many females find careers in science unappealing because accommodation to "male ways" of interacting and learning is difficult. Many culturally diverse students, even those whose families have lived in the United States for generations, are not from middle class communities. Indeed, many of these students exhibit the same characteristics as bilingual/bicultural students who have recently arrived in this country. Students who are from lower socioeconomic backgrounds and those who are bidialectic (i.e., speaking a dialect of English such as Appalachian English or the language of the "hood" or *barrio*) or bicultural find assimilation to the "white male" science model very difficult, both academically and culturally. Changing the ways that we teach science and related technology courses involves changing the ways that we view knowledge and the ways we view the teaching and learning process.

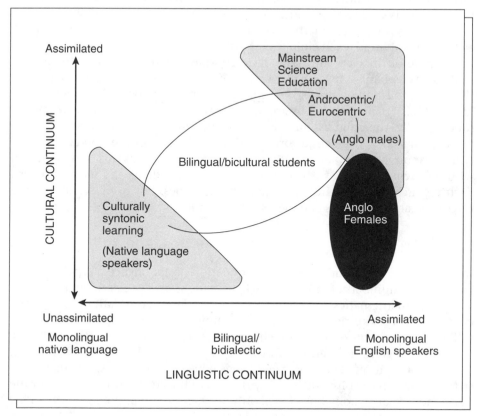

FIGURE 1.2   Linguistic Continuum

MINORITY PARTICIPATION IN SCIENCE CAREERS

Recent literature has attributed the **underrepresentation** of minority students and white females in science fields to several variables, including (1) lack of student interest in science, (2) science anxiety, (3) personality factors, (4) white male-dominated images of science, (5) lack of minority role models in science and related technology careers, (6) socioeconomic barriers, (7) improper counseling regarding academic track course work at the high school level, (8) teacher attitudes and expectations, and (9) lack of proper academic preparation. While all of these variables are salient in the education of culturally diverse individuals and white females, they are each part of an encompassing cultural history, a history that extends from a child's earliest years of schooling through the final years of schooling.

Looking at Elephants

Science education researchers working on identifying variables that impact the participation of culturally diverse individuals and white females in science careers each see part of the problem, but none seems to have "the big picture." Helen Keller is credited by modern folklore with telling the story of blind children visiting the circus for the first time. When the children arrived at the elephant compound, each child was assigned by the teacher to stand at a different portion of the elephant. The blind child assigned to stand by the ear described an elephant as being a giant piece of warm paper. The child assigned by the teacher to stand by the leg described the elephant as being like a tree trunk. The child assigned to stand by the tail described the elephant as being like a rope. Finally, the child assigned to the trunk described the elephant as being like a giant snake. Each child correctly described a part of the elephant, but no child was correct in that none had the total picture. Perhaps this is the situation with researchers dealing with culturally diverse individuals and science careers. Each researcher is right in what she or he describes, but none seems to have integrated all of the parts and pieces into a unified whole.

Pipeline Theory

In recent years, the National Science Foundation has published a **pipeline** chart based on the numbers of individuals who at various ages "declare" an interest in a career in mathematics and science (National Science Foundation, 1987). The chart begins on the right-hand side and shows a vast supply of some 4 or 5 million high school sophomores who are potential scientists, mathematicians, computer programmers, and so forth. "Drips" and "leaks" in the pipeline, in the form of attrition at various stages of the educational process, gradually constrict the flow in the pipeline until, by the end of the educational process (or the left-hand side of the pipeline chart), only 9,700 individuals emerge with a PhD degree in a science or mathematics discipline.

By extrapolating from this model, one could increase the numbers of culturally diverse individuals and females receiving degrees in science and mathematics simply by "plugging up the leaks." Indeed, vast amounts of money is currently being spent in this country to identify white females and culturally diverse students who show an interest in mathematics and science careers in the elementary, middle school, and high school grades and to instill in these children "the right stuff." The underlying philosophy of these programs is that, once these students are identified, given some remediation and a little mentoring, they will stay in the pipeline and emerge as successful scientists, mathematicians, or computer programmers. The major flaw inherent in this pipeline model is the assumption that females and culturally diverse students are deficient and that "correction of their deficiencies" will repair the problem.

Remember Javier (mentioned earlier in this chapter), who "opted out" of science in eighth grade, who elected not to pursue a rigorous program of science studies in high school. Two years before the National Science Foundation study begins to keep track of him, Javier has already left the "pipeline." His elementary and middle school science experiences influenced him not to continue his study of science. It may be that "calling the plumber to fix the leaks" is not a viable educational solution. For a long time science educators have been asking the question "What's wrong with the children?" Perhaps they should have been asking "What's wrong with the system?"

What's Wrong with the System?

A hint as to problems with the system comes from the work of Sheila Tobias. Tobias, in her book *They're not Dumb, They're Different* (1990), pointed out that mathematics and science instruction is frequently distasteful even for mainstream accomplished scholars. In her study, Tobias recruited graduate students and professors (from disciplines other than science) to audit science courses at the university level and keep journals and diaries of their experiences. The scholars that she recruited described science instruction as being "user unfriendly" in three specific areas: (1) student/teacher interactions, (2) physical environment, and (3) content presentation.

The subjects in Tobias's study pointed out that science is presented primarily through the use of expository teaching techniques with little student/teacher interaction. In addition, there was a well-established hierarchy within the classroom such that students were in the lowest caste, teaching assistants were in the middle caste, and professors were in the highest caste. Interactions between students and teachers rarely occurred in the classroom. When students had difficulty with the course content, they were referred to the middle level managers or teaching assistants instead of being allowed to interact directly with the professor, the implication being that only a select group of individuals had a sufficient knowledge base to interact with the professor. Participants in this study described the university level science classes as being devoid of human contact, an environment in which each student works alone without the support and guidance of a mentor or other human contact. Human contact and interaction seemed to be missing in science classes observed in this study. The textbooks presented factual information without explanatory narrative sections. The professors occasionally talked of famous men of science, but the exemplary models they used came from the domain of Western science (i.e., Eurocentric science), and the examples focused on androcentric (male-centered as opposed to female-centered or human-centered) models.

The physical environment of science classrooms and laboratories was a hostile environment according to the subjects in Tobias's study. In addition to being isolated from each other by the nature of the work, the students in science classes were physically isolated from each other by the seating arrangement in the classroom. Students sat in rows in large lecture halls, usually with an empty seat on either side of them. The "sage on stage" (i.e., the teacher standing in the front of the room lecturing to the class) learning model used so commonly for introductory courses in mathematics and sciences did not lend itself to social interactions among students.

Finally, the subjects in Tobias's study found science courses to be dull, dry, factual, and computationally oriented. The instructors observed by Tobias in her study emphasized computation before concepts. "How" questions, rather than "Why" questions were the benchmarks of the science classes observed in this study. The insistence on performance before competence combined with a rapid instructional rate and a lack of explanations resulted in high anxiety and a lack of class attendance among students. The problems of science instruction that Tobias described in her study have been reported previously by other researchers and are typical of elementary and secondary schools, as well as university science classrooms.

ADDRESSING EQUITY ISSUES

You may well ask, how does one address equity issues? How do schools respond to the needs of culturally diverse students? Many teachers believe that culturally diverse children come from culturally deficient communities and environments. In the United States where cultural assimilation has been an important movement, people who speak a language other than English or who have different patterns of interacting are sometimes considered to be less advanced than those who are part of the mainstream culture (Pang, 1988). Sometimes teachers believe that culturally diverse children do not excel because they come from families and communities that do not properly prepare students for learning. Teachers occasionally believe that some students do not care if they do well in school, and that these students are not properly prepared to succeed in an academic environment and are not motivated to learn. The cultural deficit model as described by Sleeter and Grant (1990) assumes that schools should change learners, should help them assimilate to mainstream culture, including the "culture of science." From this viewpoint, children need remedial work to compensate for their lack of knowledge, skills, and attitudes in science and mathematics. Those who advocate the use of this world view regard students as being "at risk" when they do not share American mainstream language and culture. The National Science Foundation pipeline approach typifies this world view. If we just call the plumber, if we just plug the leaks, then we can "fix the students."

Multicultural Approach

In contrast to the deficit model, those who adhere to a **multicultural model** (Sleeter & Grant, 1990) see the cultural and linguistic backgrounds of diverse students as being valuable educational resources. A "multicultural approach to education promotes cultural pluralism and social equality by reforming the school program for all students to make it reflect diversity" (Sleeter & Grant, 1990, p. 139). If one adopts this world view, children who speak a primary language other than English are considered an asset in the classroom because they have constructed a knowledge of science in a different sociocultural context than others in the class and thus bring added resources to the classroom. Those who advocate the use of a multicultural approach to education see diversity as a strength in the classroom, as a vehicle for increasing the learning of all students.

Culturally Syntonic Variables

Mastery of content knowledge has been shown to include an interplay between culture (which includes language) and concept formation. Historically, many culturally diverse children have encountered school-taught science in a culturally unfamiliar manner as well as in an unfamiliar language. As a result, these students never acquire the desired level of language proficiency and do not understand the science and mathematics concepts taught in the classroom.

Culture and Learning.   In a study of the learning patterns of Hmong students, Hvitfeldt (1986) found that cultural variables influenced verbal interaction patterns in the classroom, students' preferred learning modes, and students' concept acquisition. Studies of Hawaiian-American (Au, 1980; Spring, 1950; Weisner, Gallimore & Jordan, 1988), Asian-American (Cheng, 1992), African-American (Stewart & Benson, 1988) and Native-American (Harris, 1985) children indicated that the child's culture influences interactions with teachers and the way(s) they construct knowledge in the classroom. Many Native-American children have been socialized to divert their gaze (as a means of respect) when they speak to an elder. Teachers who are unaware of this habit may tend to regard children as inattentive or impolite, rather than as extremely courteous and respectful. As children grow into adults, their ways of interacting become ingrained in the fabric of their personalities. Culturally diverse learners sometimes find that their ways of thinking, knowing, and interacting are unacceptable in the elementary science classroom. For many culturally diverse children, the rules of social interaction and the patterns of learning acquired at home become an impediment as they struggle to "make sense" of "school learning".

Culturally syntonic stimuli were first defined in the medical literature over a hundred years ago as "stimuli which oscillate in harmony with one's culture" (Spitler, 1889, p. 2). The existence of culturally syntonic variables which impact the education of Hispanic/Latino adults was delineated by Valle (1978) within a neuropsychological context. Valle has since redefined culturally syntonic variables as "those factors or influences which are in harmony with normative behaviors, values and attitudes of a particular ethnic or cultural group" (1986, p.30). Ensuing research has shown that these variables impact not only learning, but also the teaching and testing of students. Elementary science teachers should view culturally syntonic or culturally harmonious variables as those culture-of-origin beliefs, attitudes, and practices which influence (both positively and negatively, functionally and dysfunctionally) the teaching/learning process.

In the science classroom culturally syntonic or culturally harmonious variables for diverse learners would include variables such as the format of printed materials, preferred instructional mode, instructional language, level of peer interaction, the use of culturally familiar role models, culturally familiar elaboration and context, and level of interactivity with manipulative materials. In identifying culturally syntonic variables, we must be careful to recognize that culturally diverse students represent many different cultures and belief systems. Mexican-American, Puerto Rican-American, Central-American, South-American, and Cuban-American students may share a common language, but beliefs, values, attitudes, and cultural histories of those students differ from one individual to another. In addition, we all need to be cautious to avoid stereotyping all members of a particular ethnic group as having the same attributes. For example, while most culturally and linguistically unassimilated Hispanic/Latino children prefer a *fotonovela* format (e.g., a highly visualized presentation of declarative knowledge) for reading materials, not all Hispanic/Latino students share the same preference for this type of textual material. Country-of-origin, level of assimilation into mainstream culture, degree of acculturation, socioeconomic status, and individual differences must be considered when identifying culturally syntonic variables.

Format of Printed Materials.   Research involving the format of printed materials has shown that the *fotonovela* or photonovel (a highly visual story book format) is the most effective means known for conveying verbal information to most unassimilated Hispanic/Latino and certain Southeast-Asian learners (Comes-Diaz, 1984; Costantino, Malgady & Rogler, 1988; Flora, 1980; Hill & Browner, 1982; Horn, 1983; le Boterf, 1984). These studies have shown that unassimilated students learn more declarative knowledge (knowledge we can state) from textual materials printed in a *fotonovela* format than from traditional textbooks. In addition, culturally unassimilated Hispanic/Latino and Southeast-Asian learners have been shown to prefer *fotonovela* format (which is commonly used in Third World literacy campaigns) over the text format used in traditional Eurocentric textbooks.

While elementary science textbooks used in the United States include many pictures, charts, and diagrams, the books are not structured in a way that tells a story through the pictures. Children accustomed to constructing meaning from a sequence of photographs, sketches, or drawings find the format used in American science textbooks to be unfamiliar and difficult to understand. *The Popcorn Book* (DePaolo, 1978) is probably the best known example of a *fotonovela* or photonovel format in American children's literature. This book tells the story of popcorn through colored line drawings, "balloons" containing information about popcorn written at an early elementary reading level, and script boxes with additional information written at an upper elementary reading level. *The Popcorn Book* allows for the use of a scaffolding technique for learning. The teacher or parent encourages the child to talk about the pictures showing the history of popcorn and the uses of popcorn. Older children or those who can read at an early elementary school level add to the information about popcorn by reading the words in the "balloon." Finally, the teacher or the parent reads the detailed information about popcorn, written at an upper elementary reading level, from the bottom of the page. This format, by which information is conveyed through a sequence of pictures, simple reading words, and complicated textual passages, is common in *fotonovelas* and is widely used in Third World literacy campaigns. Elementary science textbooks used in the United States do not incorporate this type of text format.

Instructional Language. For content area concept acquisition, access to instruction in the "home language" for purposes of cued recall benefits those students who are not fully assimilated linguistically into mainstream culture (Cortes, 1986; Cummins, 1979; Ehindero, 1980; Olson, 1986; Ortiz & Maldonado-Colon, 1986; Watts, 1986). Research shows that the use of native language in the classroom: (1) builds students' self-esteem, (2) improves students' attitudes towards schooling, (3) facilitates content area acquisition of declarative knowledge, and (4) aids in mainstream English language development. New knowledge can be integrated with existing knowledge only when existing knowledge (which may have been constructed in the student's native language) is restructured and students elaborate on what they already know. Allowing students to use their "home language" in small group settings for purposes of cued recall is rarely encouraged in "traditional" elementary classrooms. Culturally syntonic classrooms are those in which students are encouraged to bring their "home learning" to class and combine it with their "school learning."

Level of Peer Interactivity. Peer tutoring, especially when new concepts or vocabulary are introduced in a class, improves students' concept acquisition (Cohen & Lotan, 1990; Cohen, Knight & Kagan, 1977; Lotan & Catanzarite, 1990; Ortiz, 1988; Watson, 1991). Negotiating meaning, that is, building a personal rendition of knowledge through social interactions is foundational in the learning process. All of us have had the experience of sharing the meaning of a word in a group setting, of contributing our ideas to the collective body of knowl-

Many culturally diverse learners prefer group environments. (© Stephen Marks)

edge, and of finally reaching agreement about a new expanded definition for a term. Research with unassimilated, culturally diverse students has shown that many children prefer peer tutoring environments to large group instructional situations. Peer tutoring appears to be an effective means of bridging linguistic barriers for bilingual/bicultural students and for conferring status to unassimilated students. Previous research indicates that most culturally diverse learners profit from cooperative group work and peer tutoring in terms of cognitive growth, attitude change, and self-esteem.

The works of Ramirez and Castaneda (1974); Rodriguez and Bethel (1983); Valle (1978; 1986); Cohen, Lotan, and Catanzarite (1990); and Watson (1991) indicate that use of cooperative learning or *familia* (cross-age tutoring) groups increases students' science concept acquisition. When culturally diverse students are allowed to work in cooperative groups, their attitudes towards science and school in general improve. Finally, students' self-esteem is increased through use of cooperative activities. While research has shown that cooperative learning is highly effective in meeting the educational needs of culturally diverse learners, studies have shown that cooperative learning is rarely used in practice in elementary schools. Similarly, peer tutoring, if it occurs at all, is seen as the domain of the student—to be accomplished in out of class settings and not as part of the regular instructional program.

Role Models.   The presence of culturally familiar role models or significant others, both in person and as represented in printed materials or textbooks, constitutes an important variable which impacts the cognitive learning of all students, including culturally diverse students (Bandura, 1962; Cicourel, 1974; Kahle, 1985; Pearson & Bechtel, 1989; Shade, 1982; Tanner & Lindgren, 1971; Van Sertima, 1986). I remember reading the life story of Marie Curie as a child. For years, I aspired to be like Curie, to win a Nobel Prize for the discovery of a new element. Children need successful role models to emulate.

Studies by Tanner & Lindgren (1971), Cicourel (1974), Pitman (1989), and Healy (1990) demonstrated that the presence of culturally familiar role models in textual materials significantly increases students' self-esteem, concept acquisition, and motivation to pursue science careers. Few if any culturally diverse role models are presented to students in elementary science classrooms (a discussion of culturally diverse scientists is presented in Chapter 3).

Elaboration and Context.   Culturally familiar elaborations, which use culturally familiar objects, environments or contexts, examples, and analogies function as powerful variables in terms of culturally diverse students' concept acquisition. Culturally familiar contexts significantly increase students' acquisition of declarative knowledge (Halpern, Hansen & Riefer, 1990; Kessler & Quinn, 1980; Rodriguez & Bethel, 1983). Previous research has shown that culturally familiar examples proportionally benefit those students who are not yet cultur-

Marie Curie has served as a role model for generations of women in science. (North Wind Picture Archives)

ally or linguistically assimilated into mainstream American culture. In addition, research supports the notion that culturally familiar objects, contexts, examples, and analogies increase students' self-esteem and increase the rate at which students master content area concepts. Culturally familiar examples and elaborations append new learning to existing schema. Cued recall serves to activate prior knowledge and allow students to connect new knowledge to existing schema.

As teachers, we tend to use examples and analogies from our own mainstream American experience. Sometimes, students do not share our frame of reference. Because the examples we use are not part of the child's milieu, children do not understand our explanations. When we use culturally familiar objects and examples, we help students connect their "home learning" to "school learning." Recently, I observed a kindergarten teacher present a lesson on seeds. The teacher had asked students to bring seeds from home. Each child came to class with seeds that their families ate. Some children proudly exhibited pinto beans, while others displayed sesame seeds, long-grained rice, and black-eyed peas gathered from their families' gardens and pantries. Each child contributed to the classes' knowledge of seeds by bringing objects familiar to their families.

Interactivity with Manipulative Materials.   Finally, interaction with laboratory equipment and manipulative materials increases the learning of conceptual or declarative knowledge among students. Interaction with manipulative materials positively impacts students' attitudes towards science. Research by Ornstein-Galicia (1981), Comes-Diaz (1984), Kessler and Quinn (1980), and Brown, Fournier, and Moyer (1977) indicates that use of laboratory or manipulative materials significantly increases the pace at which students master concepts and assists students in developing problem-solving skills. While many teachers know the value of laboratory investigations, these activities are rarely considered part of the main instructional program. Research has shown that multiple means of knowledge representation benefits all learners, but teachers rarely hold hands-on manipulative activities in the same regard that they view textbook-based activities.

Other culturally syntonic variables such as the talk story (Au & Jordan, 1977), holistic learning (Rhodes, 1988), students' geocentric perspectives (Van Otten & Tsutsui, 1983), bidialectic expression (Hochel, 1983; Cronnel, 1981; Levine, 1976), and stage setting behaviors (Longstreet, 1987; Shade, 1979) have been identified as being salient for the education of culturally diverse learners.

Constructing a Knowledge of Science

From a **constructivist** viewpoint, conceptual knowledge of science is constructed (1) gradually over time, (2) by the learners within a social context, (3) through a series of interactions with the content, (4) when new information is integrated with old information, and (5) such that the result is an awareness of what is being learned. Constructivists hold that knowledge is constructed, not transmitted. Learning occurs within a social context as students share their ideas with peers, both in small groups and within the total society of the classroom. From a multicultural perspective, schools rather than students are considered to be "at risk," especially when they do not capitalize on the richness of experience that culturally diverse learners bring to classroom social interactions.

For many students, especially culturally diverse students, mathematics and science classes are hostile environments. Making these instructional environments user friendly requires changes in three areas: teacher/student interactions, instructional methods, and curriculum content. Improving the teacher/student interactions in the classroom requires an awareness on the part of the teacher of the way(s) in which students learn. For many culturally diverse students, a "mugs and jugs," or purely expository teaching models having their origins in the essentialist theories of education, are culturally unfamiliar learning models. Personal interactions with teachers are vital to the learning process for many students. The instructional methods used in classrooms with culturally diverse learners need to be models in which students are free to interact with others in way(s) that are culturally familiar and comfortable. Large group interactions in which students are expected to receive information are ineffective pedagogical teaching strategies for many culturally diverse learners. Personalization of instruction, small group interactions, and opportunities for hands-on experiences are vitally needed in science classrooms. Finally, the science curriculum, that is, the way(s) that knowledge is presented to students, must be addressed in science and related technology content areas. For students to actualize an interest in science, students must feel that learning in those content areas is relevant to their lives. For science instruction to be effective, it must be personalized to meet the needs of the students.

Constructivist learning models (Cobern, 1991; Driver & Bell, 1986; Driver & Oldham, 1986; Roth, 1991; Wheatley, 1991), models which use problem-solving thematic approaches to learning, appear to be highly appropriate pedagogical approaches for use with culturally diverse learners in that they (1) provide multiple means of data representation, (2) allow for peer tutoring, (3) provide for the use of home language in small groups, (4) allow students to bring culturally familiar examples and elaborations into the classroom, (5) permit students to interact with manipulative materials, (6) encourage students to work cooperatively in constructing new knowledge, and (7) "fit" with what is known of the learning/teaching process (from research in cognitive psychology).

CLASSROOM PRACTICE

The lack of achievement of culturally diverse learners in science and technology-related content areas is of grave concern to all of us. In making culturally affirming schools, our ways of viewing students and the teaching/learning process itself need to change dramatically. Students cannot be "fixed" in the way that flat tires are fixed on automobiles. Rather, what is needed is a view of students and schools which affirms everyone. First, we must begin with an assumption that students are not deficient but rather bring a wealth of knowledge of the world around them to the classroom and to their academic endeavors. Second, we must allow students to bring their culture and experiences to each new learning experience. We must affirm our students to assist them in adding new knowledge to that which they already possess. Third, our teaching models must be changed from teacher-centered to student-centered learning models, especially in the science content area. Problem-solving or problem-centered learning must comprise the core of our instructional program. "Doing" science rather than hearing or reading about science must be central to our educational process.

If elementary science instruction is to become culturally affirming instruction, we must understand that often our schools are deficient in the way(s) knowledge is presented to students, rather than assuming that the students are deficient. One goal of science education is to develop an environmental ethic in our citizens, a belief that we must conserve our natural resources. As a nation, our students are our most valuable resource. It is imperative that we preserve and protect this resource with even more vigor than we protect our planet. If we are to ensure that culturally diverse men and women do not become an "endangered species" in science, mathematics, and related technology careers, we must create user friendly environments in which instruction in these subjects can take place.

  ## CHAPTER SUMMARY

Culturally diverse students participate in science, mathematics, and related technology careers in proportionally fewer numbers than do other individuals in our society. Traditionally, schools have viewed bilingual/bicultural and bidialectic students as deficient, that is, as needing remediation to participate fully in mainstream science instruction. The purpose of this book is to propose culturally affirming instructional strategies; that is, a way of viewing children and schools and science curriculum that is affirming for all children.

  ## TOPICS TO REVIEW

REFLECTIVE PRACTICE

1. From the perspective of culturally diverse learners, what are some of the problems of "traditional" science instruction? What might be done to "correct" these problems?
2. In your opinion, how might classrooms be modified such that they would be culturally affirming places of learning?
3. What type(s) of instructional materials might be best for use with culturally diverse learners? Justify your answers.
4. Has your perception of the needs of culturally diverse learners changed as a result of reading this chapter? If so, how? If not, why?
5. In your opinion, why have schools failed to "reach" culturally diverse learners?
6. Assume that you are in charge of purchasing instructional materials, supplies, and so forth for a school with a large population of culturally diverse learners. What type(s) of science materials would you purchase? Why?
7. Based on what you have read so far, how might elementary science instruction be modified to meet the needs of culturally diverse learners?
8. Based on your prior knowledge and what you have read in this chapter, how might children's language and culture influence how they construct a knowledge of science?

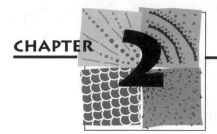

CHAPTER **2**

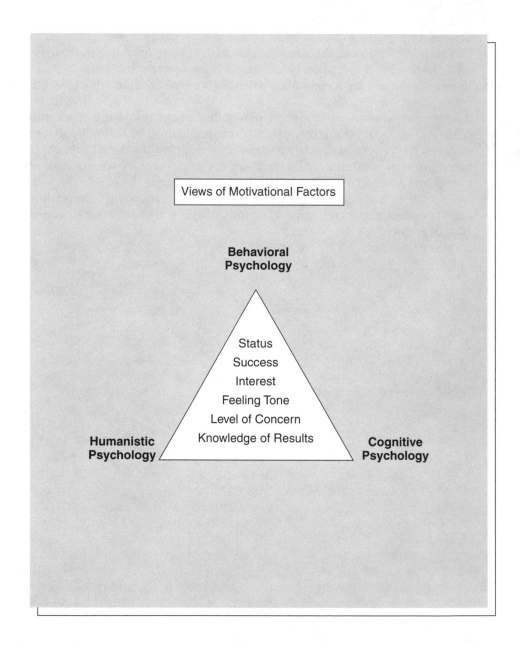

Views of Motivational Factors

**Behavioral
Psychology**

Status
Success
Interest
Feeling Tone
Level of Concern
Knowledge of Results

**Humanistic
Psychology**

**Cognitive
Psychology**

MOTIVATION IN THE MULTICULTURAL CLASSROOM

 POINTS TO PONDER

1. What factors motivate children to learn science?
2. How can we encourage children to learn science?
3. What strategies can encourage children to develop an interest in science?

ome students stand out in our memories in spite of the passage of years. Carolyn was one of those students in my life. I met Carolyn during my second year of teaching. She was a beautiful 17-year-old, African-American woman who had been placed in the eighth grade. Carolyn was a daily topic of discussion among the "lounge lizards," the teachers who spent a considerable portion of each day sitting in the faculty lounge. This group perceived her to be short-tempered, foul-mouthed, and feisty. I met Carolyn because she was assigned to me by the principal as a teacher's helper during my planning period. Apparently, most of the teachers in the building had prior experience working with Carolyn and did not care to have her in their classes a second time. Ignoring the advice of these peers, I accepted Carolyn as a teacher's helper and agreed to provide her a quasi-supervised work experience in the science lab.

During the year that I knew Carolyn, I found her to be polite, considerate, dependable, and very personable. In the course of our year together, I came to respect and trust her. One day in particular sticks in my memory. A parent of another student had come unexpectedly to the office seeking a conference regarding her child's academic progress. I had to leave Carolyn unsupervised while I met with the parent. As I left the room, I directed Carolyn to get out supplies and materials for the next class, and asked the teacher next door to look in on her from time to time. The conference lasted longer than I expected, and by the time I returned to my classroom, the bell had rung and Carolyn had gone on to her next class.

About an hour after the conference, I began to smell something. It was an overpowering odor of rotten eggs in my classroom. At first, I suspected that the school cafeteria had served pork and beans for lunch and that some "poor little darling" had expelled gas. Unobtrusively, I opened the windows of the classroom, one after another. The odor persisted and grew in intensity. Soon all of the children were holding their noses and pointing accusing fingers at each other. Mercifully, class finally ended, and yet the odor lingered. As I walked around the room, I noticed that the stench seemed to be coming from the back corner of the classroom, in the lab prep area. I continued to search for the source of the obnoxious gas. When I opened the acid cabinet under the sink, I noticed that all of the acid bottles were empty and that a large portion of my drain pipe was missing.

At about that same time, Carolyn came bounding in the door of my classroom. "Hey, Ms. B.," she called, "I forgot to tell you, while I was getting out the equipment, I emptied out those old bottles under your sink. I'll wash 'em for you tomorrow." Carolyn ran out the door, pleased with the job she had done. Voluntarily cleaning out my storage cabinets was Carolyn's way of showing her friendship; she was internally motivated to clean out my acid cabinet. Unfortunately, she had worked without adult supervision and had disposed of the acids improperly; my drain pipe was eaten away. As I stood in the office after school explaining why I wanted to requisition a new drain pipe, I thought about children and motivation.

My experience with Carolyn wonderfully illustrates some ideas about motivation and culturally diverse children. First, she performed the task of helping me on that particular day, not because she had to, but because she wanted to be helpful. Her results surprised both of us. Many children are internally motivated to learn, to share, and to help, but sometimes we do not allow them that opportunity. Second, we need to remember to avoid prejudging students, or judging them based on what others have told us. Carolyn had a reputation for being unmotivated and a trouble maker. In reality, she was a kind and sensitive person who had great difficulty learning in school and who covered up her educational difficulties with acting-out behaviors. Finally, what motivates one child may not motivate another child. Based on what I could learn of her, it seemed that Carolyn found "school learning" difficult. While Carolyn was motivated to work and learn in an informal setting, she had great difficulty in a formal class setting.

ENCOURAGING CHILDREN TO LEARN

In stating its position regarding the education of children in the multicultural science classroom, the National Science Teachers Association's Board of Directors wrote that "culturally diverse children must have access to quality science education experiences that enhance success and provide the knowledge and opportunities required for them to become successful participants in our democratic society" (1991). Implementation of this goal requires that children be motivated to learn science, to participate in activities that will enable them to fully participate in science and related technology careers. A student's motivation to learn science is, therefore, critical in the science classroom.

We can broadly define **motivation** in this context as being a student's intent or desire to learn. Gagné has stated that motivation includes a consideration of the motives that make the student want to seek knowledge, to use his/her talents, to desire self-fulfillment as a human being, to relate to other people in a satisfying manner, and to become an effective member of society (1965, p. 207). In writing of the role motivation plays among culturally diverse students, Gay states that variables associated with learning, such as ability, motivation, interest, and classroom climate, must be understood and applied within the contexts of culture and ethnicity (p. 329). Ogbu (1992) echoes those sentiments when he observes that teachers often do not recognize the meaning and value that culturally diverse students associate with school learning and achievement. Motivation plays a significant role in all children's learning, and particularly that of minority students. A knowledge of motivational factors is vital for elementary science teachers who work with culturally diverse students. Unless students are motivated to learn science, the pattern of underrepresentation of culturally diverse students in science and related technology fields will persist.

Perspectives on Motivation

At one time, a student's motivation to learn was considered to be almost totally dependent on individual personality or disposition. This view arose from the notion that academic involvement and achievement rested primarily with the individual student. From this perspective, if a student was unwilling to learn, there was little that teachers, parents, or the community could do to change the student's motivation. In challenging this belief system, Maehr (1978) points out that, if one assumes that motivational change only comes through personality change, one accepts a certain fatalistic outlook as a teacher (p. 223). Maehr's writing focuses our attention on the fact that there are many ways to view motivation and that each view depends on our basic assumptions about the ways that children learn science.

Behavioral Psychology View of Motivation.   If we hold a **behavioral psychology** view of teaching and learning, we consider motivation to learn science or any subject to be closely aligned with stimulus-response learning theories. Within this framework, motivation is believed to be based on a system of extrinsic or external rewards (teacher praise, grades, points, prizes, special privileges). The experiments of B. F. Skinner demonstrated that organisms tend to repeat actions that are reinforced and behavior can be shaped by reinforcement (Biehler & Snowman, 1986, p. 469). Advocates of stimulus-response learning theories have developed behavior modification plans for motivating students to complete a task by promising them a reward.

Within the strict behavioral framework, to motivate students is really to apply the principles of contiguity, reinforcement, punishment, and modeling in order to increase, decrease, or develop behaviors. Behavioral psychologists rely on tangible rewards as the primary means for motivating students. Premack's (1965) principle is an example of a behaviorist world view concerning motivation. Premack stated that a high-frequency behavior (a preferred activity) may be an effective reinforcer for a low-frequency behavior (a less preferred activity). In other words, "first do what I want you to do; then you may do what you want to do." In my role as a parent, there are times when I have used this principle of motivation with great success. When my teenage sons want to go out on a date, I frequently step in and say, "Not until your room is clean." It's amazing how quickly a teenaged boy can clean a bedroom when a teenaged girl is expecting his companionship. Cleaning is a less preferred activity and dating is a preferred activity.

Behaviorist principles of motivation are normally founded on "dangling carrots"; that is, providing external rewards which students are expected to internalize. Behaviorists hold that the teacher should supply rewards in response to students' "appropriate" behaviors. Teachers who provide students with stars, lollipops, smiley faces, and extra time on the playground are practicing behaviorist motivational principles. For example, if you wanted to encourage sixth-grade students to learn the symbols and spellings for the 20 most common elements of the periodic table of elements, you could set up a "star chart" system and give students colored stars for each element learned. You would be using behaviorist learning principles in a classroom setting.

Humanistic Psychology View of Motivation.   Humanistic psychologists (Maslow, Rogers, and Combs), on the other hand, have stressed that teachers should trust pupils enough to permit them to make choices about their own learning. **Humanistic psychologists**, especially Maslow, view motivation as arising from a hierarchy of needs within the student (Table 2.1). A **need**, according to Kolesnik (1978, p. 149), is any type of deficiency in the human organism or the absence of anything the person requires, or believes is required, for overall well being. In Maslow's theory of human motivation, referred to as growth motivation or need gratification, human needs are arranged in order from physiologic needs to aesthetic needs. Physiologic needs (food, clothing, and shelter) are the bottom rung of Maslow's hierarchy. Personal needs for safety, belonging, esteem, intellectual achievement, aesthetic appreciation, and self-fulfillment complete this hierarchy.

Within Maslow's hierarchy, students' desires to fill low-level needs could supersede their higher-level educational needs. If, for instance, a student comes to school hungry, the student is motivated to fill that need prior to engaging in academic work. Likewise, belonging to a social group and maintaining esteem within that group are important to students. If doing what the teacher says conflicts with group rules, students may choose to ignore or even defy the teacher. This type of behavior is most commonly found among prepubescent middle school or junior high school students. Occasionally, small groups of students in this age group begin to take pride in failure rather than success. Normally, the flirtation with the "failure fad" is short lived in most children's lives.

Cognitive Psychology View of Motivation.   Cognitive psychologists often highlight intrinsic or internal motivation. One central assumption of **cognitive psychology** is that persons do not respond automatically to external events or to physical conditions; rather, they respond to their perceptions of these events. Those who adhere to a cognitive psychology paradigm emphasize that motivation is intrinsic and, as such, is activated by an internal satisfaction with learning as a form of self-achievement. Cognitivists see the student as active and curious, searching for information to solve personally relevant problems, and sometimes capable of ignoring personal discomfort in order to achieve self-selected goals. Motivation, from a cognitive psychology viewpoint, is based on choices, decisions, plans, interests, goals, and calculations of likely success or failure.

TABLE 2.1 Maslow's Hierarchy of Needs	
Need	*Description*
Self-fulfillment	Self actualization and realization of all that a person is capable of being
Aesthetic appreciation	The search for structure, order, and beauty.
Intellectual achievement	The need to know, to explore and to understand.
Self-esteem	The desire to gain recognition and approval from others.
Belonging	The need to be loved and to be accepted among one's peers or family.
Safety	The need to feel psychologically and physically secure, free from danger.
Physiological	Survival needs—food, water, air, and shelter.

Source: Adapted from Maslow, A.M. (1970). *Motivation and Personality*

Attribution theory (Weiner, 1980) and social learning theory (Bandura, 1977), theories derived from the cognitive psychology tradition, offer insights into factors which impact students' learning in the classroom. In observing students' ability to handle stress associated with success and failure, Weiner asked students to identify the reasons for their success or lack of success in the classroom. Students attributed their success or failure to four common variables: ability, effort, task difficulty, and luck.

Children with long histories of academic failure routinely attribute their success to easy questions or luck, while attributing their failures to lack of ability. Because low achieving students attribute failure to their own low ability, these children consider future failure to be more likely than future success. High achievers, on the other hand, attribute their success to their ability and effort, and their failures to their lack of effort. When high achievers fail, they view the failure as a temporary set back, and resolve to try harder or to exert more effort in the future. From the standpoint of attribution theory, external rewards will probably not be effective with low achieving students because these children tend to view success as being attributable to factors (namely, what they perceive to be a lack of ability) that are beyond their personal control.

Bandura's social learning theory (1977) suggests that personal goal setting is a critical variable in a student's motivation or desire to learn. In the first part of his theory, Bandura states that we evaluate tasks in terms of our perceptions of future outcomes. Am I likely to be successful or to fail at this? How will my peers perceive me if I am successful (or a failure) at this? According to Bandura, the goals we set become our standards for evaluating our own performance. Individuals tend to persist in their endeavors until they meet the standards or goals that they have set for themselves. As we work toward our self-selected goals, we evaluate our performance in terms of the positive things that will occur when we achieve the goal and in terms of the negative consequences of not reaching our goals. When we have achieved a goal, we tend to be satisfied for a short time and then begin the process of setting new goals, thus raising our level of aspiration. Within the context of Bandura's social-learning theory, the teacher assists students in setting goals, reflecting on performance, and self-reinforcement.

Motivating Students

Based on what is known of student characteristics, how can we best motivate students to learn science? In truth, it is probably impossible for one person to motivate another. Research indicates that motivation is intrinsic or internal, and not extrinsic or external. However, it is possible to change the ways things are done in the elementary science classroom, to make our classroom environments more appealing to students, to encourage students to set goals, and to increase their effort and intent to learn science. Six factors have been shown to increase a student's effort and desire to learn: (1) level of concern, (2) feeling tone, (3) success, (4) interest, (5) status, and (6) knowledge of results.

Level of Concern.   Level of concern is the first factor that has been shown to impact culturally diverse students' motivation to learn science. **Level of concern** may be broadly defined as a student's level of concern about achieving in the classroom. The concept of level of concern is based on Weiner's (1980) attribution theory and on Bandura's (1977) social-learning theory. When presented with a task, or new learning, each student evaluates the task for him- or herself to determine each's ability to "do the work." If a task is viewed by the child as being too easy and unchallenging, the child may begin to engage in "off-task" behaviors. Teachers are encouragers. We use persuasive communication to encourage children to attempt tasks, to try new learning. For example, the child who is asked to plant a couple of bean seeds in a paper cup and adjust the variables which control plant growth would probably regard this task as a fun and challenging learning activity. However, if we asked children to plant an acre of bean seeds by hand, most children would regard such a chore as dull, boring, repetitive, and devoid of new learning.

Ideal learning environments are those that offer accomplishable tasks. A moderate level of concern stimulates our effort to learn, but anxiety interferes with students' performance. As you attend to the needs of culturally diverse learners, remember to present tasks that are "doable," tasks that children can accomplish with a moderate amount of effort. In describing the characteristics of a "good task," Wheatley states that teachers should select tasks which have a high probability of being problematic for students—tasks which may cause students to find a problem (1991, p. 15). According to Wheatley, **rich educational activities** or tasks should (1) be accessible to everyone at the start, (2) invite students to make decisions, (3) encourage "what if" questions, (4) encourage students to use their own methods, (5) promote discussion and communication, (6) lead somewhere, (7) have an element of surprise, (8) be enjoyable, and (9) be extendable (1991, p. 16).

Educational researchers (Gonzales, 1989; Sieber, O'Neill & Tobias, 1977) and sociologists (Gay, 1988; Ogbu, 1992; Suzuki, 1984;) who work with culturally diverse learners point out that all children want to learn. Success in school depends not only on what schools and teachers do, but also on what students do. A student's level of concern about learning science determines his or her desire to learn. An excellent example of this principle is illustrated by the life of Jaime Escalante (a Los Angeles mathematics teacher whose life is depicted in the movie *Stand and Deliver*). Although Escalante's students were among the poorest Hispanic students in the city of Los Angeles, Escalante encouraged students to learn calculus by making it seem "learnable." In the movie and in real life, Escalante states that students need to have the *ganas* (a concept which embodies self-concept, self-efficacy, and motivation) to learn.

Feeling Tone.   Feeling tone is another motivating factor in the elementary science classroom. Hunter (1982) has defined **feeling tone** as the way a student feels in a particular situation that affects the amount of effort (s)he is willing to put forth to achieve learning (p. 12). She goes on to say that feeling tones exist on a continuum which extends from pleasant through neutral to unpleasant. The overall classroom climate, the environment that a teacher establishes for culturally diverse children, greatly impacts the learning that occurs in the classroom. The establishment of a positive feeling tone, that is, the development of a motivating learning environment for children, requires a sensitivity to children's home culture and home learning. Culturally diverse students view schools as places of learning when they are allowed to bring "home culture" to school and to append new learning to existing learning.

In writing of the motivational principle of feeling tone, Gay states that research in sociopsychology, learning theory, ethnicity, and educational anthropology informs us that students differ both individually and by social, ethnic, and cultural group membership (1988, p. 331). Gay also writes that, historically, efforts to incorporate ethnic and cultural diversity in the core of all school curricula, and to make instructional programs more responsive to the unique needs of diverse learners, have been neither impressive nor comprehensive. How do you bring children's "home learning" and "home culture" into a school environment? How can science classrooms be modified such that they are culturally affirming environments (i.e., exhibit positive feeling tones for culturally diverse learners)?

Culturally diverse learners (indeed, all children) come to schools with a wealth of prior knowledge, ready to negotiate meaning from the educational environment. Teachers can facilitate children's motivation to learn science by providing positive feeling tone in the forms of culturally affirming content and contexts. Geneva Gay has pointed out that the means appropriate for teaching poor, urban black students differ from those appropriate for teaching other students because teaching and learning are sociocultural processes that take place within given social systems. Feeling tone is a multifaceted construct that is facilitated by culturally familiar instructional strategies and content including (1) interactional patterns, (2) group processes, (3) analogies, (4) materials, and (5) the physical environment. Some culturally diverse children may be more comfortable observing demonstration lessons and modeling their performance after the teacher, while others are more attentive when they engage in hands-on exploratory learning. Finally, some children may prefer interacting with others in a group setting rather than answering teacher-directed questions during expository teaching sessions.

In creating culturally affirming classrooms, that is, classrooms with positive feeling tones, you should incorporate culturally familiar analogies, themes, and curricular materials as part of the instructional program. The use of these elaborative strategies builds bridges that connect the student's prior knowledge with new knowledge. Culturally familiar analogies are examples or stories that may be used to illustrate concepts taught in the classroom. For example, when introducing the concept of a myelin sheath to a group of Chicano students, you could say that a myelin sheath surrounds the nerve cell in the way that a corn husk surrounds a tamale. The use of this analogy vali-

Culturally familiar analogies and elaborations increase student learning. (© Stephen Marks)

dates the child's home learning and assists the child in appending new learning to existing knowledge structures.

Culturally familiar materials can help students make linkages between their real world experiences and abstract scientific concepts. When you bring culturally based materials, whether pinto beans, origami paper, bagels, milk cartons, tires, or paper kites, into the classroom, you are valuing the child's real world learning experiences while providing conceptual bridges to link the child's prior knowledge to new learning. Certainly, *all* new learning does not have to be culturally relevant or linked to culturally familiar objects and events. However, children are motivated to learn when classroom environments establish a positive feeling tone.

Success.   Success is the third motivational factor that has been shown to improve the learning of culturally diverse students in the elementary science classroom. There is a popular adage which states that "success breeds success." Within the context of children's learning, this adage could be worded as follows: the more success students have experienced in the past, the more optimistic they are about their future academic performance. The corollary to this statement reads, on the other hand, the more that children have failed in the past, the less willing they are to expose themselves to risk, because their prediction is that they will not be successful.

Success as a motivational principle is grounded in the affiliative drive and ego-enhancing components of achievement motivation theory. Ausubel, Novak, and Hanesian point out that children need to do well in school in order to retain the approval of the superordinate figure (i.e., a significant other) with whom the child emotionally identifies (1978, p. 398). Success in school contributes to a child's ego enhancement, another component of achievement motivation theory. McClelland (1965) and Atkinson (1964), in formulating achievement motivation theories, stated that achievement behavior is based on two competing needs: the need to achieve success versus the need to avoid failure. The desire to achieve adult approval (including the approval of the teacher) is very strong in young children. Toward the end of elementary school, the approval of a superordinate figure diminishes in most children's lives, to be gradually replaced by peer approval in the middle school years.

Studies of children show that those with high expectancies of success generally persist longer in attempting new learning than students with lower expectancies of success. Highly motivated students, those who expect to be successful, are rarely a problem in the classroom. These students typically enjoy challenging assignments and corrective feedback from the teacher, and respond with greater effort and enthusiasm when they meet temporary failure. Students concerned with avoiding failure will present the greatest challenge to a teacher. Typically, these students prefer to work in cooperative learning groups, thus avoiding individual failure. Assistance in goal-setting is also vital for the success of students with low expectancy states. You can assist students to break the cycle of academic failure by (1) separating large tasks into manageable pieces, (2) restating tasks in terms of subtasks, (3) helping students to set reasonable goals, (4) providing ample reinforcement for success, (5) avoiding public recognition of children's mistakes or failures, and (6) providing supportive instructional environments (i.e., cooperative or *familial* learning groups).

Closely related to personal success is the concept of successful role models. Ausubel's writings regarding significant others and Bandura's writings regarding role models speak to the need for culturally diverse role models in the elementary science classroom. All children need successful role models to emulate. Sometimes teachers become significant others in the lives of students; at

Teachers are frequently significant others in the lives of children. (© Stephen Marks)

other times parents or other adults in the community become role models for young children. Role models are vital in actualizing a child's interest in science. If students see that other culturally diverse men and women have been successful in science careers, students are able to project themselves into those same careers (see Activity 2-8 and Chapter 3). Success in the elementary science classroom is highly related to other motivational factors, including level of concern and feeling tone. Learning is maximized when these three motivational factors work in concert.

Interest.   Interest or curiosity is the fourth factor shown to improve students' motivation to learn science. **Interest** is a multifaceted motivational construct that includes real world connections of learning, novelty, surprise, ego-enhancement, personal preferences, curiosity, and intellectual needs. Maehr (1984) points out that some tasks or topics by their very nature are more interesting and inherently motivating than other tasks. Most children would rather learn about the life and times of dinosaurs than about regrouping numbers. This is not to say that both are not equally "good learning"; rather, children tend to be motivated to learn some things more readily than others. Children's interests can be readily inventoried through the use of interest surveys. See Activity 2-1 at the end of this chapter.

From the perspective of cognitive psychology, interest as a motivational factor is grounded in theories of cognitive dissonance or cognitive disequilibrium. Wadsworth (1978) states that children of all ages need to have opportunities to select activities that interest them. He goes on to point out that what is desirable is that children experience disequilibrium; to put it another way, they must come to realize that their conception(s) is no longer adequate in some sense (Wadsworth, 1978, p. 79). Disequilibrium is intrinsic motivation. Piaget states that equilibrium can be thought of as a more or less temporary state of balance or stability between the processes of assimilation and accommodation in the child's cognitive system (Wadsworth, 1978, p. 79). Equilibrium may be thought of as a self-regulating factor in the development of a child's knowledge. Assimilation (taking new knowledge into an existing knowledge structure without altering that schema) and accommodation (taking new knowledge into a knowledge structure with minor modifications of the knowledge structure) allow the child to remain in a state of cognitive equilibrium.

A child raised on a dairy farm who is used to seeing Brown Swiss cows every day would probably not be upset at the sight of a black and white Holstein cow. In other words, the child takes in the information that cows come in more than one color and incorporates that information into his or her knowledge structure regarding cows. The child accommodates new information and remains in a state of cognitive equilibrium. If, on the other hand, a young inner-city child (who is used to seeing dogs and cats) encounters a live cow for the first time, the child might be thrown into a state of cognitive disequilibrium. The inner-city child would not have an existing schema to accommodate the concept of "cows." In this instance, the child would move from a state of cognitive equilibrium to a state of cognitive disequilibrium. Interest and curiosity are aroused when we encounter a new phenomenon. We are motivated to learn when we are presented with information that we can not assimilate or accommodate with our existing knowledge structures.

A knowledge of relationships between classroom learning and real world experiences increases our interest or motivation to learn. We become interested or "reinterested" in something when we see its usefulness or practical applications. Most of us, as children, were interested in learning about electricity: in constructing circuits from bulbs, batteries, and wire. As adults, our interest in electricity is rekindled each year when we are faced with replacing burned out bulbs on strings of Christmas "twinky lights." As we realize that our prior knowledge of parallel and series circuits is useful in solving the problem of "Which bulb is the 'bad' bulb?" our interest in or appreciation of our knowledge of electrical circuits increases. The relevancy or usefulness of learning increases our interest and our motivation to learn.

Science educators have come to rely on discrepant events as motivational tools in the science classroom. A **discrepant event** is a "phenomenon which occurs that seems to run contrary to our first line of reasoning; it is a device to stimulate student's interest in learning science concepts and principles" (Wright,

1981, p. 575). The "Kung Fu" demonstration developed by Wright (1981) illustrates the concept of a discrepant event (Figure 2.1). In this activity, the teacher places a slat of wood on a desk. Two pieces of newspaper are placed smoothly over the portion of the slat that is resting on the desk. The teacher hits the overhanging portion of the slat with the side of his/her hand and the slat snaps. This activity illustrates the concept of air pressure, or, as Wright says, "the tremendous pressure exerted on the newspaper and transmitted to the slat by atmospheric pressure" (1981, p. 579). The "Kung Fu" activity also illustrates the concept of a discrepant event. As the teacher hits the slat, students expect that the paper will fly up in the air; however, the unexpected happens: the slat breaks. Discrepant events move students from a state of cognitive equilibrium to a state of cognitive dissonance or disequilibrium; they motivate us (see Activity 2-4 and Activity 2-5).

Status.   Status is a fifth factor vital in motivating culturally diverse students to learn science in the elementary classroom. **Status** may be defined within a humanistic psychology tradition as the need to belong or the need for self-esteem. Within Maslow's hierarchy of needs, belonging involves being loved and accepted in one's peer group or family. The need for self-esteem is closely related to the need for belonging, in that self-esteem involves the desire to gain recognition and approval from others. Status may be broadly defined as one's social position or rank within a group.

In writing from a cognitive psychology viewpoint of a students' status within the peer group, Ausubel states that an adolescent's exaggerated need to conform to peer group values is a function of the students' marginal and prolonged interim status in our culture (Ausubel, Novak & Hanesian, 1978, p.

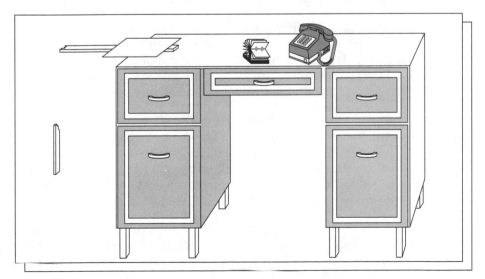

FIGURE 2.1   Discrepant Event

463). He further points out that adolescents are highly dependent on their peers for much of their social status. Status is a function of a child's social class, ethnicity, peer acceptance, and academic role in the classroom.

Cohen (1991) explains the motivational aspects of status in terms of expectation states theory. She points out that academic status characteristics are the most powerful of the status characteristics in the classroom because of their relevance to classroom activities. Cohen and her associates have investigated the effect of teacher intervention in the motivational process through a series of experiments in which teachers orally "confer status" on students through the use of praise. Findings from her study support the notion that teachers can increase the participation of low-status students in classroom activities through the verbal feedback that they provide to students. Improving students' status in the classroom increases their motivation to learn science (see Activity 2-6).

Knowledge of Results.   A knowledge of results is the final motivational factor which has been shown to impact students' learning of science. A knowledge of results may also be thought of as feedback. As a rule of thumb, when you give students a knowledge of results, for instance, of test results, give them the correct answer with an explanation of why it is correct (Hunter, 1982, p. 22). Research from cognitive psychology demonstrates that students are very logical and intelligent in making errors—few errors are randomly made (Woolfolk & McCune-Nicolich, 1984, p. 560). Feedback assists students in restructuring their schema, their perceptions of the world around them.

Schimmel (1988) points out that feedback is a powerful force, which has both motivational and cognitive effects in students' learning. He writes that three types of feedback are commonly used in the elementary classroom: (1) confirmatory feedback, (2) corrective feedback, and (3) explanatory feedback.

Confirmatory Feedback.   **Confirmatory feedback** provides students with information as to the "correctness" of an answer. Confirmatory feedback answers the question, "Is the answer correct?" The response to corrective feedback is a simple yes or no answer. An "x" marked on a spelling paper next to a word indicates to the student that the word is incorrectly spelled.

Corrective Feedback.   **Corrective feedback**, on the other hand, not only provides the student with a knowledge of whether an answer is right or wrong but also of what the "correct" answer ought to be. Assume that a teacher has asked students to identify the parts of a plant cell on a quiz. The teacher could provide corrective feedback by writing statements such as "No, that's not the nucleus, it's the chloroplast" on the child's paper.

Explanatory Feedback.   **Explanatory feedback** is the most reflective and corrective type of feedback. Explanatory feedback is usually provided to students when higher-order thinking skills are being taught in the classroom. This type of feedback provides students with knowledge of the accuracy of their answer, knowledge of the correct answer, and understanding of how they went wrong. For example, assume a teacher has asked students to compare and contrast monocot and dicot plants in terms of their leaves and seeds. In writing a journal entry to contrast the two types of plants, the student missed some of the salient information about the differences between the plants. The teacher might write the following comment:

> "Your answer is good, but you need to spend some more time looking at the leaves of the plant. Why not go back and compare the monocot leaf with the dicot leaf? Pay particular attention to the veins in the leaves of the plants."

Explanatory feedback provides the student with a knowledge that their answer was incomplete, that they need to reflect more on what they have learned and what they need to learn. In the aforementioned explanatory feedback, the teacher has focused the attention of the student on the critical attribute (the vein structure of the leaf). The feedback is motivating, since the student is challenged to go back and look at the leaves and determine the difference(s) that exist between them.

CLASSROOM PRACTICE

As a teacher, you will sometimes introduce activities in the classroom for their motivational as well as for their educational value. Discrepant events, games, and activity corners capitalize on the motivational factors of level of concern, feeling tone, success, interest, status, and knowledge of results. In this section of the chapter, examples of some field-tested motivational devices are presented to give you ideas for activities that you can replicate in the elementary science classroom. When using motivational devices, remember to inventory your students first to determine their interests (see Activity 2-1).

A knowledge of your students and the community that they come from is vital in assisting students to acquire a knowledge of science. Some students have been socialized to enjoy games and competition, while other children have been socialized to enjoy cooperative group work. This section of the chapter focuses on practical everyday suggestions for activities that may encourage children to acquire or build a knowledge of science. The activities include (1) games for individuals, small groups, and large groups; (2) interest and esteem-building activities; (3) discrepant events; (4) role model building; and (5) parental involvement.

ACTIVITY 2-1 ■ STUDENT INTEREST INVENTORY

Grade Level: All

Purpose: Students' science survey—motivational activity.

Directions for the Student: Read the list of science topics. Rank the topics from the one that you would most like to learn about (1) to the one that you would least like to learn about (10).

_____ dinosaurs
_____ plants
_____ human body
_____ animals without backbones
_____ environment
_____ oceans
_____ weather
_____ magnetism and electricity
_____ space travel
_____ solar system

ACTIVITY 2-2 ■ CHEMISTRY BINGO

Grade Level: Upper elementary

Purpose: Large group motivational activity.

Directions for the Teacher: Prepare blank "Chemo" (chemistry bingo cards with a 5 x 5 grid) cards for the students. On the day of the game, place a list of chemical symbols for elements on the chalkboard and ask the students to select 24 symbols from the list and place them randomly on their cards. Prior to playing the game, make a set of chemical symbol cards by placing the name of the element on one side of the card and the symbol on the other.

Ca	H	Na	Fe	N
Ag	Au	K	Ni	Cl
O	Al	Chemo	Br	Zn
Cu	I	S	P	U
Mg	Mn	F	Cd	He

Playing the Game: When students have marked the symbols for 24 elements on their playing cards, have them tear markers from a sheet of scrap paper. Conduct the game as a Bingo game, except that the name of an element is called out and the student is to cover the symbol. Prizes for the game would typically include edible rewards such as granola bars and small prizes such as balloons or pencils.

ACTIVITY 2-3 ■ LIFE IN THE ESTUARY

Grade Level: Intermediate to upper elementary

Purpose: Small group board game—motivational activity.

Teacher Preparation: Duplicate the "Life in the Estuary" game board and the paper spinners.

Life in the Estuary

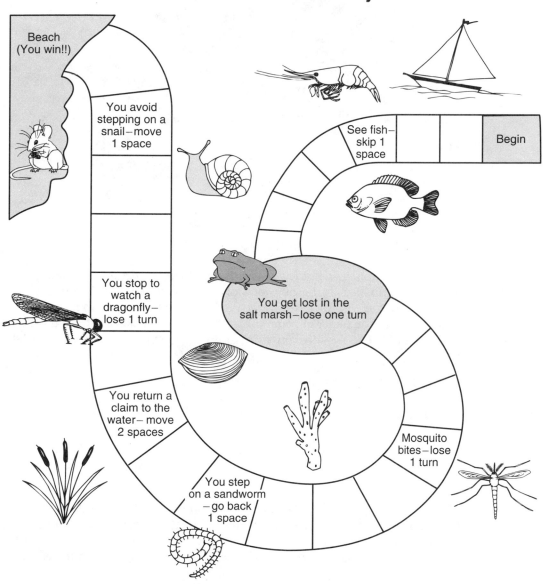

Beach (You win!!)

You avoid stepping on a snail—move 1 space

You stop to watch a dragonfly—lose 1 turn

You return a claim to the water—move 2 spaces

You step on a sandworm—go back 1 space

You get lost in the salt marsh—lose one turn

Mosquito bites—lose 1 turn

See fish—skip 1 space

Begin

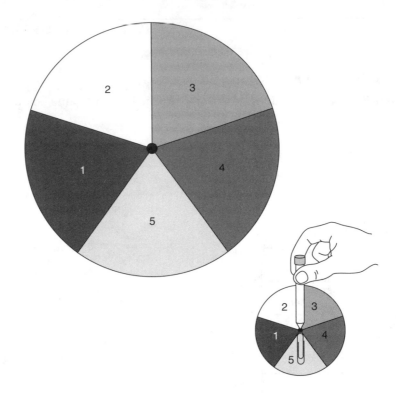

Student Directions: The object of the game is to be the first one in your group (students are divided into groups of 3 or 4) to travel through the estuary. On your journey you will travel from a boat offshore to the beach. To move across the board, spin the paper clip and move the number of spaces directed on the playing board. The first person successfully to touch the flag on the beach wins.

Materials (for each group):

1 paper clip   1 pencil
1 playing board   1 spinner

Material (for each student):

1 marker (e.g., coin, piece of colored paper)

Notes:

1. For durability, tape the game board and spinner inside a manila file folder.
2. If students do not have access to game boards at home, run extra copies and allow students to color and take home a copy to play with parents or siblings. This affords students the opportunity to share what they are learning and provides a board game for the home.

ACTIVITY 2-4 ▪ CARTESIAN DIVER

Grade Level: Primary to upper elementary

Purpose: Discrepant event—motivational activity.

Materials (for each group):

1 plastic soda bottle   1 eye dropper

Student Directions: Fill the plastic soda bottle completely full of water. Squeeze the bulb of the eye dropper and suck up half a dropper full of water. Lightly place the dropper upright in the soda bottle and **tightly** cap the bottle.

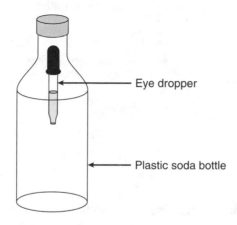

Eye dropper

Plastic soda bottle

Operational Questions: (Teacher directed questions to guide student's investigations.)

1. What happens when you squeeze the bottle?
2. What happens with a one-handed squeeze?
3. What happens with a two-handed squeeze?
4. Can you make the diver stay on the bottom of the container?
5. As you squeeze the bottle, what happens to the level of water in the eye dropper?
6. Can you make the diver rise and sink faster? If so, how?
7. What happens to the diver if you loosen the cap on the bottle?

Note: This apparatus demonstrates the concept of the Cartesian diver.

ACTIVITY 2-5 ▪ STANDING VORTEX

Grade Level: Intermediate to upper elementary

Purpose: Discrepant event—motivational activity.

Materials (for each group):

2 plastic soda bottles
1 piece of rubber tubing (heavy duct tape may be substituted for the tubing)

Teacher Preparation: Fill one soda bottle completely full of tap water and stand it on a table. Invert the second bottle on top of the first one. Connect the bottles with rubber tubing or heavy duct tape.

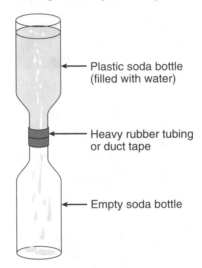

Plastic soda bottle
(filled with water)

Heavy rubber tubing
or duct tape

Empty soda bottle

Student Directions: Instruct the students to turn the bottles such that the one full of water is on top.

Operational Questions:

1. What happens when the bottle full of water is placed on top?
2. What happens if you gently swirl the bottle?
3. Can you make the vortex move faster? How?
4. How can you make the vortex move slower?

Note: This activity illustrates the principle of a standing vortex or a Coriolis effect.

ACTIVITY 2-6 ■ MINI MUSEUM

Grade Level: Primary to upper elementary

Purpose: Interest and curiosity—motivational activity.

Materials:

plain index cards   marking pen
science field guides

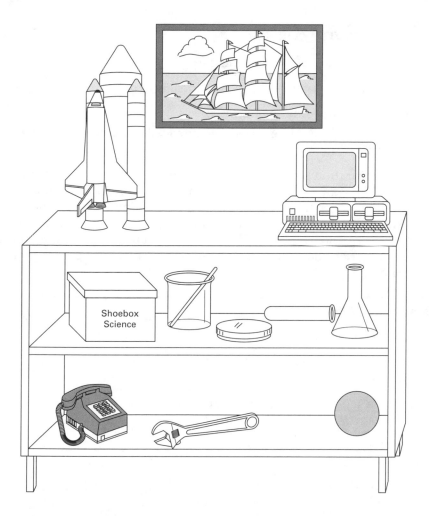

Teacher Preparation: Set aside a corner of the classroom for a mini museum or a science activity corner.

Mini Museum: A mini museum is a student-centered motivational device used to build students' self-esteem and involve parents in children's education. At the beginning of each unit of study, the teacher should clean out existing displays and explain the next unit of study to students. Students should be encouraged to bring *realia* associated with the new unit of study to the classroom. Exhibits should be marked with their name and the name of the contributing student. Exhibits involve students in identifying objects in the natural world. In addition, a mini museum involves parents in children's education.

ACTIVITY 2-7 ■ ACTIVITY CORNER

Grade Level: Primary to upper elementary

Purpose: Interest and curiosity—motivational activity.

Materials (These are only suggestions):

shoebox science kits (Chapter 7) teacher provided *realia*, computer software learning stations, library books

Teacher Preparation: Prior to beginning a unit of study, the teacher should "round up" filmstrips, library books, computer software, posters, models, and *realia* associated with the new unit of study. The purpose of these materials is to provide the opportunity for students to pursue their own interests when time permits. An activity corner is a teaching resource, a place where students can go during transitional times and "unassigned" time to engage in independent learning.

ACTIVITY 2-8 ■ GRAND PRIX

Grade Level: Primary to upper elementary

Purpose: Large group motivational activity.

Materials:

1 grand prix race car for each group in the classroom (cut from colored construction paper)

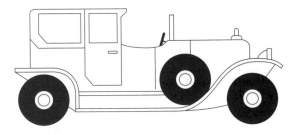

masking tape
1 grand prix race course drawn on the chalkboard

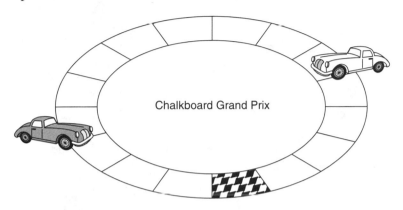

Chalkboard Grand Prix

Teacher Preparation: This is a large group board game designed to involve all students in the class. Before the students begin the activity, draw the race course on the chalkboard and cut out race cars, one for each group of students. This activity works well as an end of unit review of low-level knowledge.

Conducting the Activity: Divide the students into groups (4–8 per group). Select or allow the students to select a captain for each group (official answers must come from the group captain). Ask the students questions derived from the current unit of study. When a group gets a correct response, their car moves forward 1 space on the race course. The first car across the finish line "wins."

ACTIVITY 2-9 ■ CONCENTRATION

Grade Level: Primary to upper elementary

Purpose: Large or small group instructional activity.

Materials:

1 concentration game board (a 5 × 6 grid of numbers) with detachable numbers and *questions* behind each number (see figure on next page)

Notes on Questions:

Older students: A concentration game using famous culturally diverse scientists and their contributions is shown on the next page. The object is for students to match each scientist with the contribution. The student calls off two numbers. If the name under the number matches the contribution, the students are given the covering number cards; if not, the next group gets a chance to select two numbers. The game continues until all matches have been made.

A
C
T
I
V
I
T
I
E
S

1	2	3	4	5
6	7	8	9	10
11	12	13	14	15
16	17	18	19	20
21	22	23	24	25
26	27	28	29	30

Value of pi	Al Khwarizmi	Beta disintegration	Semiconductors	Ramon y Cajal
Smallpox inoculation	Synthesized RNA	Plant genetics	Invented paper	Invented algebra
Burbank	Ochoa	Filament for light bulb	Chang Heng	Jumping genes
D'Elhuyar	Discovered tungsten	Esaki	Wu	Discovered neuron
Tsai Lun	Discovered radium & polonium	Latimer	Heavy metal poisoning	Shen Kua
McClintock	Discovered magnetic compass	Ishimure	Onesimus	M. Curie

See the appendix at the end of Chapter 3 for a list of culturally diverse scientists and their contributions.

Younger Students: For younger students match objects and their names. The version below shows living things and their names. When students match the picture with the name of the picture, a match is made.

		Rose	Mouse	
Palm tree	Fish	Ostrich		Elephant
Pine tree			Owl	Beetle
		Penguin		Dolphin
	Spider			Snail
Oak tree		Butterfly		

ACTIVITY 2-10 ▪ TRIVIAL PURSUIT

Grade Level: Intermediate to upper elementary

Purpose: Large group motivational activity.

Materials:

bank of quiz questions (see Table 2.3) and category cards

TABLE 2.3   Trivial Pursuit Question Bank

Question	Answer
Category: Animals	
1. Name for a group of animals with 6 legs.	insects
2. Name of a soft bodied animal that carries its "house" on its back.	snail
3. Name for the world's largest animal.	whale
4. An insect that lives in a hive, lives in colonies.	honeybees
5. Animal that lays eggs in nests, warm blooded.	bird
Category: Plants	
1. Name of trees that are green all year long, keep their leaves.	evergreen
2. The part of the plant that takes in water.	root
3. The part of the plant that makes almost all of the food.	leaf
4. The container that holds a baby plant and its food.	seed
5. What part of the carrot plant do we normally eat?	root
Category: Magnetism	
1. The name of the ends of a magnet.	poles
2. The opposite end from the North Pole.	South
3. In magnets, like poles _____.	repel
4. In magnets, unlike poles _____.	attract
5. Type of material picked up by a magnet.	iron (steel)
Category: Human Body	
1. The organ that pumps blood.	heart
2. The organ responsible for thinking.	brain
3. Structures which hold up or support the body.	bones
4. Largest organ in the body.	skin
5. The main organ of vision.	eye

Teacher Preparation: Prepare a list of low-level questions for the game. Questions should be related to information that has been taught. Divide the students into groups and have each group select a captain. Give each group a question in rotation. Each time a group correctly answers the question, the group receives a point. The group with the most points at the end of the game "wins."

ACTIVITY 2-11 ▪ DINOSAUR EXTINCTION

Grade Level: Intermediate to upper elementary

Purpose: Large or small group instructional activity.

Materials:

bank of vocabulary words for   dinosaur puzzle
  current unit of study   masking tape

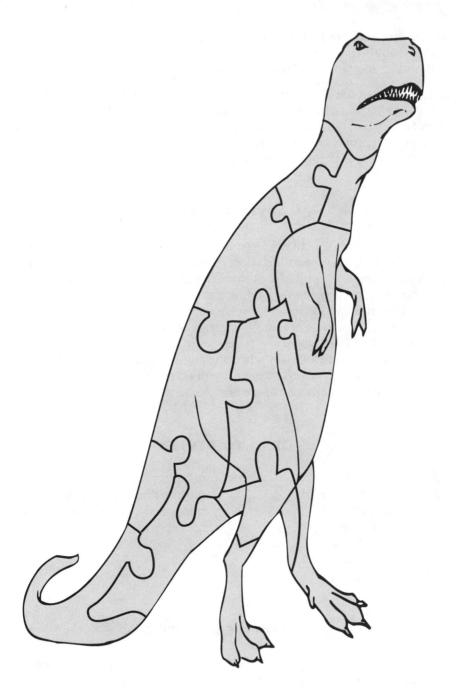

ACTIVITIES

Teacher Preparation: Prepare the dinosaur model by coloring and cutting out the figure on the preceding page. Place a tape roll on the back of each piece of the dinosaur and tape the dinosaur on the blackboard.

Student Directions: Dinosaur Extinction is played like the old game of Hangman. Put a row of dashes on the blackboard, with each dash representing one letter of a vocabulary word that is being used. For each incorrect guess, remove one piece of the dinosaur from the board. The objective is to guess the word before the dinosaur becomes extinct (all pieces are removed from the board).

 CHAPTER SUMMARY

One of the primary objectives of elementary science education is to interest and involve students in learning science and considering participation in science-related careers in adult life. Motivational factors are rooted in behavioristic, humanistic, and cognitive psychology traditions. Research indicates that the use of six motivation factors—level of concern, feeling tone, success, interest, status, and knowledge of results—increase the likelihood that children will be encouraged to learn science. The use of motivating factors also increases the likelihood that classrooms will become culturally affirming environments, places where culturally diverse students will be encouraged to continue their study of science and perhaps engage in science careers in adult life.

 TOPICS TO REVIEW

discrepant event, 34
nine characteristics of rich
   educational tasks, 29
six factors that increase
   motivation, 28
six steps to break the cycle of
   failure, 32

psychology viewpoints on
   motivation (behavioral,
   humanistic, and cognitive), 25
three types of feedback, 36

 REFLECTIVE PRACTICE

1. How are humanistic, cognitive, and behavioristic views on motivation similar? How do they differ?
2. What is meant by "making classrooms culturally affirming environments"? What specific ways can you identify that could be used to produce such environments?
3. Identify six "strategies" for motivating culturally diverse students. How could

each of these be used to make your classroom more appealing to culturally diverse students?

4. How can you modify assignments such that they are motivating for culturally diverse students?

5. In your opinion, why are all motivational factors not equally effective for all students?

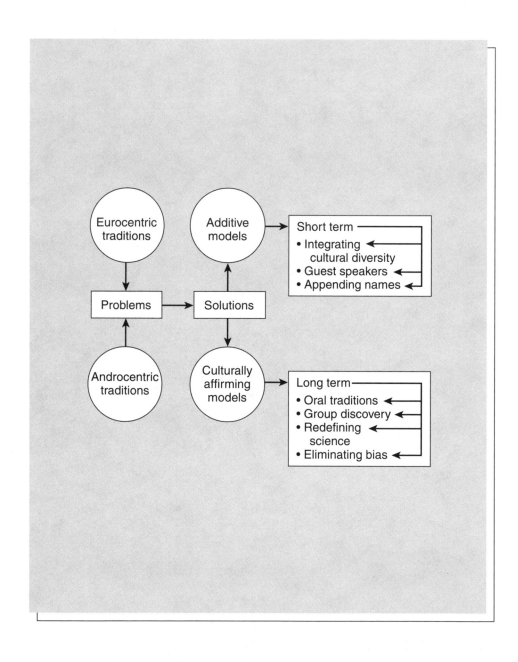

CHAPTER 3

THE HISTORY OF SCIENCE: A CULTURALLY AFFIRMING PERSPECTIVE

 POINTS TO PONDER

1. How many women scientists can you name?
2. How many culturally diverse scientists can you name?
3. What are the roots of modern science and medicine?
4. Do all cultures view "discovery" in the same manner?
5. What can be done to make the history of science more culturally affirming for all students?

y mother-in-law is a curandera, *a healer. Her yard is a beautiful, aromatic pharmacy, filled with plant species garnered from remote corners of the desert, where she has spent her entire life. As a young bride, she moved from the city of El Paso, Texas, to the isolated, rural railroad section where my father-in-law worked. The rail section at Swanee, New Mexico, has long since been bulldozed to the ground, but once it was home to a dozen Chicano families. Four or five decades ago, Swanee was located in the middle of nowhere, 50 miles from the nearest town and the nearest doctor.*

The women and men who lived in this remote area developed a special kinship with the land; they came to regard the desert as a source of food, housing, and medicine. The desert was the source of clay with which to make adobes and to build homes capable of withstanding the heat of summer and the cold of winter. If properly irrigated and cultivated, the desert soil was a source of food for their families. Finally, the desert was a source of medicine in a time when a trip to the doctor was undertaken only in the case of a life-threatening illness. During her years in Swanee, my mother-in-law learned the skills of midwifery through hands-on practice. She also learned the uses of the plants that grew around her home. Aloe, yucca, peppermint, ironweed, and stink weed abound in the New Mexican desert. Soap to disinfect wounds, salves to soothe cuts, teas to reduce fevers, and liniments to ease the pain of muscle strains can be derived from desert flora.

Modern medicine has its roots in traditional folk medicine. The current rush of pharmaceutical companies to the vanishing rain forests of the world is modern testimony to the curative value of plant species (caution needs to be exercised to avoid assuming that all folk medicine is good medicine). As we speak to children of science careers, we often forget to tell them of their heritage, of their families' and communities' historical place in science and medicine. We forget to validate their scientific traditions and to remind them that science is for all Americans.

OUR POINT OF VIEW

Traditionally, science has been taught in American schools from a Eurocentric and/or androcentric viewpoint. In the past, emphasis in the science curricula in schools has been placed on "the scientific method" and on famous scientists (primarily of European extraction) as the originators of our knowledge base regarding science. This view of the history of science excludes the historical contributions of many culturally diverse individuals and history and deprives children of vitally needed role models. One goal of science education, as expressed in *The Liberal Art of Science*, is "to increase the numbers of women, Blacks, and Hispanic/Latino students who major in natural sciences and pursue science and science-related careers" (AAAS, 1990, p. 64). Achieving this goal will require that culturally diverse children be involved in learning and doing science.

This chapter seeks to examine the historical, axiologic, and epistemologic roots of science as it is presented in "traditional" science textbooks and curricula in American public schools and to propose a culturally transforming model of science for incorporation into science education classes and instructional materials. A colleague of mine, who teaches social studies at a large Western university, begins his course each semester by asking the question, "Who discovered America?" He gets the usual answers about Columbus and Leif Erikson and other early European discoverers from his students. Then he asks a second question, "Was America ever lost?" From a Native-American perspective, the United States of America could not have been found because it was never lost. Many of us

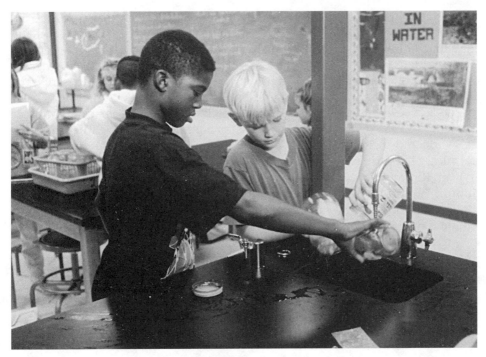

Science is for all Americans. (© Jim Pickerell)

tend to view U.S. history from a European viewpoint, while ignoring our Native-American heritage. It is as if life began when European explorers and settlers arrived on these shores.

The history of science has also been shaped and presented to American school children in our current science education programs from a European, white male-dominated viewpoint. American children find few examples of culturally diverse role models in their textbooks or classrooms. A classic study of textbooks revealed that the most widely used elementary texts in science, math, reading, spelling, and social studies contained female and culturally diverse persons in fewer than one third of the illustrations (Sadker & Sadker, 1979). The exclusion of culturally diverse individuals and females from textbooks results in a situation in which children lack culturally diverse role models. Before children can actualize their interest in science, they must be made aware of the opportunities for their participation in scientific endeavors.

The Eurocentric Tradition in the History of Science

The European tradition in the history of science is embodied in the "scientific method" and in the contributions of European scientists (and those of European heritage) to that body of knowledge (Al-Daffa & Stroyls, 1984). The questions that scientists ask, the ways that they explore the world around them, their sources of data, and the ways that they view truth and knowledge are derived from this European tradition. Writers of textbooks and curricular materials for children are normally trained in this Eurocentric scientific tradition and their writings, that is, the textbooks and instructional materials provided to American children reflect their training. The **scientific method** is described in many older science textbooks (Bierer, Lien, & Silberstein, 1987; American Chemical Society, 1988; Merrill Publishing; Slesnick, Balzer, McCormack, Newton & Rasmussen, 1985; Oram, 1986) as a five-step method for investigating the natural world and includes (1) stating the problem, (2) collecting information, (3) forming a hypothesis, (4) testing the hypothesis, and (5) drawing a conclusion. Within this tradition, Jean Lamarck is credited with discovering a theory of evolution, Watson and Crick discovered the structure of the DNA molecule, and Boyle discovered the gas laws. Frequently, science is presented to children as a single way of investigating the world rather than as a multifaceted construct.

If a scientist or a group of people does not follow this formula, is any resulting discovery science? Probably not, at least according to our science textbooks

Native Americans conducted genetic experiments on corn. (North Wind Picture Archives)

and curricular materials. For thousands of years, the Native Americans of the Southwestern United States and Central America have cultivated corn. Each year the biggest and the best ears of maize were saved by the harvesters and used as seed the following year. The tradition of sowing only genetically superior seeds resulted in the improvement of maize from a stubby little weed into the well formed ears of corn that we know today. The Native Americans certainly followed the scientific method in that they identified the problem, collected information about which ears of maize were the best, formed the hypothesis that planting the biggest seeds would result in an improved plant, conducted experiments in plant growth for thousands of years, and passed on their findings orally to their children. However, we do not view Native Americans as the founders of genetics research.

Native Americans did not keep written records of their research, nor did they present their findings for peer review in the scientific community. Credit for the discovery of genetics research is given to Gregor Mendel. Did Gregor Mendel alone discover genetics research or were there others who walked down that same path before he did? Who discovered genetics research? Our Eurocentric view of science, which includes the notion that the scientific method must be used (e.g., keeping copious notes, writing reports of findings, and reporting findings to scientific societies), excludes the research of generations of Native Americans.

Eurocentric science is not only dominated by the scientific method, but is also dominated by discoveries attributed to white males. In 1721, Onesimus, an African-American slave, explained to his master, Cotton Mather, how he had been inoculated against smallpox when he was a child (Sammons, 1990). Everyone in Onesimus's tribe knew that it was common sense to transmit a less virulent form of smallpox to children to prevent them from getting a deadly form of the disease. African parents taught their children this simple inoculation procedure through a tradition of oral history and learning. Cotton Mather wrote a letter to Dr. Boylston explaining the smallpox inoculation procedure which his slave Onesimus had shown him. Boylston tried the procedure on his son and two slaves and reported his findings in a letter to a colleague. For his discovery, Boylston was called to London and honored in the scientific community by being made a fellow of the Royal Society. Onesimus, the slave who bridged the knowledge gap between the oral medical practices of his homeland and the European world, received no such credit. Who then discovered the smallpox vaccination?

It can indeed be argued that the genetics research of Native Americans and the discovery of a smallpox vaccination by the Banyoro tribe in Africa were prescientific revolution discoveries and thus fall into a category of quasi-scientific discovery. However, even when culturally diverse scientists and women did make scientific discoveries using the scientific method, those discoveries were frequently claimed by white male colleagues. Discoveries regarding the functions of the honeybee's antennae, the expulsion of drones from the beehive, and the fertilization flight of the queen bee made by Maria Aimee Lullin (1750–

Annie Jump Cannon (1863–1941), Astronomer, Harvard University
(Harvard College Observatory)

1831) were published under the name of her husband, Francois Huber (Alic, 1986). As sometimes was the practice during this period, discoveries made by women were not acknowledged to be as credible as those made by men, which led to women publishing under male names. The lack of female and minority role models in currently used science textbooks is, in part, both a function of our Eurocentric view of the world and a reflection of the role that women and culturally diverse individuals held in our society in the past.

The Androcentric Tradition in the History of Science

The androcentric model of the history of science credits scientific discoveries to particular individuals. Within this tradition, Dimitri Mendeleev is credited as being the discoverer of the periodic table of elements, Joseph Priestley is credited with the discovery that plants produce oxygen gas, and Henri Becquerel is credited with the discovery of the x-ray. Group discoveries of knowledge are rarely acknowledged within the androcentric tradition of science.

Charles Finch has recorded a story of obstetrical procedures from the history of science in East Africa (Van Sertima, 1986). In 1879, a missionary doctor named Felkin observed a Banyoro surgeon in Uganda performing a Caesarean section. A young woman was lying in a hut preparing to deliver her first child. The delivery had been particularly difficult and the tribal surgeon had given the young mother-to-be some banana wine to ease the pain of childbirth. Banana wine was commonly used by the Banyoro as a pain killing drug. When it became apparent that both the mother and child were in difficulty and that both might die, the surgeon poured banana wine on the mother's abdomen and on his surgical knife. The wine acted as an antiseptic and killed germs on the mother's skin and on the knife which the surgeon would use. Next, the surgeon made an incision in the mother's abdomen and lifted the baby from its mother's abdomen. The cut in the mother's abdomen was sealed with hot irons, a procedure that we call cauterization today. Finally, the sides of the abdomen were reattached with sharp cactus spikes (in place of stitches) and the wound was bound with a hand woven grass mat soaked in the same banana wine. Did Lister alone invent antiseptic? Who invented pain killers? The cesarean section? Cauterization? Staples to close a surgical wound? Were they "invented" at all, or are they part of a long heritage of healing passed from one generation to the next? By insisting on identifying a particular individual as being a "discoverer" of knowledge, we neglect to acknowledge that many cultures do not value individualism and discovery, but rather see the group good as being the important consideration.

Moving Towards a Multicultural Perspective

There is little information readily available in currently used science textbooks, filmstrips, videos, and available supplementary science education materials which describes the contributions to science made by culturally diverse men and women. In fact, sometimes women and those from culturally diverse backgrounds are relegated to footnote status in science textbooks. Although these omissions may not be intentional, the hidden message is that women and culturally diverse individuals were and are not important scientists. This message victimizes all of us. Persons of color and white girls and women lack successful science role models while white boys and men develop a feeling of unfounded superiority. All human beings are being short-changed by this lack of knowledge and narrow perspective (world view orientation).

Additive Models

One strategy for handling the lack of culturally diverse role models in science education materials is through the use of an additive model (Gilbert & Gay, 1985). The additive model of history holds that providing underrepresented minority students with successful culturally diverse scientists as role models addresses the needs of students to have significant others in their lives. When using the additive method of restructuring the history of science in textbooks or classes, one could mention that an ancient Chinese scholar (Shen Kua) had invented the compass in approximately 1070 A.D. (Daintith, Mitchell & Tootill, 1981). One could mention that Percy Julian, an African-American man, had synthesized cortisone from soybeans and that cortisone is routinely used in the treatment of many illnesses including arthritis. In addition, we could include women in the history of science by adding the names of Chien-Shiung Wu,

Anna Comstock, Annie Jump Cannon, and Barbara McClintock to a list of famous scientists contained in science textbooks or on special "Scientist of the Day" bulletin boards.

The additive model appends culturally diverse role models and women to the list of white male European scientists already mentioned in textbooks, filmstrips, and instructional materials, thus perpetuating the androcentric nature of science. While the addition of information about the contributions of women and culturally diverse individuals may improve the quality of instruction for children, this action alone does not address the Eurocentric bias of science. Only when the contributions of women and culturally diverse individuals are woven into the fabric of our instruction will the basic axiologic and epistemologic foundations of science become inclusive rather than exclusive.

A Culturally Diverse Viewpoint

If the history of science taught in our schools is to be truly inclusive in nature rather than exclusive, certain fundamental changes must be made in the way(s) that we view science and scientific discovery. Suzuki (1984) suggests that we use a **culturally transforming model** for education. In science, a culturally transforming model would require the addition of culturally diverse individuals and groups to our current curricular materials and a review of the structure and values on which the discipline is based. First, science instruction needs to include the oral tradition of recording information in the history of science that we present to children. Second, we should tell children that scientific discovery does not always center on individual men and women. Some cultures value group discovery and not individual initiative. Third, our instruction should include a broadened definition of the scientific method to contain valid discoveries which research has shown to be effective and which may not have been derived through traditional Eurocentric channels. Finally, the bias in reporting the discoveries of culturally diverse individuals and women (e.g., attributing discoveries to the wrong author or ignoring the contributions of certain individuals or groups) needs to be eliminated from our curricular materials.

Oral Tradition of Science.   The oral tradition is often not recognized as a valid method for transmitting information in the scientific community. The basic axiologic and epistemologic assumptions of science hold that oral traditions are not valid sources of information. Thus, some individuals have labeled traditional scientific practices from culturally diverse groups as folk medicine. Some scientists and historians of science discount these contributions as "old wives' tales" because these discoveries were made without the controls and written documentation that accompany scientific discoveries. Certainly, there are folk medicine practices which are scientifically unfounded and unjustified in the scientific realm, but this should not discount all folk practices as being "bad science" and unworthy of note by the scientific community.

Many Hispanic parents know that the flowers of the daisy fleabane plant can be boiled into a tea which is used as a medicine to cure children's illnesses. For hundreds, probably thousands, of years, parents have been passing this oral tradition on to their children. *Manzanilla* is a mild analgesic which contains acetylsalicylic acid. In herbal tea form, *manzanilla* is a traditional cure of healers or *curanderos* for fevers, aches, and pains in children. In 1853, the German chemist, Charles Gerhardt, discovered acetylsalicylic acid ($C_9H_8O_4$) as a natural byproduct of coal tar: he called his discovery aspirin. If the history of science is to be made meaningful for Hispanic children, the discovery of aspirin by *curanderos* needs to be validated. The oral tradition as a means of communicating information from one generation to another needs to be included in our discussions of the nature of science that we hold with children.

Group Discoveries in the History of Science.　For centuries the Quechua-speaking Incas of the Andes had used *quina-quina* or the "bark of barks" to cure cramps, chills, heart-rhythm disorders, and a variety of illnesses. When Europeans arrived in the Americas, they brought with them malaria, a disease carried by the *anopheles* mosquito. Malaria is characterized by chills and fever and was a dreaded disease during medieval and colonial times. It is estimated that about 20% of the colonists of the Virginia colony were infected with malaria and died within a year of the disease (Weatherford, 1988). Historians estimate that approximately 2 million people a year died from malaria during the period of European colonization.

When malaria arrived in Peru, the Quechua-speaking Incas used their traditional "Peruvian bark" as a cure for the disease. Peruvian bark or quinine became a standard cure for the disease. Quinine was exported from Peru to Europe, North America, and throughout the world. In 1902, Sir Ronald Ross was awarded the Nobel Prize in medicine for discovering that the Anopheles mosquito carried malaria from one person to another. The discovery of the cure for malaria made by the Native Americans 300 years earlier was never honored. Surely, Sir Ronald Ross was deserving of the Nobel Prize for the discovery of the method of malaria transmission, but the Quechua-speaking Incas are also worthy of recognition for their cure of a disease that killed 2 million people a year. The inclusion of discoveries of groups into the mainstream fabric of science instruction will enhance the quality of science education for all students.

Broadening the Definition of Scientific Method.　There is a snobbery within the scientific community about the type of scientific discoveries which are considered to be worthy of note. Many scientists and historians of science give weight only to scientific discoveries which use the European language and standards of science as legitimate indicators of merit and deny the merit of discoveries which are derived from other investigative methods. In China, historically, when women gave birth, a dish of boiled pig's feet was prepared for the mother to eat. The dish

George Washington Carver, Biochemist.

is made by combining the pig's feet with a strong concentrated black vinegar. During the preparation, the vinegar dissolves the bone tissue in the pork and produces a thick broth, rich in calcium ions. When the newly delivered mother eats the pork, the calcium serves to replenish the minerals lost during childbirth and to stimulate lactation in the mother's body. In Asian communities throughout the United States this tradition of nourishing new mothers with a sweet and sour pork dish is still practiced.

If a licensed physician were to prescribe a calcium supplement for a new mother, we would tend to call this medicine. Homemade calcium supplements such as the one provided by the dish of pig's feet are commonly viewed as products of quackery and folklore. Both the prescription bottle of calcium pills and the homemade pork dish are effective in addressing the calcium deficiency in the new mother's body, but one is considered "sound medical practice" and the other "folklore." Validated discoveries derived through investigative means other than a five-step scientific method need to be included in discussions of the history of science designed for children.

Eliminate Bias in Reporting Discoveries.   The fourth barrier to the inclusion of culturally diverse individuals and women scientists in mainstream science is much more complicated because it derives from the oppressive nature of our society. Many women and culturally diverse researchers have been plagued by a lack of financial resources, lack of collegiality, and lack of opportunity to participate in mainstream science activities. For example, George Washington Carver taught only in black colleges and his laboratory was furnished with discards collected from the city dump, while the laboratories of his white peers were equipped by endowments from their universities. Carver was forced to work within an industrial arts setting, rather than within a mainstream science laboratory. The lack of a properly equipped working environment crippled Carver's ability to conduct the in-depth studies he wished to pursue.

Culturally diverse scientists and women have frequently been isolated from the rest of the scientific community. Scientists like George Washington Carver taught primarily in black institutions where they were isolated from their colleagues. Black research scientists like Charles Turner, Percy Julian, and Ernest Just were excluded from full participation in the American scientific community, as were white women like Annie Jump Cannon and Katharine Burr Blodgett. They were denied the professional interactions, laboratories, and access to public libraries accorded their white male counterparts and denied the opportunity to serve as mentors for the next generation of scientists.

Addressing the Needs of Culturally Diverse Learners

Just as they are learning that it is unclear that Columbus discovered America, our students need to know that people from all cultures have contributed to our knowledge of science. Some scientific practices have been handed down through oral tradition for hundreds of years, and these practices were often shaped by many individuals from specific communities. Because our society as a nation has strong Eurocentric roots, discoveries are often credited to white male members of our society. Unfortunately, Pearson and Bechtel (1989) point out that culturally diverse scientists and women have traditionally worked in isolation, have lacked the advanced training afforded to other scholars, have had their scholarly works usurped by others, have had their works relegated to footnotes, and have been excluded from full participation in the scientific community. Our science curriculum could become more accurate and alive if teachers and their students were to have better access to information about the contributions of culturally diverse individuals and women (see Table 3-1).

TABLE 3.1   Culturally Diverse Scientists

Name	Dates	Field	Country	Contribution
Al Khwarizmi	(800– 847)	Mathematics	Khiva, SSR	Invented algebra—1st and 2nd degree equations
Albategnius	(858– 929)	Astronomy	Turkey	Sine tables used for astronomical calculations
Albuzjani	(940– 998)	Mathematics	Persia	Trigonometry—tangents and cotangents
Alhazen	(965–1038)	Physics	Iraq	Spherical and parabolic mirrors
Alvarez, Luis	(1911–)	Physics	United States	Liquid hydrogen bubble chamber
Anderson, Elizabeth	(1836–1917)	Medicine	England	First woman physician in England
Arnald of Villanova	(1235–1313)	Chemistry	Spain	Alchemist—tinctures, carbon monoxide
Arzachel	(1080)	Astronomy	Spain	Planetary orbits are ellipses
Ashby, Winifred	(1879–1975)	Medicine	United States	Hematology techniques with red blood cells
Averroes	(1126–1198)	Medicine	Spain	Commentaries on Aristotle
Avicenna	(980–1037)	Medicine	Iran	Encyclopedia on medicine, function of human eye
Ayala, Francisco	(1934–)	Biology	Spain	Molecular evolution—genetic variation
Banneker, Benjamin	(1731–1806)	Physics	United States	Honeybee research, wooden striking clock
Bascom, Florence	(1862–1945)	Geology	United States	Optical crystallography
Bhabha, Homi	(1909–)	Physics	India	Cascade theory—cosmic rays
Blodgett, Katharine	(1898–1979)	Physics	United States	Nonreflecting glass
Bose, Jagadis	(1858–1937)	Physics	India	Short radio waves, plant tropisms
Bose, Stayendra	(1894–1974)	Physics	India	Electromagnetic properties of ionosphere
Brahmagupta	(598– 665)	Astronomy	India	Cyclic quadrilateral equation
Burbank, Luther	(1849–1926)	Botanist	United States	Plant genetics
Callinicus	(c. 670)	Chemistry	Egypt	Nature of combustion, "Greek fire"
Cannon, Annie	(1863–1941)	Astronomy	United States	Spectroscopic analysis of stars
Cano, Juan	(1460–1526)	Astronomy	Spain	First to circumnavigate the globe (not Magellan)
Carson, Rachel	(1907–1964)	Ecology	United States	Interdependence of plants and animals
Carver, George W.	(1864–1943)	Biochemistry	United States	Uses for peanuts, sweet potatoes; soil sciences
Chandrasekhar, Subrahmanyan	(1910–)	Astronomy	Pakistan	Stellar evolution, structure, and energy transfer
Chang, Min	(1908–)	Biology	China	In vitro fertilization, oral contraception
Chang Heng	(78– 142)	Astronomy	China	Value of pi, armilliary sphere, 1st seismograph
Chern, Shiing-shen	(1911–)	Mathematics	China	Differential geometry
Chou Kung	(c. 1200 B.C.)	Mathematics	China	Proofs for Pythagorean theorem, square root
Chu Shih-Chieh	(c. 1300)	Mathematics	China	Algebraic signs—negative numbers
Clarke, Edith	(1883–1959)	Mathematics	United States	Theory of symmetrical components
Comstock, Anna	(1854–1930)	Zoology	United States	Entomological drawings and illustrations
Cori, Gerty	(1896–1957)	Medicine	Czechoslovakia	Heredity of glycogen-storage diseases
Curie, Marie	(1867–1934)	Physics	Poland	Discovered radium and polonium
D'Elhuyar, Don Fausto	(1755–1833)	Geology	Spain	Discovered tungsten and wolframite

(Continued)

Name	Dates	Field	Country	Contribution
Del Rio, Andres	(1764–1849)	Geology	Spain	Discovered Vanadium
Drew, Charles	(1904–1950)	Medicine	United States	Established blood banks
Ebashi, Setsuro	(1922–)	Biochemistry	Japan	Relaxing factor (contraction) in muscle tissue
Egas Moniz, Antonio	(1874–1955)	Medicine	Portugal	Angiography, prefrontal leukotomy
Esaki, Leo	(1925–)	Physics	Japan	Semiconductors—electron tunneling
Esau, Katherine	(1898–1990)	Botany	United States	Ontogeny of Phlegm in plants
Fell, Dame Honor	(1900–1989)	Biology	England	In vitro cultivation of cells
Fernandez-Moran, Humberto	(1924–)	Biophysics	Venezuela	Brain research
Finlay, Carlos	(1833–1915)	Medicine	Cuba	Yellow fever virus research
Fleming, Williamina	(1857–1911)	Astronomy	Scotland	Spectral classification of stars
Foot, Katherine	(1852–1920)	Biology	United States	Cytology studies—photomicrographs
Franklin, Rosalind	(1920–1958)	Chemistry	England	Graphitizing and nongraphitizing carbons
Furukawa, Junji	(1912–)	Chemistry	Japan	Chemistry of oligomerication—polymers
Garcia, Manuel	(1805–1905)	Medicine	Spain	Inventor of the laryngoscope
Geber	(721– 815)	Chemistry	Iran	Father of Arabian chemistry
Geber	(c. 1300)	Chemistry	Spain	Spread of Arabian chemistry to Europe
Gilbreth, Lillian	(1878–1972)	Engineering	United States	Founded the discipline of industrial psychology
Gleason, Kate	(1865–1933)	Engineering	United States	Designed worm gear, low cost housing
Hagihara, Yusuke	(1897–1989)	Astrophysics	Japan	Stability of satellite systems
Hall, Julia	(1859–1925)	Chemistry	United States	Electrolytic reduction of alumina to aluminum
Harvey, Ethel	(1885–1965)	Biology	United States	Embryology studies with hydra
Herschel, Caroline	(1750–1848)	Astronomy	England	Discovered 8 comets
Hironaka, Heisuke	(1931–)	Mathematics	Japan	Singularity of algebraic varieties
Hodgkin, Dorothy	(1910–)	Biochemistry	United States	X-ray diffraction of penicillin, vit. B-12, insulin
Honda, Kotaro	(1870–1954)	Chemistry	Japan	Magnetic alloys
Houssay, Bernardo	(1887–1971)	Medicine	Argentina	Internal secretions of adrenal and thyroid glands
Hyde, Ida	(1854–1945)	Medicine	United States	Inventor of the microelectrode
Hyman, Libbie	(1888–1969)	Biology	United States	Invertebrate studies, embryology, morphology
Hypatia	(370– 415)	Mathematics	Greece	Neoplatonic school in Alexandria
I-Hsing	(681– 727)	Astronomy	China	Length of meridional line
Ishimure, Michiko	(1927–)	Medicine	Japan	Heavy metal poisoning
Isidore of Seville	(560– 636)	Biology	Spain	Encyclopedia of natural world
Joliot-Curie, Irene	(1897–1956)	Physics	France	Formation of electrons and positrons, alpha rays
Julian, Percy	(1899–1975)	Chemistry	United States	Synthesis of physostigmine, chemistry of indole
Karie, Isabella	(1921–)	Physics	United States	Structural analysis by X-ray diffraction
Kaufman, Joyce	(1929–)	Chemistry	United States	Three-dimensional quantum chemical calculations
Khan, Fazlur	(1929–)	Engineering	Bangladesh	Structural-architectural—tube buildings
Khorana, Har	(1922–)	Chemistry	India	Synthesis nucleotide triplets, 1st artificial gene
Kihara, Hitoshi	(1893–1988)	Biology	Japan	Cell studies of wheat

TABLE 3.1 Culturally Diverse Scientists (continued)				
Name	Dates	Country	Field	Contribution
Kimura, Motoo	(1924–)	Japan	Biology	Random drift—Mutant genes
Kitasato, Shibasburo	(1852–1931)	Japan	Biology	Antitoxins of diphtheria and tetanus
Ko Jung	(283– 343)	China	Chemistry	Alchemist—elixir of gold cinnabar, tin sulfide
Kovalevskaya, Sofya	(1850–1891)	Russia	Mathematics	Partial differential equations
Kuno, Hisashi	(1910–)	Japan	Geology	Crystallization of pyroxenes from magmas
Lamme, Bergha	(1869–1954)	United States	Engineering	Theory and design of motors and generators
Latimer, Lewis	(1848–1928)	United States	Physics	Carbon filament for electric light bulb
Lee, Tsung	(1926–)	China	Physics	"Weak" interaction of particles—nuclear physics
Leloir, Luis	(1906–)	Argentina	Biochemistry	Glycogen synthesis
Li, Choh	(1913–)	China	Biochemistry	Pituitary hormones—adrenocorticotropic hormone (ACTH)
Lim, Robert	(1897–1969)	Singapore	Physiology	Nerve receptors are chemosensitive
Lin, Chia-Chiao	(1916–)	China	Mathematics	Hydrodynamics and turbulent flow
Lonsdale, Kathleen	(1903–1971)	Ireland	Physics	Crystal structure analyses hexamethylbenzene
Maloney, Arnold	(1888–1955)	Trinidad	Medicine	Action of picrotoxin on barbiturate poisoning
Manton, Sidnie	(1902–)	England	Biology	Embryology and morphology of crustacea
Matuyama, Motonori	(1884–1958)	Japan	Geology	Magnetic field reversals of Earth
Maury, Antonia	(1866–1952)	United States	Physics	Spectral analysis of northern stars
Mayer, Maria	(1906–1972)	United States	Chemistry	Nuclear shell structure—atomic structure
McClintock, Barbara	(1902–)	United States	Biology	Behavior of chromosomes—jumping genes
Meitner, Lise	(1878–1968)	Germany	Chemistry	Discovered thorium C and protactinium
Mela Pomponius	(c. 44)	Spain	Geology	Climatic regions, first geographical work
Milstein, Cesar	(1927–)	Argentina	Biology	Structure of immunoglobulins, phosphoenzymes
Minoka-Hill	(1876–1952)	United States	Medicine	Medicine—nutrition research
Moniz, Antonio	(1874–1955)	Portugal	Medicine	Inventor of cerebral angiography
Noether, Emmy	(1882–1935)	Germany	Physics	Noether's theorem—law in particle physics
Noguchi, Hideyo	(1876–1928)	Japan	Biology	Cultivated syphilis and yellow fever bacterium
Nomura, Masyasu	(1927–)	Japan	Biology	Ribosomes contain RNA (ribonucleic acid)
Ochoa, Severo	(1905–)	Spain	Chemistry	Synthesized RNA
Omar Khyyam	(1050–1123)	Iran	Astronomy	Quadratic equations and astronomical tables
Onesimus	(c. 1700)	Africa	Medicine	Inoculation for smallpox
Paulze, Marie	(1758–1836)	France	Chemistry	Chemical nature of respiration
Perlmann, Gertrude	(1912–1974)	Czechoslovakia	Biochemist	Protein chemistry—phosphoproteins
Ponnamperuma, Cyril	(1923–)	Sri Lanka	Chemistry	Synthesized adenosine triphosphate (ATP), adenine

Name	Dates	Field	Country	Contribution
Raman, Chandrasekhara	(1888–1970)	Physics	India	Molecular spectroscopy and acoustics
Ramanujan, Srinivasa	(1887–1920)	Mathematics	India	Real analysis and number theory
Ramon y Cabal, Santiago	(1852–1934)	Biology	Spain	Discovered the neuron—nerve cell
Reed, Dorothy	(1874–1964)	Medicine	United States	Reed-Sternberg cells in Hodgkin's disease
Reynolds, Doris	(1899–1987)	Geology	England	Granitization of rock
Rhazes	(850– 923)	Chemistry	Iran	Differentiated between smallpox and measles
Sabin, Florence	(1871–1953)	Medicine	United States	Origin of lymphatic vessels
Sager, Ruth	(1918–)	Medicine	United States	Non-Mendelian inheritance
Saha, Meghmad	(1894–1956)	Physics	India	Thermal ionization of stars
Salam Abdus	(1926–)	Physics	Pakistan	Weak and electromagnet interactions
Santos Dumont, Alberto	(1873–1932)	Engineering	Brazil	Invented tail-first pusher biplane
Scharrer, Berta	(1906–)	Medicine	Germany	Invented neuroendocrinology
Servetus, Michael	(1511–1553)	Medicine	Spain	Circulation in heart and lungs
Shen Kua	(1031–1095)	Geology	China	Discovery of the magnetic compass
Shirane, Gen	(1924–)	Physics	United States	Phase transitions in solids
Slye, Maude	(1879–1954)	Medicine	United States	Hereditary basis of cancer
Stearns, Mary	(1925–)	Physics	United States	Photonuclear reactions and meson spectroscopy
Stevens, Nettie	(1861–1912)	Biology	United States	Chromosome is the basis for sex determination
Su Sung	(1020–1101)	Astronomy	China	Astronomical clock (escapement)
Takamine, Jokichi	(1854–1922)	Chemistry	Japan	Superphosphates, starch-digesting enzyme
Tamiya, Hiroshi	(1903–)	Biology	Japan	Physiology of mold—*Aspergillus oryzae*
Taussig, Helen	(1898–1980)	Medicine	United States	Surgical correction of congenital malformations
Ting, Samule	(1936–)	Physics	United States	Discovered J particle in the atom
Tomonaga, Sin-itiro	(1906–1979)	Physics	Japan	Theory of relativistic quantum electrodynamics
Trotter, Mildred	(1899–)	Medicine	United States	Comparatic anatomy by skeletal structure
Tsai Lun	(50– 118)	Chemistry	China	Inventor of paper
Uyede, Seiya	(1929–)	Geophysics	Japan	Paleomagnetism—ancient magnetic fields
Vennesland, Birgit	(1913–)	Biochemistry	Norway	Radioactive carbon as a tracer
Williams, Cicely	(1893–1980)	Medicine	United States	Described kwashiorkor
Wrincy, Dorothy	(1894–1980)	Chemistry	Argentina	Specificity of genes resides in amino acids
Wu, Chine-Shiung	(1912–)	Physics	China	Beta disintegration (radioactive decay)
Yalow, Rosalyn	(1921–)	Physics	United States	Radioimmunoassay
Yang, Chen	(1922–)	Physics	China	Yang-Mills theory
Yukawa, Hideki	(1907–)	Physics	Japan	Binding force in nucleus—strong force

CLASSROOM PRACTICE

Changing the presentation of information in science textbooks from a Eurocentric/androcentric model of science to a model of science that affirms diverse cultures will take time. In the interim, there are steps that you as a teacher can take to make science education an inclusive experience for all children. These steps include:

- Including the contributions of culturally diverse scientists and groups of individuals in each science unit.
- Setting up bulletin boards featuring the Scientist of the Day or of the Week (Table 3-1).
- Selecting filmstrips and audio-visual materials which focus on the contributions of culturally diverse scientists.
- Inviting culturally diverse and women scientists to the classroom and having them speak about their work and training.
- Selecting instructional materials that include the contributions of culturally diverse individuals.
- Assigning students to research the life and works of culturally diverse individuals and having the students present the information orally or in written form for others in their class.
- Having students make a notebook of "famous scientists" and include the names of culturally diverse individuals in that list.
- Reading biographies of culturally diverse scientists to students when working with listening skills.
- Having the students write journal entries in which they each role play the life of a famous scientist.
- Selecting reading materials, filmstrips, and so forth for the school library which feature the life stories of culturally diverse men and women of science.

 ## CHAPTER SUMMARY

Modern day science is often presented to children through a Eurocentric/androcentric model of reporting, that is, an instructional model which focuses primarily on the contributions of white men and those of European descent. The contributions to the history of science made by groups, culturally diverse individuals, and white women are rarely mentioned in science classrooms. If all children are to be actively engaged in "doing science," the way(s) that we present information to children must be restructured. Restructuring science education to make it inclusive will require that science curriculum materials include information on oral traditions and group discoveries, redefine the definition of science, and eliminate bias in reporting the contributions of culturally diverse individuals. In the short term, as a teacher you can include the contributions of culturally diverse individuals in your instructional program to ensure that all children find role models in science.

 TOPICS TO REVIEW

additive models, 59
culturally transforming models, 60
scientific method, 56

 REFLECTIVE PRACTICE

1. Why is the presentation of information about famous scientists important to students?
2. What images or perceptions of science do you hold? How were those images formed?
3. Is there a former teacher or person in your life who helped you make your career decision? What did this person do to influence your career choice?
4. If you were making specific recommendations to publishing companies regarding the historical content of their science textbooks, what recommendations would you make? Why?
5. Beyond the suggestions made in this chapter, what strategies can you identify as being appropriate to provide information about famous scientists to culturally diverse learners?

Approaches to Educational Psychology

Theory	Writers	Focus	Concepts
Behaviorism	Pavlov Thorndike Skinner Gagné	Human behavior	Reinforcement Punishment Behavior modification
Humanism	Rogers Combs Maslow	Human attributes	Self-esteem Self-worth Self- actualization
Cognitive	Piaget Ausubel Vygotsky Norman	Knowing and learning	Structure of knowledge Organization Learning

WAYS OF KNOWING SCIENCE

 POINTS TO PONDER

1. How do children learn?
2. What assumptions do you hold about teaching and learning?
3. Do all children learn in the same way?

bout a decade ago, I worked with some colleagues to develop a series of science and math, problem-solving activities for use in the middle school science and mathematics classrooms. After a year of work, we were ready to field test the materials with real kids. We finished developing the materials at the beginning of summer, and the only children we could round up for our field test were those enrolled in summer school. Based on personal experience, I have observed that children typically attend summer school for two reasons: either they are bright-eyed, bushy-tailed little darlings eager to get ahead in the academic world or they are reluctant learners, children who need extra time to master the content of the course. We selected the reluctant learners for our study, thinking that if the materials would work with them they ought to work with any students.

One lesson in particular delighted us. It was a study on the mathematics of fruit. In this activity, the children were divided into teams and each team was assigned the task of describing the physical attributes of their piece of fruit. The children were asked to determine the length, width, mass, volume, seed to mass ratio, and so forth for their particular piece of fruit. The apple, grape, tangerine, pear, avocado, lemon, and orange teams had little difficulty with the tasks. Throughout the morning, they weighed and measured their pieces of fruit and prepared presentations to share with the rest of the class. The watermelon team was a different story.

Our watermelon team was comprised of two boys and two girls, delightful young men and women who were intent on solving the problems that we presented to them. The first difficulty they encountered was the question, "What is the mass of your piece of fruit?" The other groups had been able to weigh their fruits using the pan balances that we had provided. The watermelon was so large that it "maxed out" the balance; thus, the group had to use a bathroom balance. There was one new difficulty: the watermelon kept rolling off the balance. The group tried many ways of standing and placing the watermelon on the balance, all to no avail.

Finally, Kizzy, one of the Native American girls in the group, thought of a solution. We watched as an expression of delight filled her face. She held the watermelon in her arms and looked down at the bathroom balance. She started to place her foot on the balance and then stopped. Kizzy examined the other members of her group for a moment and finally grabbed the smallest of the boys by the arms and stood him on the balance. She noted his weight and wrote it down. Next, she dropped the watermelon into his arms and wrote down the weight of Matt plus watermelon. She subtracted Matt's weight from the weight of Matt plus watermelon and smiled as she recorded the mass of the melon.

Another dilemma experienced by the watermelon group was the question, "What is the volume of your piece of fruit?" By now, the watermelon group was behind the other groups in data collection, so they watched the other groups, hoping to find some short cuts to lighten their work load. They had observed the orange group as they solved the volume problem by using the formula for the volume of a sphere (volume of a sphere = 3/4 π r³), found in the appendices of their mathematics textbook. The watermelon group had also observed the solution worked out by the pear group. The pear group had solved the volume problem by water displacement. That is, they had filled a large beaker full of water, submerged their pear, and measured the volume of water displaced by the pear. The water displacement solution seemed to be a viable solution; after all, they could not find the formula for the volume of a watermelon in the math book.

It was obvious to everyone in the watermelon group that their piece of fruit would not fit into the beaker of water. Every beaker they picked up was simply too small and delicate for the task. Jason noticed the hall trash can out of the corner of his eye. He quickly emptied the papers from the large trash can into another can and signaled for his group to follow him outside. Jason directed the group to fill the trash can with buckets of water. Finally, he dropped the watermelon into the trash can and watched in horror as the water gushed out in all directions, thoroughly soaking everyone's sneakers.

Kizzy again came to her group's rescue. She located a large kitchen knife in the lab area and walked over to her melon. With quick thrusts of the knife she cut the ends from the watermelon, placed the two dismembered ends together, and said, "If we put the ends together, we have a sphere, the rest of the melon is a cylinder." The group

quickly located the formulae for spheres and cylinders in their math books and pro-
ceeded to calculate the volume of a watermelon.

At the end of the day's lesson, I spoke to Kizzy and asked her about her problem-
solving abilities. Kizzy was a wonderful teacher. She taught me that there are many
ways to think and to solve problems, ways that I had not thought of before.   When I
asked how she had figured out how to weigh the watermelon, Kizzy explained that she
had seen her grandmother weigh new born lambs in this manner. Her grandmother
weighed each lamb in order to identify those that were sickly and would need extra care.
I asked Kizzy some questions about the volume of a watermelon. How had she figured
out that a watermelon could be divided into a sphere and a cylinder? Kizzy smiled and
said, "Oh that's easy, it's just like pottery." Kizzy related to me how she had learned to
make pottery from her mother. Her mother had shown her how to break complicated
designs into simpler ones. By her own admission, Kizzy was a terrible math and science
student. She could not understand math and science as they were presented in class
(thus, her enrollment in summer school). In reality, she was a wonderfully talented
problem solver. The way(s) that we view teaching and learning determine the way(s)
that we present information to children. This chapter deals with views of teaching and
learning and about ideas on teaching children.

TEACHING AND LEARNING

Teaching and learning are independent but highly related processes. Frequently, teaching leads to learning, but not always. **Teaching** may be operationally defined as a system of actions by the teacher intended to encourage learning on the part of the student. **Learning** may be defined as a process by which knowledge, behavior, values, attitudes, and beliefs are formulated, modified, or changed. The ways that we view teaching and learning depend on our sociological, historical, and psychological assumptions.

THINKING AND LEARNING

From a neurobiological viewpoint, learning science or any subject involves the processes by which sensory input is transformed, reduced, elaborated, stored, recovered, and used (Reed, 1988, p. 3). Learning begins with **sensory stimuli** from the physical environment (Figure 4.1). The human body is constantly receiving information about the physical world from the eyes, ears, skin, tongue, and nose. Most of the information that is received by human senses is lost or goes unnoticed. As we actively listen to someone speak, we focus on receiving information through aural means. However, at the same time, our bodies continue to receive visual, tactile, olfactory, and gustatory input: information which is permanently lost or not attended to.

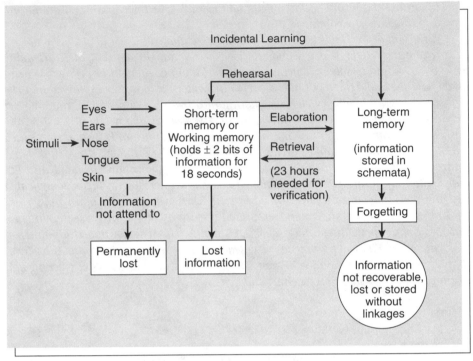

FIGURE 4.1   Physical Environment Sensory Stimuli

Many of us have had the experience of getting up from bed in the middle of the night and walking across a darkened room. In the process, we have stubbed our big toe on a piece of furniture. In that moment, our entire body seems to focus on tactile input. Pain sensors in the toe take precedence over all other sensory receptors in the body, and we block out incoming information from the nose, eyes, ears, and tongue. We focus on the big toe. **Selective perception**, that is, attending to one stimulus rather than all stimuli, is the first step in learning. By attending to sensory input from one set of receptors rather than all receptors, we "filter" information. Selective perception is the first step in the learning process.

After selective perception has occurred, information moves into **short-term memory**. A series of mental processes has already altered incoming information from the moment of perception. Changes in perception may be small or large. Short-term memory may be thought of as a temporary receptacle for information. Information may be retained in short-term memory for approximately 18 seconds. Short-term memory has a very limited holding capacity, such that only seven plus or minus two bits of information may be retained at a time. After 18 seconds, information may be retained in short-term memory only if it has been **rehearsed**. Information that is not rehearsed is permanently lost or forgotten.

Thus, when we want to remember a telephone number, we need to repeat it over and over to ourselves, rehearsing it until we use the information to dial the phone, write the number down, or transfer it to long-term memory.

When information passes from short-term memory into **long-term memory** it again has been transformed by mental processes. These mental processes include **chunking** of similar information, extracting meanings from words, and identifying patterns or relationships in the information. Long-term memory may be viewed as a **semantic network**, as a web of interconnected words or concepts. Information in long-term memory is organized into schema or data structures. **Schemata** (plural is schema) may be defined as a cognitive structure that may be created through the abstraction of previous experiences or acquired through instruction.

Schema provide an organizational structure into which new information may be "fitted." Typically, new information is linked to existing information in long-term memory. Norman (1982) states that **schema** are organized packets of knowledge gathered together to represent single units of self-contained knowledge (p. 54). Information that moves from short-term memory into long-term memory has been transformed by mental processes involved with elaboration. **Elaboration** involves adding meaning by connecting one bit of new information with other associations or with existing knowledge (Woolfolk & McCune-Nicolich, 1984, p. 208). Short-term memory has a limited capacity. In addition, data can be retained in short-term memory for only a brief period. In addition, short-term memory has the capacity for rapid input. By contrast, long-term memory has a nearly limitless capacity. Access to information in long-term memory is dependent on the way that information is stored. Finally, the input capacity of long-term memory is relatively slow. Short-term memory or working memory can retain information only for a short time, whereas long-term memory has the capacity to retain information for the life of the organism.

Learning involves moving information from short-term memory into long-term memory. Remembering or **retrieval** involves the movement of information from long-term memory into working memory or short-term memory. To remember is to have managed three things successfully: the acquisition, retention, and retrieval of information. Failure to remember means failure to manage one of these three things. Forgetting something may mean that we never learned the information in the first place. It may also mean that information was not organized for easy access. Finally, forgetting may mean that information was learned in a limited context and cannot be retrieved outside that context.

Learning and Culturally Diverse Children

Research indicates that culture may have something to do with the stimuli that we attend to, to our focus in the learning process. For a long time, there was a popular belief that all children learn in the same way. However, the opening vignette about Kizzy and the watermelon may help to dispel this myth. While it is true that the same neurobiological processes occur in all human beings, each of us has been socialized to learn within a cultural context. Consideration of the cultural learning context also requires that teachers avoid stereotypical assumptions about children and their learning styles. While many unassimilated Hispanic/Latino children prefer a *photonovela* (a highly visualized comic book-like textbook featuring embedded scaffolding techniques) format for printed materials, not all Latino children share this preference regarding textual materials. Level of assimilation with mainstream culture; country-of-origin; and family beliefs, values, and attitudes all influence the degree to which children are culturally and linguistically socialized to "home culture" and "school culture."

Erickson (1984, p. 528) reports that Polynesian children are taught to navigate ships through an apprenticeship model. In this situation, children are taught to model after an experienced navigator. Polynesian children are taught to watch the characteristics of the waves, color of the water, movement of the water, and position of the stars for navigating across hundreds of miles. While these neophyte navigators are incapable of "passing" traditional Western pencil-and-paper tests of mental abilities associated with navigational expertise, they are completely capable of sailing a boat from one place to another. Polynesian children in this situation have been socialized to attend to visual phenomena associated with water movement and stellar positioning in the learning process.

Hvitfeldt (1986) found that Hmong students have been socialized to learn in a manner different from Western/European learners. In her study with unassimilated adult learners, Hvitfeldt found that Hmong students have been socialized to work in cooperative groups and that students automatically engage in peer tutoring in order to ensure the performance of all members of the community. Hmong learners typically rely more heavily on oral learning than do their Western counterparts. In addition, unassimilated Hmong learners tended to rely heavily on external motivational factors in classroom learning rather than internal motivational devices. Hmong learners have been socialized to view the world holistically and thus tend to have difficulty "wrestling" with ideas and concepts unless they are presented in context.

Researchers working with unassimilated Native-American children have found that these children rely heavily upon oral communication as their primary means of learning. Many Native-American children have been socialized to observe adults' performance as a means of learning. Olion and Gillis-Olion (1984) point out that Native-American children are taught to listen and to wait until their years of experience have prepared them to learn enough and to be influential enough to attract listeners. In addition, Native-American children have been socialized to depend upon memory rather than written notes in the learning process. Social mores such as cooperation, anonymity, submissiveness, humility, and sharing valued in the Native-American community sometimes conflict with school ways of doing and knowing.

The interrelationship between culture and learning is frequently overlooked in the classroom. Teachers need to develop a sensitivity to the fact that not all children have been socialized to learn in the same fashion. While some children

Many Native American children are socialized to learn in group settings. (© Gale Zucker/Stock, Boston)

have been taught by their parents and community to value reading books, other children have been taught to value listening to elders. An understanding of the connection between "home culture" and "school culture" is vital in understanding the learning process. Learning occurs within a sociocultural context. The **sociocultural aspect** of learning includes the culture of the classroom, as well as the culture that the child brings to the classroom from the home environment. A consideration of the psychological assumptions which underpin learning theories must consider the child as well as the culture of the child.

Behavioral Psychology

Behavioral psychology is grounded in theories of stimulus-response learning. Behavioral psychologists and teachers socialized to teach children from this viewpoint place a heavy emphasis on external rewards and reinforcement; on controlling the educational environment to maximize the learning of children. From a behavioral perspective, the job of the teacher is to construct a learning environment which will have a high probability of reinforcing students' correct responses and behaviors, while extinguishing undesirable behaviors. Educational goals within this context focus on organizing, sequencing, and presenting information to children such that learning is achieved. Writers ascribing to behavioral psychology traditions include Pavlov, Thorndike, Skinner, Guthrie, and Gagné.

Pavlov. Ivan Pavlov, a Russian psychologist, conducted most of his studies of learning in the context of animal research. Experimentation with dogs (e.g., Pavlov's puppies) form some of the empirical evidence for behaviorist learning models. Pavlov identified food as a stimulus and salivation as a response in his experiments. In his experiments, Pavlov gave dogs bowls of food at the same time that he rang a bell (Figure 4.2). After a time, he discovered that the dogs responded to the sound of the bell (i.e., salivated) as well as to the sight and smell of the food. The dogs became conditioned to associate the ringing of the bell with the presence of food, whether food was offered or not.

In Pavlov's experiments, the food was an unconditioned stimulus, one that dogs responded to without previous training. Salivation was an unconditioned response, that is, an automatic response as opposed to a trained response. After a time, the dogs responded to the sound of the bell and associated it with food; therefore, the ringing of the bell became a conditioned stimulus. Pavlov referred to this type of stimulus-response learning as conditioning. Conditioning is still used as an acceptable education model, especially in military training.

Thorndike. E.L. Thorndike was noted for his theory of connectionism. Thorndike was a behaviorist who believed that connections between stimuli and responses became ingrained or stamped on human memory. While Pavlov's work focused on the learning of dogs, Thorndike's work involved the learning of cats. His first principle of learning, the law of effect, states that, when a connection is made between a situation and a satisfying state of affairs, a connection is formed. Rewards or extrinsic motivational devices increase the strength of these connections. His law of effect was based on Thorndike's observations of a cat in a cage pulling a string to obtain a food reward.

FIGURE 4.2   A Pavlovian Experiment

Thorndike's second principle of learning, the law of exercise, states that the more a stimulus-response connection is practiced, the stronger it becomes. Likewise, if a stimulus-response connection is not practiced, the bond becomes weaker. In educational terms, Thorndike's principles lead to drill and practice activities, including computer-assisted instruction, and to tangible rewards such as stars on students' papers to reinforce "good" work.

Skinner.   Among all behavioral psychologists, B.F. Skinner is perhaps the best known. Skinner's animal research involved the behavior of rats in mazes. In terms of human learning, Skinner's writings focused on operant conditioning. Skinner believed that most human behavior takes the form of operant responses, which include behaviors such as driving a car, reading a book, writing a letter, and talking with others.

At the beginning, an individual's responses tend to be random in any given situation. When some responses are reinforced as appropriate, the child will perform these with greater frequency. Thus, operant conditioning is taking place. For example, a young child tends to explore the world in a rather random fashion. The young child may touch the toilet brush, put toy blocks in his or her mouth, open a story book, and bite the family dog. While the parent will smile and offer to pick up the child when the child opens the story book, the parent typically will say "No" and remove the seductive object when the child plays with the toilet brush or bites the family dog. After a time, certain responses become more dominant than others: operant conditioning.

Guthrie.   E.R. Guthrie was an American psychologist who is most noted for his law of association. Guthrie pointed out the connection between a stimulus and a response and stated that, if one performs a certain act under a particular set of circumstances with a good result, the next time one is in the same situation, one will tend to perform in the same manner. Guthrie believed that, if a stimulus and response occurred together, learning would occur. Guthrie also believed that by breaking a complex task into simpler tasks that a child could be conditioned to perform complex learning.

For example, if a child has a tendency to remove his or her clothes and throw them around the bedroom, the child could be taught to practice a proper set of sequences to correct the problem. In this instance, the child should be made to redress and reenter the bedroom. Entering the bedroom becomes a stimulus which will set off a chain of correct responses. The child should be taught to remove shoes and place them in the closet. Next, the child should be taught to hang up the outer clothing. Dirty clothing should be placed in a clothes hamper and so forth. Guthrie believed that if a child learns behaviors correctly, he or she will no longer be messy.

Gagné.   Robert Gagné's writings (1987, 1988) build a bridge between traditional behavioral psychologists and cognitive psychologists. Much of his work has been used as the basis of industrial and military training models. Gagné believes that

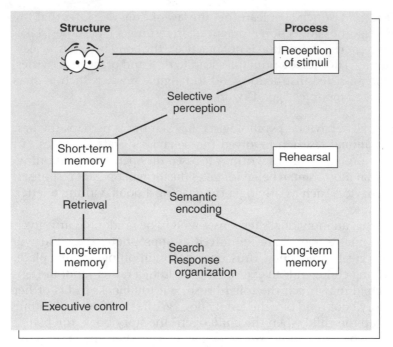

FIGURE 4.3   Events of Instruction

the purpose of instruction is to provide support to the internal processes of learning. In addition, Gagné believes that learning occurs in five domains: **attitudes, motor skills, verbal information, intellectual skills, and cognitive strategies**. By arranging the events of instruction (Figure 4.3), the teacher can control or influence the learning of the student.

According to Gagné, learning begins with stimulation of neural receptors (eyes, ears, nose, skin, and tongue) by external stimuli. This stimulation produces patterns of neural activity which are briefly registered by the sensory registers. Information from the physical environment is transformed into a form that is usable in short-term memory. Since information may be lost from short-term memory due to decay, rehearsal strategies are necessary to maintain information in memory until it can be transformed by semantic encoding into long-term memory. Gagné summarizes the events of instruction as follows:

- *Attention* determines the extent and nature of reception of incoming stimuli;
- *Pattern recognition* or *selective perception* transforms stimuli into information which can be stored in short-term memory;
- *Rehearsal* maintains items stored in short-term memory;
- *Semantic encoding* prepares information for long-term memory;
- *Retrieval* or *search* moves information into working memory;

- *Response organization* selects and organizes performance;
- *Feedback* provides the learner with information about performances; and
- *Executive control* selects and activates cognitive strategies.

The products of learning according to Gagné include intellectual skills, cognitive strategies, verbal information, motor skills, and changes in attitudes (Table 4.1). Gagné has defined **intellectual skills** as those which enable individuals to interact with the environment in terms of symbols or conceptualizations (Gagné, Briggs, & Wager, 1988, p. 43). Gagné points out that intellectual skills are the most basic and pervasive structures of formal education. Cognitive strategies are a second product of schooling. Intellectual skills, according to Gagné, may be arranged in a hierarchy to include (1) signal learning, (2) stimulus-response learning, (3) chaining, (4) verbal learning, (5) discrimination learning, (6) concept learning, (7) rule learning, and (8) problem solving. Cognitive strategies are the capabilities that govern the individual's own learning, remembering, and thinking behaviors. The third outcome of learning is the development of verbal information in the learner. Gagné states that verbal information is the kind of knowledge that we are able to state; it is declarative knowledge. The fourth outcome of learning, according to Gagné, is the development of motor skills in the learner. Motor skills may include making a microscope slide, determining the mass of an object using a pan balance, and assembling water displacement apparatus. The final outcome of learning is a change in the learner's attitudes towards objects, persons, or situations, or changes in the affective domain. Robert Gagné's writings build a bridge between information processing theories of cognitive psychology and traditional behavioral psychology.

TABLE 4.1   Gagné's Products of Learning

Outcomes or Capabilities	Examples of Performance
Intellectual skill	Identifying the diagonal of a rectangle. Demonstrating that water freezes at 0° C. Predicting plant growth based on water, soil, sunlight, etc.
Cognitive strategy	Constructing a chart to organize data. Working backwards to solve a problem. Breaking a problem into its component parts
Verbal information	Naming the parts of a plant cell and their functions. Identifying common insect vectors. Stating Newton's Laws of Thermodynamics.
Motor skill	Constructing a microscope slide, wet mount. Assembling a distillation apparatus. Determining the mass of an object using a pan balance.
Attitude	Electing to sign out a book on dinosaurs from the library. Voluntarily visiting a space museum on a Saturday. Choosing to make an insect collection.

Behavioral Psychology in the Science Classroom.   Behavioral psychologists typically advocate using social reinforcers (smiles, hugs, and social acceptance), tokens (points, grades, prizes, and play money), and activities (music listening time, free play, computer time) as motivational devices in the classroom. Theories of behavior modification, according to which "good" or desirable behaviors are reinforced while "bad" or negative behaviors are ignored, is also a vestige of behavioral psychology theories in the classroom. In terms of instruction, programmed instruction, drill and practice activities, computer-assisted instruction, and mastery learning have their origins in theories of behavioral psychology.

Operant conditioning typically involves five specific steps: (1) specifying the desired behavioral objectives or educational outcomes; (2) dividing the lesson or task into small, incremental steps; (3) sequencing instruction with a consideration of prerequisite learnings; (4) providing instruction with accompanying feedback; and (5) reinforcing correct responses (answers, study habits, and classroom behaviors). Practitioners of operant conditioning consider schedules of instruction and schedules of feedback to be vital components of instruction.

Critics of behavioral learning models point out that these models rely heavily on drill and practice activities and low levels of information processing. Second, not all teachers are skilled in identifying prerequisite skills and breaking down complex tasks into simple components. Third, the use of behavioral or mastery learning models encourages students to develop poor study habits by learning only the information necessary to pass the test. Next, the use of mastery learning models or drill and practice models may lead students to assume that they have mastered the content in a particular academic area, when indeed they have only a superficial understanding of the concepts. Finally, some critics of behavioral learning models point out that the heavy reliance on extrinsic reward structures and on behavioral modification techniques raises ethical concerns about the misuse of these instructional models.

Humanistic Psychology

Most humanistic psychologists adhere to the belief that concern for the individual's feelings, perceptions, beliefs, and purposes is the foundation of the teaching and learning process. Humanistics believe that, to understand another person, it is necessary to see the world from the same viewpoint. In order for a teacher to understand the behavior of a student, the teacher must first determine how the child perceives their actions in a particular situation. To the teacher, the wearing of "colors" by an African-American or Hispanic/Latino child (that is, wearing a Raider's jacket, "bagging" trousers, and wearing a handkerchief as a hat) is seen as gang-related activity. To the child, this behavior is seen as gaining approval from one's peers or sometimes as simply a survival technique for life on the harsh inner-city streets.

Humanistic psychologists believe that the way a person feels is as important as how the person thinks or behaves. Humanistic psychology is sometimes referred to as existential psychology, phenomenological psychology, or perceptual

The wearing of colors is often an attempt to achieve peer acceptance, not antisocial behavior. (© Alon Reininger/Woodfin Camp & Associates)

psychology. It is an attempt to understand human behavior from the viewpoint of the learner, rather than from the viewpoint of the teacher. The major proponents of humanistic psychology include Carl R. Rogers, Arthur Combs, Abraham H. Maslow, George Brown, and William Glasser.

Rogers.   Carl Rogers is a psychologist who advocates making learning and teaching more humanistic, more personal, and more meaningful. Rogers's notions of teaching and learning include learning principles which speak of (1) the desire to learn, (2) learning and change, (3) the learning environment, (4) self-directed learning, and (5) the significance of learning. Rogers's approach to educational psychology can be characterized as being person-centered or child-centered learning.

In writing of the desire to learn, Rogers points out that all human beings are endowed with a natural curiosity or desire to learn. Rogers states that this desire is evidenced in the eagerness of young children to explore their natural surroundings. Classrooms which are based on humanistic psychological principles provide opportunities for children to satisfy their curiosity, explore for themselves, and pursue their own academic endeavors.

Rogers's second principle of learning involves learning and change. Rogers states that children need to be taught to accept change as a natural part of learning. What children learn in school is soon outdated; therefore, children need to be encouraged to be lifelong learners to fill gaps in their knowledge base as new technologies produce new products. Rogers would argue that schools ought to produce individuals who are capable of learning in a changing environment.

The third principle of learning advocated by Rogers involves the learning environment. Rogers points out that learning is best acquired and retained in an environment free from threat. From a humanistic perspective, learning occurs best when children are free to fail without penalty. Effective learning environments are those in which children can test their skills, talents, and abilities without fear of criticism or ridicule.

Self-directed or self-initiated learning is Rogers's fourth principle of successful schooling. Learning how to learn is a major goal of humanistic educational advocates. Rogers would say that being able to choose the direction of one's learning is highly motivating for children. In addition, he would point out that self-directed learning focuses the child's attention on the process of learning as well as on the product of learning. In terms of outcomes, Rogers would state that self-directed learning teaches children to be self-reliant and independent.

Rogers's final learning principle, significance of learning, focuses on the child's perceptions of the value of learning. Humanistic psychologists point out that learning is meaningful when children perceive it as being relevant to their own needs and to their own world. According to Rogers, children learn best and most rapidly when learning is significant or of personal value to them. Rogers would point out that the teacher is a facilitator of learning in the classroom, not a dispenser of knowledge.

Combs.   Arthur Combs is another humanistic psychologist who writes from a student-centered perspective on the acquisition of new information and on the personalization of information. Combs would point out that, when teachers say that children are not motivated, what they really mean is that children are not motivated to do what the teacher wants them to do. Combs believes that, to understand another person's behavior, it is necessary to see the world as they do: to determine how the person thinks and feels about him- or herself and his or her world (Dembo, 1988, p. 389).

To the humanistic psychologist, learning must have personal meaning. Combs believes that children will learn new information when it is personally relevant to them. According to this author, teachers make the mistake of believing that children will learn if information is properly organized and presented. When children fail to learn, it is because they are not interested in the subject at hand. According to Combs, if teachers selected different activities, they could expect totally different reactions from their students. Combs writes that there is a personal meaning or "perception of the self" and a second level of meaning: that by which the world views the individual. Meaning is not inherent in the content area but resides in the individual student. In summary, Combs's writings emphasize that understanding the way(s) that individuals perceive their actions is the key to understanding their behavior(s).

Maslow. Abraham Maslow has long been recognized as a proponent of humanistic psychology. Most of Maslow's work has dealt with the area of gratification of needs as a motivational force in the educational process. Maslow's hierarchy of needs (Maslow, 1963) is an attempt to prioritize human needs in educational terms (Figure 4.4). Within the **hierarchy of needs**, physiologic needs for food, shelter, water, and sleep are the most primary. Once these needs have been attended to, other needs can be satisfied. At the second level of the hierarchy, Maslow is concerned with safety needs. These needs could include the desire for security from danger and the desire for good health. Maslow's third level of need includes the desire to belong to a group and the desire for affection or love. All children desire to be accepted in the family and peer group. All desire the respect, admiration, and confidence of the social group. The need for esteem is highly related to the need for belonging and constitutes the fourth level of the hierarchy. Self-actualization or self-fulfillment is the fifth level of Maslow's hierarchy. At this level of need, children focus on their need to develop to their full potential, to become "all they can be." At the self-actualization level, children engage in the pursuit of hobbies, in developing their athletic prowess to the

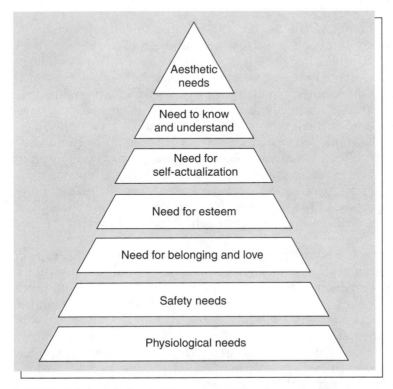

FIGURE 4.4   Maslow's Hierarchy of Needs

maximum possible, and in developing expertise in the performance of some skill, job, or talent. The need to know and to understand is placed at the sixth level of Maslow's continuum. Knowing and understanding embrace the concepts of curiosity, acquiring understanding, and the pursuit of knowledge. The final level of Maslow's hierarchy is concerned with aesthetic values and appreciations. At the highest level of the hierarchy, children have a need to fulfill aesthetic needs, including closure, order, and symmetry. Maslow has defined the first four levels of needs (physiologic, safety, belonging, and esteem) as being deficiency needs, while the higher levels of the hierarchy (self-actualization, knowing, and aesthetic needs) are growth needs or being needs.

Maslow's work in humanistic psychology emphasizes the intrinsic nature of motivation. In addition, Maslow's work provides explanations as to why students' requirement to fulfill their personal deficiency needs may at times be in conflict with teacher's educational goals. Students who come to school tired, hungry, or feeling rejected at home may have difficulty learning until the basic physiologic, safety, or belonging needs in their lives have been filled. Teachers who ascribe to Maslow's theory would seek to move students from lower-order needs to higher-order needs or needs associated with self-fulfillment and aesthetic appreciations.

Humanistic Psychology in the Science Classroom.   In general, humanistic psychologists value educational goals that help students to learn more about themselves, relate to others, and make independent decisions. This psychological perspective is concerned with the feelings and perceptions of the individual learner. Translating the writings of humanistic psychologists into classroom practice has produced the confluent educational movement, open education environments, values clarification activities, and an emphasis on social skills training. Confluent education, developed by Brown at the Center for Humanistic Education at the University of California, Santa Barbara, is a process of integrating affective experiences with cognitive learning. This humanistic psychology-based approach to instruction seeks to involve students personally in the subject matter. The purpose of this approach to learning is to involve students in understanding the content while personalizing the information in terms of their individual experiences.

Open education is a humanistic approach to education which differs from traditional education in terms of instruction, diagnosis, evaluation, provisions, and humanness. Proponents of open education encourage children to move freely around the classroom and use manipulative materials to learn about the physical world. Most open education proponents encourage children to work on their own, to pursue their own interests. Typically, open classrooms are highly individualized learning environments where tests are minimal and where teacher-directed learning occurs infrequently. Open education provides students the freedom to select their own activities and encourages teachers to serve as facilitators of learning rather than as dispensers of information.

Values clarification activities (mentioned in Chapter 14) are derived from humanistic psychology foundations. In terms of science education, values clarification is incorporated into science/technology/society instruction. This vestige of humanistic psychology is a vital part of producing scientifically literate citizens, those capable of decision making in a democratic society. Values clarification assists students in examining their personal value system such that they can arrive at informed decisions.

Social skills development, the ability to work with others, is closely akin to values clarification. Modeling, role playing, peer tutoring, and cooperative learning activities are part of social skills training from the humanistic psychology tradition which have been infused into modern elementary science education. The use of social skills training strategies improves students' social behavior in the elementary classroom.

Criticism of Humanistic Approaches.   Over the years, humanistic psychology approaches to education have been criticized regarding (1) self-directed learning, (2) goals, (3) program planning, (4) evaluation, and (5) affective components. With regard to self-directed learning, many critics of humanistic learning point out that students are not always capable of directing their own learning in that students may lack understanding of the "big picture" regarding what is relevant and necessary for lifelong learning. In terms of goals, proponents of humanistic psychology traditions point out that there is frequently a lack of direction or purpose in many humanistic classrooms. Within the same context, humanistic educational programs are criticized as lacking conceptual frameworks for students' learning. Evaluation of learning in humanistic classrooms is difficult because appropriate assessment tools or tests are lacking. It is difficult for humanistic educators to "show" that their programs have made a difference in terms of children's concept acquisition and attitudes, values, and beliefs. Finally, the reliance on affective components makes the outcomes of humanistic education difficult to quantify. It is difficult to show that children have truly learned in a humanistic classroom when the emphasis is on internal control of learning.

Cognitive Psychology

In writing of teaching and learning, Anderson (1992) points out that a "complete theory of education should eventually include a synthesis of neurobiological and cognitive scientific principles in addition to philosophical and cultural contexts" (p. 1039). Modern cognitive psychology viewpoints on teaching and learning combine a knowledge of information processing derived from medical literature. They also combine a knowledge of human cognitive development derived from the tradition of Piaget and Bruner. Further, modern cognitive psychologists consider the sociocultural context of learning, the culture of the child, and the culture of the classroom. Finally, cognitive psychology is based on theories of schema formation, such as those advocated by Norman.

Piaget.   In terms of cognitive psychology, Jean Piaget (1896–1980) may be viewed as being a pioneer in describing how children think and make sense of their world. By studying vast numbers of children and their behavior, Piaget developed his **stage theory of learning**. Piaget believed that all children move through a series of four cognitive or developmental stages (Table 4.2). Piaget is frequently referred to as a developmental psychologist, as one who focused on children's stages of intellectual development.

According to Piaget, the earliest stage of learning is the **sensorimotor stage**. This stage is so named because development focuses on sensory input and resultant body movements. Object permanence, that is, that objects exist only when they are within the visual range of the child, is the dominant mental indicator of this stage. Learning occurs at this stage of mental development through imitation of the behaviors of others.

Piaget's second developmental stage, the **preoperational stage**, is characterized by the development of language and the ability to think in symbolic form. Symbolic manipulation, that is, using pictures or symbols to represent real world objects, is first developed during this stage. Piaget theorized that children operating at the preoperational stage were egocentric or self-oriented in their thinking. In addition, he believed that children functioning at the preoperational stage were capable of using one-way logic, yet they lacked the ability to conserve matter.

As children move from the sensorimotor to preoperational stage, they develop the ability to engage in one-way logic. **One-way logic** can be operationally defined as the ability to sequence objects or events. For example, if a child is presented with a "road" and a set of objects, the child should be able to ar-

TABLE 4.2   Piaget's Stages of Learning

Stage	Age	Characteristics
Sensorimotor	0–2 yrs	Child begins to use imitation, memory, and thought. Objects cease to exist when they are hidden from view. Child moves from reflex actions to goal-directed learning.
Preoperational	2–7 yrs	Child experiences language development and gradual ability to think in symbolic form. Undirectional thinking is possible. Difficulty using multiple perspectives.
Concrete	7–11 yrs	Child is able to solve concrete or hands-on problems in a logical fashion. Child understands the laws of conservation and reversibility. Child is able to classify and seriate.
Formal	11–15 yrs	Child is able to solve abstract problems in a logical fashion. Thinking becomes more scientific at this age. Child develops concern for societal problems and issues.

Teacher's Map of the Neighborhood

Child's Map of the Neighborhood

FIGURE 4.5   Neighborhood Maps

range the objects in sequence. In this Piagetian task, the teacher presents the child with a map of the neighborhood (Figure 4.5) and a set of manipulative materials. Children functioning at the preoperational stage typically are capable of completing this task.

When teachers work with students at the preoperational stage, lessons must include concrete props and visual aids whenever possible. Because children operating at this stage have difficulty following instructions, directions need to be relatively short. Most kindergarten programs feature the use of manipulative materials which encourage children to move from operating at a preoperational stage of mental functioning to a concrete stage of functioning. In addition, programs for early elementary children include opportunities for children to develop experiences in exploring and operating in the physical world.

Most children in the early grades of elementary school function at the pre-operational stage. These children have not yet mastered conservation of matter. For example, if a child sees a teacher pour a glass of water into another container, the child is unable to understand that the volume does not change, although the shape of the liquid has changed. In this Piagetian task, the teacher fills one container with liquid and then pours it into another container in the presence of a child. Children at the preoperational stage will say that one container holds more liquid than the other (Figure 4.6), although both containers actually hold the same amount of liquid.

Conservation of liquids and length is an indicator that a child is function-ing at the **concrete operational stage**. Other indicators of this stage of mental reasoning include development of the ability to solve problems in a logical fash-ion using concrete, "hands-on" manipulative materials. Just as children are able to understand the conservation of quantity at this age, they are also able to understand reversibility (recounting events backwards). In teaching students at this stage of mental development, teachers must continue to supply manipula-tive materials to students. In addition, students learn best when lectures and readings are well organized and of short duration. The use of concrete examples from the physical world benefits all students operating at this cognitive stage, especially students who have not yet acquired English language proficiency.

Formal reasoning is the last level of Piaget's stage theory. At the formal level of reasoning, students are able to solve abstract problems in a logical and sequential manner. In addition, students' thinking at this age becomes more

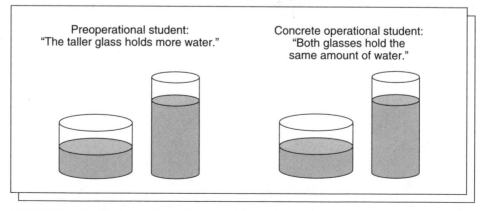

FIGURE 4.6   Preoperational Stage of Learning

scientific. Children typically become concerned with societal issues when they reach this level of mental ability. When teaching students who are operating at this stage of mental reasoning, teachers should encourage students to engage in problem solving activities and should ask students to explain their solution paths. When possible, teachers should encourage students to "get the big picture," that is, wrestle with broad concepts.

In addition to his observations of children's developmental stages, Piaget pointed out that certain environmental factors may influence a child's mental development. Piaget believed that physical maturation, physical experience, social interaction, and equilibrium (the self-control or regulation of learning) were salient variables in children's intellectual development. Many of Piaget's beliefs and theories about children's learning continue to be widely used in classrooms, as is evidenced by the chapter on SCALing in this text.

Ausubel.   David Ausubel is a cognitive psychologist who favors expository teaching techniques and reception learning. Many cognitive psychologists favor inquiry-based learning, including discovery learning. Ausubel emphasizes the idea that expository teaching is useful in helping teachers to present large amounts of information to students while focusing on the relationships between the content. Ausubel's theory explains how lecture and textual material, when properly organized, can lead to as much retention and understanding as discovery or inquiry learning. Ausubel explains that, in the process of meaningful learning, the student relates new information to existing knowledge structures. Meaningful learning occurs when students understand (as opposed to reciting from rote memory) that which is to be learned, and when they connect new information to existing knowledge structures.

Ausubel's theory of teaching is based on a **three-phase model**: (1) advance organizer, (2) presentation of the information or task, and (3) strengthening the cognitive organization. During the first phase of learning, information can be communicated to learners either by some form of reception learning (that presents the information in its final format) or by some type of discovery learning that obligates learners to discover all or part of the information independently of the teacher. In the first phase of learning, the teacher clarifies the aim of the lesson and presents an advance organizer. The **advance organizer** serves to identify the attributes of the concept, provide examples of the concept, and use the concept in context. The use of advance organizers does not automatically increase students' learning. Rather, advance organizers seem to benefit students most when information is poorly organized or when students lack prerequisite skills, abilities, or conceptual knowledge.

During the second phase of teaching, the teacher presents the material or task to be learned to the students. At this time, the teacher makes the organization of the material explicit for the students. In addition, the teacher uses the process of progressive differentiation to help students assimilate and retain new information. **Progressive differentiation** is a strategy by which teachers present the most general applications of the concept first and then less inclusive applications of the concept. For example, if a teacher were teaching the concept of insect, the teacher would begin with the broad definition that an insect is an arthropod (an animal with jointed legs), with three body segments, six legs, two eyes, two antennae, and usually one or two pairs of wings. The teacher could mention that bees, butterflies, and grasshoppers were insects. Next, the teacher would mention that ants (which in most cases have no wings) are also insects. Finally, the teacher would mention less commonly known examples of insects, such as bedbugs, lice, and springtails. By the time the teacher reaches the less well known examples of the concept, students have a cognitive structure in place to accommodate the new information.

The final phase of Ausubel's teaching and learning model involves strengthening the cognitive organization. Ausubel refers to this stage as **integrative reconciliation**. Integrative reconciliation involves the learner in integrating new information with existing information. This phase of learning promotes active reception learning, clarifies information for the learner, and prepares the student for new learning. In the case of the concept insect, the teacher would encourage students to compare insects with centipedes, millipedes, and spiders. Are these organisms insects? Why or why not?

According to Ausubel, reception learning is meaningful learning. Information is logically organized when it is presented to the learner in its final form. Students are encouraged to relate new information to existing cognitive structures. It should be noted that Ausubel is not opposed to discovery learning. In fact, he is a strong advocate of the occasional use of discovery learning, particularly for elementary school children. Ausubel points out that young children still functioning at a concrete level need tactile, kinesthetic learning experiences. Much of Ausubel's writing has been incorporated into Madeline Hunter's mastery teaching model (Hunter, 1982).

Vygotsky.   Much of Vygotsky's writing deals with the sociocultural context of learning, that is, the culture that the child brings to school and the culture of the classroom. Lev Vygotsky was a Russian cognitive psychologist who was concerned with the influence of culture on children's learning. Vygotsky's work focused on combining what was known of the neurologic and physiologic functioning of the brain with knowledge acquisition. His writings focus on the importance of culture, the role of language in learning, and the development of higher mental functioning.

Vygotsky pointed out that children under guidance, in groups, and in collaboration with one another can perform at levels which they have not achieved independently (Vygotsky, 1978, p. 87). He points out that learning has two aspects, an external one and an internal one. When children learn, they negotiate meaning. They assign meaning to objects and events as they speak with each other and with adults. Children solve practical tasks with the help of their speech, as well as with their hands, eyes, and other senses. Learning is dependent on the external environment but also on the child's internal processing of information. Vygotsky pointed out that culture makes social processes possible. Social processes bring about the learning of language (sometimes referred to as signs by Vygotsky). Ultimately, language makes thought possible.

Children's play, according to Vygotsky, is the primary means of children's cultural development. In their play, children project themselves into adult activities typical of the culture and rehearse their future roles and values. Play is a means by which children begin to acquire the motivation, skills, and attitudes necessary for their social participation. By the time children enter school, they have developed a way of learning based on their culture of origin. In terms of culturally diverse children in American schools, this means that children have frequently been socialized to learning at home in a way that may be different from school ways of "knowing" and "learning." From a Vygotskian perspective, a child's level of assimilation with mainstream American culture may have a tremendous impact on the child's learning at school.

Language, according to Vygotsky, not only makes thought possible but also regulates behavior. Vygotsky describes three stages in the development of language: social, egocentric, and inner. Social language or external speech is the first stage of language development. During this stage children typically utter words such as "juice," "milk," or "cookie." Egocentric language or speech is the second stage of language development and typically occurs between ages 3 and 7. During this developmental language stage, children talk to themselves in an effort to guide their own behavior. Children at this stage may say things like, "I'm going to the bathroom," "I'm going outside," "I'm a good girl." Inner speech, the last stage of language development, is silent self-talk; inner speech makes all higher mental functioning possible.

Norman.   If one were to summarize writings in cognitive psychology, one would say that Piaget's works have added to our knowledge of the influence of a child's physical and mental development on the child's learning. Ausubel's writings, on the other hand, deal with the area of verbal reception learning. Vygotsky's writings are concerned with the influence of the child's culture on learning, and Gagne's writings build a bridge between traditional behavioral psychology and modern cognitive psychology. Norman's works are typical of cognitive psychology writings which focus on information processing approaches to teaching and learning.

Donald Norman states that learning involves purposeful remembering and skillful performance. According to his theory of cognitive psychology, learning involves at least three distinct modes: accretion, structuring, and tuning. **Accretion** is the addition of new knowledge to existing knowledge structures. It is the process of gradually accumulating new knowledge and of appending that knowledge to existing conceptual frameworks. **Structuring**, according to Norman, involves the formation of new knowledge structures. Structuring occurs when existing schema will no longer suffice, when new knowledge cannot be appended to existing knowledge, when new conceptualizations occur. Finally, **tuning** is the last mode of learning. Tuning is the fine adjustment of knowledge to a task.

Norman points out that learning, memory, and performance are interrelated. Learning, according to Norman, tends to emphasize the acquisition of information. Memory tends to emphasize how information is retained and then retrieved when needed. Performance, on the other hand, emphasizes how information is used. As children learn, they gain expertise in certain areas of their lives. Expertise is characterized by smoothness, automaticity, decreased mental effort, performance under stress, and the point of view that children hold.

Smoothness, according to Norman's definition, is the apparent ease with which a professional or an accomplished learner performs. **Automaticity** refers to the lack of conscious awareness that characterizes expert performance. As students become expert in performing a particular task, or as they master a skill, they show a decreased mental effort. Norman points out that once something is learned, it is performed under stressful conditions without a deterioration in the quality of the performance. Finally, Norman asserts that a person's point of view changes as expertise is gained. The writings of cognitive psychologists focus on how children acquire new knowledge, organize that knowledge, and feel about what they have learned.

Special Needs Students

Within every elementary school in this nation, there are children who in one or more ways are different from the norm. Sometimes these children are more creative, are more intelligent, have superior artistic ability, or have exceptionally well-developed motor skills. At other times there are children in our classrooms who seem to be less creative, less intelligent, lacking in motor skills, or otherwise physically impaired. These children may be described as being exceptional in some way or another. With the passage of Public Law 94-142 in 1975, schools were required to provide the least restrictive environment possible for all children.

The passage of Public Law 94-142 meant that children who had previously been isolated from the rest of the academic community were to be included in the educational mainstream of the school to the greatest extent possible. This law protects a child's right to due process in educational placement, thus eliminating arbitrary placement in "special educational programs." Second, the law attempts to protect exceptional children from undue bias and discriminatory practices in testing and educational placement. Finally, the law mandates that every exceptional child is entitled to an individual educational plan to meet his or her unique educational needs. The result of this legislative act is that more children are included in mainstream science education activities than ever before. Accommodating the needs of exceptional children requires that teachers understand the educational needs of children and attend to those needs.

Physical Exceptionality. From a neurobiological perspective, children with physical exceptionalities simply have fewer sensory receptors with which to receive information than do other children. Many times, children with physical handicaps, sensory deficits, and cerebral palsy are perfectly capable of functioning in a regular elementary science classroom. At other times, students may need the support and assistance of resource teachers, classroom aids, or peer tutors. Many of the activities described in this book provide for multiple means of knowledge representation and are, therefore, appropriate for children with a wide range of abilities or capabilities. For example, hearing-impaired children, even with the aid of a hearing aid, may not be able to hear what is being said in the classroom. These same children are capable of exploring their natural environment through the use of written words, pictures, icons, and *realia*. In providing the least restrictive environment possible for physically impaired children, teachers should use multiple means of representing information.

For accommodating the needs of physically impaired children, many educational materials and supplies are readily available. Most elementary science reading materials are available in Braille editions for visually impaired children. Hearing aids and instructional aids trained in the use of sign language are available for hearing impaired children. Minor modifications of hands-on learning activities make learning accessible to physically impaired children. Elementary science experiences enrich the lives of all children and should be a vital part of every child's educational experiences.

Social-Emotional Exceptionality.   Children with social-emotional exceptionalities may range from those with negative behaviors (autism, conduct disorders, hyperkinesis, and schizophrenia) to positive behaviors (leadership skills and invulnerability). In most cases, children with social-emotional exceptionalities are capable of functioning well in elementary science classrooms. Environments which feature cooperative learning groups provide positive and affirming peer role models for children uncertain about appropriate social behaviors. At the same time, group work provides an environment in which children who exhibit excellent leadership skills can thrive and prosper.

Intellectual Exceptionality.   Just as there is a continuum of physical ability and social-emotional abilities among children, there also exists a continuum of intellectual abilities. At one end of the continuum are children with exceptional academic giftedness: superior intellect, creativity, and motivation. At the other pole of the continuum are students with mild, moderate, or profound retardation and children with information processing disorders (learning disabilities). Research has shown that learning environments which provide open-ended tasks, that is, problems that may be solved by many solution paths, profit students at both ends of the continuum. With proper supportive services, children at both ends of the intellectual continuum can be accommodated in regular elementary science classrooms. By allowing children multiple modes of knowledge representation in learning environments, and multiple means of performance to demonstrate learning ability, teachers provide for many diverse learners.

CLASSROOM PRACTICE

In practice, most classroom teachers are highly eclectic in their beliefs about human development and human learning. Classroom teachers typically "borrow" ideas from behavioral psychology, humanistic psychology, and cognitive psychology. In practice most teachers use many teaching strategies during the course of a day, month, or academic year. Some teaching practices are derived from one school of educational psychology, while other practices are derived from other schools of educational psychology. Good teaching involves using appropriate instructional strategies; that is, finding an appropriate instructional strategy to match the instructional goal for that particular lesson or activity. A knowledge of children and the material to be learned frequently determines which instructional strategies are used.

 ## CHAPTER SUMMARY

Theories of behavioral psychology focus on the behavior of the learner. Pavlov, Thorndike, Skinner, Guthrie, and Gagné are well known behavioral psychologists. Typically, behavioral psychologists believe that teachers can increase students' learning by changing the variables in the educational environment. Educational concepts derived from behaviorist traditions include reinforcement, behavior modification, and punishment.

Humanistic psychology centers on the individual learner. Roger, Combs, and Maslow are humanistic psychologist theorists. Theories of self-actualization, self-esteem, and self-worth have their origins in humanistic literature.

Finally, cognitive psychology focuses on the way(s) that people learn and the way(s) they know about the world around them. Cognitive psychology is concerned with theories of information processing, organization of information, and learning strategies. Piaget, Ausubel, Vygotsky, and Norman are writers who reflect cognitive psychology theories and traditions.

 ## TOPICS TO REVIEW

REFLECTIVE PRACTICE

1. What are the basic tenets or assumptions of behavioral psychology? Which of these assumptions do you hold?
2. What are the basic tenets or assumptions of humanistic psychology? Which of these assumptions do you hold?
3. What are the basic tenets or assumptions of cognitive psychology? Which of these assumptions do you hold?
4. What current educational practices used in elementary schools reflect behavioral psychology traditions? Explain your answer.
5. What current educational practices used in elementary schools reflect humanistic psychology traditions? Explain your answer.
6. What current educational practices used in elementary schools reflect cognitive psychology traditions? Explain your answer.
7. The author has written that most teachers are very pragmatic in their educational practices and thus combine behavioral, humanistic, and cognitive psychology traditions in their classrooms. Would you agree or disagree with this statement? Justify your answer.

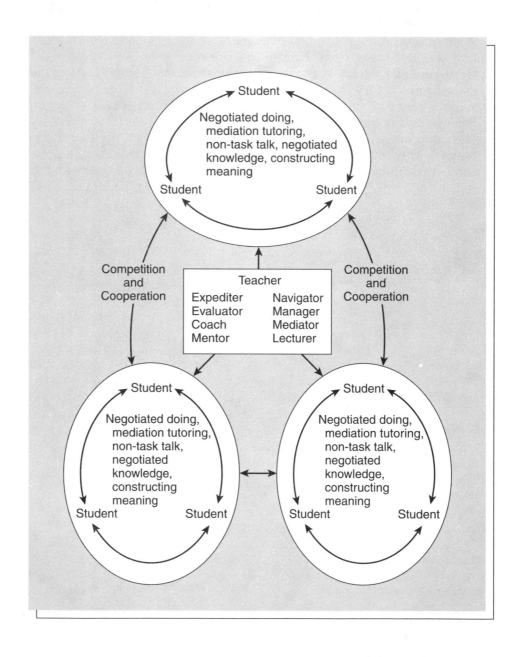

GROUPS IN THE SCIENCE CLASSROOM

  POINTS TO PONDER

1. In what situations is group learning appropriate?
2. In what situations is individualized learning appropriate?
3. Do you personally prefer individual or group learning activities? Why do you feel that way?

onnie Rausch is a wonderful and dynamic kindergarten teacher who makes learning fun for her students and for all who enter her classroom. Each August, during the first week of school, Connie conducts the Baggie Lift Activity (Activity 5-7 in this chapter) with her students. She begins the Baggie Lift by challenging the students in her class to lift her off the floor. One after another, the kindergartners come forward, place their arms around Connie's waist, and attempt to move her 145-pound frame off the floor. No one is successful.

With the class watching, Connie places a gigantic plastic bag on the floor of the classroom. She tapes the bag to the floor with duct tape and covers the center of it with a sheet of cardboard. Connie sits on the cardboard and passes out straws to her students. She instructs the students to insert the straws into the top layer of the plastic and to blow on the straws. Within two to three minutes, she calls to the students to stop and to observe what has happened. Alone, none of the students were able to lift her; work-

ing together, they are able to lift her about 30 to 40 centimeters off the floor. The Baggie Lift Activity is a wonderful way to illustrate the power of cooperative learning (the subject of this chapter); it is also a wonderful example of good science teaching in its illustration of the effects of air pressure.

LEARNING AS A SOCIAL PROCESS

In writing guidelines for school redesign and reform, the American Psychological Association (1992) has stated that learning is facilitated by social interactions and by communication with others in various flexible, diverse, and adaptive instructional settings. This same sentiment was expressed by Johnson and Johnson (1994) when they wrote that the classroom climate consists of ways in which people within a classroom interact with each other. **Learning** is a social process, based on the interactions of teachers and students.

Constructivist View of Groups

Most culturally diverse learners find that cooperative learning activities address their academic needs far better than do individual learning activities. Fields (1988) asserts that cooperative learning activities foster social skills, positive peer relationships, and higher levels of self-esteem in students. From a sociological perspective, many culturally diverse children are socialized to prefer group or extended family settings as primary learning environments. Constructivists, such as Lorsbach and Tobin (1992), believe that students individually construct a knowledge of science within a sociocultural context. They point out that cooperative learning strategies allow individuals to test the fit of their experiential world with a community of others. Social psychologists assert that no aspect of human experience is more important than cooperative interaction with others.

The sociocultural aspects of learning involve constructing a knowledge of a given subject area in a group setting. Students need the opportunity to make sense of what they are learning, to compare the knowledge that they have constructed with the knowledge that others have constructed. Discussion, active listening, discovering differences between one's knowledge and the knowledge of others, justifying one's position, and arriving at a group consensus are all part of the social process of constructing meaning, that is, part of **cooperative learning**. Knowledge is constructed and modified by individuals within a group context. Learning is not simply the act of an individual learner, but a product of social interactions between groups of learners.

Research on Group Learning

Why are so many teachers and science educators excited about group learning? Why is a transition occurring in American schools from individual goal structures to group goal structures? What is the research base concerning cooperative learning? As was not the case with many science education trends of the past, cooperative learning activities conducted in group settings are a research-based approach to science teaching and learning. Much is now known of the impact of group activities on children's science learning.

Problem Solving. Researchers commenting on the effectiveness of cooperative learning situations indicate that the use of cooperative learning groups improves students' problem-solving abilities (Tobin, 1990; Stasson, Kameda, Parks, Zimmerman, & Davis, 1991). As a university student, I remember learning computer programming for the first time. Our second class assignment was to write a BASIC program to generate the Fibonacci sequence (1, 1, 2, 3, 5, 8, 13, 21, and so forth). I understood that the sequence resulted from adding the two previous numbers together to generate the next number in the series. I spent an entire weekend working on that project, but no matter how hard I tried, I could not get my program to work. Finally, on Monday morning, a classmate showed me an error in my program; I had forgotten to initialize my variables. Had it not been for peer tutoring and sharing, I would not have been able to get a working program. Cooperation and sharing increase our problem-solving abilities.

Retention of Knowledge. Cooperative learning activities promote mastery and retention of declarative or conceptual knowledge among many groups of learners (Humphreys, Johnson, & Johnson, 1982). Walking is a wonderful illustration of this idea. I go for a walk nearly every day, but if you were to ask me what I saw and learned on the previous day's walk, I probably would not remember much about it. However, several years ago, I went on a walk with some visiting friends who belong to the Audubon Society. As we walked through the woods, they named the birds that we saw, whistled imitations of the birds' songs so that I might remember their calls, and told beautiful and wonderful stories about the habits and habitats of the birds that we encountered. That walk differed from others in that my knowledge base grew; it grew because others shared their knowledge and expertise with me. Group interaction helps us to increase our knowledge base, to remember what we have learned.

Academic Achievement. The use of cooperative groups benefits culturally diverse students in terms of academic achievement (Okebukola & Ogunniyi, 1984; Sharan, 1985; Watson, 1991). For example, some culturally diverse learners lack knowledge of the English language. Cooperative groups provide children with the opportunity to engage in peer tutoring in their native language or "home language," while increasing their understanding of English vocabulary and usage through social interaction. Group work also affords us the opportunity for active learning, a type of learning that appeals to children accustomed to learning through tactile and kinesthetic experiences.

Attitudes toward Learning. Cooperative learning activities have been shown to improve students' attitudes toward learning (Humphreys, Johnson & Johnson, 1982). So long as I can remember, I have had a fear of high open places. For this reason, I have always tried to avoid walking on roofs, climbing trees, and ascending ladders. In other words, I have had a terrible attitude toward high places. My oldest son, Ray, developed an interest in rock climbing during his freshman year of college, and he was bound and determined that he would share his joy of rappelling with his mother. I remember trudging up the side of Glorieta Baldy (Glorieta, New Mexico) with my son and his friends, who were thrilled with the occasion, and being filled with apprehension and fear. With a lot of coaxing, coaching, and outright lying, my son and his friends convinced me that rappelling was just like climbing out of my bed in the morning. It was not, but I did learn that rock climbing was not as horrible as I had thought. My attitude changed due to a group effort. Cooperating with others can help us change our attitudes toward learning new tasks.

Self-Concept.   Cooperative learning improves culturally diverse students' self-concepts (Johnson, Johnson, Scott, & Ramolae, 1985; Sharan, 1985). Many culturally diverse children have been socialized to work in groups. Feedback from peers and members of the social group are far more important than letter grades or other types of rewards for many of us. Recently, I watched a group of children build Puffmobiles (Activity 5-2) as part of a unit of study on alternative energy sources. Fernando, a shy Chicano boy, gained social status in his group during the construction process. The other students in Fernando's group were having great difficulty attaching the wheels (beads) to the axles (straws) of their Puffmobile. To the delight of his group, Fernando picked up the straws and pins and proceeded to attach the wheels such that they stayed on the Puffmobile: a task the rest of the group had been unable to perform. While Fernando's English-speaking ability was weak, his hands-on problem-solving ability was strong. Fernando was suddenly a valued member of the group. Peer praise and acceptance are important factors in improving one's self-esteem and self-concept.

Race Relations. Studies (Johnson, Johnson, Scott & Ramolae, 1985; Okebukola & Ogunniyi, 1984; Sharan, 1985) with culturally diverse learners indicate that the use of cooperative groups improves students' abilities to work with others and improves race relationships in classrooms. When we work with others, our viewpoint frequently changes. Recently, I observed a group of children newly arrived from Somalia during their first year in Southern California schools. On the first day of school, the Somalian children sat by themselves on one side of the classroom, while their American peers sat on the other side of the room. Both groups of children thought that the other group looked strange, spoke with a dialect, and wore "funny" clothing. When I returned to the classroom several months later, I found the American and Somalian children fully integrated and working together. Strangeness and distrust had given way to respect and friendship. Daily contact with one another had changed the children's perceptions and their level of racial tolerance.

Student Preferences.   Okebukola (1986) suggests that most culturally diverse students prefer cooperative learning situations to competitive learning environ-

Cooperative groups improve race relations. (© Will Faller)

ments. Okebukola's work in cooperative or group learning was conducted among tribal groups in Africa, but his findings are probably generalizable to children in this country. Although most children prefer to work with others, they do not like to be graded according to the performance of others but on their own accomplishments. When group work is used as an instructional strategy, teachers should allow children to produce individually a record of the learning activity. For example, Connie, the kindergarten teacher with the Baggie Lift Activity, should allow students to report individually on their learning even though everyone in the class participated in the activity. Cooperative learning activities improve students' learning in terms of cognitive knowledge, social skills, motor skills, and attitudes.

Competitive Learning Situations

While most teachers today advocate a cooperative or group approach to learning, the reality is that many of these teachers still rely heavily on individualized or competitive goal structures in their classrooms. Learning and working alone are firmly ingrained in the American educational system. Before continuing the discussion of cooperative learning structures as viable instructional strategies for use in the multicultural classroom, it is necessary to examine the arguments for the use of competitive learning strategies. Many of us, whether we admit it publicly or not, continue to view learning as an individual act. Therefore, it is good to examine our attitudes towards competition and toward individualized learning before turning our attention to cooperative learning strategies.

The view of learning as an individual endeavor is firmly rooted in the sociological, psychological, and historical foundations of education. Johnson and Johnson (1994) report that there are five traditional arguments for individual learning activities in schools: (1) the competitive nature of our society, (2) development of leadership skills in students, (3) real world applications of the process of schooling, (4) student preferences for instructional strategies, and (5) building self-confidence and self-esteem in children.

Competitive Nature of Society?   Johnson and Johnson (1994) first pointed out that advocates of competition insist that schools must emphasize a dog-eat-

dog theory of survival in the occupational world. Teachers who use competition in their classrooms frequently do so because they believe that the job market is highly competitive and that they are preparing students for competition in adult society. Based on these assumptions, we set up games, competitions, and individual learning activities to prepare students for "real world" applications. While this argument for competition appears to make sense, in reality, modern corporations depend on cooperation and team work rather than competition as a means of survival in the world marketplace.

Developing Leadership Skills?   A second reason that teachers frequently give for the use of individual competitive activities in the classroom is to develop leadership skills in students. Ashley Montagu (1965) pointed out that competition in schools is based on the ideas of Social Darwinism, and on concepts such as survival of the most "fit," the struggle for existence, and competition as the life-blood of the nation. Advocates of classroom competition believe that achievement, success, outstanding performance, and superhuman effort give rise to leaders with drive, ambition, and motivation: to individuals who enjoy competing with others. Those who advocate the use of individual learning activities believe these activities will produce rugged individuals capable of competing in a vast array of human endeavors. Fernando, the Chicano boy mentioned in the Puffmobile activity earlier in this chapter, developed leadership skills during a group activity but not through competition. Most successful athletes pause at the moment of their greatest victories and acknowledge the roles of parents and coaches in their achievements. Contrary to popular opinion, leadership, whether in the athletic or academic arena, comes only with a well-developed support network: through the efforts of caring, loving others who help us meet our goals.

Real World Applications of Schooling?   Johnson and Johnson (1994) point out that supporters of individual goal structures believe that competition is character building and that it toughens the young for life in the real world. Enjoying the thrill of victory and learning to endure the agony of defeat are sometimes thought to be character building activities. In our society, some businesses thrive and prosper, while others become bankrupt. Teachers who observe this economic phenomena believe that they can prepare students for adult living by teaching individual competition to children at an early age, and that competition is preparation for life in the real world. In response to this position, we could point out that all of us experience temporary failure in our lives. We learn from our mistakes only when others support us in our temporary failures and show us how we went wrong and what lessons we can learn from our mistakes.

Children Prefer Competition?   A fourth reason for individual competition in the classroom stems from the "homegrown" or naive belief held by some teachers which supports the notion that children prefer to compete with each other in the classroom. Greenberg (1932), in a classic study of children's goal structures, found that children seem to enjoy competitive reward structures so long as they are winning. Frequently, teachers use classroom competitions such as spelling bees, chess tournaments, bulletin boards of exemplary work, and honor student competitions believing that these activities will encourage students to strive for academic excellence and that all students academically profit from such activities. During my elementary school years, I dreaded spelling bees. It was not that I was a bad speller, but that I was terribly shy and hated standing in front of my peers. I frequently became nervous when it was my turn to spell a word and forgot what I was doing. I am sure my teachers meant well, but I cannot say I liked the competition of the classroom spelling bees.

Competition Builds Self Esteem?   Greenberg's classic study (1932) further pointed out that, while children enjoy winning, they do not enjoy losing. Since Greenberg's time, we have learned the devastating effects of "losing" on children's emotional development. Children who perceive themselves to be "losers" frequently spend years trying to develop positive feelings of self-worth. In discussing individual learning activities conducted in competitive environments, Johnson and Johnson (1994) point out that under appropriate circumstances competition can be exciting and enjoyable. On the other hand, they note that the inappropriate use or overuse of competition (due, in part, to questionable practices and attitudes passed down from one generation of teachers to the next) may result in destructive outcomes that interfere with successful instruction. In addition, these authors point out that prejudice and discrimination against minority groups increase and are perpetuated under competitive conditions.

Growing up, I had a uncle who ate Wheaties® breakfast cereal every morning. When I asked him about this, he used to reply that he liked Wheaties®. No matter how much we enjoy an activity or a food, a steady diet of the same thing becomes boring for most of us. Group work every minute of every school day can be just as dull and boring as constant competition. Good teachers tend to balance the classroom diet by providing a mixture of small group and large group activities for students.

Sociocultural Aspects of Learning

Schooling is a social process in the sense that students are placed in groups called classes and an adult or teacher is given the responsibility for managing their instruction. In the typical classroom, a series of social interactions occurs daily, including (1) student-to-student, (2) teacher-to-student, and (3) group-to-group interactions.

Student-to-Student Interactions.   Few studies in education have dealt with social interactions in small group settings. One of the first such studies was conducted by June Wallace (1986) in British schools. By watching children interact with each other in dyads and triads (i.e., cooperative groups of two or three students) over a protracted period, Wallace developed a system for classifying children's interactions with one another. Wallace contends that children engage

in six types of student-to-student communications, including (1) negotiated doing, (2) social mediation, (3) tutoring, (4) non-task talk, (5) negotiated knowledge, and (6) constructing meaning.

Negotiated Doing.   Wallace has defined negotiated doing to include arranging
apparatus and taking turns in conducting "experiments." Cheng (1992) points
out that approximately 65% of language is conveyed through nonverbal channels. **Negotiated doing**, according to which students hand materials to each
other, exchange supplies and equipment, and take turns using manipulatives, is
a primary means of nonverbal communication between children. Subtle negotiations about who touches the materials, who hands materials to whom, and so
forth are frequently worked out among students without overt verbal negotiations.

Social Mediation.   Removing tension is a second type of student-to-student communication commonly found in small groups. Any time social interactions occur, disappointments and disputes can arise between the participants. Removing tension, agreeing on who will perform what "job" in the group, is a vital part
of the learning experience and part of **social mediation**. Even when teachers
assign jobs to specific individuals within the group (e.g., facilitator, equipment
manager, clean-up person, recorder), students will still need to define their job
function and parameters within the small group setting. Does the clean-up person "clean up" after everyone in the group, or just check to make certain that
the work area has been cleaned? Does the recorder take one set of notes for the
entire group, or make certain that everyone has performed this task? How are
minor disputes to be handled in the group? What happens when someone goes
"out of turn"? Removing tension is a social mediation that allows learning to
take place in a group environment.

Tutoring.   A third type of student-to-student communication may be defined in
terms of giving and receiving help. For Limited English Proficient students, **linguistic tutoring** is perhaps the most useful function of small group work. Peer
tutoring allows students to append new knowledge to existing knowledge structures. Limited English Proficient students find that a small group environment
allows them the opportunity to develop new vocabulary and to try their oral
communication skills in a "friendly" or nonthreatening small group environment. Peer tutoring allows students the opportunity to teach what they have
just learned to each other. Finally, it allows students the chance to restate information to each other in terms of culturally familiar examples and analogies.

Nontask Talk.   Nontask talk is the fourth type of student-to-student communication identified by Wallace as occurring in cooperative settings. Wallace has
operationally defined **nontask talk** to include greetings and "strokings" as students settle into their small groups. Adults would probably refer to nontask talk
as "small talk" (i.e., talk about the weather, Saturday's football game results, a

television show, and the school lunch menu). While nontask talk is necessary for social interactions, it is not known to have particular educational value, other than allowing children the opportunity to begin social discourse with each other.

Negotiated Meaning.   A fifth type of student-to-student communication is referred to as negotiated meaning. **Negotiated meaning** (which is also discussed in Chapter 7) involves a give and take between children as they struggle to make sense of the world and attempt to compare the knowledge they have constructed with that constructed by their peers. For Limited English Proficient students, negotiated meaning may also entail defining terms in English and/or the student's "home" language, and appending English name tags to concepts that they have formed in their "home" language.

Constructed Meaning.   Constructed meaning is the final type of student-to-student communication mentioned by Wallace in her study of group interactions. Solomon (1989) points out that, while teacher interaction through brainstorming or question and answer periods has long been advocated to help pupils understand new learning, this style of teaching brings another message to students, namely, "getting it right" or winning the teacher's approval. Edwards and Mercer (1987) point out that teacher-led classroom discussions might appear to be relatively open and pupil-oriented, but in reality most teachers manage to maintain a close control over the selection, expression, and direction of ideas and activities.

   Constructing meaning in a small group setting involves students in corroboration and active participation with others. Group environments are places in which students examine their personal rendering of information and restructure that knowledge based on the notions, perceptions, and feedback provided to them by others in the group. A consensus effect (Solomon, 1989) is tangible evidence that the group process is "working" and that students are restructuring their conceptions of the natural world based on their interactions with their peers.

Teacher-to-Student Interactions.   When cooperative group activities are introduced in classrooms, the role of the teacher changes from that of a dispenser of knowledge to a facilitator of learning. From the viewpoint of the classroom teacher, Fields (1988) points out that the use of cooperative learning groups (1) allows teachers to use hands-on learning activities with a minimum of materials, (2) provides teachers more opportunity to interact with groups and individuals, (3) fosters social skill development in students, (4) encourages peer tutoring, and (5) produces higher levels of self-esteem in students. In their daily interactions with students, teachers serve in many different capacities and function in many different roles. Typically, when cooperative learning groups are used in the classroom, teachers function as expediters, evaluators, coaches, mentors, navigators, managers, mediators, and lecturers.

Teacher as Expediter.   One role of the teacher is to function as an expediter. As **expediter**, the teacher becomes the person who brings together children and objects from the physical world in a way that will facilitate the learning of each child. The teacher is the one who establishes the physical environment in which learning can occur. She/he defines the task that will facilitate the learning of the child. As Wheatley (1991) states, the teacher's role is to provide stimulating and motivational experiences. According to Wheatley, appropriate tasks for cooperative learning experiences are those which (1) are accessible to all students at the start, (2) invite students to make decisions, (3) encourage students to ask "what if" questions, (4) prompt students to use their prior knowledge, (5) promote discussion and communication, (6) lead students somewhere, (7) contain an element of surprise, (8) are enjoyable, and (9) can be extended to other learning situations. Finally, as an expediter, the teacher provides the materials, physical space, and "work" time which allow children to complete the task at hand.

Teacher as Evaluator.   As **evaluators**, teachers function as judges, as those who evaluate children's learning. By watching what the child does and says, the teacher gains insights into the way(s) that children have constructed knowledge. Teachers are able to make inferences about children's thinking, development, and the knowledge that they have constructed. At times teachers evaluate children in formal testing situations and at other times teachers assess children informally in an attempt to determine what children are capable of understanding. Information gained from assessing or evaluating children's understandings of science influences (1) the choice of concepts that are taught, (2) the choice of learning experiences made available to children, and (3) the presentation of the purposes of the proposed activities (Driver, Guesne & Tiberghien, 1985).

Teacher as Coach.   High school football **coaches** demonstrate, encourage, and provide feedback to football players. Elementary science teachers use these same strategies to coach children in acquiring a knowledge of the physical world. Sometimes teachers model a performance that they want children to emulate and watch while children perform the skill or task. At other times teachers encourage children to try again or attempt a different solution path when they have met with temporary "failure." Finally, teachers coach by providing corrective or reinforcing feedback.

Recently, I observed Gwen, a third-grade teacher, teaching a lesson on dinosaurs. Gwen had designed a lesson which combined science and art, an activity in which children were to make three-dimensional clay models of dinosaurs from black-and-white line drawings. As Gwen approached Sarah's desk, she noticed that Sarah had constructed a stegosaurus-shaped pancake rather than a three-dimensional dinosaur model. No matter what she said to Sarah, Gwen could not convey the idea that dinosaurs were round, not flat. Finally, Gwen picked up a ball of clay and made a round body. Suddenly, Sarah got the idea. She modeled a Stegosaurus body after Gwen's dinosaur model and began to attach the legs and plates to her model. Gwen had encouraged, modeled, and provided feedback to Sarah until she mastered the skill. She had coached her to perform spatial visualization skills.

Teacher as Mentor.   In the role of **mentor**, the teacher functions as a master learner, while students function as apprentices. This teaching role is based on theories of motivation and modeling. In the framework of the apprenticeship setting, a teacher models learning, problem solving, social interactions, investigation of the natural world, and so forth in the elementary multicultural science classroom. The following conversation from a fourth grade classroom illustrates this concept:

Ms. Kitano: Suppose that I went on a camping trip to the mountains and forgot to take along matches or a lighter, what would I do? I have a package of frozen hot dogs in my cooler ready to eat for lunch and, suddenly, I don't have any way to start a fire. Can anyone give me some ideas about what to do?

Jenny: Maybe you could start a fire with sticks or rocks.

Ms. Kitano: That's one way I could solve the problem. That's a real good idea, Jenny. Does anyone know how to start a fire with sticks?

Jenny: Not really, I heard it on TV, but I think we could get it to work.

Ms. Kitano: Maybe we could work with sticks and rocks to figure out how to start a fire. Before we try that, does anyone else have another possible solution to my problem?

Mark: You could eat the hot dogs raw. I think hot dogs are already cooked before they're sold.

Ms. Kitano: Now that's an idea I hadn't thought of, Mark. That's a second way that I could use to solve my problem. I believe Mark is correct. I could safely eat frozen hot dogs if I needed to do so. But, suppose I don't care for frozen hot dogs. Does anyone have another idea how to cook them or warm them up if I don't have matches to start a fire?

Ricardo: You could make a solar cooker. We did that in scouts last year. We took a sheet of aluminum foil and some cardboard and string and made a big curved mirror type of hot dog cooker. Then we tried to find the place where the sun's rays focused and we placed a hot dog on a stick at that point. It worked pretty well. It took a while to get it working, but we were able to cook our food without making a fire.

Ms. Kitano: Good Ricardo, you've given us a way to heat the food without building a fire. Solar cooking is a third way to solve my problem.

In this vignette, Ms. Kitano is modeling brainstorming or identifying multiple solution paths for the students. Ms. Kitano is mentoring students in problem-solving skills by acting as a master learner, as one who identifies possible solution paths and evaluates them before solving the problem.

Teacher as Navigator.   The fifth role for the teacher in the cooperative learning classroom is that of **navigator**. Teachers are accustomed to thinking of themselves in this capacity, in that they are used to determining goals or "charting the course" for students. In a cooperative group setting, however, the term navigator also refers to the analogy of a ship's navigator. On a cruise ship, a navigator is also a passenger in the sense that she or he is traveling on the ship along with others. The ship's navigator and the passengers experience the journey together. Just as the splendor of sunrises and sunsets may be enjoyed by all aboard the ship, so too everyone aboard experiences the rough waves and stormy conditions. In a cooperatively grouped classroom, the teacher charts the course, but everyone, including the students, experiences the adventure of exploring the natural world.

Teacher as Manager.   In their sixth role, teachers function as **managers** in the classroom. Teachers structure the learning environment to maximize the learning of all students. Managerial tasks in the cooperative classroom include (1) arranging the physical layout of the classroom, (2) maintaining records of student performance and task completion, (3) establishing and coordinating cooperative learning groups, (4) assigning roles to individuals in groups, (5) requisitioning supplies and materials, (6) establishing minimal performance and behavior standards, and (7) coordinating activities of the classroom with outside agencies (e.g., the entire school community and the student's homes).

When teachers function as managers, they may inform students when the work atmosphere becomes too boisterous or when students are off task. In addition, consistent with their managerial role, teachers may assign tasks to specific individuals in a group. The Inquiry Role Approach developed by Seymour, Padberg, Bingman, and Koutrick (1974) stresses the importance of assigning roles, such as coordinator, technical advisor, data recorder, and process evaluator, to specific individuals in a group. According to this model, part of a teacher's managerial role is to transfer responsibility for learning to specific individuals in each group.

Teacher as Mediator.   When teachers function as **mediators**, they are serving in a counseling or advising capacity in the classroom. In this seventh role, a teacher serves to mediate disputes between students and address longstanding social inequities which may separate students. Teacher as mediator is a concept familiar to most educators, and most teachers feel comfortable with settling disputes, the traditional mediation role in the classroom. However, there is a second facet to mediation which involves a concern for the educational and social needs of low income and/or "minority" students.

Cohen, Lotan, and Catanzarite (1990) point out that a student's status characteristics may be altered by the actions of the classroom teacher. **Status characteristics** according to these authors are socially evaluated attributes which are based on qualities associated with a student's ethnicity and social class. A child from a lower socioeconomic background may be held in low esteem by students from more affluent social classes. Teachers can confer status on such students by providing feedback to a child's peers regarding the student's contributions to the group's activities. If a teacher is standing by a group and hears a "low status" student make a suggestion to the group, the teacher could make a statement such as, "That's a really good idea, Mary. You've provided the group with another way to solve the problem." The teacher is valuing Mary's contribution to the group and in the process is attending to a sociological problem, namely, differential status between students.

Teacher as Lecturer.   The teacher as **lecturer** is the final role of the teacher in the cooperative classroom. Direction giving is necessary in all educational settings. Even in the most child-centered learning situations, there must be an adult in charge, someone responsible for the health and safety of the children. In the role of lecturer, the teacher provides instructions which insure the well being of the children in the classroom. If an activity involves the use of a flame or heat source, the teacher might give instructions such as, "Be sure to wear your safety goggles," "Be careful not to touch hot glassware," and so forth. Matters of health and safety cannot be left to discovery learning but need to be addressed by the teacher in a straightforward expository manner.

Group-to-Group Interactions.   Just as there are social interactions within groups, there are interactions between groups. Social interactions between groups may be of a cooperative, neutral, or competitive nature. Neutral interactions between groups imply that there are no formal or informal interactions between groups in the classroom. In such situations, students work within their own groups and their group activities are independent of other groups in the classroom. Traditional reading groups are an illustration of this type of intergroup interaction. When using reading groups, the teacher typically meets with one reading group while other groups of students in the classroom work on some other task, either independently or under the direction of a classroom aide.

Research Team Approach.   Cooperative interactions between groups imply the sharing of responsibility for the parts of a learning task. One model of this type of intergroup sharing is illustrated by the Research Team Approach developed by DelGiorno (1969). When using this approach, the teacher and students distribute the responsibility for the learning task across many groups in the classroom. Each group develops expertise in some part of the learning task and reports its findings to other groups in the class. For example, suppose a class was studying the behavior of mealworms. One group might investigate the preference of mealworms for wet or dry conditions. Another group might investigate the behavior of mealworms in light and dark environments. A third group might attempt to determine whether mealworms prefer oat or wheat bran flakes as a food source. Each group would develop expertise in a specific area and would then share this knowledge with other groups in the classroom.

DelGiorno (1969) identified four phases as being vital in the Research Team Approach: (1) lecture, (2) independent study, (3) experimentation, and (4) discussion. In the mealworm example just discussed, the teacher would introduce the concept of habitat through a large group lecture. The teacher would also establish the task (i.e., determining the habitat of the mealworm) for the class. Groups of students would assume responsibility for developing expertise in a particular area of the subject. During the second phase, the independent study phase, each group would search out resource persons, books, and so forth as sources of information about the assigned topic. Students would also plan a way to investigate the environment to find answers to their particular question. The experimental phase, the third phase of DelGiorno's model, would be the time when the group would manipulate materials to learn about mealworms. During the fourth phase of learning, each group would report its findings to the other groups in the class. The last phase of the Research Team Approach may also serve as a time of evaluation, when the teacher and/or other groups of students can evaluate the findings of each group and critique its performance. The Jigsaw Approach (Lucker, Rosenfield, Sikes, & Aronson, 1976; Slavin, 1982) to cooperative group work contains many of the same elements of shared responsibility for learning and disseminating of findings as are found in the Research Team Approach.

Team Competition.   In addition to intergroup cooperation, intergroup rivalry has been found to be a highly effective approach to instruction in the classroom (Slavin, 1982). Group or team competition seems to be preferred by many culturally diverse students (Hadfield, Martin, & Wooden, 1992; Okebukola, 1985). In group competition settings, students enjoy intragroup cooperation while competing with other groups in the classroom. A team environment is created when students collaborate in solving a problem and then compete against other groups in the classroom. The Puffmobile (Activity 5-2) mentioned later in this chapter is an example of a team competition activity. In this activity, students collaborate to build a wind-propelled vehicle which will travel faster or farther than similar vehicles made by other groups in the classroom. By working together, students tackle the problems of friction, wind propulsion, navigation, and so forth. The contest is "fair" in the sense that every group is supplied with the same raw materials as every other group in the classroom. Win or lose, competition in a Puffmobile derby is a nonthreatening experience for students. Competing together in a group is a culturally familiar learning experience for many culturally diverse students in the multicultural science classroom.

CLASSROOM PRACTICE

The decision as to whether students should work individually or in groups is a pedagogical decision best left to each individual classroom teacher. The decision as to which pedagogical strategies are to be used in the classroom depends on the characteristics of the students, the information to be learned, and the goals or purpose that you as a teacher have in mind. Indeed, there is no one right way to learn anything. In this next section, a series of activities are presented which are designed for use in competitive and cooperative learning environments.

ACTIVITY 5-1 ■ EGG DROP CONTEST

Purpose: Individual competition in spatial visualization skills.

Type of Activity: Competition (individual)

Materials:

25 plastic straws   100 straight pins
1 raw egg for each person   1 meter stick to measure heights

Problem: Using the straws and pins, construct a container which will protect the egg during free fall and landings. The container which successfully protects the egg from the greatest height is the winner.

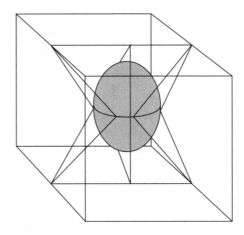

Teacher Notes (How to conduct the activity):

1. Allow students to construct their containers at home prior to the egg drop contest. (Note: the use of straws and pins addresses equity issues since nearly all students have access to these simple materials).
2. On the day of the egg drop, cover an area of the school yard with a plastic tarp or large plastic bags. Bring garbage bags to contain the losers and a bucket of warm, soapy water to rinse the target area. Access to a ladder is also advisable.
3. Drop the containers in a uniform manner starting with a height of about 2 meters.

ACTIVITY 5-2 ▪ PUFFMOBILES

Purpose: Team competition to develop a wind driven vehicle, alternative energy sources.

Type of Activity: Cooperation (team competition)

Materials (for each group):

10 soda straws	25 straight pins
1 sheet of 8 1/2" x 11" paper	4 macramé beads (with holes large enough to fit over the straws)

Problem: Construction of a wind-powered vehicle that is capable of traveling the fastest over the race course.

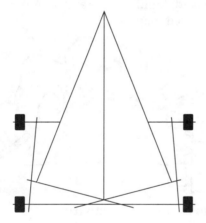

Teacher Notes (How to conduct the activity):

1. Allow students to construct and field test their Puffmobiles in small cooperative groups.
2. Remind students that one straw needs to be kept for the propulsion system.
3. All materials must be attached to the car. No "leftovers" are allowed.
4. Set up a race course on a smooth surface (concrete pad, gymnasium floor, tiled hallway). Use masking tape to denote a start and finish line. Set the lines about 10 meters or 25 to 30 feet apart.
5. Have students place all "wheels" of the puffmobile behind the starting line. The first to get all of its tires across the finish line wins. Students are allowed to follow their puffmobiles down the race course using their straws to blow air at the puffmobiles, thus supplying wind power.

ACTIVITY 5-3 ■ BOXOSAURUS

Purpose: Cooperative learning activity to develop a dinosaur model from recycled materials.

Type of Activity: Cooperative (groups)

Materials:

assorted cardboard boxes	paints
scissors	yarn
egg cartons	milk cartons
paper cups	colored photographs of modern day
dinosaur sketches	reptiles
glue	

Problem: Using cardboard, build a boxosaurus. A boxosaurus is a model of a dinosaur built using recycled materials.

Teacher Notes (How to conduct the activity):

1. Allow each group to "adopt" a dinosaur from the sketches or drawings.
2. Students should be encouraged to research their dinosaur and learn about its physical characteristics.
3. In group settings, allow students to build models of dinosaurs from the scrap materials.
4. Prior to having them paint the dinosaurs, show students photographs of present day reptiles or modern descendants of dinosaurs (e.g., coral snakes, Gila monsters, Pine lizards). Have the students note the patterns on the skin of the modern day reptiles and allow students to make inferences about dinosaur skin colors and patterns based on their knowledge of living reptiles.

ACTIVITY 5-4 ■ CLAY BOATS

Purpose: Team competition to develop a clay boat that illustrates surface area.

Type of Activity: Competition (teams)

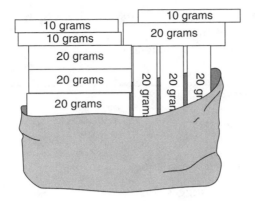

Materials:

clay
metric stacking masses (or washers
   or metric weight set)

bucket of water (or small swimming
   pool)

Problem: Build a boat out of clay that holds the largest possible mass.

Teacher Notes (How to conduct the activity):

1. It may be useful to show students pictures or drawings of boats before beginning the activity (e.g., rowboats, canoes, sailboats, barges).
2. Instruct the students to form the clay ball into a boat. Allow students to test their boats to determine the amount of mass that the boat will hold prior to sinking.
3. Conduct a contest in which students add stacking masses slowly to their boats until they sink. The group whose boat holds the greatest mass prior to sinking wins.

ACTIVITY 5-5 ■ MAGNET SCAVENGER HUNT

Purpose: Individual competition to explore properties of a magnet.

Type of Activity: Competition (individual or teams)

Materials: 1 magnet per person or per group

Problem: Identify as many objects as possible, during the time allowed by your teacher, that are attracted to your magnet.

Teacher Notes (How to conduct the activity):

1. Give each student a magnet and have each one generate a list of objects which are attracted to the magnet. A period of 15 to 30 minutes is sufficient for the activity.

2. Modify the activity for early elementary students by having them draw each of the objects attracted to the magnet. Older students will be able to generate a list of objects attracted to the magnet.

ACTIVITY 5-6 ■ MELTATHON

Purpose: Team competition to investigate the properties of insulating materials.

Type of Activity: Competition (teams)

Materials (These are just suggestions.):

ice cubes   metric balance
paper towels   newspapers
wax paper   aluminum foil
plastic wrap

Problem: Insulate the ice cube so that it melts as little as possible during a given time. The objective of the contest is to prevent meltdown.

Teacher Notes (How to conduct the activity):

1. Give each group of students an ice cube. Weigh the ice cube before handing it to the students.
2. Instruct the students to wrap the ice in materials so that it is insulated as much as possible.
3. After about 1 hour, ask the students to weigh in their ice cubes. The group that has "lost" the least amount of ice wins.

ACTIVITY 5-7 ■ BAGGIE LIFT

Purpose: Cooperative activity to investigate air pressure.

Type of Activity: Cooperative

Materials:

one heavy duty garbage bag   soda straws (1 for each child in the
duct tape   group)

Problem: To lift a classmate off the floor without touching him or her.

Teacher Notes (How to conduct the activity):

1. Place the children in groups of six to eight students.
2. Tape the plastic garbage bag flat to the floor using the duct tape.
3. Have one student sit or lie down on the garbage bag.
4. Ask the other students to insert their straws into the top layer of the garbage

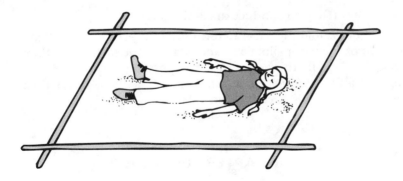

bag. Instruct the students in the group to blow air into the bag. Observe the student sitting on top of the bag.

ACTIVITY 5-8 ■ PAPER AIRPLANES

Purpose: Competitive activity to investigate properties of an airfoil.

Type of Activity: Competition

Materials:

1 sheet of notebook paper   1 paper clip (per student)
1 metric measuring tape

Problem: The objective is to make a paper airplane that will fly the farthest distance.

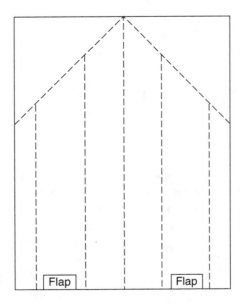

A C T I V I T I E S

Teacher Notes (How to conduct the activity):

1. Have students fold the paper to form paper airplanes. Have them adjust the position of the paper clip, flaps, and edges of the plane until they develop a model that will fly the farthest distance possible.
2. Conduct a paper airplane contest. Allow students to throw their airplanes and measure the distance that each plane flew.

 CHAPTER SUMMARY

Learning is a social process involving interactions between students and teachers. Student-to-student interactions in group situations include negotiated doing, mediation, tutoring, nontask talk, negotiated knowledge, and constructing meaning. When group activities are used in the elementary science classroom, teachers function as expediters, evaluators, coaches, mentors, navigators, managers, mediators, and lecturers. In cooperatively grouped classrooms, interactions between groups may be competitive, cooperative, or neutral in nature. The use of group activities has been found to benefit many culturally diverse learners in terms of students' academic achievement, problem-solving skills, attitudes toward science, self-concepts, and social growth and development.

 TOPICS TO REVIEW

five arguments for competitive
   learning, 104
research team approach, 112
six research-based reasons for
   cooperative learning, 101

six types of student-to-student
   interactions, 107
types of group interactions, 112

 REFLECTIVE PRACTICE

1. Compare and contrast individual learning activities and cooperative group activities in terms of student learning and social interactions.
2. What are the "traditional" arguments for competitive learning environments. Do you agree or disagree with these arguments? Why or why not?
3. In your opinion, when are competitive learning environments useful in the classroom? When are cooperative learning environments useful? Justify your answers.
4. It has been said that "cooperative learning environments proportionally benefit culturally diverse students." Do you agree or disagree with this statement? Justify your answer.

5. What is the role of the teacher in the competitive classroom? The cooperative classroom? Compare and contrast the role of the teacher in competitive and cooperative classrooms.
6. A classic argument against the extended use of cooperative learning environments is that "bright students are objectified" (that is, they carry a disproportionate burden or responsibility for the learning of slower students). How do you react to this statement? Do you agree or disagree? Justify your answer.

Affective Domain

Unobtrusive	*Obtrusive*
Library	Drawings
Mini museum	Likert
	Semantic
	differential
	Essays
Social	Surveys
interactions	Checklists

Cognitive Domain

Traditional	*Authentic*
Norm-	Portfolio
referenced	Concept
Criterion-	mapping
referenced	Task tests
Self-	Journal
referenced	writing
	Group
	discussion

Psychomotor Domain

Laboratory Activities

Checklists
Rubrics

ASSESSING KNOWLEDGE IN THE SCIENCE CLASSROOM

 POINTS TO PONDER

1. What is the purpose of testing or evaluation?
2. How can we assess what children have learned?
3. How can assessment be made more free of cultural bias and/or culture fair?

ON KNOWLEDGE

*O*ld Jack was a wonderful, kind, elderly gentleman. During my childhood years, he used to hunt for squirrels, rabbits, opossum, and pheasants on our family farm. Towards sunset one beautiful autumn day, Old Jack came to the door of our farmhouse and handed me a fistful of freshly picked pheasants. Being a rather rude teenager, I informed him that I did not care for pheasants, that I would rather eat a McDonald's® hamburger, but that I would take the pheasants to my parents. Knowing that Old Jack had only a grade school education, I deliberately spoke in 25¢ words rather than my normal 5¢ words. My father was standing behind the kitchen door listening to my remarks. As I went into the house, my father bolted over to Old Jack and apologized for my rude behavior and lack of manners.

When my father entered the house, he scolded me for my conduct and informed me that he would personally oversee my education the following day. When I protested that

I could not possibly stay home from school, my father told me that he would personally talk to the high school principal about my absence. At 4:00 a.m. the next morning, my father woke me and ordered me to get dressed. It was a moonless night that greeted us as we walked into the woods together in those predawn hours. I remember being cold and angry. Why had my father kept me home from school? Why were we walking about in the woods at this ridiculous hour? A dozen similar thoughts flashed through my mind. Finally, we reached the banks of the White Clay Creek that ran behind the edge of our property. My father sat on a rock, lit his pipe, and said, "Okay, get me some breakfast."

I protested that there wasn't any food, that we didn't have any pots and pans, and I couldn't possibly fix a meal under such primitive conditions. My father informed me that when he and Old Jack went hunting, they always paused here for breakfast, that Old Jack could whip up a tasty, freshly cooked meal in about an hour using the same basic ingredients that I now had at hand. Well, I stormed around, stamped my feet, and generally made a fool of myself. When I was done, my father told me to get started on gathering food for his breakfast. Thinking this was one of the worst mornings of my life, I gathered some old berries and a handful of mushrooms and defiantly marched back to my father. My father looked up and smiled, "Dear, those pokeberries are poisonous and so are those mushrooms."

By now, I was reduced to tears. My father sat me down, patted me on the head, and began to teach me some of the life lessons that I had not gotten in school. He informed me that, although Old Jack did not have much "school learning," he held a wealth of knowledge or a "fund of knowledge" about the natural world. You cannot judge someone's education or knowledge level by their degrees or a test score. He told me about Old Jack, how he hunted and fished to support his family, and how Old Jack always gave the best of what he killed to the farmer whose land he used. The night before, I had turned up my nose at Old Jack's gift: pheasants that I wished I had at this minute. Old Jack always took care of others before himself. He acted out of love and gave because he wanted to, not because he had to. Finally, my father gave me some words to live by, words that remain with me still, "The more education you have, the more people you ought to be able to communicate with, not fewer."

My father took me into school later that day. Looking back, I can say that I probably reflected on the learning I gained on that one morning than on any other morning of my school years. Many months later, I had the opportunity to go hunting with Old Jack. He taught me about blackberries, raspberries, and pokeberries: which were edible and which were not. I learned to eat the greens of the fields, roots of the cattail, acorns, persimmons, and fish from the creek. Once in a while, I still fix his recipe for pheasant with wild rice and chestnut stuffing. My memory of Old Jack wonderfully illustrates the value of assessment in the educational process. Sometimes, we really do not measure what people know and what they have learned. Traditionally, schools have measured only a small part of the knowledge that children have acquired.

ASSESSMENT AND EVALUATION

Assessment or evaluation is "a process that people perform in order to gather data that will enable them to decide whether to accept, change, or eliminate something" (Ornstein & Hunkins, 1988, p. 250). Most teachers tend to regard evaluation and assessment as processes of gathering information to make judgments and decisions about specific individuals in their classrooms. In actuality, evaluation and assessment involve a consideration of the child, the curriculum, and the teacher. Certainly teachers want to evaluate students to determine their academic progress, grade placement, and promotion from one grade to another, but teachers also need to use assessment tools to reflect on their own teaching and on the curriculum they are using as part of the evaluation process.

EVALUATING CHILDREN'S UNDERSTANDING

Grading papers and reporting academic growth or achievement to parents are only a small part of the total assessment process. Evaluation of children's understanding of the world around them involves an assessment of the **affective** (attitudes, values, and beliefs), **cognitive** (facts, concepts, rules and principles, and problem solving), and **psychomotor** (motor skills including science processes) domains. For culturally diverse students, nontraditional assessment tools such as oral interviews, portfolios, concept mapping, and authentic assessment tools are vitally needed in most elementary schools to assess changes in children's knowledge structures in all three domains.

Affective Domain

Throughout our lives we are constantly thrilled with the beauty of sunrises and sunsets, starry nights replete with shooting "stars," wildflowers blooming in the spring, and the splendor of autumnal foliage in deciduous hardwood forests. Science is the study of the natural world, of a physical world that affects the lives of all who share this planet. Every child is affected by natural phenomena, yet children's values, attitudes, and beliefs are infrequently assessed in the typical elementary school science curriculum. Measurements of the affective domain were rarely undertaken in the past because attitude constructs are difficult to define and measure.

Bloom (1971) divided the affective domain into five categories: (1) receiving, (2) responding, (3) valuing, (4) organizing, and (5) internalizing a value system. **Receiving**, the first level of the affective domain, involves a sensitivity to or an awareness of stimuli and events. If you watch a public television show on the plight of whales, you are receiving information. At the second or **responding** level of Bloom's affective domain, students do something about or respond to the stimuli. If, after viewing a show on whales, I decide to go to the library and sign out a book on whales to learn more about them, I am functioning at a responding level. At the third level of Bloom's taxonomy (**valuing**), the student develops criteria or a standard for determining the worth of behaviors, things, and events. According to Bloom, students functioning at the fourth level (**organizing**) of his affective taxonomy begin to formulate a value system. The final step or stage of the affective domain involves the **internalization** of a value system. It is only when students act on their interests, appreciations, attitudes, and values that teachers are able to assess those attributes.

Feelings and values are also incorporated into McCormack and Yager's (1989) taxonomy of science education. These authors divide knowledge into five domains: (1) knowing and understanding, (2) exploring and discovering, (3) imagining and creating, (4) feeling and valuing, and (5) using and applying. In this classification system, knowing and understanding include the learning of facts, concepts, laws, and theories of science. These authors define exploring and discovering as the processes of science. Imagining and creating are defined in this taxonomy as including the abilities to (1) produce a mental image, (2) visualize, (3) produce alternate or unusual uses for objects, (4) solve problems and puzzles, (5) fantasize, and (6) dream. McCormack and Yager have defined feeling and valuing in much the same manner as Bloom, that is, assessment of students' values, attitudes, and beliefs. The final domain in this taxonomic system for science education includes using and applying knowledge.

In recent years, advances in **psychometric** or test design procedures have resulted in new instruments with which to assess the affective domain. These instruments allow classroom teachers to measure readily students' values, attitudes, and beliefs and to determine if those attitudes and beliefs change as a result of instruction. Whether one uses a three- or five-domain taxonomic system for classifying knowledge, assessment of children's attitudes is vital in the evaluation process. Assessing children's attitudes before, during, and following instruction is vital to understanding students' attitudes and how those attitudes change over time and as a result of instruction.

Unobtrusive Measures.   Unobtrusive or indirect measurements of students' attitudes have long been used as a means of assessing students' attitudes or preferences. School cafeteria workers in most elementary schools are proficient in measuring students' attitudes towards particular foods. As children walk through the cafeteria line and select entrees, the workers inventory their food preferences. Cafeteria managers prepare greater quantities of foods that students like, while avoiding waste by cooking smaller quantities of foods that children avoid. This same principle of unobtrusive assessment may be used in a classroom setting.

Library Selections.   If children visit the school library and are allowed to select books for their own reading pleasure, teachers may get a crude indicator of children's interests. Suppose Mr. Hun, a fourth grade teacher, wants to determine if his unit on dinosaurs is making a difference in children's attitudes towards the study of ancient life. At the end of the weekly library period, he could

Children's reading patterns are an unobtrusive measure of their interests. (© Jim Pickerell)

unobtrusively observe and tally the topics and numbers of the books that his students had voluntarily checked out. After several weeks of teaching a dinosaur unit, Mr. Hun could again use a simple tally count of library books to determine if children's reading habits had changed as a result of his instruction. If his first survey revealed that only two children in his class of 30 students had checked out books on dinosaurs, he would conclude that only a few children were interested in the topic. Mr. Hun could conclude that his instruction had made a difference in his students' attitudes towards dinosaurs if half of the students in the same class signed out books on dinosaurs after his unit of instruction. Unobtrusive observation of voluntary performance is one way to assess students' affective domains.

Mini Museums.   A second unobtrusive measure sometimes used to assess students' attitudes towards a particular topic is the mini-museum concept. Sometimes teachers establish a museum corner in their classrooms and allow students to make voluntary contributions to the museum. Each morning as students bring in objects, the items are labeled with their names and the name of the student contributor. After each unit of study, the teacher allows students to take the *realia* home. Using this idea, a teacher could keep an informal tally of the percentage of students who voluntarily contribute materials to a particular unit of study.

Using mini-museum contributions to assess attitude is an imprecise measure since real world objects are more readily available for some units of study (e.g., plant materials are far easier for children to obtain than *realia* associated with chemistry) than others. Other unobtrusive measures of children's attitudes could include materials self-selected for reading during silent reading periods, computer software self-selected for study during a class activity time, students' choices of book report topics, and children's self-selected activities carried out in a learning center environment. Unobtrusive measures of voluntary performance are powerful devices for determining children's attitudes towards school and the subjects taught in the classroom.

Obtrusive Measures.   Purposeful measurement of children's attitudes towards science and related topics has become easier in recent years with the development of new assessment tools. Newer psychometric tools described in this chapter have allowed teachers to assess the affective domain with an ease of test administration and scoring. Drawing tests, pictorial tests, iconic response categories, and oral test administrations allow teachers to assess children's attitudes even though the children may not be highly proficient in the use of the English language. In addition, many of these tests eliminate much of the cultural bias associated with traditional pencil-and-paper assessment tools. While no test is completely "culture-free" or "culture-fair," recently developed attitude instruments do seem to minimize the testing bias which has flawed many older instruments.

Drawing Tests.   The Draw-A-Scientist Test (Mason, Kahle, & Gardner 1991) is one of the easiest attitude instruments to administer to elementary school-aged children. In this test, the child is given a blank sheet of paper and directed to "Draw a scientist." Children are allowed 15 to 30 minutes to draw their perceptions of a scientist. Since this is a drawing instrument, it is not language dependent and thus it is appropriate for younger children and for children with limited proficiency in the use of the English language. An upper elementary child's perception of a scientist is shown in Figure 6.1.

This test is scored by counting the number of standard stereotypical indicators in the drawing. A child may score from 0 to 11 points on the standard indicator scale. A list of standard indicators is presented in Figure 6.2. A high score indicates the child holds a strong negative stereotype of a scientist, while a lower score indicates that the child holds a more realistic or less stereotypical image of a scientist. Teachers may administer this test as a pretest and a posttest either on a yearly basis, or during a particular unit of study.

Likert Instruments.   Among all attitude instruments, the most reliable and valid are **Likert instruments**. Likert instruments normally feature five response categories ranging from "strongly agree" to "strongly disagree." Likert-type instruments are developed in a highly constrained environment and are subjected to numerous reliability and validity checks prior to their publication. They are, therefore, sensitive to even slight changes in student's attitudes. Among Likert instruments used in science education, perhaps the most widely known is the Science Attitude Scale (Shrigley, 1974; Thompson & Shrigley, 1986). Numerous

FIGURE 6.1   Perception of a Scientist by Elementary Student

versions of this science attitude scale have been produced over the years (Figure 6.3).

The science attitude scale has been translated into approximately 20 languages and has been administered throughout the world. It has been used in its traditional pencil-and-paper form with older elementary children and in oral administrations with younger children. In addition, iconic response categories, featuring "smiley" and "frowny" faces, have been developed over the years for early elementary school-aged children and for limited English proficient students (Figure 6.4).

Checklists. For older elementary children, attitude checklists are highly effective devices for measuring attitudes towards science. One such easily administered

1. Laboratory coat
2. Eyeglasses
3. Facial hair
4. Symbols of research
   a. flasks
   b. test tubes
   c. microscope
   d. bunsen burner
   e. other laboratory equipment
5. Symbols of knowledge
   a. books
   b. filing cabinets
   c. chalkboard
   d. other educational supplies
6. Symbols of technology (the products of science)
   a. solutions in glassware
   b. machines
   c. robots
   d. computers
   e. other inventions
7. Captions (e.g., "Eureka, I've got it!!!", "He's a nerd.")
8. Male
9. Signs and labeling (e.g., Fire Exit, Poison)
10. Pencils and pens in chest pocket
11. Unkempt appearance (e.g., uncombed hair, dirty lab coat, "high water" trousers)

FIGURE 6.2   Standard Indicators

instrument is Zuckerman's Affect Adjective Checklist (Docking, 1978). This checklist may be used to measure anxiety towards the study of science. Zuckerman's Affect Adjective Checklist (Figure 6.5) consists of 21 key words which are embedded in a total of 60 adjectives. Students are instructed to circle as many or as few words which describe how they feel about science. The 11 words designated (+) are scored as 1 if they are circled and 0 if they are not circled. The 10 words designated as (–) are scored 0 if they are circled and 1 if they are not circled. Each child's anxiety level is obtained by summing the scores for the 21 key words. The remaining 39 adjectives are ignored in the scoring process. The instrument exhibits good validity and reliability characteristics. Children's scores on the Zuckerman instrument might range from 0 (no anxiety) to 21 (extreme anxiety). This instrument can be used as a pretest and posttest to measure the effectiveness of science instruction in the affective domain.

Semantic Differential Scales.   **Semantic differential scales** have been used for several decades as a means of assessing students' attitudes towards a variety of topics. Semantic scales typically consist of a list of bipolar adjectives (e.g., beautiful/ugly, wonderful/awful) which can be applied to a particular topic. A five- or

1. I feel uncomfortable in the science classroom.

1_____ 2_____ 3_____ 4_____ 5_____
Strongly agree Agree   Undecided   Disagree   Strongly disagree

2. Learning science is important to me.

1_____ 2_____ 3_____ 4_____ 5_____
Strongly agree Agree   Undecided   Disagree   Strongly disagree

3. I fear that I will be unable to learn science adequately.

1_____ 2_____ 3_____ 4_____ 5_____
Strongly agree Agree   Undecided   Disagree   Strongly disagree

4. Learning science takes too much time.

1_____ 2_____ 3_____ 4_____ 5_____
Strongly agree Agree   Undecided   Disagree   Strongly disagree

5. I enjoy the lab period in science classes.

1_____ 2_____ 3_____ 4_____ 5_____
Strongly agree Agree   Undecided   Disagree   Strongly disagree

6. I have a difficult time understanding science.

1_____ 2_____ 3_____ 4_____ 5_____
Strongly agree Agree   Undecided   Disagree   Strongly disagree

7. I feel comfortable with the subjects in my science class.

1_____ 2_____ 3_____ 4_____ 5_____
Strongly agree Agree   Undecided   Disagree   Strongly disagree

8. I would be interested in working in a science lab.

1_____ 2_____ 3_____ 4_____ 5_____
Strongly agree Agree   Undecided   Disagree   Strongly disagree

9. I look forward to coming to science class.

1_____ 2_____ 3_____ 4_____ 5_____
Strongly agree Agree   Undecided   Disagree   Strongly disagree

FIGURE 6.3   Science Attitude Scale

FIGURE 6.4   Iconic Response Categories

Zuckerman's Affect Adjective Checklist

Directions: The words below could describe how you feel about school science. Read through the list of words and underline those which describe how you generally feel about multicultural education. You may underline as many or as few words as you wish.

absorbed	afraid	aimless	ambitious	annoyed
aware	bored	calm	careless	cautious
challenged	cheerful	cheated	comfortable	confused
contented	creative	curious	dedicated	desperate
disappointed	efficient	entertained	excited	fearful
fortunate	frightened	happy	hopeless	impatient
incapable	inspired	interested	joyful	lazy
loving	miserable	misplaced	nervous	organized
overloaded	panicky	pleasant	pleased	productive
pushed	refreshed	regretful	rewarded	satisfied
secure	serious	shaky	steady	tense
terrified	thoughtful	upset	weary	worried

FIGURE 6.5   Affect Adjective Checklist

seven-point continuum is placed between the two adjectives. Students indicate the strength of their feelings about the subject by circling the appropriate response category. Information about a student's attitudes can be determined at the beginning of a course and again at the end of the course or unit of study. From these measures a determination can be made about changes in students' attitudes. A sample of a semantic differential instrument is shown in Figure 6.6.

Essays and Surveys.   Open-ended essay questions or interviews may also be useful in assessing students' attitudes towards science. "Writing starters" such as, "Some people dislike science. Do you agree or disagree with this statement?" and "Do you think endangered animals such as the whale ought to be preserved? Why or why not?" are effective devices for assessing students attitudes. Oral interviews about the unit under study are useful for students who have difficulty communicating in written English language. Interview questions such as, "Have you gone to a science museum lately?" "Have you visited a state or national park recently?" and "What science movies have you seen during the past month on television?" provide insights into students' attitudes and interests.

Social Interactions.   Social skills are foundational to the process of schooling. Social interactions are vital to each child's success in the multicultural science classroom, in the total school community, and in the community at large. Historically, most teachers have used a simple rating of "satisfactory" or "unsatisfactory" under a vague category of "citizenship skills" to summarize all of a

SCIENCE IS...						
Exciting	1	2	3	4	5	Boring
Good	1	2	3	4	5	Bad
Fun	1	2	3	4	5	Dull
Useful	1	2	3	4	5	Useless
Important	1	2	3	4	5	Unimportant
Easy	1	2	3	4	5	Hard

FIGURE 6.6   Semantic Differential Scale

child's progress in the area of socialization. However, social skills are a complex construct and may be operationally defined as consisting of cluster skills, task skills, and camaraderie skills (Ostlund, 1992).

Cluster skills include the ability to move into small groups, sharing materials in a small group setting, taking turns, contributing ideas, and active listening. **Task skills** in a social context could include such skills as asking questions, receiving and giving peer tutoring, asking clarifying questions, elaborating on the ideas of others, justifying answers, and assisting the group in reaching consensus. Finally, **camaraderie skills** include encouraging the learning of others, avoiding negative feedback to peers, providing verbal support to others, and sharing feelings with others when appropriate. Each of these clusters of social skills can be evaluated with checklists as teachers circulate from one group to another, or they can be evaluated by the children themselves as they work in their groups.

Cognitive Domain

Assessing declarative knowledge or knowledge that we can state is the most common form of evaluation in elementary schools. Tremendous attention has been paid to cognitive assessment instruments during the past several decades. The "back to basics" movement of the 1980s focused national attention on children's mastery of declarative knowledge. Historically, most cognitive assessment has taken the form of end of the unit or **summative evaluation. Formative evaluation** (in process evaluation) or knowledge of how children are progressing is also necessary in informing students of their progress in mastering new knowledge.

Benjamin Bloom (1971) classified knowledge in the cognitive domain into a hierarchy consisting of (1) knowledge, (2) comprehension, (3) application, (4) analysis, (5) synthesis, and (6) evaluation levels. Within Bloom's taxonomic system, information at the **knowledge** stage consists of recall of facts and principles. Bloom defined **comprehension** level knowledge as the understanding of facts and ideas. Applying facts and ideas to new situations is included in the

Questioning skills are vital in the multicultural classroom. (© Frank Siteman)

application or third level of Bloom's taxonomy. **Analysis** or the ability to break concepts down into parts and see their relationships is the fourth level of Bloom's taxonomy. According to Bloom, **synthesis** or the fifth level of knowledge is the ability to put facts and ideas together to make a new whole. Finally, Bloom classifies **evaluation**, that is, the ability to judge the value of facts and ideas, as the highest level of thinking skill.

Other authors have defined the cognitive domain to include intellectual strategies and information. McCormack and Yager (1989) refer to the cognitive domain as including knowledge and understanding. Gagné, Briggs, and Wager (1988) define the cognitive domain by the level of complexity of intellectual skills. These authors define the cognitive domain as consisting of (1) discriminations, (2) concrete concepts, (3) rules and defined concepts, (4) higher-order rules, and (5) problem solving. Within this taxonomic system, **discriminations** involve responding to stimuli in ways that differ from each other along one or more physical dimensions (Gagné, Briggs, & Wager, 1988, p. 57). **Concrete concepts** according to Gagné, Briggs, and Wager are object properties or attributes (e.g., color, shape). **Defined concepts** and rules according to these authors involve attributing particular characteristics to objects, events, or relations. When a learner shows that he or she is able to respond with a class of relationships among classes of objects or events, these authors describe the child as functioning at the **rule using level**. Finally, when a student is able to generalize previously learned knowledge to a new situation, Gagné, Briggs, and Wager describe the learner as functioning at the **problem-solving level**. Regardless of how we classify knowledge in the cognitive domain, the assessment of that domain has long been central to assessment in elementary classrooms.

Traditional Assessment Tools.   Pencil-and-paper tests have long been a staple in elementary schools in the United States. Weekly spelling tests, end of unit tests, and annual achievement tests are familiar to all students and former students of America's public schools. The reported purpose of these instruments is to determine students' progress in mastering the curriculum and compare students to others at the same age and grade level. Many conventional pencil-and-paper assessment instruments come from a tradition of **objectivism**. There is an underlying assumption in these tests that there is a basic body of knowledge that students are to master and that the purpose of testing is to determine how successful students have been at this endeavor.

Norm-referenced Tests.   **Norm-referenced tests** are used to rank and compare students in such areas as scholastic aptitude, language proficiency, and academic attainment. The Scholastic Aptitude Test, the Iowa Test of Basic Skills, and the California Achievement Test are examples of norm-referenced tests. The purpose of these instruments is to compare individual students to other students of the same age and grade level. Data from these instruments has been used as a source of information for comparing individuals, schools, and school districts with others in the same locality and throughout the nation. In addition, these instruments are commonly used to identify gifted and talented students and students who qualify for special education programs.

From a multicultural perspective a great deal of attention has focused on the primacy of these instruments in assessing the achievement and aptitude of culturally diverse students. In spite of years of test analysis and construction, many norm-referenced tests remain biased against poor children and those from ethnic minority groups. Underlying norm-referenced instruments is an assumption that all children have been exposed to certain educational experiences during their lifetimes.

One commonly used neuropsychological measure uses black-and-white line drawings to assess children's knowledge of real world objects. One test item uses a black-and-white line drawing to depict an igloo. When presented with this line drawing, the child is expected to respond with its name. Many unassimilated Hispanic/Latino and Native American students from the Southwestern part of the United States see this icon and identify it as an "horno," an outside bake oven. The bake oven is familiar to Southwestern children living in rural areas. Since this particular test consists of 60 such items, incorrectly labeling just a few may mean that a child scores significantly lower than his or her actual intellectual level. Not all children have had the same mainstream educational experiences, and cultural bias in testing, therefore, may systematically alter the achievement levels of certain groups of culturally diverse children.

Criterion-referenced Tests.   **Criterion-referenced tests** measure how well a particular student is progressing or achieving the objectives of the course of study. Criterion measures are normally constructed by textbook publishing companies or by individual teachers. For example, suppose Mrs. Deal, a sixth grade teacher, wants students to label the parts of a plant cell as an objective for a unit of study on cells. The objective might be that "given a line drawing of a plant cell, the student will be able to label the nucleus, cell wall, cell membrane, chloroplasts, and cytoplasm with 80% accuracy." Mrs. Deal would pretest the students prior to beginning instruction to determine if they knew the parts of the cell. She would then present a series of activities designed to teach students the parts of the cell. Finally, she would administer a criterion-referenced posttest which would include a question about labeling the parts of the plant cell. The test would inform Mrs. Deal as to her students' progress in mastering the objective. Those students in Mrs. Deal's class who did not meet the objective would be provided with remedial instruction and additional opportunities to master the objective. An example of a criterion-referenced test is shown in Figure 6.7.

Criterion-referenced tests became very popular with the development of individualized instruction during the 1960s. They experienced a resurgence of interest within the educational community during the early part of the 1980s: the "mastery learning" decade. Criterion-referenced assessment instruments are grounded in a tradition of "training models." They are based on philosophies and theories of education which hold that children may be trained to respond to certain educational stimuli, and that children will perform learning under certain conditions. This behaviorist worldview holds that children learn best under stimulus/response instructional strategies. Aside from being used in mastery learning programs in elementary schools, criterion-referenced assessments are also widely used in military training modules and in corporate training programs.

Criterion-referenced tests have tended to focus on low levels of cognitive knowledge, since questions at these levels are easier to construct than higher level questions. Programmed instructional units are the most familiar context of criterion-referenced tests. Many textbook companies produce criterion-referenced assessments to accompany their textbooks. From a multicultural perspective, criterion-referenced tests have frequently been criticized as an impediment to student learning, especially when students must perform at a particular level prior to moving on to new instruction. For limited English proficient students, and for students who find mastery learning dull, repetitious, and boring, the criterion-referenced test has frequently become a barrier to advancement to higher level mathematics and science courses.

Multiple choice, true and false, short answer, and short essay questions are the primary means by which teachers assess students' knowledge in the cognitive domain. These test items are commonly used since most teachers view them as being (1) easy to administer, (2) easy to score, and (3) flexible. They are easily used to assess a wide range of content-area knowledge. Pencil-and-paper assessments using these formats are deemed by many to be highly effective for assessing students' prior knowledge.

Self-referenced Assessments. **Self-referenced assessments** are most frequently found associated with Individual Educational Plans (IEPs) in special education programs. Self-referenced assessments are used primarily as goals for individual students to attain before moving to the next level of instruction. When self-referenced assessment is used, the student is typically administered a pretest, given instruction, and administered a posttest. A student's achievement in meeting a particular goal is carefully assessed.

Suppose one goal for a particular fifth-grade student is that he or she successfully construct a bar graph from a table of data. The student would be assessed regarding his or her ability to construct a bar graph prior to instruction. Next, the student would be given a series of activities designed to help develop competency in graph construction. Finally, the student would be assessed to

---

Cell Test

Part A. Cell Drawings
Directions: Draw a "typical" animal cell and label the nucleus, cell membrane and cytoplasm.

Part B. Multiple Choice
Directions: Select the letter for the correct answer and place it on the line at the left.

___ 1. Which of these is not a basic need of all living cells?
   a. energy   b. space   c. oxygen   d. blood

___ 2. Plant cells make food in the process of _____.
   a. reproduction   b. photosynthesis   c. metabolism   d. competition

___ 3. Cell reproduction takes place in the cell _____.
   a. membrane   b. wall   c. cytoplasm   d. nucleus

___ 4. Plant cells obtain energy from the _____.
   a. soil   b. sun   c. chlorophyll   d. fertilizer

___ 5. The protective layer of the cell is called the _____.
   a. cell membrane   b. cytoplasm   c. vacuole   d. meiosis

___ 6. Which of these is not a basic cell process?
   a. movement   b. reproduction   c. metabolism   d. growth

Part C. Compare and Contrast
Directions: Write a paragraph or two telling how plant and animal cells are alike and how they are different.

FIGURE 6.7   Criterion-referenced Test

determine if he or she could construct a graph. If the student is found to be capable of constructing a bar graph, a new goal in graphing skills would be generated for the student. If the student were unable to perform the bar graphing task, remedial activities would be undertaken to assist the student in performing the particular skill. Self-referenced assessment is most useful when teaching skills to one particular student.

Authentic Assessment Tools.   From a constructivist viewpoint, the purpose of assessment is to identify the way(s) that students have constructed knowledge. The focus of assessment ought to be to assess accurately students' ability to do science. Former Secretary of Education William Bennett stated:

> The problem of assessment also constrains the spread of "hands-on" science. It is relatively easy to test children's knowledge when they have been asked to memorize lists of data for a test. It is much harder to design tests that measure learning derived from experience. (1986)

Certainly diagnostic testing is necessary to determine students' entry level knowledge and experience. It is also necessary to monitor instructional processes to determine if children are receiving information as the teacher envisioned. However, most traditional assessment and evaluation procedures have little to do with what children are learning in the science classroom.

The purpose of "authentic assessment" is to match assessment procedures with what children are learning and provide students with feedback about their progress in mastering new knowledge. If children have been learning to classify living insects to order using a dichotomous key, a pencil-and-paper question which asks students to select a dictionary definition for the term "dichotomous key" from a list of definitions in a multiple choice format is a difficult task. Classifying insects to order using a dichotomous insect key is a multifaceted construct which involves observation, a knowledge of insect anatomy, gathering data, and evaluating the quality of one's answer. Asking students to identify a formal definition of the term "dichotomous key" has little to do with the actual instruction. In this instance, we would say that there is little **congruency** and **consistency** between instruction and assessment. The methods of authentic assessment mentioned in this chapter are performance-based approaches to assessment which seek to provide the teachers and students with insights into the ways that children have constructed a knowledge of science.

Portfolios.   Using a **portfolio** to assess children's understanding of science is an idea that is gaining popularity among elementary science teachers. The use of problem-solving, thematic approaches to learning dictates that teachers find appropriate means to assess what children are learning. In defining the term portfolio, Hamm and Adams stated that, "a portfolio is a container of evidence of a person's skills" (1992, p.18). Most adults are familiar with an artist's or a photographer's portfolio. For children, a portfolio is a collection of the child's work. It is evidence of what the child can do in science and of the child's growth as a learner. A portfolio should show a child's growth in acquiring scientific knowledge, skills or processes, and attitudes, as well as a child's mastery of knowledge.

When portfolios are used as assessment tools, four questions need to be addressed by the teacher: (1) What is being measured? (2) What is the evidence? (3) Who determines what goes in the portfolio? and (4) How will portfolios be assessed? Typically, portfolios are used to show growth in acquiring a knowledge of science and science processes. The first question about specific science content areas and processes needs to be determined by the teacher and/or students before a portfolio project is undertaken. The second question involves the matter of evidence or proof of learning and is best addressed by a discussion and negotiation between students and their teacher. Typically, portfolios may include students' written work, journal entries, laboratory notebooks, records of students' investigations and laboratory activities, data entries and logs, rough drafts and finished products, and samples of students' individual and group assignments. The third question about portfolio use involves who determines the content of the portfolio. Most teachers negotiate a shared responsibility for this decision with their students. Some entries in the portfolio may be mandated by the teacher, while other entries are left to the discretion of the students. Finally, there is the matter of portfolio evaluation. Scoring rubrics have been shown to be one device which is useful for assessing the content of a students' portfolio.

Portfolios are devices which encourage students to collect, organize, and reflect on their own learning: to identify their strengths and weaknesses. For limited English proficient students, the portfolio offers the opportunity for students to perform in nontraditional and nonlanguage-dependent media. Videotapes, audiotapes, drawings, and projects may be used to show evidence of learning in science. The portfolio may allow students to show competency in mastering science concepts through multiple means of knowledge representation.

Concept Mapping.   Concept mapping or word webbing is a second authentic assessment tool in which students try to convey to teachers the way(s) that they have constructed knowledge of a particular concept or idea. Novak (1992) states that a "**concept map** can be used to organize and represent knowledge." The visual organizer used at the beginning of each chapter of this book may be thought of as a concept map. If the purpose of assessment is to determine what science knowledge students have constructed and how that information is organized, a concept map is a valuable tool in assisting teachers in understanding students' perceptions of the world. Figure 6.8 shows a third grade students' concept map of plants.

From this concept map, the teacher could infer that the student has some prior knowledge of plants, of edible plants, and of the parts of a plant. If a goal of the unit is to have students develop an understanding of the interdependence of plants and animals, then the teacher would use concept maps at the end of the unit to determine if students had incorporated this new information

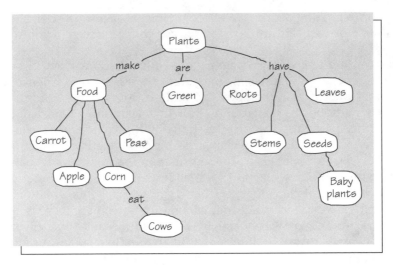

FIGURE 6.8 Concept Map of Plants

into their existing schema. Students who indicated in their concept maps that plants produce food and oxygen for animals to use, while animals produce carbon dioxide and fertilizer necessary for plant growth, would show an understanding of this content. Concept maps and word webs provide teachers with insights into the way(s) that students have constructed knowledge and into the way(s) that students integrate new knowledge into their existing schema.

Task Tests. Task tests are a third tool for assessing the state of students' reasoning abilities. Typically, **task tests** elicit a performance illustrating a science process from the student and require students to justify or explain their answers. The purpose of this authentic assessment tool is to gain insights into the way(s) that students engage in problem-solving skills. A typical Piagetian task is shown in Figure 6.9.

The purpose of this task is to determine students' abilities to engage in proportional reasoning. In this problem the student is given a small paper clip and asked to measure the height of Mr. Short. Next, the student is given a large paper clip and is asked to predict the height of Mr. Short without actually measuring the figure. Students who can function at a formal operational level are able to establish a ratio between the size of the paper clips and determine the height of Mr. Short by comparing the large paper clip to the small one. If a student is functioning at a concrete operational level, the student will be unable to write an algebraic statement or ratio comparing the lengths of the two paper clips. Other task tests may be used to determine students' abilities to engage in conservation of matter, seriation, classification, combinatorial reasoning, identification and control of variables, and hypothetical-deductive reasoning. Task tests

FIGURE 6.9   Typical Piagetian Task

are normally used to determine a child's level of cognitive development at different Piagetian stages.

Clarkson (1991) points out that task tests are highly appropriate for culturally diverse students in that Piagetian measures are highly correlated with mathematical achievement, particularly problem-solving skills. Task tests allow bilingual students to demonstrate computation, measurement, and mathematical language abilities far better than other assessment instruments. In addition, these instruments are well correlated with a student's language ability (whether home language or English). For culturally diverse learners, task tests may provide an alternative form of assessment which provides the teacher with an understanding of the way(s) that students have constructed a knowledge of science.

Journal Writing.   **Journal writing** is the fourth authentic assessment tool identified in this section. Journal writing encourages reflective learning. The process of writing about learning encourages students to (1) assess their prior knowledge, (2) think about the process of schooling, (3) formally state what they have learned in the classroom, and (4) integrate language arts and science skills in the classroom. Journal writing is highly beneficial in the science classroom because persuasive writing requires the analysis and presentation of data in an organized manner. In addition, descriptive writing requires the student to make detailed observations, organize information in a logical pattern, and assist students in developing precision in their writing styles.

Journal writing entries provide teachers with insights into the way(s) that students have constructed knowledge and into their levels of conceptual understanding. Liftig, Liftig, and Eaker (1992) point out that students need practice in journal writing skills. Specifically, students (1) are unaccustomed to responding in a written fashion, (2) have been coached in schools to respond to low level questions, (3) need practice in elaborating answers, and (4) have difficulty communicating with the intended audience. As teachers change from traditional pencil-and-paper measures to authentic assessment tools, they must mentor children in the use of these assessment devices.

Group Discussion and Projects.   **Group discussions** and projects are the final authentic assessment tool identified in this chapter. Group work and products have been infrequently used as a means of assessing students' understandings of science. Projects such as posters, videos, drama productions, interactive bulletin boards, songs, poems, debates, and so forth may be used to assess children's understanding of science. For many culturally diverse students, group performance is a more comfortable means of demonstrating knowledge than individual testing situations. Care must be taken with group work to provide each individual the opportunity to be individually accountable for his or her portion of the project.

Students who do not contribute to a group project and yet reap the benefits of the work of others present a problem in this type of grading situation. Projects provide a viable alternative for assessing students' growth, but grading of these projects must reflect concern for the contributions of each individual student. Allowing students to participate in the grading process is one technique which may be used to counteract this difficulty. Students may be asked to rate each other and their personal participation in the project. Teachers frequently use a multitiered scoring system to evaluate group work, with part of the grade derived from the total project and a portion of the work based on each individual's contributions to the work.

Recently, an upper elementary teacher wanted to assess her students' understandings of water. She assigned groups of students in the class to draw science fiction cartoons about water. Students were instructed to incorporate their knowledge of the properties of water into their cartoons. Cartoons were scored on scientific content, creativity, and grammatical skills. In addition, each student received a second grade from the teacher based on the teacher's observations of the student's ability to work in the group. One of the products of this activity is shown in Figure 6.10. The cartoon illustrates the use of authentic or alternative

The Story of Wally Water

Once upon a time, there was a drop of water named Wally.
Wally lived in a beaker of water in Dr. Lightfoot's laboratory with
his brothers and sisters.

Wally was a favorite among the other
drops of water because he was slow to anger.
He had a high boiling point (about 100 degrees Celsius).

Wally enjoyed hanging around with the other drops of water in
his family. They were a very cohesive group.

(continued)

FIGURE 6.10   Assessment Procedures in a Group Setting

One day Dr. Lightfoot was working with some soil samples in
his laboratory. Dirt, a mean and vicious little monster, got all over the sleeve
of Dr. Lightfoot's lab coat. The dirt monster was ugly, sticky,
and caused Dr. Lightfoot a lot of discomfort.

At first Dr. Lightfoot called upon his old friend Al Cohol
to help get rid of Dirt. Al tried; no matter what he did Dirt wouldn't move.

 Al    Dirt

Then a great idea struck Dr. Lightfoot, "Wally Water will help me."

Dr. Lightfoot poured Wally out of the beaker. Wally went right to work.
He had been weight lifting and working out his bipolar muscles.
Wally hit the Dirt with his positive end, and then his negative end.
Time after time, Wally Water threw punches at Dirt.

The fight was long and hard, but Wally overcame the Dirt. His electrons spun
with joy, as he claimed the victory. Dr. Lightfoot's lab coat gleamed
like new and Wally was still the Champion of Polar Solvents.

The End

FIGURE 6.10 Assessment Procedures in a Group Setting (continued)

assessment procedures in a group setting. Authentic assessment instruments provide teachers with additional tools for assessing students' cognitive knowledge of science.

Psychomotor Domain

Assessment of the psychomotor domain involves an evaluation of children's motor skills or manipulation of materials. Simpson (1972) devised a taxonomy of the psychomotor domain, which is shown in Figure 6.11. This domain can be used to identify certain "hands-on" science activities as corresponding to the levels of motor development. For example, at the **perception level** students are able to recognize that there are different sizes for insects. Students functioning at the **set level** have a knowledge of which insect is bigger than another. At the **adaptation level**, students can correctly identify an insect that they had not previously encountered.

Laboratory Activities.   Laboratory practical examinations are commonly used to assess students' psychomotor skills in the science content area. Normally these instruments assess children's competency in using science processes. During laboratory skills tests, students are asked to manipulate equipment and materials; to observe, reason, record data, and interpret results. Hands-on testing allows the teacher to assess students' abilities to (1) work with basic science equipment

---

Taxonomy of the Psychomotor Domain

1. Perception. Using sense organs to obtain cues needed to guide motor activity.
   1.1. Sensory stimulation
   1.2. Cue selection
   1.3. Translation

2. Set. Being ready to perform a particular action.
   2.1. Mental set
   2.2. Physical set
   2.3. Emotional set

3. Guided response. Performing under guidance of a model.
   3.1. Imitation
   3.2. Trial and error

4. Mechanism. Being able to perform a task habitually with some degree of confidence and proficiency.

5. Complex or overt response. Performing a task with a high degree of proficiency and skill.

6. Adaptation. Using previously learned skills to perform new but related tasks.

7. Origination. Creating new performances after having developed skills.

FIGURE 6.11   Taxonomy of the Psychomotor Domain

(e.g., thermometers, balances), (2) manipulate objects (e.g., simple laboratory equipment), (3) collect data, (4) record data, (5) observe and classify, (6) perform laboratory procedures, and (7) communicate.

Assume that Ms. Czienski, a fifth grade teacher, had completed a unit of instruction on the metric system. During this unit, her students had learned to measure linear distances using a metric ruler and a meter stick. In addition, these students had learned to measure volume with a graduated cylinder, and had learned to determine the mass of an object using a spring balance and a pan balance. To assess her students' knowledge of measuring, Ms. Czienski could set up a rotating laboratory test while the students were at recess. The test might consist of 35 laboratory stations, and the students could move from station to station once each minute. Each station would assess each individual student's ability to use metric measuring tools. A portion of this rotating lab test on the metric system is shown in Table 6.1.

In this testing situation, students move from station to station performing specific measuring skills. Laboratory examinations can measure performance, including the processes of observing, manipulating, and measuring. They can measure investigative processes, including planning and designing investigations or experiments. Finally, laboratory practical examinations can be used to assess students' reasoning abilities, including interpreting data, formulating generalizations, and developing models.

Assessment in the psychomotor domain is frequently overlooked in the elementary science classroom. Laboratory practical examinations (1) require more planning time than pencil-and-paper examinations, (2) necessitate access to manipulative materials, (3) require more space than other instructional activities, (4) involve clean-up time, and (5) commit the teacher to a lengthy set-up process. However, in spite of the difficulties attending test preparation, laboratory practical examinations do accurately assess students' learning. From the viewpoint of limited English proficient students, hands-on manipulative testing tends

TABLE 6.1   Portion of a Rotating Lab Test on Metrics

Station Number	Question Card	Materials
1	What is the height of the chair at this station?	Meter stick
2	What is the length of this line segment?	Metric ruler Paper with line segment
3	How much water does this container hold?	Bucket of water Container Graduated cylinder
4	What is the mass of this object?	Spring balance Object to weigh
5	What is the mass of this object?	Pan balance Object to weigh

to present the teacher with a more accurate picture of the child's learning than "traditional" pencil-and-paper instruments.

Checklists and Scoring Rubrics.   At times, teachers seek to evaluate just one skill or science process at a time. In such instances, checklists and scoring rubrics are highly effective evaluation tools. In most instances, evaluation is seen as a summative activity to be conducted at the end of a period of instruction. If assessment is to be effective in providing students with feedback, for example, corrective in nature, it must also be formative in nature. Assessment ought to be part of the learning process, not an end in itself. Checklists assist teachers to provide feedback to students and are a tool for reflective learning, that is, helping students to "get a handle" on what they know and what they need to learn. Observation checklists are among the easiest ways to implement different assessment methods, and also the most flexible (Nott, Reeve & Reeve, 1992).

Suppose a teacher wishes to assess students' abilities to use a Bunsen burner. The teacher could develop a checklist of specific behavioral objectives and assess each student on those skills as each one moves from group to group (see Figure 6.12 for an example). Using this checklist, the teacher could evaluate the student's knowledge of safety rules, ability to light a burner and adjust the flame, and skill in handling hot materials. This checklist establishes a standard for performance and judges the student's skills against that standard. Does the student wear safety goggles? If so, how often? Always? Sometimes? Never? From this data, the teacher and the student can begin a dialogue about the student's progress in mastering science processes.

In addition to checklists, teachers may wish to use scoring rubrics as a means of assessing students' progress in the psychomotor domain. Scoring rubrics typically contain a limited number of well-defined categories for describing a student's performance. Suppose a teacher wants to evaluate a student's ability to observe and record data on a table of data during a laboratory investigation. The teacher

Behavioral Objective	Always	Sometimes	Never
Wears safety goggles			
Lights burner properly			
Adjusts flame correctly			
Heats objects carefully			
Handles hot materials carefully			
Cleans work area			

FIGURE 6.12   Checklist of Behavioral Objectives

TABLE 6.2 Observing and Recording Data

Points	Characteristics
0	Fails to observe or record data
1	Seems to observe correctly; does not record data accurately
2	Observes and records data accurately
3	Observes and records data with great expertise

could use a scoring rubric, such as that shown in Table 6.2 to assess a child's ability in this area.

By using this rubric, the teacher can translate observations of a student's behavior into a numerical grade. In addition, this rubric allows the teacher to distinguish between students who are minimally performing the process and those who perform with expertise. When properly used, rubrics and performance checklists have great potential for providing productive feedback to students and their teachers about the appropriateness of each student's performance.

Evaluating Teaching and Curriculum

As teachers evaluate and assess students, they also must reflect on their own teaching practices and the instructional materials they are using. Sometimes children fail to learn because of their own lack of effort and motivation. At other times, students fail to learn because the teaching materials are inappropriate for the students. Finally, students sometimes fail to learn because the teacher has used inappropriate teaching strategies with the students or because the teacher has failed to provide an appropriate classroom environment for learning to occur. A child's failure in the science classroom is a two-edged sword. Failure of a student indicates that the child has failed to learn at this particular time, but it also indicates that the teacher has failed to reach the child. Just as teachers evaluate and assess students, they also need to evaluate themselves and the curriculum materials that they use with children.

Reflective Teaching. Reflectivity is part of every teacher's professional growth and development. Four basic questions should guide the teaching process and teachers' reflections on that process: (1) What do my students know? (2) What do I want my students to learn? (3) How will I help them learn? and (4) What have they learned?. The first question, "What do my students know?" refers to the prior knowledge that students bring to the classroom. Assessment of prior knowledge may involve formal pretesting, concept mapping, or simple conversations. "What do my students know?" also involves an assessment of children's language abilities and their experiences in the real world. Frequently, teachers may find that students need to broaden their background before they are "ready" to learn new material or information. For example, many kindergarten science programs introduce students to a study of common farm animals, or use farm animals as a basis for building a knowledge of living things. Because inner city students may not have been exposed to life in rural America, these students may need to visit a farm and gain experience in seeing, touching, and hearing animals before they are ready to tackle new learning that presupposes a knowledge of these animals.

The second question, "What do I want my students to learn?" involves an examination of the goals and objectives of the teacher, the school, and school district and sometimes state curriculum frameworks and requirements. Frequently, teachers interpret local and state recommendations as defining "the course," or as a mandate for teaching, rather than as guideposts or suggestions. In schools where teachers rely heavily on textbooks, teachers need to remember that publishing companies frequently include far more material than can be mastered in a year or in a course of study. "What do I want my students to learn?" is a question that involves professional decision making based on a knowledge of the students and of the curriculum.

The third question, "How will I help them to learn?" is a pedagogical question based on a knowledge of the students, their prior knowledge, and the science concepts to be learned. For students in the multicultural classroom, a consideration of how I help them learn involves a knowledge of the way(s) that children have been socialized to learn. Not all children learn in the same manner. While a highly verbal presentation of information may be appropriate for teaching a certain topic in one setting, the same teaching strategy may not work in another setting. Many culturally diverse children are socialized to work in groups. In addition, if a teacher is working with large numbers of limited English proficient students, the teacher may choose teaching strategies that use peer tutoring, multiple modes of knowledge representation, and multiple modes of performance.

"What have they learned?" is a reflective teaching question that involves assessment. Assessment involves a knowledge of children's cognitive, affective, and psychomotor domains. Historically, schools have focused on assessing children's cognitive growth without adequately assessing changes in attitudes, values, beliefs, and science processes. Assessment ought to include classroom practice.

CLASSROOM PRACTICE

As a teacher, assessment provides you the opportunity to make students part of the teaching and learning process. Assessment provides the opportunity for you and your students to examine goals and determine the progress that you are making collectively in achieving those goals. Evaluation of the cognitive, affective, and psychomotor domains provides an opportunity for you and your students to reflect on what is being learned. Finally, assessment encourages students to become reflective learners, to assess what they are learning, why they are learning it, and how they might express what they have learned.

This section of the chapter provides specific examples of assessment devices which may be used in the multicultural classroom. Each assessment device is a model of the types of assessment activities which may be used to measure specific content knowledge, processes, or attitudes of students.

ACTIVITY 6-1 ■ PHASES OF MATTER QUIZ—TASK TEST

Materials: small container of oobleck for each child

Teacher Notes—Advance Preparation Work: Oobleck is a mixture of corn starch and water. Pour corn starch into a container and add sufficient water to moisten the corn starch completely (thick, not runny).

1. Provide each student with a paper cup or plastic container of oobleck.
2. Provide the following instructions to the students: "I have a new substance for you today. It is called oobleck. I want you to play with the oobleck for a few minutes and then answer some questions about it."
3. Write the following question on the board and also read it aloud to your students: "What phase of matter (solid, liquid or gas) is oobleck? Explain your answer."

Scoring: Students should be encouraged to write their observations about oobleck and classify oobleck as a solid, liquid, or gas based on their prior knowledge of the phases of matter. Oobleck or the mixture of corn starch and water is really a non-Newtonian fluid. Most students will classify it as a liquid. In evaluating student responses, focus on the students' knowledge of the characteristics of the phases of matter.

ACTIVITY 6-2 ■ WEATHER QUIZ—LITERARY EXPRESSION ASSESSMENT

Materials: tape players and record players

Procedure: Assign students to work in groups and write a song (including rap songs as an option) or poem that expresses some of their ideas about weather. Encourage students to incorporate as much knowledge of the weather as possible into their answer. When each student has completed the song or poem, allow each one to perform a rendition for the class. For those students who have written a poem, encourage them to perform a choral reading of the poem for the class.

Scoring: Use the rubric in Table 6.3 to assess each student's knowledge of weather.

TABLE 6.3	Scoring Rubric for Weather Activity
Points	Characteristics
0	Students did not perform any knowledge of weather.
1	Students performed an imitation of an existing song or poem.
2	Students performed an original piece, but knowledge of weather was lacking.
3	Students adequately performed a song or poem about weather which showed a conceptual understanding of the causes and/or types of weather.
4	Students expertly performed a song or poem about weather which demonstrated outstanding conceptual understanding of the causes and/ or types of weather.

ACTIVITY 6-3 ■ ENERGY QUIZ—BULLETIN BOARD QUIZ

Materials (suggestions):

Poster board or newsprint (1 per
  group or student)
magazines
scissors

felt tipped markers
glue
crayons

Procedure: Create a bulletin board that displays your knowledge of energy. Be certain that the display includes a definition of energy, and an array of the types of energy.

Scoring Rubric: See Table 6.4.

ACTIVITY 6-4 ■ INSECT TEST—PICTORIAL TESTING

Procedure (to be read to students): Examine each picture. Place an X on each drawing that is NOT an insect and explain your answer on the line below the drawing (see the next page).

TABLE 6.4	Poster Scoring Rubric
Points	Characteristics
0	Display shows no evidence of a knowledge of energy.
1	Students are able to define energy operationally.
2	Students are able to define energy operationally and show a knowledge of at least three types of energy.
3	Students are able to define energy and give examples with expertise.

ACTIVITY 6-5   ■   MAGNET TASK—TASK TEST

Procedure: Read the following problem to the students.

Mario wanted to find out which of three magnets was the strongest. He had a bar magnet, a truck-shaped refrigerator magnet, and a u magnet. He found a jar of nails in the kitchen that his mother used to make repairs around the house. How could he use these materials to find out which magnet is the strongest?

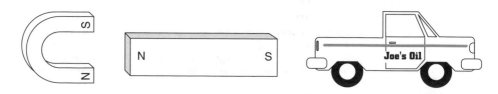

CHAPTER SUMMARY

Evaluation and assessment involve a consideration of what children know, what they will learn, how they will be exposed to new information, and what they have learned. Assessing children's learning ought to be both formative and summative in nature, involving both children and teachers in a consideration of what children are learning as well as the final product of their learning. In addition, assessment ought to consider affective and psychomotor outcomes as well as cognitive outcomes. Traditional pencil-and-paper assessment has focused on the cognitive domain, that is, on conceptual learning. For all learners, especially culturally diverse learners, assessment ought to be a means for students and their teachers to reflect on their learning, which may be expressed through multiple modes of knowledge representation. Authentic assessment, which involves multiple means of presenting information, ought to be incorporated into all elementary science classrooms.

  TOPICS TO REVIEW

  REFLECTIVE PRACTICE

1. Standardized tests have long been popular in public schools as a tool for insuring accountability of the educational system. What are the benefits of using standardized tests? What problems are associated with the use of standardized tests? (Focus your response on the needs of culturally diverse children.)
2. In what ways is "authentic assessment" more responsive to the needs of culturally diverse children than "traditional" assessment tools?
3. If you were to use "authentic assessment" tools in your classroom, what types of "public relations work" might you need to do with parents before implementing the use of such tools? Elaborate on your answer.
4. Assume you have been given the responsibility for developing a new "report card" for your school that would report to parents on the progress of their children. Based on what you have learned in this chapter, how might that report card look? Explain a rationale for your decision making.
5. Assume that you have just completed a unit of instruction on rocks and minerals. Design an assessment tool that will assess children's (1) attitudes towards the study of rocks and minerals, (2) ability to identify the characteristics of common minerals, and (3) knowledge of rocks and minerals.

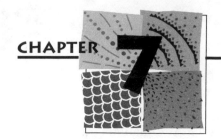

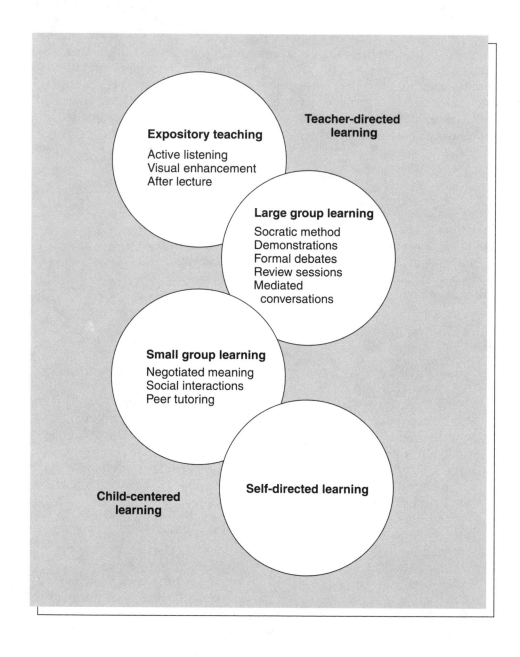

CHAPTER 7

INSTRUCTIONAL STRATEGIES FOR CULTURALLY DIVERSE LEARNERS

 POINTS TO PONDER

1. What are teaching strategies?
2. What is meant by the expression, "There's no one right way to teach any-thing"?
3. Why do many teachers use a variety of instructional strategies throughout the day and the school year?

LEARNING TO LEARN

y youngest son, Aáron, has just completed driver's education training and has received his first driver's license. As I reflect on driver's education over the years, I realize that there are many ways to learn. My son began driver's training by reading a book and memorizing the rules of the road. When he had passed a written examination on driving, he began simulator training (sitting in a car seat chair in the classroom and watching a movie about driving). Next, he advanced to the school's driving range where he practiced starting, stopping, braking, parallel parking, and a multitude of other nontraffic-related skills. Finally, he was issued a learner's permit and permitted to drive on America's highways, but only when accompanied by a licensed adult. In other words, he first acquired a strong declarative knowledge (i.e., knowledge you can state or "head knowledge") of the rules of the road and then he began to acquire a procedural knowledge (e.g., "how to" knowledge) of driving. Needless to say, it will be many months before his parents allow him to make his first solo flight.

I, on the other hand, cannot remember a day when I did not drive. As a toddler, I sat on my mother's and father's laps as they drove tractors from one field to another. I learned steering, shifting, and braking by experience by emulating my parents. By age 5, I was given the responsibility for driving a tractor and wagon from the cornfield to the house. I still remember my first solo trip on the tractor. My father told me to drive the John Deere® (a green tractor with yellow wheel rims) up to the house, disengage the hand clutch, step on the brake, and wait for my mother to come and get me. My mother came from the house quickly when she saw me. I still remember the discussion she had with my father about 5-year-olds and tractor driving. As a teenager, I learned the rules of the road and acquired a driver's license. Having driven a tractor, truck, and combine, I did not consider driving a car to be much of a treat. Unlike my son, I acquired a procedural knowledge of driving first and later acquired a declarative knowledge of the rules of the road.

Some of us learn to drive by first reading about it. Some of us learn to drive by first steering a moving vehicle. I am not advancing one method over another but simply pointing out that there are many ways to learn to drive or, for that matter, do anything. Sometimes one way is better than another, sometimes it is equally good, and sometimes it is worse. Teachers make decisions everyday of their professional careers about teaching methods: about which method or strategy is best for teaching children. This chapter is designed to introduce you to a variety of teaching strategies appropriate for use with culturally diverse learners in the elementary science classroom.

CHILDREN'S UNDERSTANDING

Children's understanding of the physical world results naturally from their ordinary interactions with adults and other children. A knowledge of the world is constructed by each individual child within a social context, that is, through their social interactions with others. Learning in the multicultural classroom, indeed in all classrooms, should "begin and end with students. This means that the teacher's understanding of students should form the basis of all instruction" (Marshall, 1989, p. 60). Children are like natural scientists bent on making sense of the world (Elementary Grades Task Force, 1992, p. 12). Instructional activities should be selected by teachers because they assist students in making sense of the world. While hands-on, experience-oriented activities conducted in heterogeneous, cooperative groups have been shown to be particularly effective with students from varied language backgrounds and achievement levels (Mechling & Oliver, 1983; Science Curriculum Framework and Criteria Committee, 1990), there are other instructional activities or strategies which are highly effective and appropriate for use in the elementary science classroom. Most teachers use a variety of instructional strategies during each class period and throughout the school day.

Variety in Teaching Strategies

If a teacher wants students to investigate the causal agents in a volcanic eruption, an inquiry approach to learning will probably not be appropriate. It is difficult to imagine finding a volcano where the variables that lead to a volcanic eruption could be controlled. Even if a teacher could find such a volcano, no one would care to have children randomly adjusting the pressure on the magma chamber or to have children causing a volcano to erupt. In this particular instance, the teacher would need to provide a means for students to acquire a knowledge of volcanoes which does not involve "hands-on" manipulation of the real world object. Filmstrips, movies, textual passages, and tutorial computer programs could be used as data sources for children as they attempted to construct a knowledge of phenomena associated with volcanic eruptions. Volcanic eruptions and the atmospheric conditions on other planets in our solar system are topics which are more appropriately taught using expository instructional strategies than inquiry-based pedagogical techniques.

INSTRUCTIONAL STRATEGIES

Four clusters of instructional strategies are commonly used in elementary science classrooms: (1) self-directed activities; (2) small group negotiations, interactions, and peer tutoring; (3) large-group verbal interactions; and (4) expository sessions. Expository instructional techniques are the most teacher-centered or teacher-directed pedagogical methods, while self-directed activities are the most child-centered strategies. A continuum of instructional strategies is shown in Figure 7.1.

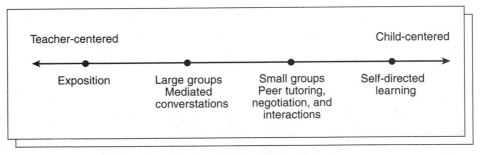

FIGURE 7.1   Continuum of Instructional Strategies

Self-directed Learning

Self-directed learning or individualized learning is most effective when it is child-initiated rather than teacher-initiated. A child working alone in the classroom completing a teacher-made ditto page is not an example of self-directed learning. Self-directed learning is self-motivated learning; it is the self-initiated act of a child who wants to explore a portion of the world alone. Teachers can support and nurture this type of learning, but it should be controlled by the child and not mandated by an adult.

Elementary classrooms should contain the elements of interactive learning commonly found in "good" museums or libraries. Science classrooms for children should "burst at the seams" with things to do and learn. Niches, nooks, crannies, and corners of classrooms should literally bulge with "stuff" (e.g., library books, interactive bulletin boards, computer workstations, listening stations, mini-museums filled with *realia*, and "activity" corners). Sometimes, elementary classrooms resemble adult work places, with rows of neat orderly workstations, professionally designed visual displays, and rigorously controlled supplies and materials. For self-directed learning to occur, there must be (1) time for self-initiated activities, (2) resource materials for individual learning, and (3) encouragement to pursue individual interests.

Time for self-initiated activities can be formally or informally provided by the teacher. Studies have shown that, when "dead time" or time between transitions (e.g., time between instructional activities or time between classes and recess) is eliminated from classrooms, student learning is increased. Physical resources in the form of library books, mini-museums, interactive bulletin boards, computer workstations, and learning centers need to be provided in each classroom for students to engage in self-directed learning. Finally, teachers need to encourage students to continue learning after the formal instructional period has ended.

It is difficult to imagine that a third grader would not want to learn more about dinosaurs, or that a first grader could avoid exploring the world with a magnet if given the opportunity. If students are to share actively with others what they have learned, they need the opportunity to develop individual expertise, to acquire new knowledge and insights which they can share with others. Self-directed learning provides the opportunity for students to pursue their interests and continue learning after the "planned" instructional activities have ended. Creativity, a sense of freedom to learn, a knowledge of science processes, and a feeling of success, are the products of self-directed learning (Wolfinger, 1984).

Small Group Learning

Small groups or cooperative groups (discussed in more detail in Chapter 5) are environments in which negotiations, interactions, and peer tutoring provide support for the learning of each child. Groups may be viewed as an extension of

Students perform in groups work they can't do by themselves. (© Jim Pickerell)

the home environment of the child into the school environment. For many culturally diverse children, working in a group in the classroom closely resembles working with family members or extended family groups that they have encountered in settings outside school. Group learning provides a culturally syntonic or culturally harmonious supportive environment for the child. In speaking of the primacy of group learning, Lev Vygotsky wrote, "children can perform under guidance, in groups, and in collaboration with one another learning which they have not mastered independently" (1978, p. 87).

In the small group environment, children have the opportunity to "try out" their ideas within a supportive, nurturing environment. A group is a place of sharing, a place in which an individual has the capacity to externalize and share with other members of his/her social group his/her understanding of their shared experience (Vygotsky, 1978, p. 132). Learning is a social process: a child's knowledge of the world is derived from social interactions with others. Children solve practical tasks with the help of their speech, as well as their eyes and hands (Vygotsky, 1978, p. 26). The use of speech in problem solving or in task completion implies group work, a sharing of possible solution paths with others. Speech is a social process rather than an individual endeavor. Groups provide places in which children can (1) negotiate meaning, (2) engage in social interactions, and (3) give and receive peer tutoring.

Negotiated Meaning.   The small group environment is a place in which children interact with peers in an attempt to make sense of the world. Group work fosters reflective learning and articulation. Within the social context of the small group, children should reflect on what they have learned and on the applications of that learning. Meaning of ideas and objects is achieved by the speaker and/or listener(s) through a process of collaboration and negotiation (Greeno, 1989, p. 51). The process of **semantic negotiation**, of using speech to make sense of the world, occurs as a collaborative act that is accomplished only when the speaker and listener(s) agree that something meaningful has been added to the collection of information that is shared in their common ground (Greeno, 1989, p. 51). An example of semantic negotiation or group collaboration to achieve meaning is shown in this scenario in which a group of second graders are attempting to apply what they know of the concept fruit:

Tom: We're supposed to look at each picture and decide if each one is a fruit. This first picture's a carrot. [Tom points to the picture while the rest of the group looks on.]

Li: I think a carrot's a vegetable because my mother buys 'em in the vegetable section of the store.

Wilma: Yeah, and when you cook 'em and eat 'em, they don't have any seeds inside.

Felipe: The teacher said fruits are supposed to have seeds in 'em.

Li: Yeah. That's right. Carrots are roots, they grow in dirt, they don't have any seeds.

Tom: Carrots grow from seeds, but the stuff we eat doesn't got any seeds.

Li: Fruits grow on trees.

Felipe: Not all the time. Tomatoes have seeds in 'em and they don't grow on a tree. My parents have a garden . . . I know that tomatoes don't grow on any old trees.

Wilma: Well some fruits grow on trees. Oranges and apples grow on trees. The teacher said they're fruits.

Tom: The teacher said a fruit is supposed to be a package of seeds. I don't think the part of the carrot we eat's a fruit.

Felipe: Yeah, that's right. This picture [Felipe points to the picture of the carrot] shows a root of the plant, not a fruit. Root, not a fruit. Hey, that rhymes.

During this conversation, each child added what he or she knew from personal experience about the concept fruit. Each contributed an interpretation of the information that the teacher provided them and their own "real world" experiences with carrots and fruits. Together, they are forming a definition of the concept fruit by reflecting on their own learning and articulating that knowledge.

Social Interactions.   A second function of the small group environment is to provide **social interactions** for children. Within the small group, the child has the opportunity to (1) develop social interaction skills (e.g., active listening and responding), (2) build self-esteem, (3) develop efficacy in the use of the English language, and (4) learn leadership skills. The socialization of children is a primary, often unmentioned goal of schooling. Small group instructional environments can be powerful environments in which children develop social skills.

In discussing the social value of small group learning, Cohen (1984) states that learning curriculum content in a peer group is positively related to the frequency of interaction within the group. In turn, frequency of interaction is correlated with social status in the classroom. Cohen also points out that teachers sometimes need to intervene on behalf of some students to encourage their participation in group activities, that is, to assist students by conferring status on those students. She points out that, when students are put into the position of using each other as resources for learning, status characteristics become salient and relevant to the social interaction (Cohen, 1984, p. 18). Within the small group, the student has the opportunity to build self-confidence and self-esteem. Each child should be viewed by his or her teacher and peers as being a valuable part of the whole. Each child brings unique skills, talents, and abilities to the group, and these attributes can enrich the learning of others and enhance the performance of the total group.

Peer Tutoring.   A third function of small group instructional settings is to provide an opportunity for peer tutoring. Educational literature has revealed that peer tutoring (1) improves students' academic performance, (2) improves students' attitudes toward the content area, (3) facilitates students' acquisition of English language proficiency, and (4) enhances students' acquisition of science processes. Both the tutor and tutee benefit when peer tutoring is used in the classroom. Every child can function as a tutor or a tutee in a group, depending on what is being taught and what is being learned.

Learning as an Apprenticeship.   When small group work is used, the function of the teacher in the classroom changes. Teachers who rely on small groups as the primary environments for teaching and learning find that their responsibilities include modeling, coaching, scaffolding, articulation, and reflection (Garcia & Pearson, 1990). The teacher is the one who models behaviors and attitudes for students. Sometimes, teachers model attitudes such as a positive attitude toward recycling natural resources. At other times, teachers model actual performance,

Learning as an apprenticeship. (© Will Faller)

such as the procedure for making a microscope slide. As teachers move from one group to another in the classroom, they engage in coaching. Coaching involves providing students with corrective feedback, as well as encouragement to continue learning. Small group work requires that the teacher provide a framework for learning or a scaffolding structure for student learning. As students become adept at guiding their own learning and in reflecting on that learning, the responsibility for learning is transferred from the teacher to the students. Teachers need to articulate what is being said or read or verbalized to the class. One job of the teacher is to explain new ideas and concepts to students. In addition, the teacher should expound on students' responses while encouraging students to apply what they are learning to new situations. Finally, teachers need to reflect on what students are learning and encourage their students to engage in their own reflective learning activities. When teachers engage in modeling, coaching, scaffolding, articulation, and reflection, they are using an apprenticeship model of teaching and learning (Garcia & Pearson, 1990). In this apprenticeship situation, the teacher becomes the "master learner" and students become "apprentices."

Large Group Interactions

Large group verbal interactions between teachers and students have long been used as an appropriate pedagogical technique in science instruction. Too frequently, large group discussions are actually lectures interspersed with review questions. In a true discussion, the students should talk as much and preferably more than the teacher (Wolfinger, 1984, p. 211). Five types of large group verbal interactions are commonly used in elementary schools: (1) Socratic teaching, (2) demonstrations, (3) formal debates, (4) review sessions, and (5) mediated conversations. Socratic teaching and demonstrations are the most teacher-directed large group verbal interactions, while mediated conversations are the most child-directed. Formal debates and review sessions allow for constrained interactions between teachers and students.

Socratic Method.   The **Socratic teaching method** is an instructional strategy according to which the teacher attempts to assist students in developing a simple concept through the use of verbal questioning. When using a Socratic teaching method, the teacher begins by asking a broad general question. The next question should begin to narrow the range of responses from the students and focus the learners on the topic. Periodically, review statements are mixed with the questions to keep the salient points in the forefront of the discussion. The final question in the sequence should bring the students to the desired concept. A sample of a sequence of Socratic questions used in a fifth grade classroom is shown in Table 7.1.

While Socratic teaching is a large group discussion activity, it rarely produces a mediated learning environment. As the teacher begins the instruction, she or he knows the desired end and verbally "forces" students toward that end. Socratic teaching, while interactive, is a highly teacher-centered instructional technique. Reciprocal teaching (e.g., when teachers and students share learning with each other), which typifies mediated conversations, is lacking when this instructional strategy is used.

Demonstrations.   A demonstration is a large group activity during which some person (typically the teacher) stands before the class and shows or demonstrates something. Typically, a demonstration is followed by a period of student-directed questioning. Demonstrations are appropriately used in the science classroom when (1) there is a danger to students due to the use of chemicals or flammables, (2) the correct use of a piece of science equipment is being demonstrated for the first time, (3) a model is used as a visual enhancement device, and (4) a discrepant event is used as an advance organizer. For a demonstration to be effective, it must be possible for the entire class to view it simultaneously and it must "work."

It has been jokingly said that, "the only one who learns from a demonstration is the teacher." To preclude this result, the teacher must use the demonstration as a motivational device to interest and involve students in the scientific process. When doing a demonstration, the teacher should gather the required materials and try out the demonstration ahead of time to be certain that the desired event indeed does happen. When a demonstration is used in the classroom, everything must be enlarged to ensure that students in the back of the room see what is occurring. If a demonstration calls for a beaker of liquid, the teacher should plan to use a large battery jar instead, so that the action is clearly

TABLE 7.1   Script from a Socratic Lesson

Teacher Question	Probable Student Answer
1. Has anyone ever seen a chicken or a picture of a chicken before?	1. (all hands are raised)
2. What do chickens eat?	2. worms, seeds, insects, corn, chicken feed
3. Yes, chickens eat a lot of different things, but what do they eat most of the time?	3. Mostly they eat grain or seeds from plants.
4. This is a gastrolith. It is a fossil. It came from a Stegosaurus, a plant eating dinosaur. This fossil was found inside the rib cage of the Stegosaurus.	4. (students examine gastrolith)
5. What can you tell me about the gastrolith?	5. They're round. They're like stone balls. They are different colors They are very smooth.
6. [Teacher summarizes what students have observed through manipulating the gastrolith.]	
7. Why do you suppose the Stegosaurus had gastroliths inside its rib cage?	7. Maybe they had something to do with eating?
8. How would round stones have something to do with eating?	8. Maybe it's like a chicken.
9. How do chickens eat differently from other animals?	9. Chickens have a gizzard.
10. What's a gizzard?	10. It's part of the digestive system used for grinding food.
11. Can you explain that a little more?	11. My grandmother raises chickens on her farm and she explained how baby chickens pick up pieces of gravel and they store them in their bodies.
12. Why would chickens store gravel in their bodies?	12. To grind up corn and other seeds.
13. How is this gastrolith from a Stegosaurus like the gravel in the chicken's gizzard?	13. The Stegosaurus was a plant eater. Maybe it ground up food in a gizzard or a similar organ like the chicken grinds up corn and grain.
14. What is a gastrolith?	14. It's probably some stones in the Stegosaurus's stomach or gizzard which grind up food.
15. How did the stones get inside the Stegosaurus?	15. Maybe the Stegosaurus picked up the stones with its food.
16. Why are the stones round?	16. The grinding made them smooth, like a rock tumbler or something.
17. Would someone summarize what we have learned about gastroliths?	17. [Teacher calls on a student to summarize the discussion.]

visible. Lengthy demonstrations should not be attempted in elementary science classrooms because inattentiveness and restlessness rather than learning are the products of dull, lengthy demonstrations. Finally, demonstrations must include a question and answer period. Children should be engaged in the demonstration by being allowed to ask questions at the conclusion of the action or activity. Demonstrations can be highly effective, large group instructional devices, but, as with salt, they enhance the "food" only when used sparingly.

Formal Debates.   The **formal debate** is a verbal teaching strategy that is highly effective but rarely used in elementary classrooms. Debates are most effective when they are used to present controversial information. "Should oil drilling be allowed off the Delaware coast?" "Should genetic engineering be used to produce new animal species?" "Should government agencies set off mild earthquakes in fault zones to prevent the likelihood of large earthquakes?" "Should people be allowed to keep threatened animal species as pets?" "Should nuclear waste from around the nation be stored in New Mexico?" These are questions which lend themselves to formal debate in classrooms. The actual debate itself is the public presentation of what has been learned. The library research, organization of information, and preparation of opening statements are normally conducted in small groups prior to the formal presentation to the large group.

When conducting a formal debate, the following modifications of the formal debating procedure seem to meet the needs of elementary-aged children best:

- Brief speech from the affirmative side;
- Brief speech from the negative side;
- Second speech from the affirmative side which rebuts the statements of the negative side;
- Second speech from the negative side which rebuts the statements of the affirmative side;
- Short period of questions from the audience for both sides;
- Summary by the affirmative side captain; and
- Summary by the negative side captain.

Formal debate is appropriate for use with culturally diverse learners when all students are encouraged to participate in the process. Each child can contribute to the data gathering and organizing efforts of the team. Many times students who have difficulty expressing themselves in written language find that the oral medium used in debating is comfortable for them. Debating provides an opportunity for students to develop oral communication skills within the science content area.

Review Sessions.   Reviewing prior knowledge or new learning is a highly effective use of the large group instructional environment. In a **review situation**, the teacher asks a series of questions that provide students with the opportunity to verbalize what they have learned. Review questions may be convergent or divergent in nature. When using **convergent questioning**, the teacher is attempting to focus the child on a single answer, that is, encouraging the child to reproduce what has been previously stated in class. When **divergent questioning** is used, the student is encouraged to combine background knowledge with new information and generate a creative or novel way of looking at things.

Wait Time. Research has shown that teachers using large group discussion techniques typically ask as many as 150 questions during the average class period (Melnik, 1968). When question and answer periods are used as an instructional technique, teachers tend to ask low-level questions in rapid-fire order (Rowe, 1974a; 1974b). For many children, the science classroom resembles a television game show in which the objective is to score points with the teacher by playing a live version of "trivial pursuit." Children who may be embarrassed by a lack of English proficiency and children who are unused to performing in front of a large group find this a very uncomfortable environment. When low-order questions become the focus of instruction, students are encouraged to "memorize" facts, to engage in shallow information processing. This type of question-asking and student-responding behavior precludes effective use of discussion sessions that emphasize reflective thinking and inquiry (Collette & Chiappetta, 1984, p. 209).

When question and answer periods are used as instructional devices, teachers should strive to ask open-ended questions, that is, questions that encourage divergent thinking on the part of students. Rowe (1974a; 1974b) proposed that teachers pause and wait 3 to 5 seconds after asking an open-ended question. This pause after a question is asked is referred to as **wait time**. The use of wait time by the teacher gives students an opportunity to think, reflect, and formulate an answer. Research (Atwood & Wilen, 1991; Riley, 1986; Rowe, 1974a; 1974b; 1983; Tobin & Capie, 1981) has shown that the use of wait time by the teacher (1) increases the length of student responses, (2) lessens the failure of students to respond, (3) increases the number of unsolicited but appropriate responses, (4) changes the number and type of questions asked by the teacher, (5) decreases the students' failure to respond, (6) improves the performance of "slow" students, (7) increases students' confidence in their answers, (8) increases the variety and type of students' verbal responses, (9) increases the students' incidence of comparing their findings with others, (10) increases the number of questions that students ask, (11) produces a higher incidence of speculative responses, and (12) results in a higher incidence of evidence-inference statements by students. In speaking of the value of wait time, Tobin (1984) states that it improves the quality of the learning environment and increases achievement in subjects such as mathematics and science for which higher cognitive level outcomes are often a concern.

The active use of wait time during question and answer periods benefits all students. When wait time is used in the classroom, students listen to one another, rather than listening for the next question. This environment reinforces the self-worth of each child and tends to build self-esteem. By allowing children time to formulate answers to questions, teachers who use wait time are encouraging children to activate their existing mental structures and are providing the opportunity for children to translate mentally information stored in their "home language" into "school language." The use of wait time allows a child time to evaluate the quality of his or her answer and builds confidence in his or her ability to respond to the question. Wait time is a vital tool for encouraging the participation of culturally diverse learners in large-group verbal interactions.

Target Students.   The interaction of the teacher and the student with the curriculum is the heart of the educational process. Research (Barba & Cardinale, 1991; Parakh, 1967; Tobin & Gallagher, 1987) has shown that students do not interact equally with their teachers in the classroom. Tobin and Gallagher (1987) reported that, in nearly every classroom, there are three to seven "salient" students who tend to monopolize or control student interactions. Parakh (1967) reported that high-ability or highly verbal students tend to interact with their teachers more often than less verbal students. According to Tobin and Gallagher (1987) and Barba and Cardinale (1991), **target students**, that is, those who engage in frequent verbal interactions with their teachers, generally tend to be assertive Anglo/European males, rather than Anglo females or culturally diverse learners. In examining the research on teachers' targeting behaviors (Connery, 1990; Gallagher & Tobin, 1987; Gooding, Kephart, Swift, Swift, & Schell, 1990; Okebukola & Ogunniyi, 1986; Tobin & Gallagher, 1987), the following trends have emerged:

- Most teachers tend to direct questions at random to the whole class, which favors those who raise their hands and those who call out responses;
- Teachers feel that students who raise their hands probably "know" the answer and deserve to be recognized;
- Teachers occasionally attempt to call on students who do not raise their hands but not in a concerted manner;
- Teachers generally ask low-level questions and random but direct high-level questions to those who they perceive to be more capable;
- Teachers generally "target" students because they feel that these students will facilitate learning and content coverage;
- Target students generally receive "better" feedback from their teachers; and
- Some target students are teacher selected, while others self-select to become target students.

In their assessment of the effect of teachers' targeting behaviors, Barba and Cardinale (1991) point out that non-targeted students have fewer interactions with their teachers and thus receive less attention in the classroom. Over time, nontargeted students may feel that the teacher avoids them because they are less capable than other students. Systematic disengagement of students during classroom verbal interactions results in a situation in which some students believe that they do not have meaningful information to contribute to the class. For Anglo females and culturally diverse students, the lack of interaction with the teacher during science instruction may result in students feeling that they have low ability in sciences and thus may remove themselves "mentally" from the study of science and from science careers. When using large group verbal interaction teaching techniques, teachers need to distribute questions equitably across the class to avoid targeting behaviors.

Levels of Questioning.   Educational journals and trade magazines frequently have articles that exalt the use of "high-order" thinking skills, while degrading the use of "low-level" thinking skills. One criticism of large group verbal interactions is that this environment fosters "low-level" learning. The terms "low level" and "high level" generally refer to Bloom's Taxonomy (1956) of the cognitive domain. Research (Barba & Cardinale, 1991; Melnik, 1968; Parakh, 1967; Riley, 1986; Rowe, 1983; & Tobin, 1984) has shown that, during verbal interactions, teachers tend to rely heavily on questions at the knowledge and comprehension levels of Bloom's taxonomy while avoiding questions at the application, analysis, synthesis, and evaluation levels.

In his taxonomy of the cognitive domain, Bloom (1956) asserted that cognitive knowledge could be classified as being at the knowledge, comprehension, application, analysis, synthesis, or evaluation levels. The knowledge level of Bloom's taxonomy includes information that emphasizes the student's recognition or recall of factual information. The comprehension level includes a determination as to whether the student understands the information. Application, according to Bloom, refers to the students' ability to use scientific knowledge in a new situation. Using cognitive knowledge at the analysis level involves the ability to break information into component parts. When students function at the synthesis level, they are, according to Bloom, able to put that information together to form a new whole. Finally, at the evaluation level, students are able to develop criteria and judge the relative worth or merit of ideas, solutions, and methods. A summary of each of the levels of Bloom's taxonomy is shown in Table 7.2.

Mediated Conversations.   Among all large group instructional techniques, the mediated conservation is the most productive in terms of student learning. A **mediated conversation** is a large group instructional technique during which teachers and students teach each other and learn from each other. In a large group situation, the teacher should serve as a mediator whose job it is to assist students in examining their mental constructions, and should guide children as they engage in cognitive restructuring. Through questioning, the teacher redirects, guides, channels, and generally assists the students in accommodating new information such that their internal mental structures are more consistent with empirical data about the external world. A constructivist learning model, modified from the works of Walter Saunders (1992, p. 139), is presented in Figure 7.2.

In this constructivist model of learning, assimilation occurs when students take data through their sensory organs into the existing cognitive structures. If these data do not "fit" with the existing mental structures, a state of cognitive dissonance or disequilibrium develops within the learner. In science education, we sometimes refer to the event which causes this cognitive dissonance as a

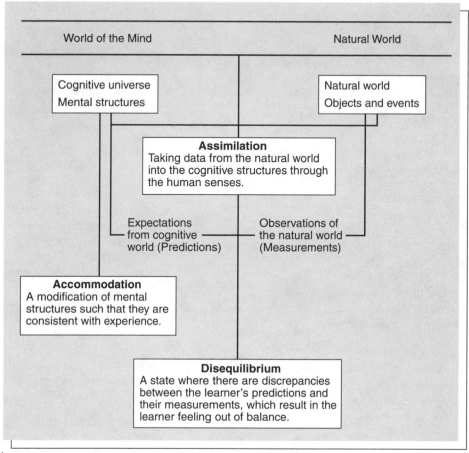

| FIGURE 7.2   Constructivist Learning Model

discrepant event. For example, all of us are familiar with the properties of rocks and minerals. If we were to see someone pick up a rock and struggle to heave it into a pond or lake, we would expect the rock to sink. If that rock floated, we might be hard pressed to explain what happened. Unless we had a prior knowledge of pumice, a rock which is normally lighter than water, we would not be able to accommodate this new information. We would be in a state of disequilibrium. After a period of "playing" with pumice, of manipulating it and determining that indeed it is a light-weight rock, we might be able to accommodate this new knowledge, in which case we would restructure our existing schema to accommodate the fact that this one rock floats, that it is less dense than water.

One job of the teacher is to assist students in restructuring their schema such that their interpretations of the natural world are more in accord with those of the community of scientists and not home-grown conceptions or mis-

TABLE 7.2   Bloom's Taxonomy of the Cognitive Domain

Descriptors	Associated Questioning Verbs		Sample Activities or Questions
Knowledge (Definition: to recall or to know)			
• Remembering terms, facts, concepts, or methods	Arrange	Quote	• Label the parts of an insect.
• Recalling information	Ask	Recall	• Write the definitions for the words.
• Lowest level of learning	Check	Recite	• Locate the parts of the animal cell.
• Bringing to mind stored knowledge	Choose	Repeat	• Write the symbols for the elements.
• Remembering previously learned material	Cite	Say	• List the names of the birds.
• Reciting learned information	Define	Select	• Group the minerals by color.
• Listing previously learned information	Describe	Show	• Locate biomes on the map.
• Bringing to memory stored knowledge	Label	Spell	• Name the parts of the microscope.
	List	State	• Label the parts of the flower.
	Match	Tell	
	Name	Touch	
	Outline	Underline	
	Pick	Write	
	Point out		
Comprehension (Definition: to understand or explain)			
• Interpret charts and graphs	Alter	Qualify	• Summarize the reading.
• Grasp the meaning of new material	Annotate	Spell out	• Give reasons for the dinosaurs becoming extinct.
• Predict consequences	Calculate	Submit	• Explain why we have lab safety rules.
• Interpret material	Change	Transform	• What factors contributed to the scientific revolution?
• Estimate future trends	Construe	Translate	• Restate the reasons for climatic changes on the earth.
• See relationships among things	Convert	Vary	• Interpret the line graph showing the heating of the liquid.
• Understand facts and principles	Define operationally		• Outline the steps in preparing a "wet" mount.
• Project effects of ideas	Demonstrate		
• Summarize material	Expand		
• Communicate in a new way	Explain		
• Explain ideas	Moderate		
	Offer		
	Project		
	Propose		
Application (Definition: to use ideas)			
• Make use of knowledge	Adopt	Organize	• How do you use simple machines at home?
• Apply concepts to new situations	Apply	Profit by	• Put this information in a bar graph.
• Requires higher levels of understanding than comprehension	Avail	Put in action	• Organize the survival gear from most needed to least needed.
• Apply scientific principles in a real world situation	Classify	Put to use	• Plan posters, skits, and activities that will promote a recycling ethic in your peers.
• Demonstrate correct use of a procedure or method	Collect	Relate	• Sketch a mural that relates your feelings about the environment.
• Construct graphs and charts	Construct	Solve	
• Solve mathematical problems	Employ	Try	
	Exercise	Use	
	Manipulate	Wield	
	Operate		

TABLE 7.2   Bloom's Taxonomy of the Cognitive Domain (continued)

Descriptors	Associated Questioning Verbs		Sample Activities or Questions

Analysis (Definition: to break down into component parts)

• Break into components • Understand the organizational structure • Analyze the elements • Analyze relationships between parts • Understand content and form • Recognize principles involved	Audit Break down Deduce Diagram Differentiate Dissect Divide Examine Include Inspect Look into	Reason Screen Search Section Separate Sift Simplify Study Subdivide Survey Take apart Test for	• Compare and contrast plants and animals. • Identify the problems associated with nuclear waste materials. • Uncover the unique characteristics of horseshoe crabs. • Examine a toy and identify the simple machines you find in it. • Compare and contrast lava and magma. • Examine a cartoon and identify the scientific errors you find.

Synthesis (Definition: to form a new whole)

• Take something apart and pattern it in a new way • Put parts together in a new whole • Create new and original things • Abstract relationships • Communicate an idea in a new way • Tell a personal experience effectively	Build Cause Combine Compile Compose Conceive Construct Create Design Develop Effect Evolve	Formulate Generate Make Mature Modify Originate Plan Produce Rearrange Reorganize Revise Structure	• Formulate a scheme for classifying wildflowers from your neighborhood. • Develop a plan for schoolwide recycling. • Using straight pins and soda straws, construct a bridge that will hold at least 500 grams of mass. • Create a rap song to tell others about the elements of the periodic table. • Write a theme describing how you would invent a new robot to help you with your schoolwork.

Evaluation (Definition: to judge or critique)

• Ability to judge the value of material • Ability to indicate logical fallacies in arguments • Use of a definite criterion for evaluations • Use of cognitive and affective domains simultaneously • Highest level of learning • Value judgments based on a defined criterion	Appraise Arbitrate Assay Classify Conclude Criticize Decide Determine Discriminate Evaluate	Grade Judge Justify Prioritize Rank Rate Referee Rule on Umpire Weigh	• Summarize what you have learned this year. • Rank the list of scientific discoveries in order of importance to you. • Decide which solution to the problem is best and why. • Determine the criteria for a "good" paper airplane and justify your selection criteria. • Read two different accounts of the "discovery" of DNA, decide which is most accurate, and tell why. • Judge your peers' science fair displays, decide which is best, and give a rationale for your decision.

conceptions about the world. Verbal interactions between students and teachers are a medium for this restructuring process.

Just as the teacher guides and directs the students, students guide and direct their teacher. Through the questions they ask and through the statements they make, students communicate to the teacher their level of understanding of scientific knowledge. Unfortunately, teachers are not always good listeners; they do not always attend to what students say about their level of understanding. The following conversation illustrates this point:

Ms. Chan: We have just finished looking at some insects. We've written a list of insect characteristics on the board. Would someone review for us the characteristics of insects? . . . . [the teacher uses wait time] . . . Carlos?

Carlos: Insects have six legs, three body parts, and some of them got wings.

Ms. Chan: Good, Carlos, that's a very good beginning. Did anyone else find some characteristics that all of the insects seemed to have in common? [the teacher again uses wait time] . . . Yes, Lisa, what did you want to add?

Lisa: Our group collected a spider. It was real yucky. When we were outside, our group noticed that insects are animals, they move from one place to another. Some of them walked and some ran.

Ms. Chan: That's right. Lisa has just told us that insects are animals, that they move from place to place. What else do we know about insects? . . . [the teacher pauses] . . . Tim?

Ms. Chan missed a "teachable moment," that is, she missed the opportunity to assist Lisa and others in the class in restructuring their knowledge of insects. In this conversation, Lisa mentioned that a spider was an insect, and Ms. Chan complimented Lisa on knowing that insects were animals, but she neglected to notice that Lisa had included spiders in the same group as insects. Many students in the class probably shared the same mental image of insects that Lisa did, that is, that insects are "small animals." Ms. Chan should have allowed Lisa and her classmates the opportunity to count the number of legs on several insects and then to count the number of legs on a spider. Had she done this, Lisa and her classmates would have been faced with a dilemma: insects have six legs and spiders have eight legs. Being placed in a state of cognitive dissonance or disequilibrium would have allowed Lisa and her peers the opportunity to accommodate new knowledge. One role of the teacher is to assist students in altering their schema in such a way that their predictions or expectations are more in line with their observations of the natural world.

A mediated conversation is a class meeting. In this large group setting, the principles of modeling, coaching, scaffolding, articulation, and reflection are practiced by students and their teacher. Large group instructional environments should be places in which students and teachers (1) develop plans to explore the natural world; (2) share their findings regarding phenomena, objects, and events in that world; (3) wrestle with explanations and interpretations of data; and (4) attempt to make sense of the world around them.

Exposition.   Exposition or expository instructional strategies may be operationally defined as those pedagogical techniques according to which some authority (e.g., teachers, textbooks, computer programs, filmstrips, or videotapes) presents oral and/or verbal information to students without active verbal interactions occurring between the students and the authority figure. While extensive use of exposition is not recommended with elementary-aged school children, expository instructional techniques certainly have a place in the multicultural science classroom. Madeline Hunter is quoted with saying that "telling is not teaching" (Hunter, 1982, p. 33). Long, monotone lectures devoid of visual enhancement are not an appropriate pedagogical strategy for use with young children. However, sometimes telling *is* teaching. Speaking frankly and succinctly to the subject is a highly effective instructional technique in certain instances. If you wish to train young children in behaviors appropriate for use in emergency situations, then expository teaching is best. During an earthquake, students should be taught to "Duck, Cover, and Hold." When crossing the street children should remember that they are to "Stop, Look, and Listen." On a field trip to a national forest, students should be encouraged to "hug a tree" and wait there until help arrives if they get separated from the rest of the group. Direction giving is one very appropriate use for exposition.

In the past, when expository instructional techniques were used in the classroom, the teacher was viewed as the controller of knowledge, the person who somehow or other transmitted knowledge to students who were blank slates and therefore must be attentive and quiet. This view of teaching and learning is based on objectivist epistemological precepts that hold that knowledge is a truth to which humans have access. From this viewpoint, the function of the teacher in the classroom is to "teach" this truth or knowledge to children. The teacher, from this perspective, is one who dispenses knowledge to children, that is, one who structures the learning environment to maximize the learning of the children. In writing about expository instructional strategies, Vygotsky (1978) stated that the mere exposure of students to new materials through oral lectures neither allows for adult guidance nor for collaboration with peers.

Extended use of expository instructional techniques is usually viewed as being inappropriate for use with elementary-aged children in the science classroom because (1) verbal presentations are difficult for children to understand, (2) children have a limited attention span and thus tend to become restless, (3) children tend to be passive learners when expository techniques are used, and (4) what is said is not always what is heard or interpreted (Wolfinger, 1984). In addition, children are typically not coached in schools to assimilate and accommodate information presented orally or verbally.

Socialization and Learning.   For culturally diverse learners, expository teaching techniques pose another set of problems, problems related to the ways that children have been taught to engage in social situations. Many culturally diverse children are socialized to interact or work in small cooperative groups or in extended family settings. For these children, sitting silently in a large group, facing front, and not interacting with peers while attending to the words of one adult is a highly unpleasant and culturally unfamiliar experience. Frequently, teachers build an invisible wall between themselves and their students when they lecture. Teachers sometimes pace the perimeter of the classroom or stand on a podium, physically removing themselves from the children in the classroom. Sometimes, children perceive these teacher actions as acts of hostility and conclude that the teacher does not like them or care about them. Learning is difficult when children view the classroom as a hostile environment. Making expository instructional periods "user friendly" for culturally diverse students can be accomplished by (1) increasing the level of student interaction through note-taking and active listening activities; (2) using multiple modes of knowledge representation or visual enhancement; (3) conducting short, concise lecture periods; and (4) incorporating small group after lecture techniques.

Active Listening and Interacting. There are times when lectures, filmstrips, textbooks, videos, and tutorial computer programs are appropriate for use in the classroom, especially in providing background information on a particular topic (e.g., the volcano example used earlier in this chapter). Expository instructional techniques are excellent for providing students with access to science content knowledge that cannot be derived easily through the use of inquiry-based instructional techniques. However, expository techniques need to include elements of active participation in order for students to receive the full benefit of this instructional strategy. In coaching elementary-aged children to attend to what is being said, the teacher may wish to design the focusing questions ahead of time, as guideposts to facilitate students' listening and processing skills. Studies (Anderson & Armbruster, 1986; Lazarus, 1991; Peper & Mayer, 1986) have shown that students benefit from expository presentations only when they actively listen, process what they have heard, and write down words or phrases which will activate their mental structures at a later time.

Visual Enhancement. When expository teaching techniques are used with elementary-aged children, especially those culturally diverse children who may have difficulty acquiring meaning from spoken or written words, visual enhancement of expository presentations is especially appropriate. When students represent their knowledge during problem-solving situations, they represent that knowledge through real-world objects (or *realia*), spoken words, written words, pictures, and icons (Lesh, Landau, & Hamilton, 1983). These modes of knowledge representation may be used to present information to children (Figure 7.3).

Since icons, *realia*, and pictures are not language dependent, their use in the multicultural classrooms profits limited English proficient students who have not yet mastered the English language. Icons, real-world objects, and pictures serve to activate a student's prior knowledge: knowledge that sometimes was constructed in the student's "home language" or native tongue. Research (Allen, 1975; Conway, 1968; Dwyer, 1978; Levie & Levie, 1975; Severin, 1967; Sless, 1983) has shown that multiple means of knowledge representation proportionally profit students who have difficulty extracting meaning from printed words,

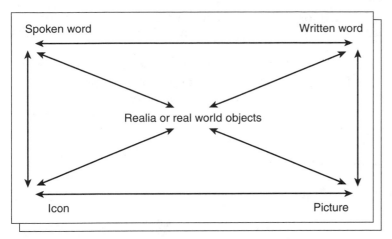

FIGURE 7.3 Modes of Knowledge Representation

that is, those students who are not high verbal learners in English. Teachers who use slides, transparencies, photographs, drawings, and diagrams to enhance their verbal presentations are attending to the linguistic needs of multicultural students.

When Lecturing. When expository teaching is used in the classroom, the classroom environment needs to be structured in such a way that students are mentally engaged in what is being said. In addition, periods of expository teaching need to be "short and sweet." Elementary teachers should remember that children at this age can attend to verbal presentations for only short periods (10 to 15 minutes). Students should know in advance what they are expected to learn from the presentation. The use of an advance organizer is a highly appropriate way to begin a lecture.

An advance organizer (Ausubel, 1963) is a verbal device which provides relevant introductory information. Advance organizers serve to assist students to explain, integrate, and interrelate prior learning with new knowledge. Short stories, analogies, and questions may be used as advance organizers. Advance organizers may be comparative or expository in nature. If a teacher is beginning a unit of study on wildflowers, the teacher may relate this to a similar experience that the students have had. The teacher could use a comparative organizer and make a statement such as, "Do you remember when we learned to group or classify insects? Today we are going to begin to learn about grouping wildflowers." A comparative organizer relates new learning to previous knowledge, to familiar experiences.

A second group of advance organizers is called expository organizers. Expository organizers exist to inform the learner of what is to be learned: knowledge with which they are unfamiliar. When introducing a unit of study on monerans, the teacher could say, "Today we are going to begin to study monerans. The name moneran refers to bacteria, tiny single-celled living things." With this statement, the teacher is informing the students of what is to be learned and is assisting students in identifying the salient information that will be presented during the lecture.

Following the introduction of the subject, the teacher should move to the body of the lecture. During this time, information should be presented in a clear, concise fashion. It must be stressed that the attention span of children is far less than that of adults. Therefore, lengthy expository presentations are inappropriate for young children. Children tend to remember what they hear at the beginning and at the end of the expository presentations. Children retain less information from what is said during the middle of the presentation. We refer to this as primacy and recency. The first words and the last words that the teacher says during an expository presentation will be best remembered by their students.

When providing understanding of a new concept, the teacher should (1) identify the critical attributes, (2) select examples from the students' own lives whenever possible, (3) provide examples that are less than ideal but still present the appropriate characteristics, and (4) provide unusual examples (Hunter, 1982; Wolfinger, 1984). Suppose a teacher wants to teach the concept "mammal" to her students in an expository manner. She should begin by stating the critical attributes: "A mammal is a warm-blooded animal whose body is covered more or less with fur. Mammals have milk glands to nourish their young, a diaphragm used in respiration, and a four-chambered heart." Next, the teacher should provide examples of mammals from the lives of her students: "Cats, dogs, and people are examples of mammals with which you are familiar." In reinforcing the concept, the teacher provides additional examples of mammals, examples that are more removed from the students' direct experiences: "Cows, monkeys, horses, deer, and pigs are also mammals." Finally, the teacher should provide little known and unusual examples of mammals: "The bat is a mammal. Even though it flies, it is a mammal and not a bird. The bat has hair rather than fur on its body. It provides milk to its young. The whale is also a mammal. The whale lives in water and looks like a fish, but it is really a mammal. The whale's body does not have scales like a fish. It feeds its young milk from its own body." Visual enhancement through photographs, slides, and transparencies is vital in expository teaching. Each example of a mammal mentioned orally by the teacher should be accompanied by a pictorial, iconic, verbal, and/or real world representation of the organism. During the conclusion of the lecture, the teacher should reiterate the main points and ask students to reflect on what they have just learned.

CLASSROOM PRACTICE

As a teacher, part of your "job" is to determine the best instructional strategy to meet the needs of your students. There are times when you will find expository teaching to be the most appropriate method for instructing students. Sometimes, you will find that students learn best in a small group setting. At other times, you will want to engage your students in a mediated conversation. Finally, there will be times when you will want to assist students in engaging in self-directed learning, of extending what they have previously learned. The decision as to which instructional strategy is appropriate is one that you will make many times a day, depending on (1) the content knowledge to be mastered by the students, (2) the characteristics of your students, and (3) your purpose in teaching a particular concept or "body of knowledge."

Fostering self-directed learning in students is perhaps the most difficult task that teachers face. This section focuses on the development of an activity corner designed to provide resources that "invite" students to engage in self-directed learning. Many times it is difficult to determine what will "excite" students, what will "turn them on" to learning.

Nearly every parent in the world shares the story of carefully selecting a Christmas or birthday gift for their child, only to find the child "unappreciative" of the gift. The parent has spent endless hours shopping for an age-appropriate toy which will actively engage the young child in meaningful play only to find that the child prefers the wrapping paper or the box as a toy. The same phenomenon occurs in classrooms in that, what teachers find engaging and interesting, students sometimes find dull and boring.

"Pogo sticking" with a purpose or exploring one "thing" after another on one's own is at the heart of self-directed learning. One vehicle for self-directed learning is the activity corner. The activity corner ought to be a place where students can continue learning begun in a larger class setting, a place where alone, or together with one or two others, students can pursue their interests. Activity corners should be stocked with materials that elicit curiosity in children: computer workstations, microscopes, library books on the current topic of study, filmstrip viewing stations, a mini-museum (e.g., displays of child-collected *realia*), and individual learning kits or shoeboxes.

Individual learning kits or shoebox science activities are normally teacher-made learning activities which the child can do on his or her own. Several shoebox science activities are provided here as examples of the type of materials which can be used with students:

SHOEBOX ACTIVITY 7-1 ■ FLOATERS AND SINKERS

Purpose: To illustrate a small group activity.

Grade Level: Primary

Teacher Preparation Directions: Assemble the materials and place them in the shoebox.

Science Concept: Some objects float while others sink.

Science Processes: Observing, classifying, collecting data, interpreting data.

Sink   Float

Student Materials (list to be taped to the lid of the shoebox):

cotton ball   penny
soda straw   small piece of paper
button   popsicle stick
ping pong ball   plastic cup

Student Directions (to be included in the shoebox):

1. Make sure that all the materials are in the shoebox.
2. Fill the plastic cup 2/3 full of water.
3. Pick up one object and place it in the water.
4. Does it float? Sink?

Directions: Draw each object in the correct column.

Floater?	**Sinker?**

---

5. Draw the object on the correct column of the data sheet.
6. Repeat for each object.

SHOEBOX ACTIVITY 7-2 ▪ FISHING WITH MAGNETS

Purpose: To illustrate an activity, thus encouraging self-directed learning.

Grade Level: Primary or intermediate grades

Teacher Preparation Directions: Assemble the materials and place them in the shoebox.

Science Concept: Some materials (e.g., those made of iron or steel) are attracted to a magnet.

Science Processes: Observing, classifying, inferring, predicting, collecting, and interpreting data

Student Materials (list to be taped to the lid of the shoebox):

20 to 30 pieces of "junk"   string
   (e.g., marble, staples, paper clip,   magnet
   erasers)   plastic tray
ruler

Student Directions (to be included in the shoebox):

1. Assemble a "fishing pole" by tying the magnet to the string and attaching it to the end of the ruler.
2. Make a "fishing hole" by placing the assorted items provided by your teacher in the plastic tray.
3. "Catch" the objects from the fishing hole. Write the names of each object that is attracted to the magnet on one side of the data sheet and the names of the objects left behind on the other.

SHOEBOX ACTIVITY 7-3 ■ HEARTBEATS

Purpose: To illustrate a small group activity.

Grade Level: Upper elementary

Teacher Preparation Directions: Assemble the materials and place them in the shoebox.

Science Concept: Variables such as the type of exercise affect heart rate.

Science Processes: Observing, using numbers, recording data, interpreting data, graphing data

Student Materials (list to be taped to the lid of the shoebox):

stopwatch, graph paper

Student Directions (to be included in the shoebox):

1. Rest for one minute. Determine your heart rate and record it on a table of data. To find your pulse, place two fingers on your neck under your chin. Move your fingers carefully, pressing gently on your neck until you feel your pulse. Count the number of heartbeats for 1 minute.
2. Jump rope for 2 minutes. Now determine your heart rate. Record your results on your table of data.
3. Jog in place for 2 minutes. Determine your heart rate. Record your results on a table of data.
4. Lie down for 2 minutes. Record your heart rate.

A
C
T
I
V
I
T
I
E
S

TABLE 7.3 Heart Rate and Exercise	
Activity	*Heart Beats/Minute*
Resting	
Jumping Rope	
Jogging	
Lying down	

5. Make a bar graph of your results.
6. What happens to your heart rate as you exercise (Table 7.3)?

  CHAPTER SUMMARY

In this chapter, four clusters of instructional strategies were discussed: (1) self-directed learning, (2) small group interactions, (3) large group instruction, and (4) expository teaching. Expository teaching techniques are the most teacher centered, whereas self-directed teaching strategies are the most child-centered. In all four clusters of teaching strategies mentioned in this chapter, the role of the teacher is to assist children in exploring the natural world. Teachers assist children by modeling, coaching, scaffolding, articulating, and reflecting on learning and how to learn. The choice of an appropriate instructional strategy is situational and depends on what is to be learned, the characteristics of the learners, and the teacher's understanding of their students and the way(s) that they learn.

 TOPICS TO REVIEW

 REFLECTIVE PRACTICE

1. Explain what is meant by the concept "appropriate use" of instructional strategies. In other words, when might a particular teaching strategy be appropriate? Inappropriate?
2. Many authors state that knowledge is "constructed within a sociocultural context." Having read this chapter, what does this expression mean to you?

3. Identify some reasons why social skills are important in science learning. Explain your reasons.
4. Reflecting on your own skills and competencies, which teaching "jobs" or functions are you most comfortable with? Least comfortable with? In which teaching roles do you have the most expertise? In which teaching roles do you need to develop expertise?

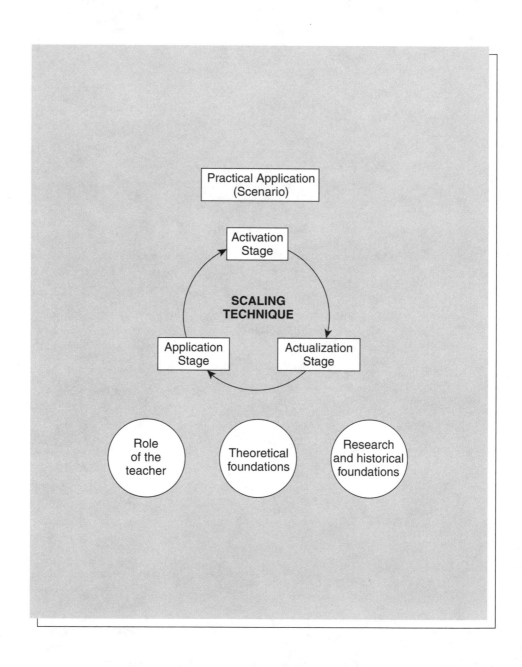

Practical Application
(Scenario)

Activation
Stage

**SCALING
TECHNIQUE**

Application
Stage

Actualization
Stage

Role
of the
teacher

Theoretical
foundations

Research
and historical
foundations

CONSTRUCTING A KNOWLEDGE OF SCIENCE AND LANGUAGE

 POINTS TO PONDER

1. How do language and hands-on experiences help children build a knowledge of science concepts?
2. How should science instruction be modified to accommodate the needs of limited English proficient children?
3. In what ways is science like children's play?

MS. GONZALES

n San Diego, California, Ms. Gonzales's 31 third graders enter their class-room after recess to find two sizes of soda straws (one with a larger diameter than the other) and a slice of raw potato on their tables. Ms. Gonzales begins class:

> "While you were at recess, I placed straws and potato slices on your tables. Today we are going to make potato pistols. To make the pistol, place your thumb over the end of the large straw and press it into the raw potato. (Ms. Gonzales waits while the students perform this action). Now pull the straw out of the potato and turn it upside down, put your thumb over the other end of the straw, and insert it into the potato. You should have a plug of potato in each end of your straw. Now take the thinner

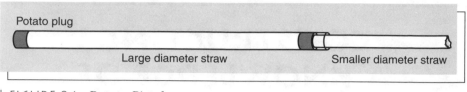

FIGURE 8.1   Potato Pistol

straw and push it into one of the potato plugs in the big straw (Figure 8.1). What happens? (Ms. Gonzales waits for the students to perform the action.)

As the students practice "shooting" their potato pistols, Ms. Gonzales walks around the room from group to group using encouraging comments to keep the students on task. At each group, Ms. Gonzales pauses and checks with the children to be certain that they have understood her instructions. When she encounters a Chicano boy who seems to be having difficulty with the task, she quickly and quietly translates her previous instructions into Spanish and encourages the child to begin manipulating the materials. As she passes a group with two Vietnamese children, Ms. Gonzales says:

> "Tran, I remember that you speak Vietnamese, would you be sure that My San understands what we are doing? Help her by translating my instructions into Vietnamese. Be sure that she knows the English names for straw and potato."

After a walk through the room and a quick visit at each group, Ms. Gonzales has determined that everyone has been successful in getting their potato pistol to "fire." Ms. Gonzales calls the class to order and begins to lead a discussion in English:

> "What happens when you push the plunger or small straw into the potato inside the larger straw? (Ms. Gonzales waits for student answers.) What would happen if we used a longer straw? A shorter straw? What happens when we push the plunger slowly? Very rapidly? What would happen if we put two or three potato plugs in the larger straw? How could we find out?" (Ms. Gonzales pauses after each question and allows the children to formulate "guesses" about what they think would happen. She encourages each child to justify his or her answer to develop a rationale for decision making.)

Ms. Gonzales encourages the students to design their own activities in their small groups. She provides the class with metric measuring tapes so they can measure the distance that the potato plugs travel. She also encourages students to record their observations and the results of their activities in a journal or a science notebook to keep a record of their investigations. As the students work in their small groups, she encourages the students to think about the activities they have just done and to formulate additional questions that they can answer by manipulating the materials (the straws and the potato plugs).

We call these child-generated questions operational questions (so named by Dorothy Alfke while she was on the faculty of The Pennsylvania State University). An **operational question** is one that either directly or by implication states what must be done with science materials to obtain an answer to a student-generated question. Ms.

Gonzales allows the students to formulate a series of activities which will help them develop the experiential background necessary for later understanding of the phenomenon they are observing. As the students work in their small groups, Ms. Gonzales encourages them to help each other, in particular, she encourages students with stronger English language skills to help others in the group in naming objects and events. In addition, Ms. Gonzales encourages every student to become actively involved in manipulating the potato pistols, in exploring the scientific phenomena.

Finally, after about 30 minutes, Ms. Gonzales asks the class to put away the materials and pick up any potato plugs that may be lying on the floor. At this point, she leads them in a large group discussion of the activity. As students speak of their experiences, Ms. Gonzales introduces the term "air pressure" to the class. Together Ms. Gonzales and her students operationally define the term "air pressure." **Operational definitions** *are working definitions as opposed to formal science definitions. They are definitions based on the child's understanding of the phenomena that they have observed and they are refined by the child as he or she grows older and has more experiences in the physical world. In this case, the students may define air pressure as a "squeezing of the air inside the large straw which causes the potato plug to shoot across the room." Ms. Gonzales asks the students to put down the manipulative materials and says:*

> *"We have been working with materials that illustrate the concept of air pressure. Can you think of another example of air pressure? What experiences or events in your past or at home could also be considered an illustration of air pressure? I want you to look for examples of air pressure around you. Tomorrow, we will have another activity or two in which we will apply our new understanding of air pressure. Right now, I would like you to share with me what you have learned about air pressure today. Some of you may choose to write a journal entry describing what you have learned, some of you may choose to draw a word web sharing your new learning, and some of you may choose to make a drawing sharing your ideas. Take about 15 minutes now and find a way to tell me what you have learned about air pressure."* *(Ms. Gonzales again moves around the classroom speaking to individual students and encouraging them to develop a plan for reporting their new learning.)*

The story of Ms. Gonzales and her third grade students is an example of a modified learning cycle lesson or scaled activity. Scaling is an instructional strategy which enables students to investigate the natural world in much the same manner that professional scientists use when investigating the world.

INTERACTIVE SCIENCE INSTRUCTION

Science is more than a collection of facts about the natural world; it is a way of thinking, of approaching problems objectively by theorizing about what might be after careful observation of what is, and then testing the hypothesis. Science instruction in U.S. public schools should help all children think as scientists, to become familiar with the laws and principles of the natural world, to develop proficiency in the use of the English language, and to become scientifically literate citizens in a democracy. Showalter (1974) has stated that a **scientifically literate** individual is one who:

1. "Understands the nature of scientific knowledge;
2. Accurately applies appropriate science concepts, principles, laws, and theories in interacting with his universe;
3. Uses process of science in solving problems, making decisions, and furthering his own understanding of the universe;
4. Interacts with the various aspects of his universe in a way that is consistent with the values that underlie science; and
5. Has developed a richer, more satisfying, and more exciting view of the universe as a result of his science education and continues to extend this education throughout his life" (p. 2).

The ability to understand and apply science concepts, processes, and vocabulary to everyday life is vital for all children. The development of scientific literacy within each child is an underlying goal for all science teaching and learning.

Historical Foundations of Scaling

Translating the work of real scientists into a pedagogical approach for children has resulted in what is termed a "learning cycle" (Karplus, 1984) or an inquiry approach to science teaching. Expanding and modifying the learning cycle to include language acquisition skills and an accommodation of the needs of culturally diverse learners has resulted in a scaling technique for teaching and learning. **SCALE** is an acronym for **S**cience **C**ontent **a**nd **L**anguage **E**xpansion. Scaling knowledge involves the acquisition of science concepts, science processes, and scientific vocabulary as a unified whole. As used in this chapter, scaling knowledge involves the use of a three-stage, inquiry-based teaching strategy which allows the child the opportunity to construct a knowledge of scientific phenomena and its associated vocabulary. Scaling allows children to build new science concepts, science processes, and vocabulary knowledge through a scientific investigation and questions. It allows children in the elementary classroom to function as scientists in investigating their natural world.

Scaling is a highly modified form of the learning cycle approach to science teaching. The learning cycle as it was designed is a three-phase inductive teaching approach which was developed by Karplus and Atkin in 1962 (Lawson & Renner, 1975). Originally, the learning cycle was developed to accompany an elementary science curriculum project, which was called the Science Curriculum Improvement Study (SCIS) project. Since the time of its development, the learning cycle has been found to be an appropriate teaching strategy for use with middle school (Barman, 1989; Lawson, Abraham, & Renner, 1989), high school (Abraham & Renner, 1986; Lawson, 1975; Lawson, Abraham, & Renner, 1989; Lawson & Renner, 1975; Purser & Renner, 1983), and university students

(Marek & Methven, 1991; Lawson, Abraham, & Renner, 1989; Schlenker, 1983). Today, modified forms of the learning cycle are used as the pedagogical foundation of the Biological Sciences Curriculum Study elementary science program (Science for Life and Living; Integrating Science, Technology, and Health) and in the Lawrence Hall of Science (Full Option Science System [FOSS]) program.

Exploration Phase.   The learning cycle as it was originally conceived consists of three distinct phases: exploration, concept introduction, and concept application (Figure 8.2). During the first phase of the learning cycle (e.g., the exploration phase), students are very active. The emphasis of the **exploration phase** is on students' learning through their own actions and reactions in a new situation. It is during this phase that students interact with materials in the physical world and with each other. The teacher functions primarily as an observer during this phase, as one who assists individual students and small groups of students. The exploration phase provides children with concrete experiences to help them build mental images of new ideas or terms.

Exploration, according to Lawson and Renner (1975), involves students in concrete, real-world experiences. As a result of the exploration phase, the learner encounters new information for which he or she does not have an available mental structure to allow for its immediate assimilation. When students do not have existing mental structures to accommodate new information, they enter into a state of disequilibrium, a state which gives rise to potential cognitive restructuring.

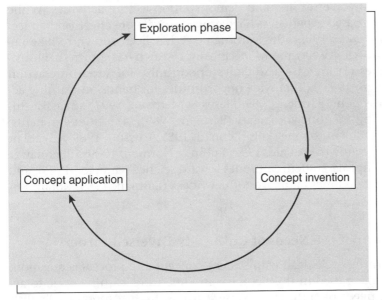

FIGURE 8.2   The Learning Cycle

Concept Invention Phase.   During the concept invention phase of the learning cycle, the teacher assists students in naming object and concept. **Concept invention** serves "to introduce a new concept or principle that leads the students to apply new patterns of reasoning to their experiences. This step, which aids in self-regulation, should always follow exploration and relate to the exploration activities" (Karplus, et al., 1977, pp. 5–9). It is during this phase that the teacher assumes a more traditional teaching role in gathering information from students about their experiences in the exploration phase.

Concept Application Phase.   During the final phase of the learning cycle, the **concept application** phase (sometimes called the expansion phase), students apply what they have learned in the first two phases of the learning cycle to new situations or problems. In this last phase of the learning cycle, the students apply the new concept and/or reasoning pattern to additional examples. The application phase provides children with the opportunity to use new ideas or terms in different situations. This phase permits students to generalize their learning, thus reinforcing the newly acquired knowledge.

Research Findings

In reviewing the literature regarding the learning cycle, Lawson, Abraham, and Renner (1989) state, "the learning cycle approach appears to have considerable promise in areas of encouraging positive attitudes toward science and science instruction, developing better content achievement by students, and improving general thinking skills. It has shown superiority over other approaches, especially those that involve reading and demonstration-lecture activities. While science laboratory-based experiences have proved to be more effective than lecture techniques (Hykle, 1992), the learning cycle has been shown to be especially useful in the science classroom. Specifically, research has shown that learning cycle activities (1) increase a student's opportunity for social interaction (Marek & Methven, 1991), (2) provide opportunities for hands-on learning activities in the classroom (Barman, 1989; Marek & Methven, 1991), (3) assist students in developing scientific vocabulary (Barman, 1989), (4) facilitate students' development of problem-solving skills (Barman, 1989; Lawson, 1989), (5) aid in students' cognitive growth (Pollard, 1992; Rubin & Norman, 1989; Silberman & Zipp, 1986), (6) improve students attitudes toward science (Granger, 1986), and (7) help students build mental images of new ideas (Barman, 1989; Koran, Koran, & Baker, 1980).

Accommodation of the Needs of Culturally Diverse Learners

The original learning cycle dealt with science concept and process acquisition. The scaling approach used in this book has modified the learning cycle to accommodate the needs of culturally diverse learners. By incorporating English language acquisition opportunities and multiple modes of performance into the structure of learning cycle, a new teaching strategy emerges. This strategy, called scaling, incorporates the strengths of a hands-on/minds-on, inquiry-based approach to learning with a language acquisition model suitable for usage in bilingual/bicultural and regular science classrooms (Figure 8.3). Scaling, like learning cycle, is a three-step inquiry-based strategy for science teaching.

Rationale for Scaling.   Scaling (Science Content And Language Expansion) accommodates the needs of culturally diverse learners by providing (1) multiple modes of declarative knowledge representation, (2) an opportunity for science process acquisition, (3) a vehicle for English language acquisition, (4) peer tutoring in the student's "home language", (5) a cooperative learning environment, (6) a means for socialization between students, (7) an avenue for students to bring home learning into the school environment, and (8) the environment in which children can demonstrate their learning orally, verbally, and visually.

The use of the three-tiered SCALE technique described in this chapter allows teachers to present declarative information to children by multiple modes of representation, that is, with real world objects or *realia*, icons, spoken words, written words, and pictures. Scaling uses an inquiry-based approach to learning which allows children to develop science process skills (e.g., observing, comparing, ordering, categorizing, relating, inferring, and applying). Limited English

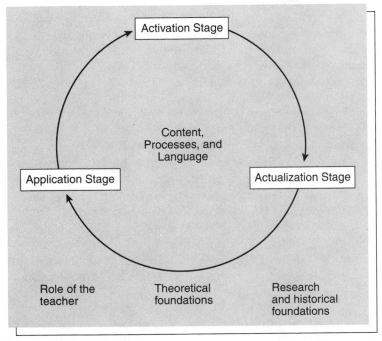

FIGURE 8.3   Scaling Strategy

proficient children in this instructional environment are paired with peers who have developed more competency in the English language; therefore, there is the opportunity for each child to acquire language skills and science concepts simultaneously. The activity-based approach fostered by scaling presents new information to children in a manner which encourages the activation of mental structures in the child's home or native language, while appending English "name tags" to objects and concepts. This approach assists children in attaching two sets of name tags to the same objects and events, one set of name tags in the child's native language and one set of name tags in English. Scaling decreases the chances that a child will develop two different mental structures for the same concept (one in English and one in the child's home language).

Scaling accommodates children's needs for social interactions by encouraging children to work in cooperative groups, in which together with others they are encouraged to negotiate meaning regarding the natural world. When scaling is used as an instructional technique, children are urged by the teacher to bring examples, analogies, metaphors, and other elaborations from their own experience into the science classroom: to connect their home learning to school learning. Finally, scaling allows students to present their new learning to the teacher and to their peers, to engage in reciprocal teaching in a manner which is culturally familiar and in keeping with their English language proficiency.

Activation Stage.   During the **activation stage** of the scaling technique, students activate their prior knowledge of the events, materials, and concepts that are being introduced in the class. Ms. Gonzales began the activation stage by allowing her students to explore the potato pistol. Each student investigated the potato pistol using his or her prior notions and knowledge. All of the students had prior experience in using straws and in eating potatoes. However, few of the students would be expected to have prior experience with "potato pistols." Most students would not possess mental structures to accommodate this new experience. There would probably be a lot of "oohing" and "aahing" in Ms. Gonzales's class as students manipulated the straws and potato plugs for the first time. The unexpected happened in class: pieces of potato shot across the classroom. Ms. Gonzales was providing a real world experience which helped students to develop a mental structure to accommodate the concept of air pressure. In addition, Ms. Gonzales was providing the opportunity for students to see, touch, hear, and in general manipulate a real world object (the potato pistol). During this stage children recall what they already know about the *realia* that they are manipulating. For bilingual students and for students not yet linguistically assimilated in the use of the English language, this is an opportunity to expand and/or develop their English vocabulary by learning the English names for physical objects and concepts.

Actualization Stage.   The **actualization stage** provides a time when the teacher assists students in building their vocabularies and using the formal language of science. Actualization is a time when students assume "ownership" of new knowl-

Activation engages students in manipulating realia. (© Jim Pickerell)

edge, a time when they construct a personal rendition of the science concept. In Ms. Gonzales's class, the students encountered the concept of "air pressure" and developed an operational definition for air pressure based on their experiences with the potato pistol. Sometimes, textbooks, audiovisual materials, and other sources of information are incorporated at this stage to assist students in developing the concept.

The actualization stage is the step in the learning process in which students first construct and name a new concept. It is a stage in the learning process that allows students to accommodate new learning. During the actualization stage, the teacher acts as a guide to channel the student's thinking, attempting to get students to construct appropriate labels for the relationships they have just discovered. The actualization stage lends itself to reciprocal teaching (Johnson & Johnson, 1987). As children share what they have learned with the teacher, the teacher shares the formal terminology of science (sometimes in more than one language) with the students. Teachers and students teach each other and learn from each other during this stage of scaling.

Application Stage.   The concept of air pressure developed in Ms. Gonzales's class could be expanded through related activities such as making a homemade barometer or an investigation into the workings of a squirt bottle. The **application stage** of scaling is necessary to extend the concept to new settings and new environments. Unless students are presented with numerous examples of the newly learned concept, their application of the concept will be constrained to the single setting in which the concept was first learned. In addition, this stage allows children to use the new concept to explain phenomena in their own lives in a different manner. A student may connect the concept of air pressure as illustrated by the potato pistol to the functioning of a staple gun that his or her father or mother uses at home or to a toy squirt gun or to a condiment dispenser stored in the refrigerator. The application stage of the scaling technique is a time for students to report formally to the teacher and to their peers what they have learned through the activity and through their interactions with their peers.

Theoretical Foundation of Scaling

Learning in the science classroom involves acquiring knowledge by means of a constructive process during which the learner interacts with the external world, mentally considers data, and renders data meaningful in terms of his or her prior knowledge. Learning is always an interpretive activity characterized by individual constructions (Tobin, 1989). Learning is the act of the individual learner. "To know" something requires that the learner receive, interpret, and relate incoming information to already existing knowledge. "Principles of constructivist epistemology are clearly evident in guided discovery science instructional models, particularly in the learning cycle" (Staver, 1991, p. 123) and in scaling techniques.

When using scaling techniques the role of the teacher is (1) to facilitate students' knowledge construction by designing learning experiences or tasks, (2) to provide the physical resources necessary to complete the tasks, (3) to establish a classroom climate in which students are free to discuss and exchange ideas, (4) to form cooperative groups for peer interactions, and (5) to foster sharing about the learning experience to mediate conversations about the new concepts. In the real world, "doing science" involves higher-order-thinking skills and problem solving, and it involves interacting and sharing with one's colleagues. Use of the scaling technique in the classroom allows children to function as scientists, formulate hypotheses, design experiments, gather data, interpret data, and make sense of the natural world.

Role of the Teacher

When scaling is used as a pedagogical strategy in the classroom, the role of the teacher changes from an authoritative source of information to a facilitator of learning. The "teacher in the science classroom is someone who understands that their role is to engage children in working with natural phenomena, someone who assists children in making sense of the world. A teacher is someone who cares about some part of the world and how it works and who wants to make it accessible to children" (Duckworth, 1987). During the activation stage of scaling technique, the teacher functions as an expediter and observer: someone who supplies the manipulative or instructional materials and watches and encourages children as they interact with those materials. The role of the teacher changes to that of a conductor or guide during the actualization stage of the

Scaling builds science concept knowledge, science processes, and language skills. (© Will Faller)

scaling process. During this stage, the teacher channels or focuses the students on the concept and vocabulary that they have just learned. Finally, during the application stage, the teacher serves as a controller, mediator, or reference librarian, directing students to new sources of learning or new places where the concept may be applied. The use of a scaling technique transforms the role of the teacher from a "sage on stage" to a facilitator of learning. Scaling allows the teacher to assist the child in building linguistic and cultural bridges between the home environment of the child and the school environment of the child.

CLASSROOM PRACTICE

This section describes a series of lessons which are appropriate for use with all learners, especially culturally diverse children in multicultural classrooms. These lessons provide specific examples of the scaling technique previously mentioned in this chapter. Note that these lessons are written in far more detail than normal. The reason for this detail is to provide a model of the types of questioning, coaching, mentoring, and so forth that should be used when working with students. While these lessons have been widely used with children in classrooms, they have been modified in this chapter to show their usefulness with culturally diverse learners. You are encouraged to modify each lesson such that it is appropriate for the particular students that you are teaching. Remember that many science lessons may be used with students of different ages and ability levels. For example, we may grow seeds in paper cups in kindergarten classrooms but also grow seeds hydroponically (e.g., aquaculture or growing in water) in graduate level science classes. While the activity may be the same, the activity's level of sophistication varies with the age and intellectual development of the learner.

Older elementary students or students in gifted and talented classes are typically capable of controlling more than one independent variable at a time. Frequently, students in upper elementary classrooms are capable of determining the "average" or mean during a number of trials and are able to use more sophisticated graphing techniques than younger children. Determining the instructional level of students is a decision best left to the professional discretion of the individual teacher.

Each of the scaling lessons presented in this section provides an opportunity for you and your students to construct investigations of natural phenomena together. Keep in mind that the extra detail provided in these lessons is to give you a "flavor" of the modifications necessary for lessons to meet the needs of culturally diverse students. You are encouraged to work with your students to develop plans for exploring the natural world through the use of operational questioning. During the activation stage, you should encourage students to explore phenomena briefly on their own or in small groups. When working with culturally diverse learners, especially those who are bilingual or limited English proficient, you should place a special emphasis on social interactions that allow students opportunities to develop their English language proficiency as they work with others. The activation stage, as used in the scaling lessons presented here, is used as a vehicle for activating the child's prior knowledge and for preparing students to integrate new learning with their existing mental structures. When working with bilingual or second language students, you should strive to (1) simplify the input (e.g., use a slower but natural speech rate with clear enunciation, avoid scientific jargon); (2) focus on the manipulative materials; (3) draw on the students' prior background and experiences; (4) expand, restate, and reinforce important ideas; (5) identify the key concepts and whenever possible translate (or have a peer or classroom aide translate) the naming words for manipulative materials and/or concept names into the student's home language; (6) encourage all students to engage actively in using manipulative materials, and (7) encourage all students to interact verbally with each other (California State Board of Education, 1990).

Scaled activities provide the opportunity for all students to become actively involved in the learning process. When using manipulative materials, be sure that you encourage female students to become actively involved in the learning process. Previous research has shown that female students tend to be passive observers in laboratory or hands-on settings and watch their male peers manipulate the materials. In making your classroom a culturally affirming environment for all students, be certain to engage all students in hands-on learning.

During the actualization stage, you should encourage students to design investigations which answer "What if . . . ?" and "What happens when . . . ?" questions. In other words, you should encourage students to formulate operational questions, questions that may be answered with the manipulative materials. In the past, many teachers who use the traditional learning cycle approach have focused on operational questioning during the exploration phase of learning cycle. When working with limited English proficient students or low verbal learners, that is, those who are struggling with vocabulary development, operational questioning is best done in groups in which students receive assistance in acquiring and negotiating meaning for new vocabulary words.

Finally, during the application stage of the scaling process, you should encourage students to connect their new learning to their prior experiences. For example, if you are teaching the concept "fruit" (operationally defined as a package of seeds produced by the parent plant), you should encourage students to mention fruits with which they are familiar. What fruits has the student eaten or grown or seen? For children in the multicultural classroom, the application stage might be better viewed as an expansion stage during which the student brings home learning to class and combines it with school learning. Students should be encouraged to apply new learning to new situations. At the same time, they should be encouraged to apply new learning as an explanation for experiences they have had in life.

From a linguistics viewpoint, the activation stage should be viewed as a time when students manipulate real-world materials and activate their prior knowledge about those materials. The actualization stage should be used to invent the new science concept, while building English language proficiency. The application stage should be a time when students apply the newly learned concept to new situations and a time when they use the new concept to explain events or phenomena in their prior experience.

ACTIVITY 8-1 ■ BOTTLE ROCKET

Purpose: Scaling lesson to illustrate the concepts of air pressure or the laws of thermodynamics.

Content

Theme: energy

Basic field of study: physical science

Concept: force (A force is a push or pull.)

Related concepts and/or terms: work, energy

Processes: communicating, observing, ordering, relating, inferring, applying

Activation Stage

Teacher Preparation Work (To be done before class): Collect a sufficient supply of empty detergent bottles to ensure one for each group in the class. Using a pair of pliers, remove the cap from the bottle and the plastic "stem" from inside the center of the top of the bottle. Wash out the bottles with clean water to remove the excess soap and/or detergent. Allow the bottles to dry before using them in class.

Materials (for each group):

one empty detergent bottle (see teacher preparation work)
one ball of clay

one thin plastic soda straw

three thicker plastic soda straws (thicker than the straw used on the "rocket launcher")

Procedure:

1. Have the students assemble the "bottle rocket launcher." In assembling the launcher, place the thin straw at the top of the detergent bottle and mold the clay around the straw such that the top of the bottle is sealed off. Have the students check to be certain that air can escape only through the straw.

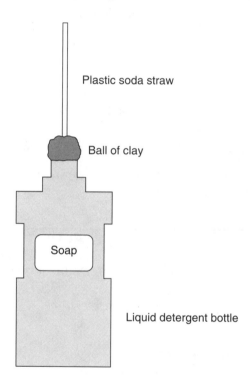

Plastic soda straw

Ball of clay

Soap

Liquid detergent bottle

2. Assemble a "rocket" by placing a small amount of clay on one end of a soda straw (a straw with a larger diameter than the straw used on the "rocket launcher" (figure on next page).
3. Instruct the students to "test fire" their bottle rockets. Place the rocket on top of the launcher and squeeze the center of the detergent bottle. What happens?
4. If you have a large number of limited English proficient students in your class, take time to name the objects that you are working with (e.g., *straw, clay, detergent bottle*). Also, explain that you are making a model of a *rocket launcher* and a *rocket* from these materials, that the clay serves as a *payload*, etc. Be sure to build the student's vocabulary as you work.
5. When all students have had the opportunity to test fire their rockets, as-

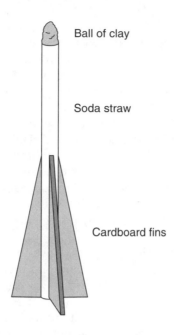

Ball of clay

Soda straw

Cardboard fins

A
C
T
I
V
I
T
I
E
S

semble the students in a large group setting and allow the students to discuss their observations about the bottle rockets.

Actualization Stage

Materials:

one empty detergent bottle (see teacher preparation work)
one ball of clay
one thin plastic soda straw
three thicker plastic soda straws (thicker than the straw used on the "rocket launcher")
metric measuring tapes
graph paper
calculators (optional for use with older students when multiple rocket "firings" will be used and the average or mean distance that the rocket travels will be calculated)

Procedure:

1. Encourage the students to generate a list of questions that they could answer with the materials that they have. For example: What would happen if the rocket were shorter? Longer? What would happen if I squeezed the squirt bottle harder? Softer? What would happen if I had a heavier payload (ball of clay) on the rocket? What would happen if I added paper "fins" to my rocket? How many fins should I add? Where should I place the fins?

**A
C
T
I
V
I
T
I
E
S**

2. Assume that the students have decided to investigate the "squeeze" as the important variable in the "bottle rocket" system. Allow the students to define operationally (e.g., formulate a working definition) a soft, medium, and hard squeeze. For example, the students may decide that a soft squeeze means a quick, light squeeze of the detergent bottle, while a hard squeeze is a two-handed squeeze.

3. After identifying the squeeze as the independent variable in the activity, allow the students to define the dependent variable (normally it would be the distance that the "rocket" travels) or responding variable.

4. Before conducting the activity, have the students identify extraneous variables (e.g., those variables which could influence the "flight" of the "rocket") which the class will all hold constant. Students might identify the angle of the launcher, the length of the straw, and the mass of the payload as extraneous variables.

5. Establish a means of recording results. Have the students decide how each group will collect and record data and present their findings to the class. You may wish to have students make a table of data or a bar graph of their results.

6. After students have had the opportunity to design and conduct an investigation using their "bottle rockets," engage students in discussing their results. Finally, introduce students to the concept of *force* (a force is a push or pull). Encourage the students to talk about the relationship between the squeeze on the "rocket launcher" and the distance that the "rocket" travels.

Application Stage

Materials:

bottle rocket launcher (assembled previously)	scissors tape
straws	miscellaneous art supplies (e.g.,
glue	string, markers)
cardboard	

Procedure:

1. Ask students the following question: Could we build a better "rocket"? Provide students with a box of scrap materials and allow the students to design and test fire rockets of other designs. When students have developed the "best possible rocket" allow them to share their designs with the rest of the class. (Note: Sharing may include drawings, graphs, diagrams, actual models and so forth: allow multiple means of reporting to accommodate the needs of limited English proficient students.)

2. The rocket travels because of air pressure: the force with which we squeeze the bottle. What is another example of a force, something that results in a push or a pull?

3. Can you think of an example of a force that you have seen or experienced?

4. How is your "rocket" like a real rocket? How is it different?

ACTIVITY 8-2 ■ BUBBLEOLOGY

Purpose: Scaling lesson to illustrate the concept of a bubble or a film.

Content

Theme: scale and structure

Basic field of study: physical science

Concept: bubble (A bubble is a thin film of liquid forming a ball around air or gas.)

Related concepts and/or terms: film, gas, surface tension

Processes: observing, communicating, comparing, applying

Activation Stage

Materials:

straw	water
liquid detergent	paper towels (for clean-up)

Procedure:

1. Instruct the students to pour some water on their tables or desks. Add four or five drops of liquid detergent to the puddle of water.
2. Insert a soda straw into the water and blow a bubble. What happens?
3. Be certain to help children with limited English proficiency name the manipulative objects.

Actualization Stage

Materials:

straw	metric measuring tapes
liquid detergent (several different brands may be desirable)	calculators (optional for older students for determining the
water	"average" size of bubble footprints
paper towels (for clean up)	

Procedure:

1. Allow the students to generate a series of operational questions about bubbles, such as, How can you make a larger bubble? A smaller bubble? What would happen if we used a larger straw? A smaller straw? What would happen if we used a stronger concentration of detergent? A weaker concentration? What would happen if we used different brands of detergent?
2. Assume that the students wanted to investigate the concentration of detergent as an independent variable. Prepare solutions of different concentrations of soap solution (e.g., one drop of soap/milliliter, two drops/milliliter).
3. A dependent variable could be the size of the bubble footprint (operationally defined as the diameter of the bubble or the "ring" left on the table after the bubble pops).

4. Have the students identify extraneous variables that everyone will control in the same fashion, such as, size of the straw, method for measuring the bubble footprint, and brand of detergent to be used.
5. Allow the students to conduct an investigation to determine how the concentration of the soap solution affects the size of bubble they make. Depending on the age of the students, tables of data and graphs are appropriate methods of recording data. With older students, you may wish to have them record the "average" size of the bubble (an average of three or five or ten trials).
6. During this phase you should develop the concept of **bubble**. (A bubble is a thin film of liquid forming a ball around air or gas.)
7. Be certain to allow students to engage in peer tutoring and assist others in their group with naming the objects and the concepts that they are encountering: in English and in the child's home language when appropriate.

Application Stage

Materials:

straw
liquid detergent (several different
    brands may be desirable)

water
pieces of insulated copper wire
paper towels

Procedure:

1. Allow students to continue investigating bubbles by asking some operational questions (have students share their answers with others in the class): Can you blow a "square" bubble? What happens when two bubbles touch? Can you make a "long lasting" bubble?
2. How are bubbles useful in the real world?
3. Where do we use films of materials in the real world?

(Note: Provide students with many opportunities for expressing what they have learned: students may use journal entries, drawings, and/or oral reporting for sharing their knowledge with teachers and with peers.)

ACTIVITY 8-3 ■ DANCING RAISINS

Purpose: Scaling activity to illustrate the concept of energy conversion.

Content

Theme: patterns of change

Basic field of study: physical science

Concept: Energy can be converted from one form to another.

Related concepts and/or terms: chemical change, gas, buoyancy

Processes: observing, communicating, comparing, ordering, relating

Activation Stage

Materials:

vinegar	beaker, or clear plastic container, or a
baking soda	glass
raisins	

Procedure:

1. Fill a beaker one-third full of vinegar and one-third full of water. Slowly add one teaspoon of baking soda to this mixture.
2. Add five or six raisins to the container. What happens?
3. Be certain to move around the classroom and assist students in naming the objects and phenomena that they are seeing and experiencing. For example, *raisins, vinegar, baking soda, beaker, foam, bubbles.*

Actualization Stage

Materials:

vinegar	beaker, or clear plastic container, or a
baking soda	glass
raisins	stopwatch or other timer

Procedure:

1. Allow the students to generate a list of operational questions (questions that can be answered using the manipulative materials), such as, What would happen if more vinegar were used? Less vinegar? What would happen if more raisins were added to the liquid? Fewer raisins? What would happen if more baking soda were used? Less baking soda?
2. Select one or more activities for the students to investigate. For example, vary the concentration of the vinegar. The concentration of the vinegar would be the independent variable and the length of time that the raisins "danced" or continued to move up and down in the container would be the dependent variable. Allow the students to identify extraneous variables which all students will control.
3. Work with the students to find ways to observe and record data. This may include producing a table of data and a graph showing the result(s) of their investigation.
4. Allow time for students to share their results with others in the class.
5. Assist students in developing the concept of **chemical change**, or the concept that energy can be changed from one form to another (e.g., chemical energy to mechanical energy).
6. Be certain that limited English proficient students receive help, peer tutoring, or teacher-assisted instruction, in expressing their ideas in English.

Application Stage

Materials:

vinegar	empty soda bottle
baking soda	cork (to fit the top of the soda bottle)

Procedure:

1. Fill a soda bottle one-fourth full of vinegar. Add two or three teaspoons of baking soda to the bottle. Immediately stopper the bottle with a cork. Observe carefully. What happens? What type of energy is produced when baking soda is added to vinegar? What kind of energy is produced by this chemical reaction? What energy transfers are involved in this activity?
2. What are some sources of energy that you have seen before?
3. Can you think of instances of energy transfer that you have seen in your life? Discuss these with others in your class.
4. Provide opportunities for students to express what they have learned in various ways. Allow for journal writing, drawings, or demonstrations and so forth.

ACTIVITY 8-4 ■ MYSTERIOUS MINERALS

Purpose: Scaling activity to illustrate the concept of mineral.

Content

Theme: patterns of change

Basic field of study: earth sciences

Concept: Minerals can be grouped based on their physical characteristics.

Related concepts and/or terms: hardness, luster, color, cleavage

Processes: observing, communicating, comparing, ordering, applying

Activation Stage

Materials:

10 to 15 mineral specimens for each group of students

Procedure:

1. Ask the students to observe the minerals and determine a list of their characteristics.
2. In what way(s) are minerals alike?
3. In what way(s) are minerals different?
4. How could minerals be grouped? Share your system of grouping minerals with the class. (Note: Be certain that limited English proficient students receive assistance in naming terms such as *mineral, hardness,* and so forth.)

Actualization Stage

Materials:

10 to 15 minerals (try to select typical specimens that are the same as those shown in the filmstrip or movie)
filmstrip or movie on minerals

Procedure:

1. Ask the students to identify the minerals they have been working with using the examples that they saw during the movie or filmstrip. Allow the students to share with others the reasons for their decision-making.
2. Following the discussion, introduce the terms **mineral**, **luster**, **hardness**, **color**, and **cleavage** and explain that these are physical characteristics which scientists use to group or classify minerals.

Application Stage

Materials:

10 to 15 different mineral specimens (specimens not previously used by the students)
mineral identification guides
field hardness testing kit (optional)

Procedure:

1. Explain to the students that they are mineral detectives and that their "job" is to identify each of the "unknown" minerals using the mineral identification guides. (Note: Allow students multiple means of performing what they have learned, such as, charts, tables of data, and oral reporting.)

ACTIVITY 8-5 ▪ WHAT COLOR IS BLACK?

Purpose: Scaling activity to illustrate the concept of color.

Content

Theme: patterns of change

Basic field of study: physical science

Concept: Chromatography is the process of separating the parts of a mixture.

Related concepts and/or terms: solutions, mixtures, capillary action, color

Processes: observing, comparing, communicating, ordering, relating, inferring

Activation Stage

Teacher Preparation Work (to be done before class): Prepare chromatography strips such that there is one strip for each group of students. Cut strips from commercially available coffee filters and mark the strips in 1 centimeter increments. Place a large "dot" of black ink from a water soluble black felt tipped pen on the "0" mark.

Materials:

beakers or clear plastic cups   chromatography strip
pencil and masking tape

ACTIVITIES

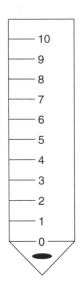

Procedure:

1. Place 1 or 2 centimeters of tap water in the bottom of the beaker or a clear plastic cup.
2. Lightly tape the coffee filter (the chromatography strip) to a pencil and suspend the pencil on the lip of the cup such that the tip of the paper just touches the surface of the water.
3. Observe for the next 10 minutes, recording your observations. What happens?
4. After the water has reached the 10 centimeter mark of the filter paper (chromatography paper), remove the paper and allow it to dry.
5. What colors were in the black ink? (Note: As students work in small groups, move around the classroom and assist limited English proficient students in naming the materials they are using.)

Actualization Stage

Materials:

filmstrip or movie on color

Procedure:

1. Allow the students to discuss their observations with others. Encourage the students to formulate a series of operational questions about this phenomenon, such as, What would happen if we used a different color ink? What would happen if we left the filter paper in the water for a longer time? What would happen if we used more ink?
2. Show the students a film or movie on light and color.
3. Ask the students to explain what happened to their black "dot" in accordance with the new knowledge presented in the filmstrip or video.

4. Following the discussion, introduce the terms **color**, **chromatography**, **mixture**, and **capillary action**. (Note: Allow for peer tutoring, especially for limited English proficient students.)

Application Stage

Materials:

coffee filters and pattern for cutting the filters (figure on page 204)	masking tape
	beakers or clear plastic cups
water soluble colored markers (several different colors)	scissors
	metric ruler

Procedure (instructions for students):

1. Using the pattern (page 204), cut out four or five chromatography strips from pieces of filter paper and mark each strip in 1 centimeter increments.
2. Place a large "dot" of ink from the felt tipped pens on each strip of paper. Place one color on each strip.
3. Predict what colors may appear as the water is absorbed by the filter paper.
4. Tape each strip to a pencil and suspend the pencil on the top of the beaker or cup as you did with the first chromatography strip.
5. Write down your observations.
6. When the water reaches the 10 centimeter mark, remove it from the beaker or cup. Were your predictions correct?
7. Share your findings with others. (Note: Allow for oral, verbal, and pictorial sharing of new learning.)

ACTIVITY 8-6 ■ MAGIC MILK

Purpose: Scaling activity to illustrate the concept of surface tension.

Content

Theme: patterns of change

Basic field of study: Physical science

Concept: surface tension

Related concepts and/or terms: molecular attraction, molecules

Processes: observing, communicating, comparing, relating, inferring, applying

Activation Stage

Teacher Preparation Work (to be done before class): Allow the milk to warm to room temperature for best results. Cold milk may be used in this activity but prior experience has shown that slightly warmed milk is best.

Materials (for each group):

milk	heavy duty paper plates or shallow
food coloring (three or four colors)	trays
liquid detergent	eye dropper

A
C
T
I
V
I
T
I
E
S

Procedure:

1. Pour some milk into a paper plate such that the bottom of the plate is covered with milk.
2. Instruct the students to place two or three drops of each color of the food coloring at different locations on the surface of the milk. For example, there would be a spot of yellow food coloring at one corner of the plate, a spot of red coloring at another location, and so forth.
3. When the surface of the milk is very still, instruct the students to add one or two drops of liquid detergent to the plate. Observe what happens. (Note: When working with limited English proficient students, be sure to name the manipulative objects, that is, paper plate, soap or liquid detergent, milk, the colors of the food coloring, and so forth.)
4. Encourage the students to present their observations to others in the class.

Actualization Stage

Materials (for each group):

heavy weight paper plates or   liquid detergent
   shallow trays   black pepper

Procedure:

1. Instruct the students to cover the bottom of their paper plates with water.
2. Cover the surface of the water lightly with black pepper.
3. When the water in the plate is very still, add one or two drops of liquid detergent. What happens?
4. Introduce the students to the term **surface tension**. Ask the students to explain how the milk activity and the pepper activity are alike? Different?
5. Allow the students to design other activities in which they investigate phenomena. For example, what would happen if we used skim milk instead of whole milk? What would happen if we used another brand of liquid detergent?
6. Encourage the students to record their activities and their findings in a journal or a science notebook, to share their findings with others.

Application Stage

Materials:

sewing needle
beaker or clear plastic cup
water

Procedure:

1. Can you get the sewing needle to float on the surface of the water? What concept does this illustrate?
2. Lead the class in a discussion of surface tension. What is surface tension? (Have the students operationally define the concept.) How is surface tension useful? Can you think of instances of surface tension that you might have

seen before? Have the students relate the new learning to their home learning.

3. Report what you have learned about surface tension through a word web, a journal entry, or a drawing.

ACTIVITY 8-7 ■ PLANTING A MOLD GARDEN

Purpose: Scaling activity to illustrate the concept of mold growth.

Content

Theme: systems and interactions

Basic field of study: life sciences

Concept: Mold is a living thing.

Related concepts and/or terms: fungi, characteristics of living things, spores, hypha, reproduction

Processes: observing, communicating, comparing, ordering, categorizing, relating, inferring, applying

Activation Stage

Teacher Preparation Work (to be done 2 to 4 days before the activity): Begin bread mold cultures for each group. Place small cubes of bread in individual plastic "baggies." Add two or three drops of water to each bread cube and seal the plastic container. Place the "baggies" in a warm, dark place to facilitate mold growth.

Materials (for each group):

Bread mold
Hand lens or tripod magnifier or dissecting microscope

Procedure:

1. Present the students with a bread mold colony. Allow the students to discuss what they see and report their observations to others in their group.
2. Have the students draw their bread mold. (For limited English proficient students, name the terms bread mold, baggie, and so forth.)
3. Lead the class in a discussion of bread mold. What is bread mold? Where does it come from? On what kind(s) of materials does mold grow?

Actualization Stage: (This activity will take several days to complete. Allow time for mold growth to occur.)

Materials:

plastic bags   magnifiers
eye droppers   bread cubes

Procedure:

1. Select materials on which you think mold will grow. Also select some materials that you think will not encourage the growth of mold. Place these materi-

als in a baggie and put several drops of water on each one. Place the sealed baggies in a dark area and allow mold to grow for several days.

2. What conditions are most favorable for mold growth? Have students design activities in which they investigate mold growth. For example, does mold grow better in light or in darkness? In hot, warm, or cold places? How much water does mold need to grow? A little? A lot? Have students identify independent variables (variables which they will control) and change those variables.

3. After several days, examine the mold gardens. Where did mold grow best? On what types of materials? Under which conditions?

4. Have students develop plans for reporting their findings to others.

5. Develop the concept that mold is a living thing and that mold grows better under certain conditions than others.

6. You might want to show a filmstrip or movie at this stage of the scaling process. Since mold is difficult to observe, even with hand lenses, it might be useful to show a filmstrip or movie which assists students in focusing on the critical attributes of the mold organism.

Application Stage

Materials:

Basic art supplies: crayons, markers, colored pencils, drawing paper

Procedure:

1. Have the students discuss mold. Have you seen mold before? Where?

2. Is mold useful? How? Is it harmful? How? Write a journal entry or make a word web or concept map describing your knowledge of mold.

3. What are the characteristics of living things? How are all living things alike? How are they different? Make a chart showing the characteristics of living things.

4. How is mold like other living things? How is it different?

5. Assist students in connecting their prior knowledge of mold to their newly gained school knowledge of mold.

ACTIVITY 8-8 ■ BOBS AND STRINGS

Purpose: Scaling activity to illustrate the law of the pendulum.

Content

Theme: systems and interactions

Basic field of study: physical science

Concept: Energy can be transformed from one kind to another.

Related concepts and/or terms: pendulum, bob, kinetic energy, potential energy, work, period of a pendulum

Processes: observing, communicating, comparing, relating, inferring, applying

A
C
T
I
V
I
T
I
E
S

Activation Stage

Materials:

bob (any objects may be used for the pendulum bobs, e.g., washers, stoppers, large paper clips)
string

Procedure:

1. Construct a hand-held pendulum by attaching a weight to a string and releasing the pendulum.
2. Lead the students in a discussion of ways to make the pendulum go faster and slower.
3. If you have a large number of limited English proficient students in your class, take time to name the objects that you are working with (e.g., bobs, washers, string). Also, explain that you are making a **pendulum** and that pendulums are sometimes used in clocks. Be sure to assist students in developing their vocabularies as they work.

Actualization Stage

Materials:

bobs
string
timer or wrist watch

Procedure:

1. Lead the students in reporting their findings on factors that influence the movement of the pendulum. Have the students formulate a series of operational questions that may be answered using the pendulum, such as, Does the mass affect the movement of the pendulum? Does the length of the string affect the movement of the pendulum? Does the color of string affect the movement of the pendulum?
2. Have the students develop investigations to determine which factors affect the movement of the pendulum. Students could vary the length of the strings on their pendulums; one group could have a string 50 centimeters long, while another has one 100 centimeters (1 meter) long, and so forth (Table 8.1). In this instance the length of the string is the independent variable and the

TABLE 8.1   Pendulum Data Sheet #1

Length of the String (centimeters)	Period of the Pendulum (swings/minute)
50	
100	
150	
200	

TABLE 8.2 Pendulum Data Sheet #2

Number of washers	Period of the Pendulum (swings/minute)
1	
2	
3	
4	
5	

number of swings per minutes is the dependent variable. Have the students construct a table of data to record their results.

3. Allow the students to discuss their results with their peers.

4. You may wish to have students investigate other variables associated with the pendulum, such as the mass attached to the pendulum. In this instance, the number of washers attached to the pendulum could be used as the independent variable, while the number of swings of the pendulum per minute would be the dependent variable. Have the students make a table of data to record their results (Table 8.2).

5. When working with the pendulum, have the students identify and control extraneous variables, that is, other factors which might influence the period of the pendulum.

6. Work with the students to develop and operationally define the concepts of potential and kinetic energy. **Potential** energy is stored energy, operationally defined as the energy that the pendulum has at its maximum release point. **Kinetic** energy is energy of motion, the energy that the pendulum has while it is moving. In a pendulum system, potential energy can be changed into kinetic energy.

7. Encourage the students to record their activities and their findings. For older children, use multiple trials and record the "average" result.

8. When working with limited English proficient children, encourage peer tutoring. Encourage children to apply English name tags to the science objects and concepts that they are encountering in class.

Application Stage

Materials:

bobs
string
timer or wrist watch

Procedure:

1. Ask the students to make the best possible pendulum: one that will make the most swings in a minute. Next, ask the students to construct another pendulum that will make the fewest possible swings in a minute.

2. Have the students report their findings to others. Allow for multiple means of reporting (writing, drawings, oral reporting, and so forth).

ACTIVITY 8-9 ■ FAIR AND UNFAIR GAMES

Purpose: Scaling activity to illustrate fair and unfair games.

Content

Theme: patterns of change

Basic field of study: life science (genetics)

Concept: Possibilities and probabilities are different entities.

Related concepts and/or terms: probability, fair games, unfair games, random selection

Processes: observing, communicating, comparing, ordering, categorizing, relating, inferring, applying

Activation Stage

Materials (per person):

1 penny (any coin will do)

Procedure:

1. Flip a penny 100 times and record each flip on a chart using "tick" marks (Table 8.3). What did you expect to happen? What actually happened?
2. What are the two possible outcomes? Does "heads" appear at the same frequency as "tails"?
3. Is flipping a coin a fair game (A fair game is one in which each outcome occurs in about the same number of times)?
4. If working with young children, a discussion of coins and their value is a natural extension of this activity at this time.

Actualization Stage

Materials (per person):

thumb tacks

TABLE 8.3   Coin Outcome Data Sheet

Number of heads	Number of tails

**A
C
T
I
V
I
T
I
E
S**

TABLE 8.4   Thumb Tack Outcome Data Sheet

Point up	Point down

Procedure:

1. Flip a thumb tack 100 times in the same fashion that you flipped the coin (Table 8.4). What are the possible outcomes (answer: point up and point down)? Will the thumb tack land point up as often as it lands point down? Record your findings on a table of data using "tick" marks.
2. Does each possibility (point up or point down) occur with equal frequency? Is flipping a thumb tack a "fair" game? Why or why not?
3. Lead students in a discussion of the concept. A **possibility** is an expected outcome. A **probability** is the chance of obtaining that outcome.

Application Stage

Procedure:

1. From your own experiences, what are some fair games? Some unfair games?

 CHAPTER SUMMARY

Through use of the scaling technique, students and teachers together can build a knowledge of science concepts, processes, and vocabulary. Scaling is a three-stage, inquiry-based approach to science instruction in which students function as scientists in investigating their physical world. During the first stage, the activation stage, students' prior knowledge is activated through the use of hands-on manipulative activities. The activation stage serves to activate students' prior knowledge and assist students in appending English name tags to existing "home language" when necessary. The actualization stage is a time when teachers and students work together to construct an understanding of natural phenomena. Through the process of asking operational questions, formulating hypotheses, controlling variables, collecting data, recording data, and interpreting data, students construct mental images of science concepts. By engaging in reciprocal teaching, through which students share their data and findings with their teacher and their peers and teachers share the formal language of science, both teachers and students together construct individual understandings of the world around them. Actualization involves each individual learner in constructing a personal rendition of scientific knowledge and its accompanying vocabulary. Finally, during the application stage, students apply newly acquired knowledge to new situations and use this same knowledge to explain events and phenomena that they have observed in the "real world." The application stage of scaling actively involves students in applying their newly formed knowledge of science and in preparing them for additional learning. The final stage of the scaling process assists students in building linguistic and cultural bridges between school learning and home learning.

TOPICS TO REVIEW

activation stage, 190
actualization stage, 190
application stage, 191

SCALE, 186
scientifically literate, 186

REFLECTIVE PRACTICE

1. Based on your previous experiences and your prior knowledge of science teaching and learning, how is scaling similar to "traditional" laboratory activities? How is scaling different from "traditional" laboratory activities?
2. Based on your previous life-long experiences, how is scaling similar to the way(s) that scientists explore the world? How is it different?
3. In your opinion, why is there an emphasis on integrating vocabulary development into scaling activities instead of teaching the vocabulary before the activity (the most commonly used model for teaching language)?
4. Many researchers have said that learning cycle (scaling is a modified form of learning cycle) activities are examples of thematic or integrated teaching. Do you agree or disagree with this statement? Justify your answer.

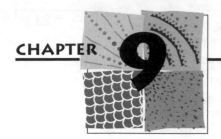

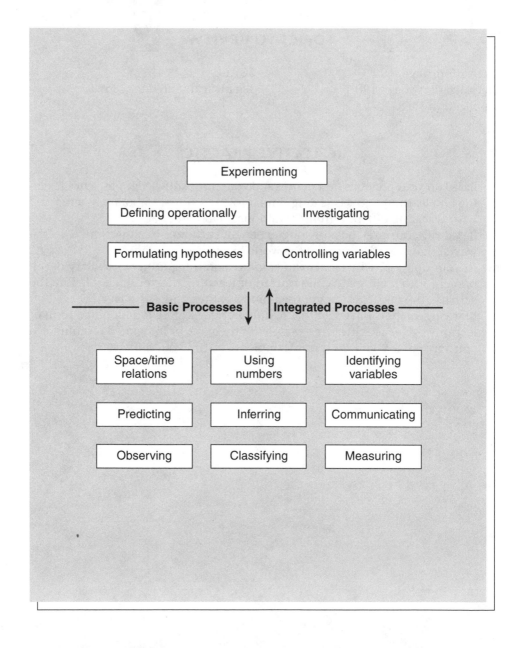

CHAPTER 9

CONSTRUCTING
A KNOWLEDGE OF
SCIENCE PROCESSES

 POINTS TO PONDER

1. What are science processes?
2. Why are science processes vital in science education?
3. What types of activities assist students in forming a knowledge of science?

HICKORY-HORNED DEVILS

y love of Hickory-horned Devils began during the summer between seventh and eighth grades. Two old majestic Walnut trees grew outside the front door of our farmhouse, which provided us with shade in the heat of summer and were a source of food during the cold winter months. These same trees were also a source of specimens for my insect collection. One warm spring day, I found a cluster of insect eggs on the underside of the leaves of one of the lower branches of the tree. Gingerly, I carried the leaf inside and placed it in a gallon-sized pickle jar with a piece of wire gauze on the top. Within a week, my eggs hatched and I was the proud owner of 20 small green larvae.

During the coming weeks, I "fed" my larvae Walnut leaves more and more frequently; once a day at first and later four or five times a day. Gradually, the larvae became recognizable as Hickory-horned Devils. At maturity, they were 8 to 10 inches

long, with green bodies covered with vibrant white and black markings and large orange "horns" curved back over their heads. When an unsuspecting stranger approached
their jar, they would rear back on their hindlegs in a defensive posture. Among all
larvae in the insect world, the Hickory-horned Devil is certainly the fiercest looking.

Toward the middle of summer, my little Devils reached their maximum size and
one after another began to pupate in the bottom of the jar. Within a few weeks, the
pupa began to hatch. From each pupa, a newborn moth emerged. Slowly, the newly
hatched moths climbed on to the sticks in the jar. Each one firmly attached itself to a
branch while they pumped "blood" into their wings. In the heat of the summer sun,
their wings hardened. By nightfall, each newly hatched Royal Walnut Moth was ready
for its maiden flight. As I released the Royal Walnut Moths back into the natural
environment, I reflected on my weeks of observation. It had been a joy to know these
creatures for a short time. From egg to larva to pupa to adult, the life cycle of Citheronia
regalis had provided me with a source wonder and delight.

Observing creatures in their natural environment is still a source of delectation in
my life. I will always be grateful to Bea Derickson, my fifth grade teacher, who encouraged us to observe the world around us. Each day after lunch, she bundled us up in
coats and jackets and walked us through the woodlot on the school grounds. We observed that woodlot with her in the sunlight of autumnal splendor; in the cold, frozen
snows of winter; and in the warming days of spring. She taught us to walk softly and
quietly, to listen carefully, to look up as well as down. Mostly, she taught us to enjoy
looking and seeing. Observing is the most basic of the science processes, a skill that is
learned over time. It is the foundation upon which all other science processes are built.

"Science should be taught as science is practiced" (AAAS, 1990, p. xi) is an underlying theme of science education reform documents such as The Liberal Art of Science. In summarizing the status of science education, the American Association for the
Advancement of Science has stated that, "conventional science teaching suppresses
students' natural curiosity and leaves them with the impression that they are incapable
of understanding science" (1990, p. 28). From Bea Derickson, I learned that, even as a
child, I could investigate the natural world on my own and seek answers to my own
questions.

Too often, teachers have viewed science as a body of facts to be memorized. Renner
and Lawson state that traditional science teaching methods embrace the beliefs that
(1) teaching is telling, (2) memorization is learning, and (3) being able to repeat something on an examination is evidence of understanding (1973). The over-reliance in
elementary schools on expository teaching techniques has resulted in a situation in
which children tend to view science as a list of vocabulary words to be committed to
memory, rather than as a way of investigating the world. In addition to a heavy reliance on expository teaching techniques, elementary schools have overdepended on textbooks as the major sources of information and knowledge about science. Bea Derickson
engaged her students in doing science, not in reading about it.

In summarizing an investigation of ten recently published elementary science textbooks, Elliott (1987) stated that textbooks do not promote or encourage the development of scientific thinking or attitudes, and do not they engage students in applying
cognitive processes that are basic to understanding the content covered. I was able to
learn about the life cycle of the Royal Walnut Moth from first hand observation. Later,

*I would go to books to increase my knowledge base about these magnificent creatures,
but only after my curiosity had been aroused through my firsthand experiences.*

RESEARCH REGARDING SCIENCE PROCESSES

The thinking processes used by scientists to investigate the natural world are
referred to as scientific thinking processes. These same processes are readily learned
by children in classrooms that foster an inquiry or discovery-based approach to
learning. Science is the process of "finding out." It is the art of interrogating
nature, a system of inquiry that requires curiosity, intellectual honesty, skepti-
cism, tolerance for ambiguity, and openness to new ideas and the sharing of
knowledge. In making sense of the natural world, students should be able to
learn from direct experience, not vicariously. "Learning science" involves careful observation, experimentation, identification of salient variables, and precise,
accurate, and reliable measurements. The cornerstone of science learning is the
discovery or "rediscovery" of the laws implicit in data, constructing and testing
hypotheses, and challenging the predictive power of theories and models.

In describing the importance of science processes, the California Department of Education stated that a knowledge of science processes is vital for all
students including those for whom considerations of gender, ethnic and cultural backgrounds, and physical disabilities are of primary importance (1990).
Science processes are dynamic, higher-level thinking skills which help students
build an understanding of the natural world and its connection to our technologically advanced society. Mechling and Oliver summarized research into science processes by saying that competence in using process skills provides children with the ability to apply knowledge, not only to science, but outside the
classroom in everyday life (1983). These authors (Mechling & Oliver, 1983)
pointed out that science processes learned in childhood are useful in adult life as
we attempt to separate inferences from evidence in a systematic fashion.

Learning for all children begins as physical experience with objects. This
experience provides the student with a mental model or record of what she or
he has done and seen. From this mental model, the student is able to develop a
conceptual understanding of science. In writing of the role of science processes
in the classroom, Lawson and Renner (1975) stated that experience in manipulating objects and learning science through a hands-on instructional model helps
students to build operational structures that can ultimately lead them to think
abstractly about the world around them. Inquiry-based laboratory investigations
conducted in small cooperative groups proportionally benefit culturally diverse
students and white females (Cohen, Lotan, & Catanzarite, 1990). In addition,
research has shown that inquiry or discovery-learning activities which emphasize science processes enhance the intellectual development of students (Herron,
1952; Lawson, 1975; Lawson & Renner, 1975; & Renner & Lawson, 1973).

BASIC SCIENCE PROCESSES

Science processes may be divided into two types: basic processes and integrated processes. Basic processes may be viewed as empirical and/or analytic procedures which have been derived from scientific practice and which may be used as part of every student's daily life. Science processes are thinking processes that foster life-long learning. The simplest science processes are referred to as basic processes, while those which incorporate more than one process are referred to as integrated processes. Basic science processes include (1) observing, (2) classifying, (3) measuring, (4) communicating, (5) inferring, (6) predicting, (7) using space/time relationships, (8) using numbers, and (9) identifying variables.

Observing

Observing involves using one's senses, that is, seeing, hearing, tasting, smelling, feeling, and in general experiencing the natural world. The process of observing involves children in identifying and naming the properties of objects and events in the world around them. In operationally defining observation, Wolfinger (1984) said, "observation is a piece of information learned directly through the senses" (p.89).

As adults we frequently assume that children have a prior knowledge of objects and events in the world when, indeed, they do not. For all children, a strong foundation of observational knowledge, knowledge derived from watching, from looking, from experiencing the world, is vital to later success in science. Observing is the most basic of the science processes. All other science processes are built directly or indirectly on this scientific thinking process. Historically, children in the United States came to school with a knowledge of plants

Observing is a basic science process. (© Jim Pickerell)

and animals built on their experiences playing, working, and living in the natural world. This experiential learning base was often derived from a rural farm experience and included a knowledge of farm animals, growing crops, ponds and streams, and the interrelationships between people and the natural world.

Today, many children live in high-rise apartment buildings in inner cities paved with asphalt and concrete. Teachers can no longer assume that children come to school with a wealth of knowledge of the natural world. For many children, their experiences with plants are limited to potted house plants or decorative trees and shrubs. Children's prior knowledge of animals may be limited to invertebrate household pests and common household pets. Children's experiences with energy sources may be limited to a knowledge of electrical appliances and battery powered toys. Observation of the natural world, the ability to observe accurately without at first making judgments from those observations, is a vital science process which must be developed and nurtured in all children. Activity 9-1 is one way to develop scientific observation.

ACTIVITY 9-1 ▪ "GROWING" A BUTTERFLY

Grade Level: Primary, Intermediate, or Upper

Science Process: Observing

Materials:
butterfly eggs (approximately 3–5 per child)
plastic vial with cap
food for butterfly larva (depends on species, e.g., Spicebush Swallowtails feed on
  Spicebush, Monarch butterflies feed on milkweed)
ruler

Procedure:
1. Supply each child or cooperative group with butterfly eggs. Have the children observe the eggs and record their observations in a journal. Encourage young

children or children with limited English proficiency to make drawings as a means of recording their observations.

2. Once the eggs hatch, instruct the children to feed the larvae daily, to "water them" by sprinkling the food with water, to clean their "habitats," and to make daily observations on the larvae.

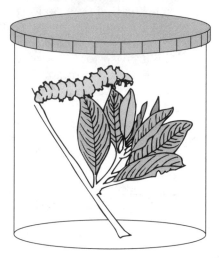

Observations:

Instruct the children to keep a journal of their observations of their butterflies. Some species will complete a life cycle in 4 to 6 weeks in warm weather.

ACTIVITY 9-2 ■ IT SMELLS LIKE . . .

Grade Level: Primary

Science Process: Observing

Materials:

10 film canisters or small opaque containers
10 food substances

Procedure:

1. Prior to the arrival of students in the class, puncture holes in the lids of 10 film canisters or similar containers. Place a different food (e.g., onion, apple, watermelon slice, cinnamon, orange peel, chocolate, oregano, banana, strawberry, celery) in the bottom of each container.
2. Have the students sniff each container and make a guess about its contents (without opening the container).
3. After students have made a guess about the contents of the container (Table 9.1), allow them to open the containers and check the accuracy of their observations.

TABLE 9.1   "It Smells Like . . ." Observations

Container Number	Guess as to Contents	Actual Contents
1		
2		
3		
4		
5		
6		

ACTIVITY 9-3 ▪ WHAT'S A BEETLE?

Grade Level: Primary or intermediate

Science Process: Observing

Materials:
beetle or drawing of a beetle

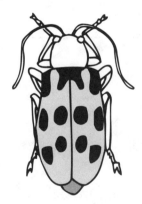

Procedure:

1. Present the students with a beetle or a drawing of a beetle.
2. Pass the beetle from person to person, asking the students to identify a characteristic of the beetle as it is passed. Make a list of observations on the board. While students at all grade levels need practice with observational processes, those in early grades need the most practice. Young children frequently lack the experiential base necessary for good observations and thus practice in making and stating scientific observations is vital at this age. Observation is the basis for almost all of the other science processes, practice in observational skills is desirable for students of all ages.

Classification

Classification is a science process which develops the ability of students to place objects into groups on the basis of the characteristics of the object. Classification can range from a simple task, such as grouping objects based on their colors, to highly complex classification systems which identify the genus and species of a living organism. Classifying may be operationally defined as arranging or distributing objects, events, or information representing objects or events in classes according to some method or system (Carin, 1993). Activities which develop classification expertise are those which involve sorting shapes, living things, and so forth by some common property.

Classification involves categorizing objects according to a predetermined property or set of properties. When working with culturally diverse learners, especially those with limited English proficiency, teachers should allow extra time to identify common attributes and build English vocabulary associated with those attributes. Names for colors, sizes, relative masses, and so forth should be mentioned as children work with real world objects. Whenever possible, *realia* (real world objects) should be used in classification activities. Older students should be encouraged to develop multistage classification systems on their own. A multistage classification system for insects is shown in Figures 9.1 and 9.2. From this picture of insects, we could develop a system for classifying insects: Some activities to develop classification skills are illustrated in the Activities 9-4 and 9-5.

ACTIVITY 9-4 ■ ATTRIBUTE BLOCKS

Grade Level: Primary Science

Science Process: Classifying

Materials:

attribute sheet or attribute blocks

Procedure:

1. Duplicate the attribute sheets (page 225) for the students.
2. Ask the student to cut out the shapes and group them by common characteristics or attributes.

Follow up Questions:

1. What are some of the ways we can group the objects?
2. What are some of the properties of the objects?
3. What shapes are the objects?
4. What sizes are the objects?
5. What patterns are there?
6. How many circles are there?

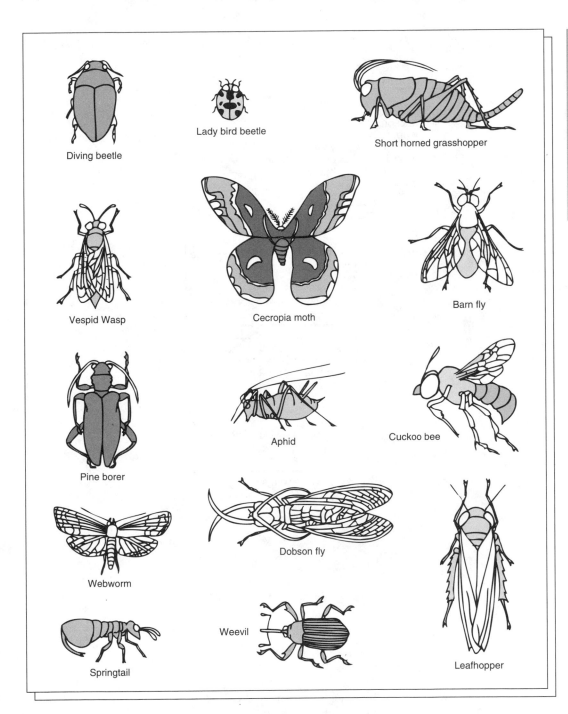

Diving beetle

Lady bird beetle

Short horned grasshopper

Vespid Wasp

Cecropia moth

Barn fly

Pine borer

Aphid

Cuckoo bee

Webworm

Dobson fly

Springtail

Weevil

Leafhopper

FIGURE 9.1   Insect Multistage Classification System

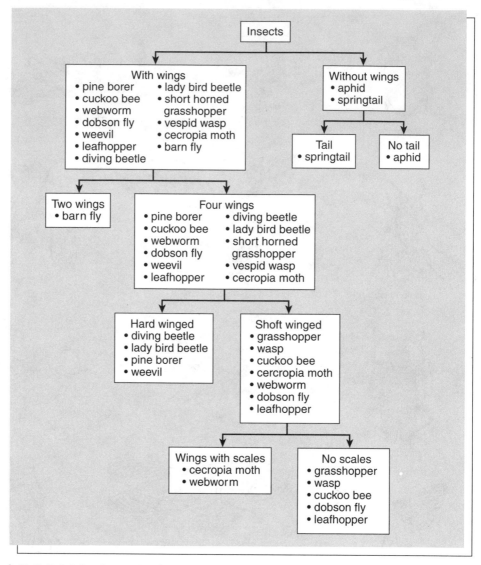

FIGURE 9.2   Insect Multistage Classification System

7. How many squares do you have?
8. How many triangles do you have?
9. How many of the objects are striped?
10. How many of the objects are spotted?
11. How many of the objects have a solid color?
12. How many of the objects are small?
13. How many of the objects are medium sized?
14. How many of the objects are large?

ACTIVITY 9-5 ▪ LEAVES

Grade Level: Intermediate or upper grades

Science Process: Classifying

Materials:
Leaves or leaf print sheet (page 226)

Procedure:
1. Using the leaf print sheet, ask the students to group the leaves.
2. Ask the students how the leaves are alike? Different? How could the leaves be grouped?

Measuring

Measuring can be defined as developing appropriate units of measurement for length, area, volume, time, and mass. Measuring at its simplest level involves comparing, that is, comparing an object of known dimensions with one of un-

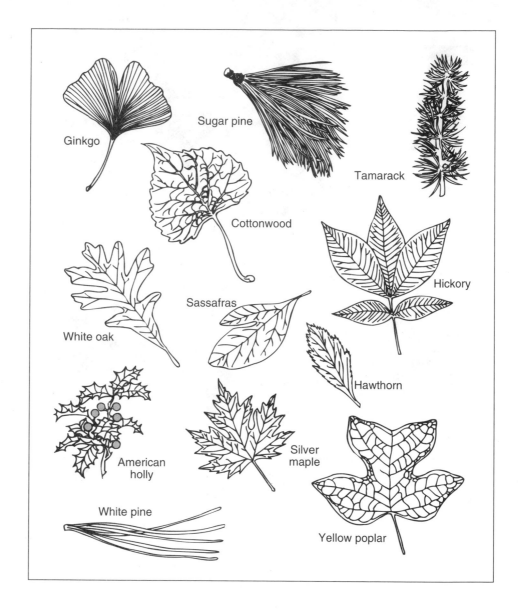

Ginkgo

Sugar pine

Tamarack

Cottonwood

Hickory

Sassafras

White oak

Hawthorn

American
holly

Silver
maple

White pine

Yellow poplar

known dimensions (California Department of Education, 1990). In measuring a line segment, a student compares the line segment (the object with unknown dimensions) with a ruler (an object with known or defined dimensions). According to Piaget, a child needs to have first attained the mental structures for conservation before he or she is able to understand measurement concepts (Wadsworth, 1978).

Conservation problems are some of the best-known illustrations of children's levels of developmental reasoning. Assume that a young child is given two rows

| FIGURE 9.3

| FIGURE 9.4

of pieces of candy. The child is allowed to count the pieces of candy and determine that each row holds exactly the same number of pieces. The adult aligns the candies such that there is a visible one-to-one correspondence between the pieces of candy in the top row and the bottom row (Figure 9.3).

The adult rearranges the candy in one row such that it is more spread out than the other row (Figure 9.4). Children who lack the mental structures for conservation will identify the spread out row of candy as containing more candies than the other row. Such children lack conservation of length. Indeed, most children learn to conserve length at about 8 years of age.

In identifying the "age appropriateness" of various measuring activities, Wadsworth (1978) points out there is a strong relationship between a child's age and the child's ability to conserve different quantities. A table showing various measurement tasks and children's typical age of mastery of conservation of such tasks is shown in Figure 9.5.

Measurement Unit	Age of Attainment
Length	6 to 7 years
Number	6 to 7 years
Area	7 to 8 years
Mass	7 to 8 years
Liquid	7 to 8 years
Weight	9 to 10 years
Volume	11 to 12 years

| FIGURE 9.5

Measurement is a basic science process. (© Jim Pickerell)

In assisting children to develop measurement proficiency, teachers should take care to be certain that the activity is appropriate for the age of the child. Young children, who have not yet mastered conservation of liquid, will have great difficulty understanding the properties of liquids (i.e., a liquid has a definite volume but will assume the shape of its container). For most children, informal measurement activities are appropriate from the kindergarten through third grade levels. Formal measurement using standard units of length, volume, and mass are appropriate for most children after the third grade level.

When working with large numbers of children who have recently arrived in this country, teachers should remember that most children in the world have been taught to use metric measurement units rather than English measuring units. For example, children who have recently arrived from Mexico are used to buying milk and gasoline by the liter (International System of Measurement [SI] spelling: litre) rather than by the gallon. These same children are accustomed to buying cloth by the meter (SI spelling: metre) rather than by the yard. Finally, they are used to buying flour and sugar by the "kilo" rather than by the pound. Since metric units of measurement are used in subsequent science instruction, teachers should encourage such children to continue using metric measuring units with which they are already familiar. Activities which assist children in mastering measurement competency are shown in Activities 9-6 and 9-7.

ACTIVITY 9-6   ■   PAPER CLIP MATH

Grade level: Primary

Science Process: Measuring

Materials:

10 small common household objects or a measuring sheet

Procedure:

1. Ask the student to measure the length of each object using a paper clip.
2. Instruct students to measure to the nearest whole paper clip.

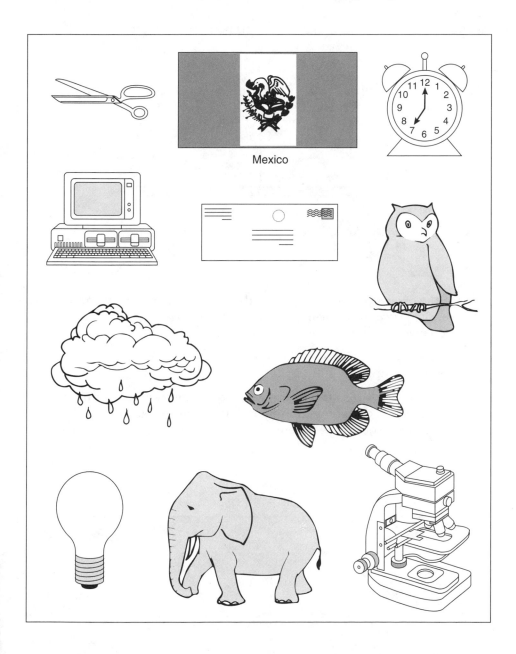

Mexico

ACTIVITY 9-7 ■ MEASURING MASS

Grade Level: Primary to Intermediate

Science Process: Measuring

Materials:

washers   ruler or stick
baking cups   10 household objects
thread

Procedure:

1. Construct a baking cup balance using the baking cups, thread, and stick. A completed balance is shown below.

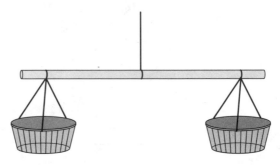

2. Place the objects in one pan (cup) of the balance. Add washers to the other cup until the two cups "balance." How heavy is each object? Record the weight of each object on a data table like Table 9.2.

Communicating

Communicating is the fourth of the basic science processes. Communicating frequently involves compiling information in graphic or pictorial form. It also involves describing objects and events in detail. Communicating is the scientific

TABLE 9.2   Baking Cup Balance Data Sheet

Object Name	Weight in Washers

thinking process that conveys ideas through social interchanges or social discourse. The process of communicating is actually the integration of language activities and mathematics in the science content area. The reporting of findings is central to the work of all scientists.

Communication can be understood as a means of passing information from one individual or group of individuals to another (Wolfinger, 1984). Communication in the elementary science classroom ought to involve multiple means for children to express what they have learned in science. Pictographs, histograms, charts, tables of data, pictures, songs, and models are alternative means for children to express what they are learning. While written and oral communication is vital in the life of every child, not all children feel comfortable expressing their knowledge in written or oral form. Teachers working with large numbers of culturally diverse learners ought to consider alternative means of communicating or sharing new learning among students. When children are presented with alternative means to express their new knowledge all children in the classroom benefit from the sharing.

ACTIVITY 9-8 ■ CANDY MATH

Grade Level: Primary to Intermediate

Science Process: Communicating

Materials (for each group):

1 bag of M & M®-like candies

Procedure:

1. Allow the students to open the bag of candy. Instruct the students to divide the candy by colors (put all red candies in one pile, all yellow in another pile, and so forth).
2. Complete the data table for the candy (Table 9.3). From the table of data, make a histogram or frequency distribution showing the distribution of colors of candy in the bag (page 232).

TABLE 9.3   Candy Color Distribution Table

Color of Candy	Number of Pieces

A C T I V I T I E S

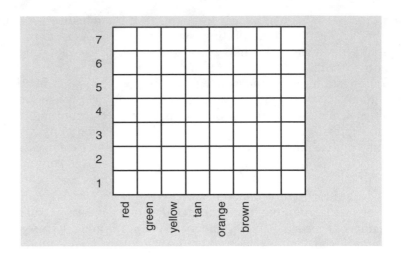

ACTIVITY 9-9 ■ ANIMAL LEGS

Grade Level: Intermediate

Science Process: Communicating

Materials (for each student):

1 animal data sheet (page 233)
1 piece of graph paper (below)

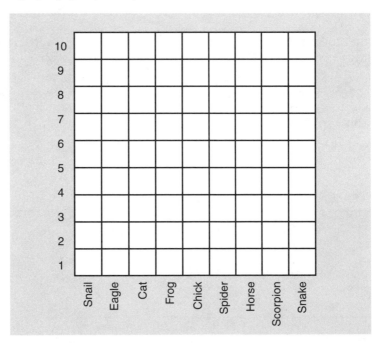

Procedure:

1. Have the students examine each animal picture and decide how many legs each animal has.
2. Make a bar graph comparing the number of legs each animal has.

Inferring

Inferring is a basic science process that deals with ideas that are remote in time and space. Inferring involves making a conclusion based on reasoning to explain a set of observations. Stating that the snow melts due to the heat of the sun is an example of an inference. Inferences are guesses. They are explanations based on observations. Questions can encourage students to make inferences.

A
C
T
I
V
I
T
I
E
S

For example: What can you infer from these data? What can you suggest is the reason? Can you give evidence to support your statement? When students have access to a large amount of data, we tend to refer to the inference as a conclusion. A conclusion is a special type of inference based on a wealth of data rather than on a few specific cases.

Making an inference involves students in conjecturing, concluding, or suggesting new relationships based on careful observations. The process of inferring involves drawing a conclusion from what we have observed. Activity 9-10, Mystery Boxes, is an example of an activity which encourages children to make inferences. In this activity, children guess the contents of the box based on their observations of the sound that the object makes as it moves inside the box, the relative mass of the box, and so forth. In this activity children are encouraged to use their observations and draw a conclusion which extends beyond their direct observations.

ACTIVITY 9-10 ■ MYSTERY BOXES

Grade Level: Primary to Upper Elementary

Science Process: Inferring

Materials:

10 mystery boxes (each box should contain an object commonly found in the classroom and should be sealed with tape so that children cannot "peek" at the object).

Procedure:

1. Pass the mystery boxes from child to child. Instruct the children to twist, turn, and generally manipulate the box.
2. Encourage children to write down (younger children may be asked to draw a picture) a guess as to the contents of the box (Table 9.4). Before opening the boxes, encourage children to share with others their "guesses" about the contents of the boxes and their reasons for making their "guesses."

TABLE 9.4 Mystery Box Recording Sheet

Box Number	Guess	Actual Contents
1		
2		
3		
4		
5		

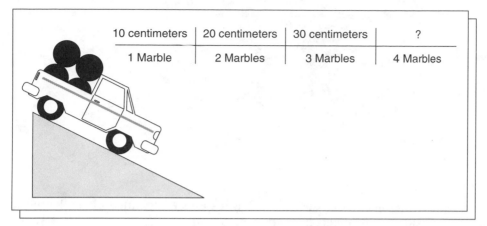

10 centimeters	20 centimeters	30 centimeters	?
1 Marble	2 Marbles	3 Marbles	4 Marbles

| FIGURE 9.6

Predicting

Predicting involves children in forecasting some future event based on solid evidence. Abruscato (1988) states that predictions are based on observations, measurements, and inferences about relationships between observed variables (p. 32). Unlike a guess, a prediction is based on careful observation. While inferring involves children in drawing a conclusion based on data, predicting involves children in making "informed guesses" (i.e., guesses based on data) about future occurrences. Inferences are an interpretation of past events, while predictions anticipate future events.

Suppose a child observed a toy truck traveling down an inclined plane (Figure 9.6). When the truck was carrying one marble, it traveled a distance of 10 centimeters. When the truck carried two marbles it traveled 20 centimeters from the ramp. Three marbles loaded in the truck resulted in a trip of 30 centimeters. Based on these data, what distance would the child predict the truck would travel if it were carrying four marbles? The child's prediction would be based on observations, that is, it would be an extrapolation or an extension beyond the existing data and it would be a prediction of a future event based on prior observation.

ACTIVITY 9-11 ■ MARBLE MANIA

Grade Level: Primary to Upper Elementary

Science Process: Predicting

Materials:

marble
1 piece of cardboard (approximately 20 cm. long)

1 ruler
1 piece of graph paper per student

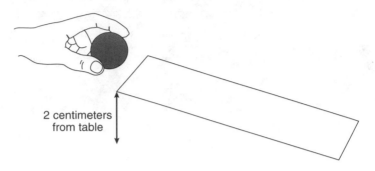

2 centimeters
from table

Procedure:

1. Elevate the piece of cardboard so that it forms an inclined plane. Raise the cardboard 2 centimeters from the table.
2. Place the marble on the cardboard and "let it go." How far does the marble travel?
3. Repeat the process, raising the cardboard 4 centimeters, 6 centimeters, and so on. Record your findings (Table 9.5) Make a line graph showing the relationship between the height of the ramp and the distance the marble traveled.

Using Space/Time Relationships

Space/time relationships are science processes that use plane and solid geometric shapes as well as length, area, mass, and volume as part of the observation. An understanding of space/time relationships includes the ability to recognize and name two-dimensional shapes (i.e., squares, rectangles, and circles), as well as the ability to identify and name three-dimensional shapes (i.e., prisms, pyramids, cubes, and ellipsoids). At its simplest level, space/time relationships may include references to ordinal numbers (first, second, third). Abruscato (1988) states that this process can be broken down into various categories, including, shapes, direction and spatial arrangement, motion and speed, symmetry, and rate of change. In terms of culturally diverse learners and white females, space/time relations are particularly important science processes since many research-

TABLE 9.5   Marble Mania Recording Sheet

Height of Ramp	Distance Traveled
2 centimeters	
4 centimeters	
6 centimeters	
8 centimeters	
10 centimeters	
12 centimeters	

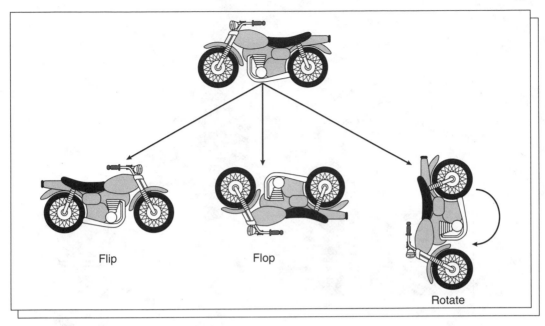

Flip   Flop   Rotate

| FIGURE 9.7

ers have identified these processes as prerequisites to success in science careers. Students who lack spatial skills are frequently unable to handle the complexity of advanced science courses. Spatial visualization skills at the lowest level include "flips," "flops," and "rotations" (Figure 9.7).

In terms of a notebook, a flip could be thought of as the position of a letter after one turns a page. A flop can be viewed as the position of a letter or numeral after one has turned up the page on a legal tablet. A rotation is the ability to turn mentally an object in a 360° plane. Mastery of spatial visualization processes includes the ability to manipulate objects mentally, for example, to twist, turn, and permute objects. At the high school and university levels, students who lack space/time relationships have extreme difficulty assembling laboratory apparatus from line drawings and in mentally flipping the structures of organic molecules. A knowledge of space/time relationships is vital for success in the advanced study of science and mathematics.

ACTIVITY 9-12 ■ SYMMETRY

Grade Level: Upper Elementary

Science Process: Space/time relationships

Materials:

1 mirror, 1 symmetry sheet (see page 238)

ACTIVITIES

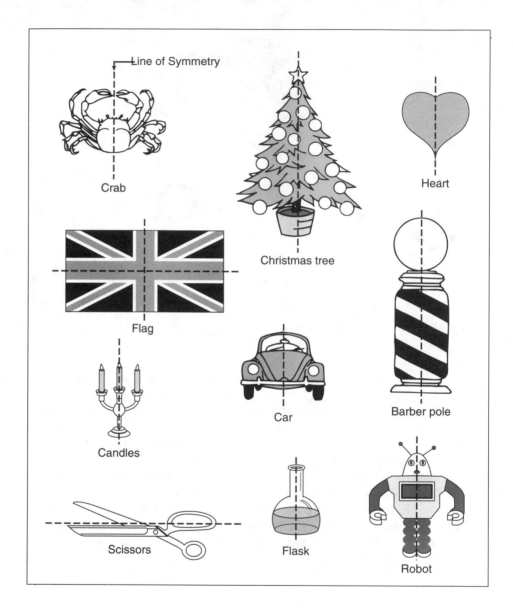

Procedure:

1. Examine each drawing and decide if the figure is symmetrical. Record your answer (Table 9.6).
2. Check your answer by placing a mirror on the dotted line on the figure. The dotted line is called the line of symmetry. If the figure is a mirror image of itself, that is, if one side is the same as the other when the figure is folded in half, then the object is symmetrical.

TABLE 9.6   Symmetry Data Sheet

Name of Object	*Symmetrical? (Yes or No)*
Crab	
Christmas tree	
Heart	
Flag	
Candles	
Car	
Barber pole	
Scissors	
Flask	
Robot	

Using Numbers

Using numbers is a basic process according to which numbers (other than those associated with the dimensions of an object) are used to describe or quantify an activity or an experiment. Processes involved with using numbers include those which apply mathematical rules or formulae to calculate quantities or determine the relationships between numbers derived from simple measurements. The computation of an arithmetic average is an example of using numbers. Using numbers is a progression of mathematical skills which can include identifying sets and their elements, ordering numbers, serial ordering, establishing one-to-one correspondence, ordering or sequencing objects or events, counting, adding, subtracting, multiplying, dividing, finding averages, using decimals, manipulating fractions, and using scientific notation.

Calculators facilitate students' computations efforts and focus the attention of learners on questions such as "What does the answer mean?" and "Is the answer reasonable?" rather than on the computation itself. When using numbers in the elementary science classroom, teachers should encourage students to use mental mathematics skills, to estimate answers, and to use technology to facilitate routine computation work.

ACTIVITY 9-13   ■   HOW BIG IS A BLOCK?

Grade Level: Upper Elementary

Science Process: Using numbers

Materials:

calculator
ruler

5 blocks of wood (different sizes)

TABLE 9.7   Volume of Solid Data Sheet

Number	Length	Width	Depth	Volume*
1				
2				
3				
4				
5				

*Volume = length × width × depth

Procedure:

1. Have the students determine the dimensions of the wooden blocks using a metric ruler (length, width, and depth).
2. Calculate the volume of the block by using the formula for volume of a rectangular solid. (Be sure to use a calculator.) Record your findings (Table 9.7).

Volume = length × height × width

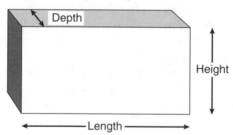

ACTIVITY 9-14 ■ HOW HEAVY IS IT?

Grade Level: Upper Elementary

Science Process: Using numbers

Materials:

calculator   ruler
5 rectangular solids (different   balance
   densities)

Procedure:

1. Have the students measure the dimensions of the rectangular solids (length, width, and volume). Volume = length × width × depth.
2. Determine the mass of each solid by weighing it on a pan balance.

TABLE 9.8 Density Data Sheet					
Number	*Length*	*Width*	*Depth*	*Volume**	*Density***
1					
2					
3					
4					
5					

*Volume = length × width × depth

**Density = mass/volume

3. Calculate the volume of the object first. Next have the students calculate the density by dividing the mass by the volume. Density = mass/volume. Have them record their findings (Table 9.8)

Identifying Variables

Identifying variables is a basic science process that involves the student in recognizing the characteristics of objects or factors in events that are constant or change under different conditions. Naming variables involves stating all the factors that affect an event. Variables are all of the factors within an experiment that can be changed by the experimenter.

Independent Variables.   Typically, variables can be classified as independent, dependent, and extraneous. An **independent variable** can be operationally defined as the variable that is changed in an experiment. Independent variables are also referred to as manipulated variables. Manipulated or independent variables can be deliberately and systematically changed by the investigator.

Dependent Variables.   **Dependent variables**, on the other hand, can be defined as "responding" variables. Dependent variables respond or change according to changes in the independent variables. For elementary aged children, dependent variables need to be those forces, actions, or quantities which are easily measured by children at this age.

Extraneous Variables.   Finally, there are other factors that can influence the outcome of the experiment. These are referred to as extraneous variables. **Extraneous variables** are frequently defined as controlled variables. They are factors or influences which can affect the outcome of the activity and which are kept constant or unchanged during an investigation.

Suppose a researcher wanted to find out whether mealworms prefer a light or dark environment. The researcher would place the mealworms in a container with a light source at one end and darkness at the other end (Figure 9.8). The

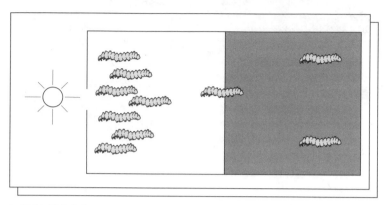

| FIGURE 9.8

presence or absence of light is the independent variable, that is, the variable that is changed. The movement of the mealworms to the light or dark end of the box is the responding variable. If most of the mealworms moved to the light end of the box, the researcher would infer that they preferred light to darkness.

However, we need to control for extraneous variables, that is, other factors which might influence the outcome of the experiment. Is the paper in the bottom of the box moist in some places and not others? Perhaps mealworms respond to moisture as well as light. Is the paper in the bottom of the box rough in some places and not in others? Perhaps the smoothness of the paper affects the movement of mealworms. Is the temperature in the box uniform? Mealworms might respond to changes in temperature. Controlling extraneous variables or factors which may influence the outcome of the experiment is vital in all scientific investigations.

Identifying variables is a science process that is a prerequisite for all science experimentation. If children are unable to identify variables, they will be unable to control those variables in experimental conditions. Activity 9-15 is typical of investigations which encourage children to construct a knowledge of variables.

ACTIVITY 9-15 ■ SODA CAN CATAPULT

Grade Level: Intermediate to Upper Elementary

Science Process: Identifying variables

Materials:

1 empty soda can (the type with the ring on the top)

3 marbles of different masses
metric measuring tape

Teacher Preparation Directions:

Before students arrive in class, pull back firmly on the tab at the top of the soda can such that the tap is at a 45°-angle to the top of the can. This forms the top of

TABLE 9.9   Soda Can Catapult

Size of the Marble	Distance It Travels
Small	
Medium	
Large	

the can into a simple catapult. Instruct the students to put the soda can on the floor and place a small marble firmly against the tab. When the spring (the inverted tab) is as far back as possible, release the marble. How far does it go? Repeat with a medium and a large marble. Record the distances that the marbles travel (Table 9.9).

Procedure:

1. After the students have had the opportunity to investigate the soda can catapult, ask them to reflect on the activity and to complete Table 9.10 based on their observations.
2. Define the terms independent, dependent, and extraneous variables for the students.

INTEGRATED PROCESSES

Integrated science processes can be considered "complex" processes or multifaceted processes. Each type combines two or more basic science processes. Integrated scientific thinking processes include (1) formulating hypotheses, (2) controlling variables, (3) investigating, (4) defining operationally, and (5) experi-

TABLE 9.10   Identifying Variables

Type of Variable	Example
Independent (changes)	
Dependent (responding)	
Extraneous (other)	

menting. **Integrated processes** can be defined as "causal" processes, that is, processes which help students establish cause and effect relationships.

Formulating Hypotheses

A **hypothesis** can be defined as an educated guess. Abruscato (1988) has defined a hypothesis as a generalization that includes all objects or events of the same class. Esler and Esler (1993) have defined hypothesis formulation as making a statement that is believed to be true about a whole class of events. In constructing a hypothesis, the student is making a statement that is tentative and testable. Hypothesis formulation is an integrated process in that it combines observation, prediction, naming variables, communicating, and using numbers.

In **formulating a hypothesis**, the student is attempting to explain a class of events in a reasonable fashion, that is, in a way that can be verified through his or her own experimentation. When adults formulate a hypothesis, they frequently express the hypothesis in the form of a Boolean statement, that is, in the form of an "if one thing, then the other" statement. For children, hypothesis formulation is best done within the context of operational questioning. An operational question is a "child-generated question" (named by Dorothy Alfke, The Pennsylvania State University): one that can be answered by children through their manipulation of simple, readily available materials. Operational questions for children could include: If I added salt to water, could I make an egg float? What would happen if I added a paper clip to the nose of a paper airplane? How could I shape a clay boat to make it hold more mass? For children, formulating a hypothesis involves the child in an attempt to explain a phenomenon in his or her world.

ACTIVITY 9-16 ■ PAPER PARACHUTE

Grade Level: Primary to Upper Elementary

Science Process: Formulating hypotheses

Materials:

piece of cloth (approximately 30 centimeters square) or a paper towel or napkin	thread washers meter stick or metric measuring tape

Procedure:

1. Assemble a toy parachute. Drop the parachute from a height of 1.5 meters. What happens?
2. Instruct the students to read each operational question, formulate a hypothesis, and conduct an investigation using the parachute which will answer the question (Table 9.11). (Hint: Use one parachute as a control before beginning to manipulate variables.)

TABLE 9.11   Parachute Data Sheet

Operational Question	Hypothesis
What would happen if the parachute were dropped from a greater height?	
What would happen if more washers were added to the parachute?	
What would happen if a larger parachute were used?	
What would happen if a smaller parachute were used?	

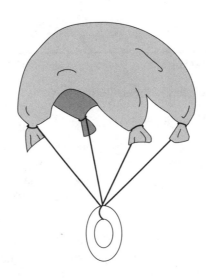

Controlling Variables

Identifying variables is a basic or simple science process that involves the students in identifying which factors affect the outcome of an investigation. **Controlling variables** involves students in manipulating variables, that is, in changing some objects or conditions while keeping others constant. Abruscato (1988) states that controlling variables means managing the conditions of an investigation. As stated earlier, a variable is an object or quantity which may be changed and which may affect the outcome of an investigation. Controlling variables is an integrated science process which combines many basic science processes, including observing, classifying, measuring, communicating, inferring, communicating, using space/time relationships, using numbers, and identifying variables.

A logical step after identifying variables is to control variables in a systematic fashion. For example, if students involved with the "mealworm" activity (see Chapter 5) believe that moisture may be a salient variable in the behavior of mealworms, then students could design an investigation to determine if mealworms prefer moist or dark environments. Likewise, if children believe that exercise might affect human heart rate or respiration rate, they could design a simple investigation which would determine if the two were related. It should be pointed out that controlling variables involves mental maturation on the part of the child. Young children are rarely able to control variables by themselves. Controlling variables only becomes possible when the child has reached the formal operational level (the final stage of development hypothesized by Piaget) of thinking.

Activity 9-17 is an activity in which children can manipulate variables and determine the relationship between them.

ACTIVITY 9-17 ■ CORK CANNON

Grade Level: Intermediate to Upper Elementary

Science Process: Controlling variables

Materials:

test tube or soda bottle   water
cork or stopper to fit   baking soda
vinegar   graduated cylinder

Procedure:

1. Place 9 milliliters of water and 1 milliliter of vinegar in a test tube. Add five grams (or a level teaspoon or measuring spoon) of baking soda. Quickly stopper the test tube. (Note: This is best done as an outdoor activity with children.)

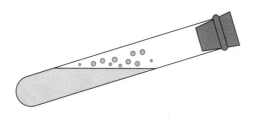

2. What happens? How far does the cork travel? Repeat for different amounts of water and vinegar while holding the amount of baking soda constant. What happens to the distance the cork travels as the concentration of vinegar increases? Record your answers (Table 9.12).

TABLE 9.12   Cork Cannon Data Sheet

Amount of Water	Amount of Vinegar	Distance
10 ml	0 ml	
8 ml	2 ml	
6 ml	4 ml	
4 ml	6 ml	
2 ml	8 ml	
0 ml	10 ml	

Investigating

Investigating is an integrated science process that incorporates manipulation of manipulative materials and recording data. This integrated process builds upon the basic processes of observing, classifying, measuring, communicating, inferring, predicting, and using space/time relationships. Typically, investigating uses science process skills to gather data in a discovery learning situation or by following teacher directions when not employing the formal scientific process.

Investigating can be understood as a replication of an activity. Investigations provide an opportunity for students to acquire expertise in handling or treating materials and equipment. As part of the manipulation of materials, students should be engaged in analyzing data, that is, in looking for patterns and relationships between variables. Activities which provide students with the opportunity to develop investigative skills might include using a microscope, noting the way(s) that it works, and manipulating bulbs and batteries to make a circuit. Investigation typically strengthens students' motor development as well as their observational proficiency.

ACTIVITY 9-18 ▪ LETTER E

Grade Level: Intermediate to Upper Elementary

Science Process: Investigating

Materials:

newspaper   cover slip
microscope   scissors
slide

Procedure:

1. Cut a letter *e* from a newspaper. Place it on a microscope slide and cover with a cover slip (this is called a "dry" mount).

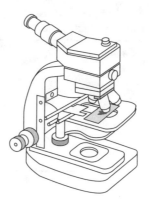

2. Place the slide on the platform of the microscope such that the letter *e* faces you. Look through the eyepiece and adjust the coarse and fine adjustment knobs such that the *e* is in focus.

3. Draw the letter *e*. What did you expect the letter *e* to look like? How is it different under the microscope? Move the slide to the left. What happens to the letter *e*? Move the slide to the right. What happens to the letter *e*? Move the slide up. What happens to the letter *e*? Move the slide down. What happens to the letter *e*?

ACTIVITY 9-19 ■ BULBS AND BATTERIES

Grade Level: Intermediate to Upper Elementary

Science Process: Investigating

Materials:

1 battery
1 bulb

1 piece of insulated copper wire

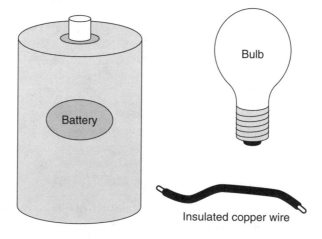

Battery

Bulb

Insulated copper wire

Procedure:

1. Connect the bulb and battery with the wire such that the bulb lights. Draw your circuit.
2. Try another way of getting the bulb to light. Draw this circuit.
3. How many different arrangements of the bulb, battery, and wire can you make that will light the bulb?

Defining Operationally

Operational definitions can be thought of as working definitions. They are based on a child's experience in the natural world and as such lack the sophistication of formal science definitions. Normally, operational definitions are associated with identifying and controlling variables. The formulation of an operational definition involves defining all variables as they are used in an experiment. For example, in the Cork Cannon activity (Activity 9-17), a "good" cannon might be defined as one which shoots the cork the greatest distance possible.

An operational definition within the context of the physical sciences is based on what is done and what is observed. Operational definitions in life sciences tend to be descriptive in nature. For example, an insect's cocoon (Figure 9.9) can be defined as being a container made by the insect which holds an insect's pupa. The formal science definition of a cocoon is as follows:

> "Cocoon—in general, any tough, protective covering which encloses the eggs or young, and sometimes adults of animals, as the silken envelope enclosing the larva or pupa of an insect." (Steen, 1971, p. 107).

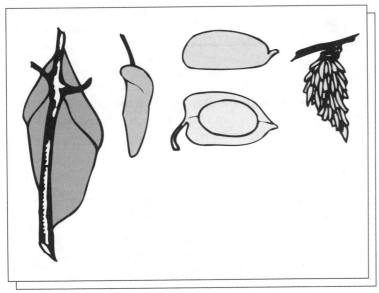

FIGURE 9.9   Cocoon

A
C
T
I
V
I
T
I
E
S

As children have the opportunity to investigate the natural world, their knowledge and understanding of the world increases and their operational definitions begin to resemble formal science definitions more closely. An operational definition can be thought of as a "working" definition, one that will be refined by the child over time.

ACTIVITY 9-20 ■ SOAP BOAT

Grade Level: Intermediate to Upper Elementary

Science Process: Defining Operationally

Materials:

3 cardboard boats
3 thin-cut slivers of different brands
  of soap from worn down soap
  bars (best done by the teacher in
  advance)

1 pan of water
1 measuring tape

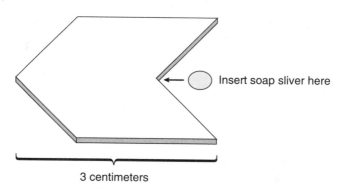

Insert soap sliver here

3 centimeters

Procedure:

1. Assemble the soap boats by inserting the soap slivers at the back of each boat.
2. Fill a shallow pan about half full of tap water. Place the three boats in the center of the pan of water at the same time.

TABLE 9.13   Soap Boat Data Sheet

Brand Soap	*Distance*

3. Observe the boats and measure the distance that they travel before stopping. Record your findings (Table 9.13)

Operationally Defining Terms:

1. Which boat was the best boat? Why?
2. Which soap is best as a fuel for soap boats? Why?
3. How do you decide how far the soap boat travels?

Experimenting

Experimenting is the last of the integrated science processes. It involves students in using all other processes. The "best" experiments are those that are student-generated activities which students want to perform because they are interested and motivated. Experimenting typically involves extending classwork into a new domain. At its simplest level, **experimenting** can be defined as "performing the activity." Experimenting is the process that encompasses all of the basic and integrated processes. Experimenting involves children in formulating their own operational questions, that is, questions that they may answer by manipulating materials. In addition, experimenting involves children in identifying and controlling variables, designing an activity which will test a hypothesis, formulating operational definitions, observing, gathering data and using numbers, making inferences, interpreting data, and drawing conclusions based on that data.

In nearly every elementary classroom there are children who do not have the opportunity to experiment on their own, that is, carry on an activity beyond the regular instructional period, due to a lack of resources and materials at home. Schools need to be places which support the learning of children, places where children are encouraged to pursue their learning beyond the scope of the curriculum. All children ought be encouraged to learn on their own, to pursue their interests, to develop expertise in a field of their own choosing.

ACTIVITY 9-21 ■ BALLOON ROCKET

Grade Level: Intermediate to Upper Elementary

Science Process: Experimenting

Materials:

balloon	scissors
string (5–10 meters)	tape
metric tape	paper clip
soda straw	

Procedure:

1. Place a thread or fine string in a short piece of soda straw.
2. Tie the ends of the thread to chairs (spaced 5–10 meters apart).

TABLE 9.14   Balloon Rocket Data Sheet

Size of Balloon	Measurement	Distance Traveled
Small		
Medium		
Large		

3. Blow up the balloon, twist the end, and temporarily close the end with a paper clip.
4. Place a piece of tape over the soda straw such that the balloon is attached to the straw.

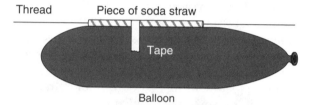

5. Place the balloon at one end of the "rocket" course, undo the paper clip, and "let go" of the balloon. How far does it travel?
6. Repeat with a balloon with a small amount of air, a medium amount of air, and a large amount of air inside. The size of the balloon can be measured by placing a string around the balloon to measure its circumference. Record your findings (Table 9.14).

Experiment:

Try to design the best balloon possible, that is, the one that will go the farthest. What happens if you add fins? A nose cone? How many fins are best? How should the nose cone be shaped? Should mass be added to the nose cone? Keep a log of your experiments and results.

CLASSROOM PRACTICE

Reflection is vital in the life of all teachers. As a teacher, you will reflect on your teaching on a daily basis. Reflection is guided by questions such as: What do my students know? What do I want my students to learn? How will I assist them to learn this? What have my students learned? Activities which encourage students to use science processes are educationally rich activities. Work through the electromagnet activity (Activity 9-22) first as a student. Experiment with constructing an electromagnet, investigate the properties of the electromagnet, and perform the activity as if you were a student. When you have finished the activity, reflect on your learning. What science processes have you used while doing this activity? What conceptual knowledge have you gained?

Each activity in this chapter is designed to enhance students' knowledge of science processes and assist students in their conceptual development. Even though activities have been listed under specific science processes, all of the activities "teach" more than one science process. Review the activities and attempt to identify all of the processes which are used in the activities.

ACTIVITY 9-22 ■ ELECTROMAGNET

Materials:

dry cell battery   nail
insulated copper wire   metal paper clips

Procedure:

1. Assemble the electromagnet as shown below.

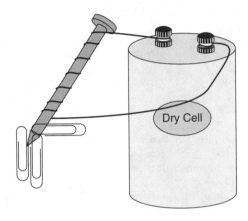

2. Conduct an investigation to determine what happens to the strength of the electromagnet as more wraps of wire are added to the nail. Record your findings (Table 9.15).

Follow-up Question:

What happens to the strength of the electromagnet as more wraps of wire are added to the nail?

TABLE 9.15   Electromagnet Data Sheet

Wraps of Wire	No. Paper Clips Lifted
5	
10	
15	
20	
25	
30	

CHAPTER SUMMARY

One role of the elementary science teacher is to assist students in developing the thinking processes that characterize the scientific enterprise. Science as it is practiced aims to be testable, objective, and consistent. The goal of developing scientific literacy in all students is best met by students who have mastered the scientific thinking processes. The basic science processes of observing, classifying,

TABLE 9.16   Overview of Science Processes

Science Process	Definition	Example
Basic Processes		
Observing	Identifying and naming the properties of objects and events in the physical world	Formulating hypotheses
Classification	Arranging objects, events, or information according to a method or system	Grouping living things
Measuring	Comparing an object of unknown dimensions to a known dimension	Measuring line segments
Communicating	Conveying ideas through social interchanges	Journal writings of findings
Inferring	Making a conclusion based on reasoning to explain a set of observations	Mystery box activity
Predicting	Forecasting some future event based on solid evidence	Weather forecasting
Using space/time relationships	Using plane and solid geometric shapes as well as length and so forth for observation	Leaf symmetry
Using numbers	Applying mathematical rules or formulae in order to calculate quantities	Computing work and force
Identifying variables	Recognizing the characteristics of objects or events which are constant or changing	Soda can catapult
Integrated Processes		
Formulating hypotheses	Making a statement believed to be true about a class of events	Paper parachute
Controlling variables	Changing objects and/or conditions while keeping others constant	Cork cannon
Investigating	Gathering data in a discovery learning situation through manipulating materials	Bulbs and batteries
Defining operationally	Generating "working" definitions in the context of an investigation	Soap boats
Experimenting	The process that encompasses other processes	Balloon rocket

measuring, communicating, inferring, predicting, using space/time relationships, using numbers, and identifying variables are vital for all students. As students grow and mature, they ought to be encouraged to develop expertise in using integrated science processes: formulating hypotheses, controlling variables, investigating, defining operationally, and experimenting (Table 9.16).

 TOPICS TO REVIEW

 REFLECTIVE PRACTICE

1. Think about the Soap Boat Activity (Activity 9-20). What science processes will students use when working through this activity? Explain when in the activity each process is used.
2. The "Growing a Butterfly" Activity (Activity 9-1) is used as an illustration of the process of observation in this chapter. Actually, other processes might be taught with this activity. Name them. Identify the points at which you see evidence of these other processes being used.
3. In your opinion, why are children discouraged from experimenting in the elementary science classroom? What could be done to change this?
4. In what ways could teaching children using process-based lessons benefit culturally diverse students? Explain your answers.

Instructional Technology Approaches

Traditional Design

• Mathemagenic models
• IDI models for design

Information Processing

• Cognitive strategies
• Visualization
• Information processing
• Feedback and motivation

Current Microcomputer
Applications in Science

• Graphic packages
• Instrument interfacing
• Simulations

FOUNDATIONS		
Historical	Pedagogical	Research

INSTRUCTIONAL TECHNOLOGY IN THE MULTICULTURAL CLASSROOM

 POINTS TO PONDER

1. What is instructional technology?
2. What is the value of instructional technology in the science classroom?
3. In your opinion, how could computers and instructional technology transform science instruction?

CHANGE AND COMPUTERS

hange is part of all of our lives. Change is good, healthy; it refreshes us, although it sometimes bewilders us. The summer that my family moved from New Mexico to Pennsylvania is an illustration of the nature of change in our lives. We traveled at the beginning of August to arrive in Pennsylvania before the start of the school year. My children had spent their entire lives in the warmth and comfort of family surroundings and were moving thousands of miles from home. As parents, we wanted to make sure that they had time to adjust to their new home before the infamous first day of school.

In spite of our efforts, the first day in a new academic environment proved to be a disaster for our sons. Our middle son, Javier, came home from school complaining that the school cooks were attempting to poison him. He had been raised on school lunches comprised of burritos, tacos, nachos, green chili stew, green chili cheeseburgers, and tort burgers. According to Javier, the cooks in Pennsylvania served rotten food. The hot dog was gray and swollen and tasted "nasty." He also asserted that the cooks must have left the potato salad out too long before serving it, because it had become warm. Finally, they served some kind of rotten, "squishy," spoiled lettuce. According to Javier, except for the hot dog bun, the entire meal was inedible. When I called the school in the late afternoon to complain about the spoiled food, I learned that he had been served a Pennsylvania Dutch meal of knackwurst on a bun, hot German potato salad, and sauerkraut. Pennsylvania food was culture shock to a boy from New Mexico.

My other son had an equally disappointing day. As a first day assignment, he was asked to write a composition about his summer vacation. Now, it seemed to me that a composition about one's summer vacation on the first day of school is a fairly routine assignment. When I pressed Aáron about the nature of his complaint, I learned that the teacher had asked him to write the composition using pencil and paper. I thought this was fairly reasonable, until I saw through Aáron's eyes. From kindergarten through fifth grade, he had done all of his composition work on a computer. He was used to writing with the assistance of a prewrite package, a spelling checker, and a primitive grammar checker. His first day in a new school seemed like a visit to another planet. Having been raised as part of the computer generation, he viewed his new school as being undeveloped and technologically illiterate. Changes in computer technologies have resulted in changes in the way(s) that we teach children.

INSTRUCTIONAL TECHNOLOGY

Movie projectors, cassette tape players, television monitors, microcomputers, and interactive video workstations are examples of audiovisual technologies that have at one time or another entered the science classroom as tools to facilitate the teaching/learning process. Since the first school museum opened in St. Louis in 1905 (Saettler, 1968), science educators have looked to technology for solutions to pedagogical problems. In 1913, Thomas Edison proclaimed that, "Books will soon be obsolete in our schools . . . . It is possible to teach every branch of human knowledge with the motion picture projector" (Saettler, 1968, p. 98) Edison went on to predict that our school systems would be radically changed (by motion picture projectors) within 10 years.

History of Audiovisual Technology in Science Instruction

Magic lanterns (stereopticons and stereoscopes) became instructional tools in the science classroom during the later half of the nineteenth century. Edison's movie projector became the visual tool of choice for science teachers during the decade of the 1910s. Following World War I, motion pictures with accompanying sound became popular instructional tools in the science classroom. Educational applications of audiovisual technology multiplied with the advent of World War II. Military applications of instructional technologies included the use of overhead projectors for large group instruction, slide projectors for teaching aircraft recognition, audiotape instruction for teaching foreign languages, and the use of multimedia flight training simulators (Olsen & Bass, 1982). Following World War II, teachers adopted these same technologies for instructional purposes in the science classroom.

The 1950s and 1960s were the decades of instructional television. Educational television during this time was viewed as a means to provide quick, efficient, and inexpensive science instruction. The National Defense Education Act: Title VII, which was in effect for one decade, spent more than $40 million dollars on 600 projects (Filep & Schramm, 1970), including instructional television. Private foundations such as the Ford Foundation, which spent $170 million dollars during this same period, supported instructional programming as a means of improving instruction nationwide. With minor exceptions, the disappearance of educational television has left science instruction fundamentally unchanged.

In 1951, Remington Rand introduced the first commercially available computer system, the UNIVAC I, which was constructed of vacuum tubes. By the middle of the 1950s, the vacuum tubes of the UNIVAC had been replaced by transistors. The second generation of computers was faster and more complex than its predecessor. Early in the 1960s, the third generation of computers run by integrated circuits became commercially available. Widespread science classroom use of microcomputer technology began in the 1970s with the invention of the fourth generation of microcomputers, which were based on microchip technology. Since the introduction of computer technologies into schools, an entire generation of children has been raised using computers as readily as textbooks.

Research into Computerized Instruction

Computer-assisted instruction (CAI) or the use of the microcomputer as an instructional tool has been available to science teachers for more than two decades. Computer-assisted technologies are the newest in a long line of instructional technologies that have appeared in the classroom. During the past two decades, literally hundreds of research studies have been conducted into the effectiveness of this electronic learning. Unfortunately, most of the studies into the effectiveness of computer-assisted instruction have been flawed by poor research designs, improper control of variables, and inappropriate use of statistics (Kracjik, Simmons, & Lunetta, 1986). From those studies which used proper controls on variables, it has been learned that computer-assisted instruction makes significant differences in student learning in four areas: achievement, learning retention, learning time, and learner attitude.

Achievement.   Perhaps the most comprehensive study of the effectiveness of computer-aided instruction was undertaken by Kulik, Bangert, and Williams

Computer technologies enhance students' acquisition of declarative knowledge. (© Will Faller)

(1983). These researchers used a metaanalysis technique to examine and synthesize 51 studies of computer-assisted instruction involving students in grades 6 through 12. They found that, generally, students who received computer-assisted instruction scored higher on objective tests than students who received "traditional" instruction. Results from their metaanalysis indicated that the average student in the control groups scored in the 50th percentile, while the average student who received with computer-assisted instruction scored in the 63rd percentile. The gain for students who receive computerized instruction was .32 of a standard deviation.

Studies conducted by the Educational Testing Service indicate that students who use computerized drill-and-practice packages for only 10 minutes a day score significantly higher on mathematics achievement tests than do students who do not have access to microcomputers (Bracey 1982). Roblyer (1985), in summarizing the results of computer-assisted instruction studies, reports that computer-based instruction achieves consistently higher effects than other instructional treatments in experimental situations.

Science teachers need to integrate this body of research into their everyday instructional practice. Information at the lowest levels of Bloom's taxonomy, that is, knowledge and comprehension levels, lends itself readily to electronic learning. Hence, factual information, such as the symbols for the elements of the periodic table or names of plant and animal structures, can be taught more efficiently with computerized drill-and-practice packages. If the objective of instruction is to have students trained to produce symbols for element names, electronic tutorial packages are highly appropriate.

Caution must be used, however, when recommending drill-and-practice software for use with culturally diverse learners and with students who are having "difficulty" mastering the content of the course. Frequently, culturally and linguistically unassimilated students and low verbal learners (e.g., mainstreamed special education students), as well as those who have difficulty in reading, speaking, and writing English, are assigned to work independently or in small groups at computer workstations. Sometimes teachers mistakenly think that this will assist students in developing "basic skills." Assigning students to work independently at a computer terminal isolates the child from his or her peers. This results in a situation in which children are physically, socially, and educationally separated from the mainstream learning activities in the classroom. While computers can be powerful tools for learning low level knowledge, they can also become tools to isolate culturally diverse students from their peers.

Retention.   Kulik, Bangert, and Williams (1983) also investigated student retention of information in their metaanalysis study. They found that computer-assisted instruction improves retention of information at the knowledge and comprehension levels of Bloom's taxonomy, and reported that four of five studies investigating retention over a period of 2 to 6 months showed greater retention of information for students who used computer-assisted instruction. Roblyer's (1985) survey of computer-assisted instruction research had different results. His research indicated that, while there were differences in the performance between computer-assisted instruction students and "traditionally" instructed students, those differences were not statistically significant. Since the results of this research into student retention were not conclusive, Robyler recommended more research in this area.

While computers can be powerful tools in helping students learn and retain information, such as the symbols for the elements of the periodic table and vocabulary terms, care needs to be taken to select software for student use carefully. Culturally diverse learners, indeed all students, learn best and retain what they learn when knowledge is presented in multiple formats, that is, written words, spoken words, and with *realia* or "real world" objects, pictures, photographs, and icons. Teachers who want to encourage lifetime learning for their students should remember that computer terminals normally present information only in written words, pictures, and icons. While some interactive multimedia workstations also present information in spoken form, there is as yet no substitution for real world objects in the electronic learning environment.

Learning Time. Blaschke and Sweeney (1977) found that computer-assisted instruction has been helpful in decreasing learning time. Their study compared the learning times of military recruits using a computer-assisted electronic training package with those using a similar programmed booklet commonly used in secondary education. The results from this study indicated that students learn the same electronics information in 10% less time using the computer-assisted instruction module. A study by Dence (1980) indicated that students who use computer-assisted instruction master content faster than students who use traditional instructional techniques. A study by Lunetta (1972) showed that students could master physics content in 88% less time using computer-assisted instruction than it took for students who used "traditional" physics instruction.

Research into instructional time indicates that computer-assisted instruction is highly effective in certain situations, namely, low-level learning tasks. Science teachers need to identify those bodies of information that can be learned more quickly using microcomputers than by traditional instructional methods. The time saved by learning low-level information on the computer should be used to teach higher-order thinking skills in the multicultural science classroom.

Attitudes.   In addition to improving students' achievement, increasing retention, and decreasing instructional time, computer-assisted instruction appears to improve students' attitudes toward learning. The metaanalysis conducted by Kulik et al. (1983) indicated that, in eight of ten studies reviewed, students' attitudes toward subject matter was more positive after students had used computer-assisted instruction. A study by Bracey (1984) indicated that students react favorably to the use of the computer for instructional purposes. In fact, Bracey found that students who have worked on microcomputers in a subject area have a more positive attitude toward that subject than do students who have not used the computer in that particular class. Other researchers (Foley, 1984; Fiber, 1987) also have reported that students' attitudes toward an academic subject, including science instruction, improve after computerized instruction. Computers have endless patience in tutorial situations. Science teachers need to capitalize on the microcomputer's ability to teach and reteach information consistently. Electronic learning frees the science teacher from the drudgery of endless drill-and-practice learning situations, but as yet does not assist students in developing higher-level thinking skills.

Beyond Drill and Practice

While drill-and-practice software is the most commonly used software in the science classroom, it is not the only computer application available to the science instructor in the multicultural classroom. Indeed, other types of software provide for higher levels of questioning skills and for deeper levels of understanding regarding content area information. Graphing packages, instrument interfacing kits, electronic simulation activities, statistical packages, database simulations, and spreadsheet simulations provide for deeper information processing on the part of the learner and for high levels of user interactivity: interaction between the learner, microcomputer, and the "real" world.

Computerized Graphing Packages.   Computerized **graphing packages** such as MECC Graph and Microsoft Works allow students to generate bar graphs, line graphs, and pie charts rapidly. The primary value of computerized graphics packages is that they change the level of questioning skills in the classroom from the lowest levels of Bloom's taxonomy to higher levels of that taxonomy, for example, application, analysis, synthesis, and evaluation. When graphing packages are introduced into the classroom, they allow students to spend time asking "what if" questions rather than questions concerning the construction of the graph itself. Graphing packages allow learners in the multicultural classroom to focus on questions such as, "What is the relationship between the variables?" rather than focusing on how to draw a graph or plot a point. This is not to say that students should not be afforded the opportunity to construct graphs on their own at some point in their educational experience, but rather that graphing packages allow teachers to focus on higher-order thinking skills after students have acquired a conceptual understanding of graphic representation of data.

In a study into the effectiveness of graphing packages, Gesshel-Green (1987) found that students who use computerized graphing packages do not differ from "traditionally" instructed students on immediate recall scores. However, students treated with computer graphing packages do show significant positive gains when compared with these students on measures of long-term retention, motivation, and cooperation. Results from a study into the use of computerized graphing packages to teach concept formation (Heid, 1988) indicated that students formulate concepts in significantly less time when using computer graphing packages.

Instrument Interfacing. Instrument to microcomputer **interfacing** is the domain of the science teacher. Connecting thermistors (temperature probes), potentiometers (stick pendulums), photoresistors (light probes), and electrically conductive styrofoam (hand grips) to microcomputers allows students and teachers to collect and analyze data in real time. Microcomputer-based laboratory (MBL) activities have been shown to improve students' understanding of science processes (Nachmias & Linn, 1987). While conducting an experiment to compare traditional laboratory activities with computer-based laboratory activities, these researchers discovered that eighth grade students engaged in computer-based activities showed greater understanding of scientific processes than did students in conventional science labs.

Krendl and Lieberman (1988) report that student motivation, involvement with the laboratory activity, and self-perception are improved as a result of computer-based laboratory instruction. Instrument interfacing allows learners to focus on science processes rather than on data collection and interpretation. Events that occur rapidly or slowly, involve minute changes in temperature or light intensity, or require extreme care in data recording can be easily observed with instruments interfaced to microcomputers (Barba, 1987). Laboratory activities that have traditionally been left out of the curriculum because they required extreme care in observation can be conducted using microcomputer interfaces. Instrument interfacing allows students to work at higher-level thinking skills and focus on the relationships between variables rather than on low-level skills such as reading a thermometer or a light meter.

Simulations. **Simulation** activities are a form of computer-assisted instruction in which the learner assumes a role within a structured environment (Lockard, Many, & Abrams 1987, p. 398) and makes decisions based on that role playing. These activities can be conducted in the science classroom with single use packages, such as *Oh, Deer!* and *Energy House,* or through the use of spreadsheets or simple computer programs. In reporting on the effectiveness of *CATLAB,* a genetics simulation activity, Krajcik, Simmons, and Lunetta (1988, p. 151) pointed out that computer simulations facilitate student problem-solving skills by allowing students to: (1) generate their own questions; (2) control variables; (3) gather, record, and interpret data; and (4) draw conclusions to support or reject hypotheses. Experiments which are dangerous or time consuming can be performed quickly and easily by computer simulation.

Spreadsheets also allow students to engage in simulation activities. While investigating the use of spreadsheets as simulation tools, Dubitsky (1986) discovered that sixth grade students can transfer understanding and methods of solutions from one problem to another. In assessing the value of spreadsheets in the science classroom, Pogge and Lunetta (1987) noted that spreadsheets allow students to spend extra time collecting and interpreting data, rather than spend time on routine computational work. The use of spreadsheets allows students in the multicultural science classroom to develop science processes, especially in inferring, predicting, and hypothesizing.

Multimedia. **Multimedia** and/or hypermedia is one of the most exciting new advances in instructional software. Typically with this type of technology, CD-ROM drives or laser disk readers are connected to computers. Since the storage capacity of these devices is far greater than that of traditional floppy diskettes, computer programs can now feature segments of on-screen movies, on-screen dictionaries, glossaries, embedded electronic notebooks, and on-line encyclopedias. The availability of text screens, embedded graphics, movies, and multiple language channels means that software is better able to address the needs of culturally and linguistically diverse learners.

Multimedia is particularly appealing for use with culturally diverse learners since it allows for multiple means of knowledge representation, that is, written words, spoken words, line drawings, icons, and movie segments. In addition, many multimedia products are being produced with multiple sound tracks that allow the user to control the instructional language. For students socialized to learn from spoken language or pictorial presentations of knowledge, multimedia is particularly appropriate.

Networking or Telecommunications. **Networking** or connecting computers from around the world through existing telecommunication channels is another example of computer applications that benefit science teachers. By using electronic mail connections, teachers may access satellite images of weather patterns, stored NASA documents from previous space flights, botanical and zoological databases, and information about earth resources. Electronic servers, such as Ecogopher, provide updated information about a wealth of subjects. Libraries, taxonomic keys, science research reports, and electronic images are a few key strokes away from students and teachers.

In addition to the resources available from electronic servers, telecommunications allows students to communicate with others in their native languages. Bulletin boards around the world provide the chance for students to interact in cyberspace by sending messages to others. Distance education affords students the opportunity to use the entire planet as a classroom and extend their resources globally.

The Traditional Role of Educational Technology

In the past, science software has been developed using an instructional systems design or educational technologies approach. **Educational technology** is "an approach that has been directed toward expanding the range of resources used for learning, emphasizing the individual learner and his unique needs, and using a systematic approach to the development of learning resources" (Definition and Terminology Committee of the Association for Educational Communications and Technology, 1972, p. 36). An **instructional systems design** approach to software development involves identifying and controlling the variables which lead to increased information processing on the part of the learner. It is an approach that involves applying principles of behavioral psychology to computer applications and to off-line courseware development. The melding of audiovisual technologies and a systematic approach to courseware design have resulted in the production of mathemagenic software or electronic stimulus-response learning models.

Systematic design of instruction, such as the systems approach model designed by Dick and Carey (1985), includes: (1) identification of instructional goals, (2) task analysis for each learning outcome, (3) identification of the entry behaviors, and (4) consideration of the learner characteristics of students in the science classroom. Dick and Carey's model of instructional design (Figure 10.1) allows the program designer to communicate the performance objectives expected of students in the science classroom as a part of the software development process.

Criterion-referenced test items are used in systematically designed science software. Instructional strategies and instructional materials are identified in terms of observable behavioral outcomes. Formative and summative evaluation are used to assess learner outcomes in this approach to instruction. An instructional systems approach to the design of science software considers the resources, constraints, delivery system, and teacher preparation (Gagne, 1988, p. 31) in hopes of manipulating the instructional environment to produce desired outcomes in the learner. In other words, the traditional instructional systems design approach is often regarded as "training" the child rather than "teaching" the child.

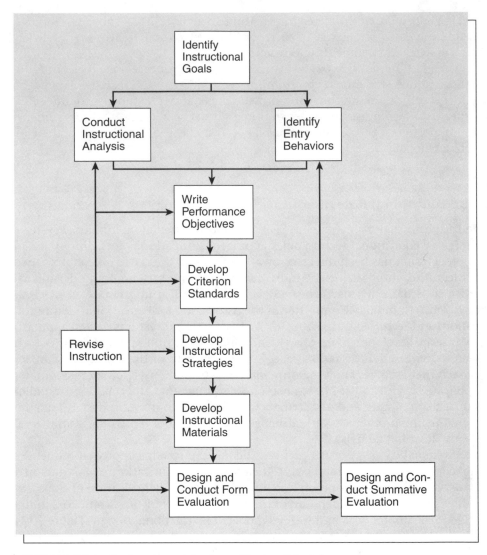

FIGURE 10.1   Instructional Systems Design Model
(*Source:* Dick, W. & Carey, L.(1985).*The Systematic Design of Instruction* (2nd ed.). Glenview, IL: Scott, Foresman.)

Psychological Foundations

Just as there has been a revolution in technology which has allowed the microcomputer to become an affordable instructional tool in the science classroom, there has been an evolution in the software that runs that hardware. The first generation of educational software used in the science classroom consisted of networked programs such as PLATO, which required the computing power of mainframe computers (Denenberg, 1988, p. 313). The first microcomputer software widely used in science classrooms was written in BASIC and required the regular science teacher to have a knowledge of BASIC commands (such as "LOAD <FILENAME>" and "RUN <FILENAME>"). By the beginning of the 1980s, "Press <RETURN> to continue," had become the instructional standard of the second generation of science software (Jonassen, 1988, p. 151). Software in the early 1980s became menu driven and user friendly, but the pedagogical base of that software remained rooted in a mathemagenic, drill-and-practice model.

The model of software design used in first- and second-generation software development was rooted in stimulus/response or behaviorist learning theory. This model held that the software provides a stimulus and the learner responds or "learns." This is a "sage-on-stage" learning model in which the computer becomes the source of authority or information and the students are "empty vessels," waiting to be filled with knowledge. According to this model, information is somehow transmitted from the computer to children whose minds are receptive empty slates. Indeed, 85% of the software used in public schools in the United States today is drill-and-practice software (Cohen, 1983), written from this pedagogical perspective.

From an instructional systems design perspective, computer instruction needs to include the events of instruction, which involve (1) gaining the attention of the learner, (2) informing the learner of the objectives of instruction, (3) stimulating recall of previous learning, (4) presenting the stimulus material, (5) providing learning guidance, (6) eliciting student performance, (7) providing meaningful feedback, (8) assessing student performance, and (9) enhancing retention and transfer (Gagne, 1988, p.182). Software designed through this approach exhibits a firm behaviorist or information processing pedagogical base.

The behavioral principle of **connectionism**, which served as the basis of first- and second-generation software, assumes that enough practice ultimately produces correct performance (Jonassen, 1988, p. 151). This **mathemagenic model** for computerized instruction has failed to achieve desired results in the science classroom because (1) it fails to accommodate the principles of educational psychology, (2) it results in shallow or low levels of information processing, and (3) microcomputer and interactive video technologies have outgrown programmed instructional models. With the third-generation software, microcomputer software is evolving from stimulus-response learning, beyond information processing learning models, to a constructivist view of learning.

Improving CAI Software

A third generation of software, software that encourages high levels of user interactivity and metacognitive processing, is beginning to find its way into the science classroom. The term interactivity here refers to the user's capability to engage in direct and continual two-way communication with the computer. Third-generation science software establishes a transactional triangle among the learner, the microcomputer, and the natural world (Figure 10.2).

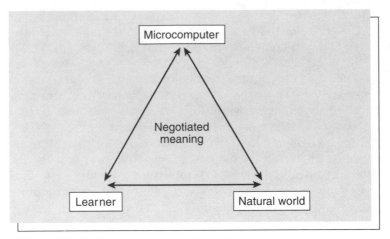

FIGURE 10.2   Transactional Triangle

In addition, third-generation software allows children to construct meaning for themselves in an electronic environment or, put another way, negotiate meaning through interactions with the computer. This newer software is built on a cognitive psychology foundation, which holds that children construct knowledge based on their experiences and interactions. From this perspective, software in the future ought to allow the learner in the multicultural classroom to explore the natural world and relationships in that natural world, that is, to "do" science, rather than to "watch" science or to "read about" science. As science software is modified and refined, microcomputers will become tools for learning rather than "teachers." The computer in the immediate future will become a resource to aid children in negotiating meaning regarding natural phenomena.

The goal of third-generation software in the science classroom ought to be to support the acquisition, retention, and retrieval of information by the individual learner. It should promote and guide active mental processing on the part of the student and foster metacognition or an "awareness of learning," in the student. To do this, science software must have embedded generative cognitive strategies (Wittrock, 1978) that facilitate the transfer of information from short-term to long-term memory. Third-generation science software should allow the learner to explore actively the natural world as it supports the activities of the learner in that world. Placing the learner in control of the software, rather than the computer in charge of the learner, is a pedagogical decision which profits all children.

Culturally diverse learners, who frequently need multiple modes of information presentation in the learning process, particularly benefit from embedded cognitive strategies. Wittrock (1978), in addressing the status of microcomputer software, states that meaning for material presented by computer or inter-active video instruction is generated by activating and altering existing knowl-edge structures within the learner. There is a recognition that learning is an active rather than a passive process. New learning comes as the individual con-sciously and intentionally relates new information to existing knowledge struc-tures. Hence, instructional materials need to facilitate this interaction through the inclusion of learning strategies.

Learning strategies generate not only learning about science, but informa-tion about how to learn science. Generative activities, such as outlining, under-lining, paraphrasing, summarizing, mnemonic devices, cognitive mapping, metaphors, categorizing, and note taking, are mental operations or procedures that the student may use to acquire, retain, and retrieve knowledge and perfor-mance (Rigney, 1978). Such learning strategies may be taught explicitly or they may be embedded in the instructional materials themselves. Embedding learn-ing strategies directly into software not only assists students with constructing meaning from the material at hand, but also facilitates students' development of metacognitive strategies for future learning.

Research has shown (Carrier, 1983) that students who engage in active note taking perform better than students who do not overtly organize information. The active use of organizational strategies, such as outlining and analyzing key ideas, and information integration strategies, such as paraphrasing and exem-plifying, increase schemata formation in learners. When students engage in ac-tive study strategies such as using electronic notebooks embedded in science software, they develop deeper levels of information processing. Electronic note-books embedded in courseware (Figure 10.3) are tools which allow students to

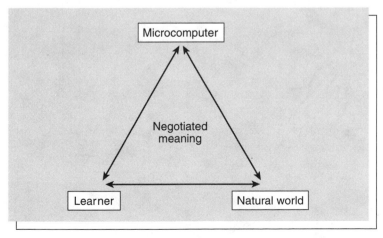

FIGURE 10.3   Electronic Notebook

organize, manipulate, and retrieve information. These tools assist the child in constructing knowledge of the physical world.

Visualization Strategies in CAI.   Visualization strategies have been recognized for several decades (Day & Beach, 1950; Allen, 1960; Chu & Schramm, 1967; Levie & Dickie, 1973) as important in the learning process. Visualization increases learner interest, motivation, curiosity, and concentration. In addition, increased visualization provides instructional feedback, facilitates information acquisition, spans linguistic barriers, increases the reliability of communication, and emphasizes and reinforces printed instruction. Research has shown that enhanced visualization, including the use of the *fotonovela* or photonovel (a highly visual story book format), is the most effective means known for conveying verbal information to culturally and linguistically unassimilated learners. Students learn more declarative knowledge from textual materials printed with enhanced visualization than with traditional textbook or screen formats.

Hockberg's (1962) research into the visualization continuum indicates that plain line drawings and shaded line drawings are the most meaningful for all classes (low, average, and high verbal) of learners. When drawings are embedded in science software, as is pictured in Figure 10.4, they can focus the attention of the learner on critical attributes and provide multiple channels of information to assist the learner in acquiring information. The inclusion of pictorial repre-

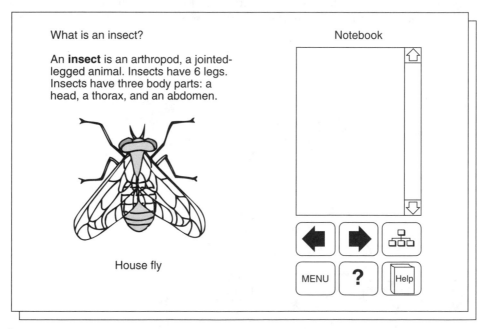

FIGURE 10.4 Embedding Drawings in Science Software

sentations of knowledge provide additional modes of conveying meaning about the subject.

Simple line drawings and shaded line drawings can be used for pictorial testing of students' knowledge and comprehension as well as for instructional purposes. In reporting on the advantages of pictorial testing, Gibson (1947) pointed out that pictorial tests are as reliable and valid as verbal instruments. Pictorial testing has not been frequently used in science classrooms in the past because it was cumbersome and time consuming to produce visual questions. Newer computer languages, such as Hypertalk (Apple Corp.) and Linkway (IBM Corp.), make visual testing as routine as traditional pencil-and-paper testing procedures. In the future, science software will routinely include questions in a visual format. Students will benefit from the change in questioning format because visual questions are (1) more accurate and more easily understood, (2) reduce the emphasis placed on reading skills, (3) provide motivating situations, and (4) assess information that is not easily evaluated through a verbal format (Lefkowith, 1955). Researchers (Dwyer, 1978; Koran, 1972; Shapiro, 1975) have recognized that visualization strategies embedded in textual material facilitates the learning and assessment of that learning among low verbal students and students for whom English is a second language.

Information-Processing Strategies.   Computerized science packages in the near future will allow the students to access on-disk encyclopedias, dictionaries, pictorial dictionaries, and a multitude of reference sources with a single key stroke or click of the mouse (Figure 10.5). In addition, software packages will allow children to control the linguistic environment in which they are working.

As the memory capacity of microcomputers has increased, and as CD-ROM technologies have developed, microcomputers are able to hold the larger bodies of information in memory. This increase in the memory capacity of computers allows for a greater individualization of instruction to accommodate the needs of the individual child. Students who need additional information on a topic will be able to access glossaries, dictionaries, or information databases readily that will assist them in constructing new knowledge. Naisbitt (1982) has pointed out that we live in an information processing age, but our pedagogical methods do not reflect the times in which we live. We have not taught students to access multiple sources of information actively as they engage in learning and we have not allowed students to control their own pace of instruction. One goal of newer software is to allow students to engage in "reflective learning" (that is, thinking about learning while it is taking place) as they work in electronic environments.

Feedback and Motivational Strategies in CAI.   "Feedback or a knowledge of results facilitates meaningful learning cognitively, primarily through clarification and correction, rather than by reinforcing correct responses" (Ausubel, 1978, p. 310). Ausubel (1978, p. 310) states that feedback is "less important for meaningful learning than for rote learning because the internal logic of meaningfully learned material allows for more self-provided feedback than do [sic] inherently

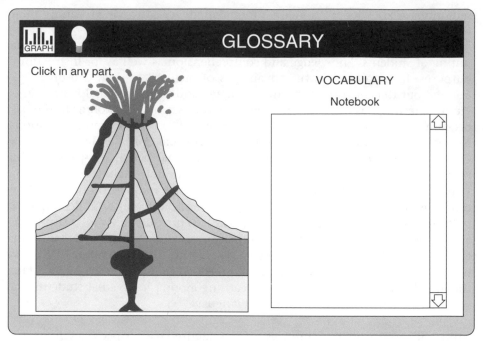

FIGURE 10.5   Accessing Information

arbitrary association." In the design of computer software, feedback needs to be confirmatory, response correcting, or explanatory depending on the nature of the learning activity. Fitting feedback to the learning activity, such that the feedback is meaningful, will be a design feature of science software in the future. Gone are the days when courseware simply flashed the words "Right" or "Wrong, try again!" onto the screen. Future software will analyze student answers and correct student responses to ensure that practice is meaningful. In addition, feedback can assist students in making sense of new information in the electronic environment.

"Motivation is absolutely necessary for the sustained type of learning involved in mastering a given subject matter discipline, such as science" (Ausubel, 1978, p. 397). Attention to motivational variables in future science software design will make these technologies more effective learning tools in the science classroom. The embedding of gaming techniques, perceptual arousal, culturally familiar elaborations, learner control over the instructional program, and metalinguistic capacities will improve the electronic environment in which students construct knowledge. Metacognitive strategies, such as the use of instructional maps embedded in science software (Figure 10.6), can be used to provide students with a knowledge of their progress in moving through the electronic microworld. Instructional maps can function as motivational devices to assist learners in structuring their learning experiences.

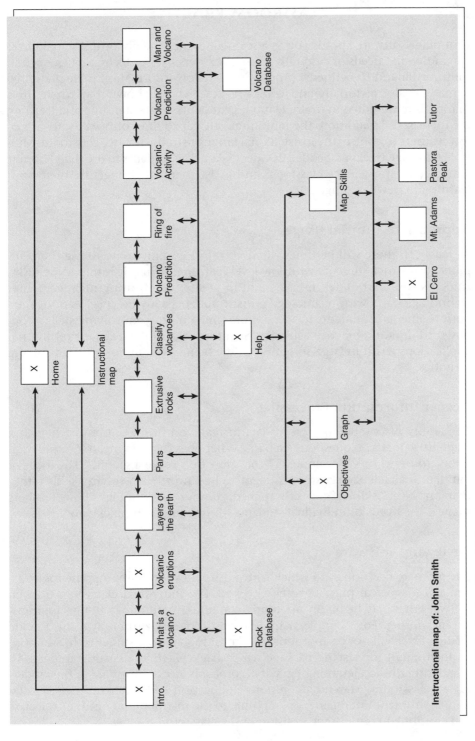

FIGURE 10.6   Instructional Map

CLASSROOM PRACTICE

Computer software affords you as a science teacher the opportunity to address the individual needs of culturally diverse learners. Newer technologies, such as multimedia and Hypermedia (Apple Corp.), allow information to be presented verbally, orally, pictorially, and iconically. Research has shown that, when information is represented in multiple modes, students' understanding and learning are increased. In addition, the multilinguistic capabilities of newer software allow learners to control the instructional language in the science classroom. Multiple language tracks embedded in videodisks allow students to use their "home" language in the science classroom and assist them in connecting their prior learning to new learning.

Appropriate Tutorial Usage

As teachers, there will be times when you find it appropriate to use the computer to instruct students with low-level learning. When learning some tasks, students will learn quicker, faster, and in greater depth using microcomputer technologies. Allowing technology to assist students with low-level learning frees both teacher and students to spend more time on problem-solving skills as opposed to drill-and-practice activities. Small amounts of time spent on tutorial applications result in large amounts of time being freed up for problem-solving activities.

Deeper Information Processing

The ability of computers to read data in real-world time allows teachers and students to focus on questions such as, "What does the data mean?" rather than "How do I read this thermometer?" or "How do I make a graph?" The focus of multicultural science classrooms ought to be on problem-solving skills rather than on "basic" skills. If correctly applied, computer technology allows teachers to meet the needs of individual students in the multicultural classroom.

Reviewing Software

The ultimate decision as to which software application is appropriate for a particular pedagogical purpose rests with you, the individual classroom teacher. Software that may be highly appropriate in one situation may not be appropriate in another. For example, a tutorial on dinosaurs written at a third grade reading level will not be appropriate for most high school students. In addition, an instrument interfacing package which is excellent in assisting students in calculating the acceleration of gravity is probably not appropriate in the kindergarten classroom. Matching computer applications, whether tutorial, simulation, instrument interfacing, or graphing, to the instructional needs of the class will continue to remain the decision of the classroom teacher.

CHAPTER SUMMARY

We know from research that computerized learning can make a significant difference in students' performance in the areas of achievement, retention of information, learning time, and student attitudes. Software of the future will feature a strong research base and rationale for pedagogical decisions. Transactional triangles (sets of interactions among learners, microcomputers, and the natural world) will be established within the science courseware of the future. Technology can assist you as a teacher to provide individualized instruction that supports individual learners in the multicultural science classroom.

  TOPICS TO REVIEW

computer-assisted instruction, 259
graphing packages, 262
instrument interfacing, 263

multimedia, 264
networking, 264
simulations, 264

  REFLECTIVE PRACTICE

1. In your opinion, what impact have computers made in elementary science instruction in public schools? Why do you think this is so?
2. What would you consider the "perfect" computerized classroom? Describe this classroom in terms of numbers of computers, types of learning environments, types of software, amount of time spent using computers, role of the teacher, role of the students, and so forth.
3. Much of the early computerized instruction in elementary science classrooms was dominated by a "drill and practice" instructional model. What improvements and innovations are needed to move teachers and students away from this instructional model?
4. In your opinion, how could instructional technologies or educational technology be most effective in improving instruction in the elementary science classroom?

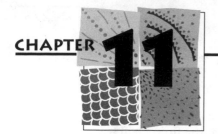

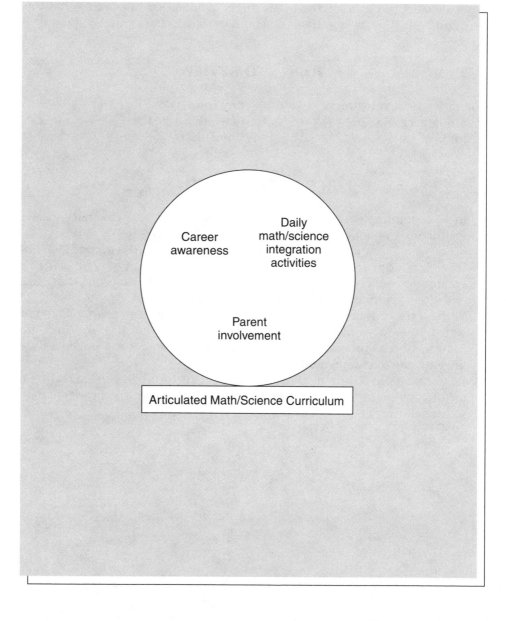

Career
awareness

Daily
math/science
integration
activities

Parent
involvement

Articulated Math/Science Curriculum

MATH/SCIENCE INTEGRATION IN THE MULTICULTURAL CLASSROOM

 POINTS TO PONDER

1. Math/science integration is one approach to thematic teaching. What is thematic teaching?
2. How does math/science integration encourage "real world" learning?
3. How does math/science integration involve parents and community members in the educational process?

CORPORATE CAREER DAY

A friend of mine, Dr. Mae Chen, recently recalled her adventures in taking her daughter to work. Her company had sponsored a "Young Women in Science" day at work. The corporation had urged each employee to bring his/her daughter or other young female relative to the workplace to provide math/science/technology awareness activities for the young women. During the morning hours the youngsters had been kept occupied learning about different products that the company researched and manufactured. They had used the company's computers to download satellite weather maps, had manufactured shaving cream and "super" balls in the company's labs, and had freeze-dried peaches and ice cream.

At lunchtime, the young women had a chance to rejoin their adult sponsors in the company dining room. Mae's daughter had described her morning's activities and her *excitement about science careers. She wanted to become a chemist like her mother. As Angie spoke with her mother, she asked one question, "Mom, I really like science, but why do I have to study math?"*

Many children are like Angie in that they do not understand the connections between academic disciplines. For a long time, schools have taught using an "egg carton" instructional model: science here, math there, and language arts someplace else. We teach children in a disjointed fashion, which results in them failing to see the connections between academic disciplines in the school environment.

THEMATIC TEACHING

In writing of the need to improve science and mathematics instruction in the United States, the National Science Board's Commission on Precollege Education in Mathematics, Science, and Technology stated:

> Alarming numbers of young Americans are ill-equipped to work in, contribute to, profit from and enjoy our increasingly technological society. Far too many emerge from the nation's elementary and secondary schools with an inadequate grounding in mathematics, science and technology. As a result, they lack sufficient knowledge to acquire the training, skills and understanding that are needed today and will be even more critically needed in the 21st century (1983, p.3).

The concern for the quality of education expressed by the National Science Board has been echoed in many school reform documents during the past decade. A survey conducted by the National Assessment of Education Progress at Educational Testing Service "suggests that a majority of 17-year-olds are poorly equipped for informed citizenship and productive performance in the workplace, let alone postsecondary studies in science" (Mullis & Jenkins, 1988, p. 6). In addition to lacking a sufficient knowledge of science to perform as citizens in a democracy, most students simply lack an interest in science, mathematics, and related technological careers. Culturally diverse students and Anglo females participate in mathematics and science careers in proportionally fewer numbers than do Anglo/European males.

Recent literature has attributed the underrepresentation of culturally diverse students and Anglo females in science fields to a variety of variables, including (1) lack of student interest in mathematics and science (Berryman, 1983; Clark, 1986; Entwistle & Duckworth, 1977); (2) mathematics and science anxiety (Clawson, Firment & Trower, 1981; Czerniak & Chiarelott, 1985); (3) personality factors (Clark, 1986; Harlen, 1985); (4) white male dominated images of mathematics, science, and technology careers (Hill, Pettus, & Heddin, 1990); (5) lack of minority role models in mathematics, science, and technology careers (Sadker & Sadker, 1979); (6) socioeconomic barriers (Patchen, 1982); (7) improper counseling regarding academic track coursework at the high school level (Marrett,

1981); (8) teacher attitudes and expectations (Karlin, Coffman, & Walter, 1969); and (9) lack of proper academic preparation (Harlen, 1985). For most children, the process of selecting or deselecting a science career begins at the elementary school level (Smith, 1983). Career awareness activities for children typically begin at the high school level (Sevenair & Carmichael, 1988; Mulkey & Ellis, 1990). There is a need, therefore, to provide science career knowledge and real world connections for mathematics and science learning at the elementary school level.

Effective science instruction should provide elementary-aged students with opportunities to investigate future careers as well as engage in activities which assist them in exploring the world in which they live. Science instruction should allow students to model the characteristics of scientists and mathematicians and enjoy the joys of discovery, creativity, curiosity, and striving to obtain a knowledge of the world around them. Effective learners are those who are actively engaged in the learning process, understand the value of what they are learning, and accept responsibility for their own learning throughout their lifetimes (Mullis & Jenkins, 1988, p. 13). Lifetime learning includes the ability to participate as a scientifically literate adult in society. In attempting to provide a knowledge of science, a knowledge of science career opportunities, and an awareness of the role of science in society, many teachers have come to use a math/science integration approach to instruction.

Math/science integration is an inquiry-based, **thematic** approach to teaching which stresses the "real world" applications of the study of science and mathematics. In speaking of this approach to teaching, the National Research Council stated that, "since mathematics is both the language of science and a science of patterns, the special links between mathematics and science are far more than just those between theory and applications. The methodology of mathematical inquiry shares with the scientific method a focus on exploration, investigation, conjecture, evidence and reasoning" (1990, p. 44). Modern day advocates of mathematics and science integration are links in a long chain of educators who have sought to bring a thematic approach to the study of these disciplines. Integrating science and mathematics is not a new idea in education. Modern math/science integration curriculum writing efforts are an eclectic approach to curriculum design in that they incorporate elements of constructivism, confluentism, humanism, and social reconstructionism.

Historical Foundations of Math/Science Integration

One of the first known attempts at math/science integration may be found in the works of Fredrich Fröebel, the inventor of the term "kindergarten." During the 1840s, Fröebel pioneered the use of manipulative materials to teach young children mathematical concepts and scientific principles simultaneously through a thematic, inquiry-based approach to learning. Around 1900, the Central Association of Science and Mathematics Teachers (parent organization of the present day School Science and Mathematics Association) was formed in the United States (Breslich, 1936). The purpose of this organization was to establish a closer relationship between mathematics and science teachers. Founders of the Central Association recommended that "algebra, geometry and physics be combined into a single, coherent course" (Breslich, 1936, p. 58). The decade of the 1960s was a time of resurgence of interest in math/science integration in elementary schools in the United States. During this decade several elementary science curriculum projects, including Science: A Process Approach (SAPA); Science Curriculum Improvement Study (SCIS); and Elementary Science Study (ESS) were written using a math/science inquiry-based approach to learning. Modern day advocates of math/science integration echo the sentiments of their predecessors in stating that it is vital that we teach young children both mathematics and science in an integrated, discovery-based environment (National Research Council, 1989). Recent elementary school math/science curriculum writing efforts have produced the Activities that Integrate Mathematics and Science (AIMS), Unified Science and Mathematics for Elementary Schools (USMES), South Central Kansas Elementary Science Math Project (SOCKEMS), and Great Explorations in Math and Science (GEMS) materials.

Research Foundations for Math/Science Integration

Math/science integration is used as a pedagogical approach with culturally diverse students because research has shown that it is effective in improving students' science process acquisition. An integrated thematic approach to mathematics and science instruction emphasizes problem-solving skills rather than computational proficiency in mathematics instruction. Thematic teaching of mathematics and science stresses the relevancy of the content area knowledge and assists students in making connections between "school learning" and the "real world." Studies have shown that the use of thematic instruction with culturally diverse learners results in more parent participation in the educational process and in the education of their children. For teachers, math/science integration is an effective way to reduce the amount of time spent on lesson planning in that it reduces the redundancy of content area presentations. In writing of the need for an integrated curriculum, Rutherford and Alhgren (1988) state, "science and mathematics have had a long and successful relationship. On the one hand, science continually provides mathematics with challenges, while on the other hand, mathematics was developed as a suitable way to analyze scientific problems" (p. 82).

The Teacher. A search of mathematics and science research literature reveals that an integrated math/science approach to teaching (1) improves teachers' attitudes toward teaching mathematics and science (Lehman & McDonald, 1988), (2) improves teachers' ability to articulate the curriculum (Bomeli, 1991; McGarry, 1986; Milson & Ball, 1986), (3) encourages teachers to teach higher-level thinking skills (Lewis, 1990; Voss, 1980), (4) emphasizes school and business partnerships to improve education (Lewis, 1990), (5) encourages the use of alternative assessment devices (Lewis, 1990), (6) promotes the introduction of technology in the mathematics and science curriculum (Winner & Holloway, 1983), (7) assists teachers in incorporating career awareness in their instruction (Voss, 1980), and (8) increases teachers' motivation to teach mathematics and science (Berlin, 1990; McGarry, 1986). When teachers use an interdisciplinary approach to mathematics and science teaching, they typically feel that their students' excitement for learning is enhanced, that the number of self-initiated learning activities undertaken by their students increases, and that their students improve in their social interaction skills.

The Student.   When mathematics and science are taught in an integrated, thematic manner, students' attitudes towards mathematics and science improve significantly (Dowd, 1990; Friend, 1985; Young, 1990). The use of a math/science approach to teaching improves students' problem-solving abilities in both subjects (Lewis, 1990; Shann, 1977). Math/science integration is highly effective in improving students' mathematical graphing skills and science process acquisition (Kren & Huntsberger, 1977). The acquisition of basic skills in reading comprehension and mathematical computation is fostered through the use of an interdisciplinary, problem-solving curriculum (Shann, 1977). In addition, the use of an integrated approach to instruction results in an improvement in students' concept acquisition in the two content areas (Friend, 1985; Kren & Huntsberger, 1977). In writing of students' concept acquisition through math/science activities, Kurtz and James (1975) stated, "children learn best when they discover concepts through concrete experiences" (p. 258).

The Parents or Guardians.   Frequently, parental or guardian involvement is not mentioned in science education literature or in teacher training activities. Research has shown that parental or guardian involvement is an important variable in children's academic success and in their future career decision-making processes (Useem, 1990). Successful math/science integration activities normally include a home involvement component, that is, an opportunity for parents and guardians to discuss with children their "school learning," assist their children in extending school knowledge, and advise their children about career options. Research has shown that parents and guardians of culturally diverse learners are willing to become involved in their children's education if given the opportunity (Mucha, 1987). When parents or guardians of culturally diverse learners become involved in their children's education, (1) children's academic performance improves (Allen, 1987; Gibb, 1989), (2) children's interest in science and mathematics increases (Beane, 1990; Gibb, 1989), and (3) children's career awareness increases (Anderson, 1989; Gibb, 1989). In addition, research (Sosa, 1986) has shown that parent or guardian involvement in schools through math/science integration activities produces positive changes in students in terms of decreased incidents of students' referrals for disciplinary reasons and increased school attendance. Students with higher science proficiency are more likely to

Parental involvement in children's learning is essential in schools.
(© Will Faller)

report home involvement in science projects and activities, access to more types of reading and reference materials in the home, and shorter periods spent television viewing (Mullis & Jenkins, 1988, p. 112). In summarizing the importance of home support for children's learning, Mullis and Jenkins (1988, p.117) state, "home support for and involvement in student's learning appears to be correlated with proficiency in various subject areas."

Social Foundations of Math/Science Integration

Math/science integration addresses the need for "relevant" curriculum in schools by incorporating social reconstructionist sociological foundations (Freire, 1970). Frequently, schools are criticized because "school knowledge" does not seem to be relevant or to have any practical value. While knowledge for the sake of knowledge may be desirable in certain instances, parents sometimes feel that schools are "out of touch" with the realities of the market place. Parents have high aspirations for their children, usually expecting their children to "do better" in life than they did. Thus, parents anticipate that schools will empower their children to participate in society by providing them with career awareness and job-related skills. Math/science integration incorporates elements of social reconstructionism in helping students to make "real world" connections between what they are learning and its practical application in the work place. Math/science integration can be viewed from a sociological perspective as a powerful tool for helping to build bridges between "school learning" and the "world of work" and as a means for empowering children to participate fully as scientifically literate adults in a democratic society.

Psychological Foundations of Math/Science Integration

As with the other pedagogical approaches discussed in this book, math/science integration contains many elements of constructivist learning theories. Problem-centered learning, which is central to constructivist instructional models, is also prevalent in math/science integration activities. Working in groups to seek possible solutions to real world problems is a constructivist psychological tenet which has been adopted for use in math/science integration instructional models. Group work, which accommodates the sociocultural aspect of constructivist learning models, is also indigenous to thematic math/science instructional activities. Sharing, reporting of findings in small group and large group settings, reflective learning, and metalearning skills are found in both constructivist and confluent educational traditions.

Philosophical Foundations of Math/Science Integration

While modern math/science integration contains elements of "constructivist" psychological and social reconstructionist sociological foundations, it is also based on confluent education philosophical foundations. **Confluent education** is the integration of the affective domain with the cognitive domain. The goals of math/science integration from a confluent education viewpoint are (1) to provide students with more alternatives to choose from in terms of their own lives, (2) to assist students in making choices, and (3) to assist students in realizing that they can make choices. Inherent in modern math/science integration programs are four confluent education principles: (1) participation, (2) integration, (3) relevance, and (4) social goals (Shapiro, 1972). From a confluent education perspective, math/science integration involves power sharing, negotiation, and joint responsibility for teaching and learning between students and teachers (Friere, 1970). The ideas of interpenetration (e.g., the mutual sharing of ideas), thematic learning, and the integration of social values into the content areas advocated by adherents of confluent education are central in math/science integration. The focus on solving real world problems and applications of mathematics and science knowledge addresses the confluentist concept of educational relevancy. Finally, the social goal of the development of a person who is able to function in a human society is strongly embedded in math/science integrated curriculum programs.

Components of an Interdisciplinary Curriculum

Math/science integration programs may be viewed as "add-on" programs in the sense that they add parental involvement, social concerns, and career awareness to the existing mathematics and science courses of study. Four types of activities are common to successful math/science integration projects: (1) articulation of the curriculum to identify opportunities for integration; (2) thematically planned, inquiry-based daily activities; (3) parental involvement; and (4) career awareness.

Articulation.   The first step in building an integrated curriculum is articulation. **Articulation** of the curriculum involves examining the mathematics and science curriculum and identifying opportunities for thematic activities. Articulation can be undertaken using concepts, themes, units of study, skills, processes, or a combination of these approaches. One approach to identifying opportunities for math/science integration is through constructing a matrix which includes mathematics topics and science "disciplines" as starting points. This approach leads to a math/science matrix such as that shown in Table 11.1.

The result is a matrix which identifies opportunities for math/science integration activities for the teacher. From this matrix, the teacher could determine when duplicate conceptual knowledge is to be presented in the two content areas; these occasions become opportunities for thematic instruction. For example, the earth science unit of a particular upper elementary science textbook series presents information on specific gravity at the sixth grade level. The mathematics curriculum materials at the same grade level present the topic of decimals and decimal notation. Since related concepts are presented in both sets of materials, an integrated approach to learning is possible in this instance. Math/science integration begins when related concepts are presented thematically to students, rather than in a fragmented or compartmentalized fashion.

A second approach to identifying opportunities for math/science integration is based on articulating the broad unifying themes of science and mathematical ideas. In the particular instance shown in Table 11.2, six science themes—energy, evolution, patterns of change, scale and structure, stability, and systems and interactions (California Department of Education, 1990)—form one axis of the integration grid. The other axis of the grid represents five broad ideas of mathematics, that is, dimension, quantity, uncertainty, shape, and change (Steen, 1990). The concepts identified in this process become the basis of math/science

TABLE 11.1   Mathematics Topic/Science Discipline Matrix

	Science Discipline		
Math Topics	*Life Science*	*Physical Science*	*Earth Science*
Measurement	Plant growth	Temperature	Map scale
Equations	Magnification	Work	Relative humidity
Probability & Statistics	Population sampling		Hurricane prediction
Ratio/Proportion	Symmetry	Balancing equations	
Graphing		Displaying data	Displaying data
Spatial Visualization	Animal drawings	Light	Mineral crystals
Geometry/Angles		Wave theory	Mineral identification
Scientific Notation	Growth curves		Geologic time
			Radioactive decay
Percent		Solutions	
Decimals		Work/force	Specific gravity

integration instruction: the chance to simultaneously fulfill the requirements of the mathematics and science curriculum.

It must be noted that it is not possible to integrate mathematics and science instruction everyday during the school year. There are certain concepts in science and mathematics which are domain specific and which have no corresponding concept in the other discipline. Frequently, math/science integration matrices will have "holes" or empty spaces in which no common concepts have been identified. "Holes" are healthy. They reflect that thematic teaching is not possible everyday in all content areas.

Thematic Activities.   Once a matrix of integration opportunities has been generated, the teacher can identify instructional activities which will build a knowledge of the science and mathematics concepts simultaneously. Math/science integration is predicated on problem solving. For example, suppose Mr. Son, a fifth grade teacher, had discovered that he taught map construction in his science curriculum and ratio and proportion in mathematics to the same students. He could begin by stating a problem to his students, "Next week is PTA Open House and let's assume your grandfather will be coming to meet me. Can you help him find my classroom?" After a period of discussion, Mr. Son could ask the students, who have been divided into small groups, to draw a map of the school. The students could measure the building and construct a map to scale showing their findings. This activity teaches mapping skills and ratio and proportion simultaneously in a meaningful manner. There is an inherent career awareness component built into this instructional activity. Surveyors, cartographers, and geologists in their everyday work use the same concepts and skills that the students are learning. Daily integration activities teach science and mathematics concepts and skills and identify their real world connections in a unified, thematic fashion.

Parental Involvement.   Successful math/science integration programs actively involve parents and guardians in children's learning. Sometimes parents may be

TABLE 11.2   Science Theme/Mathematical Idea Matrix

Science Theme	Mathematical Ideas				
	Dimension	Quantity	Uncertainty	Shape	Change
Energy		Simple machines			
Evolution			Genetics	Fossils	
Patterns of Change	Minerals	Plant growth			Geologic time
Scale and Structure		Microscope	Mapping		Astronomy
Stability	Molecules			Crystals	
Systems & Interactions		Pendulum		Landforms	
					Ecosystems

directly involved in school activities by serving as resource persons to the class, that is, parents may be guest speakers who visit with children in the classroom and tell them about their jobs and careers. At other times, parents or guardians may serve as mentors and tutors assisting students at home with math/science projects, such as the bridge building or aluminum boat building contests mentioned in the classroom practice section of this chapter. Use of any problem-solving approach allows children to bring their home knowledge to school while encouraging students to use their home as a resource in the learning process.

Career Awareness.   Career awareness is the final component of successful math/science integration activities. A knowledge of when and where science and mathematics concepts are used in adult life is vital for every student. Career awareness may be undertaken on a daily basis as well as through the use of occasional guest speakers and visitors to the classroom or through field trips to "job sites." Successful math/science integration activities assist students in making connections between classroom learning and adult work in the real world. Expanding students' knowledge base regarding preparation for various mathematics, science, and related technology careers is a primary focus of integrated instruction.

CLASSROOM PRACTICE

Four components are typically found in successful math/science integrated programs: an articulated curriculum which identifies opportunities for math/science integration, thematic daily lessons, parental involvement, and career awareness. One way to include these components is through the use of daily math/science instructional activities, monthly guest speakers or field trips to the community, and monthly contests to serve as motivational devices and to build career awareness. Daily lesson plans should provide students with a knowledge of mathematics and science concepts as well as a knowledge of when this information is useful in the real world. Guest speakers (e.g., parents, community members) and field trips to business and industry in the immediate geographic area give students an awareness of the connections between "school learning" and adult work in society. Finally, motivational contests on a weekly, monthly, or quarterly basis give students the opportunity to engage in problem solving while engaging parents and guardians in children's learning.

Daily Math/Science Activities

One foundation of teaching the math/science integrated curriculum consists of daily lessons which incorporate mathematics and science concepts, or concepts which are common to the two disciplines. Daily activities also lend themselves to the building of career awareness in each student. Grayson Wheatley's (1991) instructional model involving tasks, groups, and sharing should be central to math/science instruction. Because math/science integrated instruction involves problem solving, the task or the problem is the beginning of instruction. As problems are presented to students, students should be encouraged to work in cooperative groups in the classroom. Finally, students should be encouraged to share their solution path(s) with others in the class. The following activities show some sample math/science lesson plans.

ACTIVITY 11-1 ▪ BOUNCING BALL

Science Concept: Energy can be converted from one form to another.

Mathematics Concept: Function

Materials:

rubber ball (tennis ball)   meter stick

Procedure:

1. Ask the students to predict what will happen if a ball is dropped and allowed to continue bouncing.
2. Have the students drop a tennis ball or similar ball from a height of about 2 meters. Measure the height of each of four rebounds.
3. Make a data table of the results (Table 11.3).
4. Make a line graph of the results.
5. What happens to the height of the ball as it continues to bounce?
6. What would happen with other types of balls?

ACTIVITY 11-2 ▪ SPRINGS

Science Concept: Elasticity

Mathematics Concept: Mass

Materials:

springs (from old ballpoint pens)   washers or metric weights

TABLE 11.3   Rebound Heights of Tennis Ball

Rebound Number	Height of Bounce
0	2.0 meters
1	
2	
3	
4	

**A
C
T
I
V
I
T
I
E
S**

TABLE 11.4 Measuring Springs	
Number of Washers	*Length of Spring*
1	
2	
3	

Procedure:

1. Attach a spring to a hook (attached to a table, wall, etc.). Measure the length of the spring.
2. Add one washer or weight to the spring. Record its length.
3. Repeat for 10 or 11 washers. Make a data table (Table 11.4) and line graph from your results.
5. What happens to the length of the spring as the mass increases?
6. What is the independent variable? Dependent variable?
7. What would happen if another spring were used?

ACTIVITY 11-3 ■ SUGAR CUBES (PENTAMINOES)

Science Concept: Isomers

Mathematics Concept: Spatial visualization

Materials:

5 sugar cubes

Procedure:

1. Using the sugar cubes, determine how many different ways you can arrange the cubes so that at least one side of a cube touches another cube.

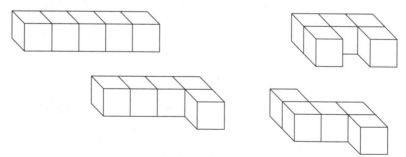

2. Draw each arrangement that you make.
3. How many different arrangements can you make with six sugar cubes? Four cubes? Three cubes?

Math/Science Contests

Contests are motivational activities which are based in problem-solving activities and should foster an interest in mathematics, science, or related technology fields in students. Typically, classroom contests should be used in lieu of other homework assignments and should encourage parental involvement. Contests are most effective when equity issues (especially those associated with socioeconomic status) are addressed. Simple, readily available materials should be used to ensure that all students have the opportunity to participate. Contests which foster career awareness in elementary school-aged students and which increase parental involvement in the process of schooling are illustrated with the next group of activities.

ACTIVITY 11-4 ■ TOWER BUILDING CONTEST

Materials:

25 soda straws   100 straight pins

Problem: The objective of this contest is to build the tallest "building" possible that will withstand hurricane force winds (an electric fan).

Teacher Materials to Conduct the Contest:

1 electric fan   1 meter stick

Teacher Notes (how to conduct the contest):

1. Allow students to construct their towers at home with parental or adult assistance (if available). Address equity issues by encouraging students to use very simple materials (regular soda straws available at stores, school cafeterias, and fast food restaurants).
2. On the day of the contest, have the students "bolt" their towers to a sheet of cardboard on the floor of the classroom.
3. Allow a student to hold a corner of the cardboard (not the building) to keep it from flying across the room.
4. Using a window fan, create a "hurricane" by setting the fan at its highest setting. Allow the "hurricane" to rage for 30 seconds before turning off the fan. If the tower does not fly apart during the "hurricane," measure its height in meters.
5. Place each child's tower in the same starting position at the same distance from the wind source. Measure each tower in the same manner.

Follow-up Activities: As each tower is measured, have the students record their peers' names and the heights of their successful towers. Make a data table and/or accompanying histogram or bar graph showing the heights of the towers.

Guest Speakers: Architects and engineers work with concepts related to this activity.

ACTIVITY 11-5 ▪ ALUMINUM BOAT CONTEST

Materials:

1 sheet of aluminum foil per student (20 × 20 centimeters)

Problem: The objective of this contest is to build a boat out of the aluminum foil which will hold the greatest mass before sinking.

Teacher Materials to Conduct the Contest:

metric stacking masses or a set of weights
container for water (plastic pan if the competition is inside or a small wading
    pool for an outside activity)

Teacher Notes (how to conduct the contest):

1. Allow students to construct their boats at home with parental or adult assistance (if available). Address equity issues by encouraging students to use simple materials. Aluminum foil is selected for this activity because it is inexpensive. One roll of foil is sufficient for an entire class of children and is a material readily available to all children.
2. On the day of the contest, establish ground rules for adding "weights" or masses to the boats. With younger children, you may wish to have them add marbles to their boats and count how many marbles are needed to "sink" the boats as opposed to using metric weights or stacking masses.
3. The aluminum boat activity is a little messy in the sense that it is difficult to avoid having some spilled water when children float an object in a container of water. This activity is most appropriately done outside, on a tiled floor, or on flat-topped tables which can be "mopped up" with a sponge or paper toweling.

Follow-up Activities: As each boat "sinks" have the students record their peers' names and the maximum mass that the boat held prior to sinking. Have the students make a data table and/or accompanying histogram or bar graph showing the masses that the boats held. For older students, computational work in determining the "average" mass is appropriate. When older children are involved, calculators can be integrated into this activity (e.g., having the students determine averages).

Guest Speakers: Container design engineers, boat captains, architects, and expeditors deal with concepts covered in this activity.

ACTIVITY 11-6 ▪ BEAN GROWING CONTEST

Materials:

3 bean seeds/student

Problem: The object is to grow a plant that has the greatest biomass during a 1-month growing period.

**A
C
T
I
V
I
T
I
E
S**

Teacher Materials to Conduct the Contest:

Provide seeds for the students at the beginning of the contest period; bean seeds are relatively inexpensive when purchased in bulk. On the day of the contest a metric balance is needed to determine the biomass (e.g., the mass of the living material: cut the plant at the soil level and determine its weight or mass) of the plants.

Teacher Notes (how to conduct the contest):

1. Allow students to plant their seeds in any manner that they choose. Have students adjust soil, fertilizer, and water, etc., on their own. Address equity issues by providing seeds for the students. By allowing students to select their own container (e.g., paper cups, pots, cans) and soil for the containers, the contest becomes open to all students.
2. On the day of the contest, instruct the students to bring their growing plants to class. Allow the student to select their largest plant.
3. Using scissors, cut off the largest plant at the surface of the soil and weigh each plant on a metric balance. The use of biomass rather than plant height discourages the use of expensive plant growth lamps and makes this a "fair" contest for all students.

Follow-up Activities: As each bean plant is weighed, have the students make a data table, histogram, or bar graph showing the biomass of each person's plant. With older students, determine the "average" biomass for the class. Calculators are appropriate for older students to use in handling "averaging" procedures. Computer graphing is also easily integrated into this activity.

Guest Speakers: Agricultural extension agents, feed store operators, farmers, gardeners, horticulturists, and those engaged in agribusiness careers work with concepts related to this contest.

ACTIVITY 11-7 ■ BRIDGE BUILDING CONTEST

Materials:

25 soda straws   100 straight pins

Problem: The object is to build a bridge that will span a distance of 30 centimeters and hold the greatest mass possible before collapsing.

Teacher Materials to Conduct the Contest:

metric weight set

Teacher Notes (how to conduct the contest):

1. Allow students to construct their "bridges" at home under adult supervision and guidance.
2. On the day of the contest, place two stacks of books on the floor of the classroom or on a table, such that the books are 30 centimeters apart. Place one bridge at a time over this span.
3. Hang weights under the bridge until the bridge breaks.

Follow-up Activities: As each bridge is tested, have the students record the names of each of their classmates and the mass that the bridge held when it "broke." Make a data table from the findings. You may also wish to have the students construct a bar graph comparing the results of their classmates. For older students, simple univariate statistics are appropriately used with this activity. Students can determine the mean, median, mode, range, and rank of the "strength" of the bridges. Calculators are especially useful in this type of activity with older elementary students.

Guest Speakers: Civil engineers, structural designers, cargo storage personnel, and container designers work with concepts related to this contest.

Guest Speakers and Field Trips

Every community, no matter how large or small, contains resources in the form of people who are willing to assist teachers with building career awareness in children. Guest speakers bring careers alive for students. Contact with successful role models is a strong and powerful device for stimulating students' interest in mathematics, science, and related technology careers. A schedule of math/science concepts, guest speakers, and related motivational contests is shown in Table 11.5.

Career awareness is vital to math/science integration activities. (© Jim Pickerell)

| TABLE 11.5   Suggested Career Awareness Plan |||
Month	Topic	Career Emphasis
September	Energy	Power plant worker
October	Simple machines	Engineer
November	Magnetism & Electricity	Recycling attendant
December	Rocks & Minerals	Jeweler
January	Landforms	Geologist
February	Tissues & Organs	Physician
March	Human Body	Exercise therapist
April	Simple plants	Farmer
May	Flowering plants	Florist
June	Ecosystems	Fish & wildlife

 CHAPTER SUMMARY

Math/science integration is a thematic approach to teaching which is based on confluentist philosophical, social reconstructionist sociological, and constructivist psychological foundations. Successful math/science integration programs share four components: articulation of the mathematics and science curriculum, parental involvement, career awareness, and daily math/science integration activities. Research has shown that this thematic approach to learning improves students' mathematics and science concept acquisition, improves students science processes, and improves students attitudes towards mathematics and science. Thematic teaching of science and mathematics is a problem-solving approach to teaching and learning which fosters tasks, groups, and sharing.

 TOPICS TO REVIEW

 REFLECTIVE PRACTICE

1. Dr. Peg House of the University of Minnesota is often quoted in speeches at professional societies as saying, "math/science integration has always made good sense." What do you suppose she means by this?
2. Successful math/science integration activities typically contain four components: (1) an articulated curriculum, (2) thematically planned daily activities, (3) parental involvement, and (4) career awareness. In your opinion, why is each component necessary for a successful program?
3. Why do you think math/science integration is not more widely used in elementary science and mathematics instruction? Justify your answers.

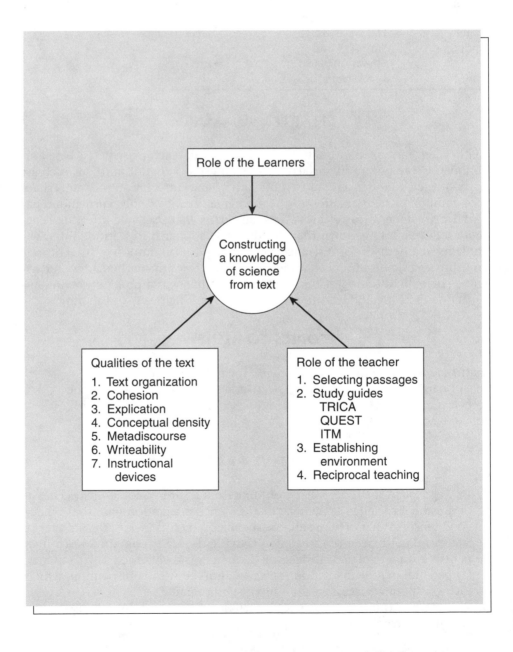

CONSTRUCTING A KNOWLEDGE OF SCIENCE FROM TEXT IN THE MULTICULTURAL SCIENCE CLASSROOM

 POINTS TO PONDER

1. How do students construct a knowledge of science from text?
2. What is a constructivist view of reading in the science classroom?
3. How do "friendly texts" differ from traditional science texts?
4. What strategies may be used to make reading in the science classroom an interactive experience?

READING IN THE SCIENCE CLASSROOM

Reading in the science classroom is not simply a matter of instructing the students to "read the book and answer the questions at the end of the chapter." Learning from text is not a passive act. Children are not tree roots; they do not learn by the process of osmosis or take in knowledge in the manner that trees take in water. A child's conceptual knowledge of science is constructed gradually. Children construct knowledge through their interactions with written material, through their experiences in the real world, and through their interactions with others. Students append new knowledge to what they already know. Grayson Wheatley has written that "knowledge is not disembodied but is intimately related to the action and experience of the learner—it is always contextual and never separated from the knower" (1991, p. 10).

In the past, emphasis in content-area reading has included reading skills, word recognition, reading comprehension, and study skills. This "traditional" approach to content-area reading has been based on two assumptions: (1) that the major way to learn an academic subject is to read about it, and (2) that the textbook is the major source of content-area knowledge. This perspective on reading is based on theories and philosophies of education which hold that textbooks are sources of authoritative information and that this information can somehow be transmitted to children.

There has arisen a belief among some segments of the science education community that reading in the science classroom is somehow counterproductive and is not "real science." Proponents of this viewpoint suggest that reading is not the domain of the science teacher and that teachers who encourage reading in the science classroom are somehow "bad" teachers. In real life, the reverse is actually true. Writing and reporting of the findings from scientific investigations are part of the "job" of every scientist. Reading the research of others and wrestling with their theories and hypotheses is part of every scientist's job. If we view reading as part of the everyday life of a scientist, and if we assume that children can construct meaning from verbal materials, then we find that indeed reading has a very valuable role in the science classroom. Textbooks are sources of information, information that cannot in many instances be accessed by hands-on activities. Historically, textbooks in the science classroom have been used as encyclopedias, and not as tools to facilitate the learning process.

Learning from Text

Problem-centered learning, according to Wheatley (1989), has three components: tasks, groups, and sharing. Reading in the science classroom should be a problem-centered activity. If we use Wheatley's model, selecting **"friendly" text** (prose which is comprehensible by all students) and developing accompanying study guides is the first component in a problem-centered reading approach in the science classroom. When presenting reading materials to students, teachers should emphasize the task, that is, the purpose of the reading material(s), to allow students to construct knowledge of scientific phenomena. Social interactions, for example, reading and discussion in small and large groups, are the second component of a problem-centered reading process. Group reporting or reciprocal teaching (for which teachers and students share the responsibility for teaching) is the final component of a problem-centered approach to reading.

Constructivist theory holds that knowledge is not transmitted to children but is constructed by children. The process of understanding written or verbal text is one in which a reader uses a combination of what is written, what he or she already knows, and various general processes to construct a plausible representation of what the author presumably had in mind. In addressing the linguistic needs of learners in the multicultural science classroom, three main concerns arise: (1) the role of the textbook, (2) the means by which children construct meaning from that textbook, and (3) the role of the teacher.

Group reading or reciprocal teaching is a highly effective strategy for culturally diverse learners. (© Frank Siteman)

The Role of the Textbook

Science textbooks historically have been described as at best packed with facts but lacking in concepts; at worst, they have been condemned as inaccurate, poorly organized, and uninteresting. In spite of this, surveys repeatedly show science teachers relying heavily on textbooks as both pedagogical guides and subject matter authorities in the modern science classroom. In addition, teachers believe the reading level of science textbooks is "too hard" for their students. Difficulties students encounter in comprehending modern science textbooks, however, may be more attributable to their being reader "unfriendly" rather than their being too difficult for the targeted age group. Low verbal learners, students with limited English proficiency, and students from culturally diverse backgrounds find science textbooks difficult to understand even when those students have a basic mastery of the English language. Singer and Donlan (1990) in studying science textbooks found that the writing style of the textbooks was more of an impediment to student learning than the science content.

Friendly textbooks help the learner recall background information, perceive relationships among ideas, make inferences, and draw conclusions. Textbooks should assist the student in constructing declarative knowledge of science facts, concepts, and rules and principles. Most currently used science textbooks are not friendly textbooks in that they do not assist learners in structuring new knowledge. Friendly textbooks are those which consider text organization, cohesion, explication of textual material, conceptual density, elements of metadiscourse, writeability, and instructional devices which increase students' overall comprehension of the reading material.

Text Organization.   **Text organization** not only includes the purpose and arrangement of textual materials, but also the choice of rhetorical patterns used to show the relationship among ideas. The five commonly used rhetorical patterns found in textbooks are (1) the question and answer format (*response pattern*), (2) the cause and effect relationship (*covariance pattern*), (3) the sequencing of events in chronological order (*temporal pattern*), (4) the comparison and contrasting of characteristics (*adversative pattern*), and (5) the listing of characteristics to define concepts and ideas (*attribution pattern*). According to textbook surveys, the most commonly used patterns for science textbooks are compare and contrast as well as cause and effect patterns. Most students in the elementary multicultural classroom have difficulty constructing meaning from textual materials which use the adversative and covariance patterns of text organization. Science textbooks and trade books which used the response, temporal, or attribution rhetorical patterns have been shown to increase student comprehension and, thus, are reader friendly.

Cohesion.   **Cohesion** refers to how writers tie information together from sentence to sentence, paragraph to paragraph, and chapter to chapter. *Cataphora* is a cohesion pattern used when cited elements point to a later referent in the text, whereas *anaphora* is used when elements point to a prior referent. Five cohesive patterns are commonly used in textual materials: (1) constructing sentences or phrases such that a word's meaning depends on a previous word (reference), (2) repetition of words or the use of synonyms (lexical cohesion), (3) deletion of previously stated words or ideas (ellipsis), (4) substitution, and (5) conjunction. Research has shown that the relative lack of cohesion makes science textbooks boring, slows the reading rate of students, lowers reading comprehension rates, and reduces student recall. Friendly textbooks employ all types of cohesive devices to tie together sentences, paragraphs, and chapters. Cohesion increases student comprehension of the written material. Writers of science textbooks need particularly to include reference, lexical, and ellipsis patterns of cohesion to benefit students who have difficulty comprehending verbal materials.

Explication.   Writers use **explication** when they state facts, ideas, and their relationships directly instead of requiring readers to infer, organize, or construct the relationships themselves. Textbooks, especially science textbooks, tend not to explicate information systematically. Explication devices include (1) vocabulary (defining new terms using language familiar to the student), (2) background knowledge (relating new ideas to students' prior knowledge), and (3) organizing ideas with real-world applications. Friendly science textbooks activate students' prior knowledge, use common analogies or analogies that are part of the child's milieu, and present students with real-world applications of new knowledge. The use of real-world knowledge, culturally familiar or culturally syntonic examples, and everyday vocabulary is especially important for students in the multicultural science classroom.

Conceptual Density.   **Conceptual density** refers to the number of new ideas and vocabulary words contained in a textbook. According to Singer and Donlan (1990), Mary Budd Rowe has determined that the average high school textbook introduces seven to ten new concepts per page and from 2,400 to 3,000 terms and symbols overall during a 1-year course. This is an average of 20 concepts per class period or one concept every 2 minutes. Research shows that friendly textbooks use wordier text, while controlling the introduction of new concepts. Explication helps students bridge the gap between their own knowledge and experience and new knowledge contained in the textbook.

Metadiscourse.   **Metadiscourse** is like a conversation between the author and the reader. It occurs when the author of a text talks directly to the reader about the information in the textbook. This book uses elements of metadiscourse in the classroom practice section of each chapter. Previous research studies have shown that the use of metadiscourse improves a reader's comprehension of information that the author is attempting to convey. Metadiscourse may include statements of textual goals, such as, "You will learn . . . ." Metadiscourse may assist the learner in previewing or recalling prior knowledge: "You recall in the first chapter that you learned . . ." or "When you were a child . . . ." Stressing the importance of an idea to the reader ("You realize that this is important . . .") is a form of metadiscourse. Finally, stressing an attitude toward a fact or an idea ("Your attitude toward . . . .") is a use of metadiscourse. Research indicates that readers prefer textual materials which use this interaction between the author and the reader, that is, material that helps them to negotiate and personalize meaning. Research also indicates that metadiscourse increases student's declarative learning.

Writeability.   **Writeability** (Fry, 1988) is the reverse side of the readability coin. Writeability answers such questions as, "Are sentences long enough to explicate adequately cause/effect relationships?" "Are sentences sufficiently long enough to define new terms?" and "Are sentences long enough to compare and contrast ideas?" Two hundred twenty common words (e.g., a, the, and, some, but, to, from) make up 75% of the textual material in elementary school science textbooks. Including these common words in readability formulae does not give an accurate picture of the level of difficulty of textual materials.

How does sentence complexity affect the friendliness of a reading passage? Psycholinguistic research has shown that "kernel" sentences (those which contain only a noun and a verb) are more easily understood by students than complex sentences. Clauses which contain cause and effect relationships should be used after the kernel portion of the sentence. Less punctuation makes textual passages easier for children to understand. In addition, variation of paragraph format makes for friendlier text.

Instructional Devices.   **Instructional devices** are those reading strategies which help the reader to focus attention to shifts in topic, the relative importance of ideas, and the relationship among elements. Such conventions as headings and subheadings, glossaries, and visualization strategies (e.g., diagrams, tables, graphs, and flow charts) are commonly used instructional devices. Research has shown that embedding instructional devices or strategies within the text supports the learning of all students and proportionally benefits bilingual/bidialectic students. Photographs, diagrams, charts, and tables of data which illustrate textual material increase the learning of students, especially low verbal students and students for whom English is a second language. There is a strong aptitude-by-treatment interaction favoring low verbal learners which supports the enhancement of textual materials with visual and graphic displays.

Summaries of textual information embedded in written materials benefit all categories of learners (e.g., low, average, and high verbal learners). Since transferring knowledge from one situation to another is a major purpose in learning, friendly textbooks or passages written in considerate prose facilitate this objective by providing suggestions for the application of the text's knowledge to new situations. No matter how "friendly" the textbook, the use of that textbook is even more vital in the learning of children in the multicultural science classroom. Science textbooks are heavily used as the primary source of science instruction in many classrooms. While the quality of those textbooks could be greatly improved through the addition of the elements of friendly text or friendly prose, the use of those textbooks is the vital concern in the reading process.

The Role of the Learner

Learners in multicultural classrooms construct meaning or a knowledge of the physical world through what they do and read. Constructing new knowledge of the physical world from verbal materials depends in large part on the existing knowledge that the reader brings to the text. Guided by one's purpose in reading and the sociocultural conditions that apply, one builds a personally renders the message intended by the author. Activity-based instruction, which is the hallmark of "good" science instruction, is also the hallmark of good reading instruction in the science content area. Reading in the science classroom should involve active mental processing in the same way that laboratory investigations involve active information processing. Students construct a knowledge of science concepts from verbal materials or from prose passages when they are actively involved in reading at the literal, interpretive, and applied levels of comprehension. Reading, like all inquiry in the science classroom, involves identification of a task and the interactions that students experience while doing the task.

The Role of the Teacher

The teacher, not the textbook, is responsible for guiding the process of learning. In orchestrating the use of printed materials for science instruction, the teacher performs four vital roles: (1) selecting of textbook passages and/or trade books

Reading is a form of inquiry learning. (© Will Faller)

that will enhance students' understandings of the concepts, (2) preparing of study guides or of questioning procedures which actively involve all students in interacting with the verbal material, (3) establishing the physical environment, and (4) assisting students in constructing meaning. In establishing a classroom atmosphere in which students can actively construct meaning from verbal materials, the teacher first needs to select passages which exhibit the characteristics of friendly text. Second, the teacher should prepare study guides or questioning procedures which will actively engage students in questioning, evaluating, criticizing, and in general "worrying about" the knowledge that the author(s) are trying to convey. Third, teachers should place children in cooperative reading groups, groups in which children are required to explain, elaborate, or defend their position to others (as well as to themselves). Striving for an explanation or meaning from a text passage forces the learner to integrate and elaborate knowledge in new ways. Finally, teachers need to engage in reciprocal teaching, that is, must allow students to assist in the teaching process. Within cooperative groups, students should question each other: For example, "Where does the author say that?" "How do you know that?" In addition, the teacher should assist students by asking clarifying or focusing questions, which encourage students to collect data from textual passages and construct new knowledge based on that data. Teachers can actively engage students in the act of reading through use of three-tiered study guides, QUEstions that Stimulate Thinking (QUEST) techniques, or inductive thinking methods (ITM) (Singer & Simonsen, 1989).

Reflective Reading

When assisting children in the learning process, a Teaching Reading in Content Areas (**TRICA**) technique is especially useful in the science classroom. One of the most widely used reflective reading techniques was developed by Harold Herber (1978). Herber's technique allows students and teachers to construct meaning from textual passages at literal, intepretive, and applied levels. When working with literal level reading activities, teachers should ask students, "What does the author say?" At the interpretive level, teachers should encourage students to consider the question, "What does the author mean?" Finally, at the applied level of reading comprehension, teachers should encourage students to think in terms of "How does this new information relate to what you already knew about the subject?" The use of reflective reading techniques (discussed in depth in the classroom practice section of this chapter) allows students to construct a knowledge of science concepts from prose passages.

QUEstions that Stimulate Thinking (QUEST)

While the use of Herber's technique is a powerful tool in assisting students in constructing meaning from prose passages, it is not the only technique which can be used to assist culturally diverse students in the elementary classroom. The **QUEST** (an acronym for QUEstions that Stimulate Thinking) technique is also a powerful device for guiding students in constructing meaning from verbal information sources. Whereas most classroom discussion of prose material is conducted at a literal level, QUEST techiques attempt to raise the questioning levels to the inferential and interpretive and finally to the generalized, applied, and evaluative levels of thinking (Singer & Simonsen, 1989, p. 45).

To use QUEST in a science lesson, the teacher first has the students read the text to obtain information. For example, the teacher could supply the students with a textbook chapter which describes the kingdoms of living things. Next, the teacher conducts a discussion that leads the students to recall information that they have just read about organisms in each kingdom. This discussion is stimulated by a *focusing* question such as, "Would someone summarize the characteristics of plants?" The teacher may subsequently ask an *extending* question: "Who can give us some more information about plants?" The teacher repeats this process for animals, protists, moneran, and fungi.

After the relevant literal level information has been reviewed, the next step is to get students to abstract the common properties or attributes of each of the kingdoms of living things. A *lifting* question is then posed for the students such as, "What do all living things have in common?" or "How are all living things alike?" After extending questions have led to a definition of "living things," the teacher can then have students evaluate the quality of their answers by asking, "Is a tomato a living thing? How do we know?" "Are bacteria living things? Explain your answer." As with TRICA techniques, QUEST techniques encourage students to work at literal, interpretive, and applied levels of reading to construct meaning from prose materials at many different levels.

Inductive Thinking Method (ITM)

The **Inductive Thinking Method** (ITM) is another tool to assist children in constructing meaning from verbal materials. In using this procedure, the teacher asks a series of hierarchically arranged questions which facilitate students' thinking about what they have read. The ITM technique moves students from concrete discussion of facts to abstract discussions of principles. Following is a list of the nine stages in the ITM procedure with sample questions:

1. *Enumeration and listing*: What were the.. . ? What did you notice?
2. *Grouping*: What belongs together?
3. *Labeling and categorizing*: What are good names for these groups?
4. *Identifying points*: What did you notice?
5. *Explaining items of identified information*: Why did this happen?
6. *Making inferences*: What does this mean?
7. *Predicting consequences and hypothesizing*: What would happen if?
8. *Explaining and/or supporting the prediction*: Why do you think this would happen?
9. *Verifying the prediction*: What could show this prediction to be true? Is there anything that you have seen that might support what you have predicted? (Singer & Simonsen, 1989, p. 46).

The first three stages of the inductive teaching method involve describing and categorizing information found in text passages. The middle stages involve interpreting information, while the final stages involve hypotheses formation and testing. The ITM method is a procedure that systematically leads students to think about information that they are acquiring or structuring from prose passages.

CLASSROOM PRACTICE

The TRICA technique advocated in this chapter is a cooperative learning model in which you, as a teacher, construct a three-tiered study guide for use by your students. The purpose of the study guide is to encourage your students to work together to construct meaning from verbal materials. The three-tiered study guide allows you to use reciprocal teaching in the science classroom. In reciprocal teaching, you and your students take turns in leading discussions of text passages as together you attempt to understand what the author(s) is saying.

THE ENERGY CRISIS: A REFLECTIVE READING AND SCIENCE ACTIVITY

What do I know about the energy crisis?

Directions: Draw a word web or concept map which shows your knowledge of the energy crisis.

What do I want to learn about the energy crisis?

Target Objectives:

1. Am I able to define the term energy crisis? How likely am I to define the word energy?

Highly unlikely   Highly likely

2. Am I able to name the ways that gasoline powered automobiles directly and indirectly impact the environment? How many ways can I now name?

1	2	3	4	5	6	7	8	9	10

3. Am I able able to name three alternate energy sources? How many alternate energy sources am I able to name?

1	2	3	4	5	6	7	8	9	10

4. Am I able to construct a model of a wind powered vehicle? How likely am I to construct a model of a wind powered vehicle?

Highly unlikely   Highly likely

5. Am I able to identify possible solutions to the energy crisis? How likely am I to identify solutions to the energy crisis?

Highly unlikely   Highly likely

6. What new information would I like to learn about the energy crisis?

ECOGOPHER NEWS—Alternate Energy Sources

WASHINGTON, DC—April 21, 1993
Secretary of Energy Hazel R. O'Leary today said President Clinton's Executive Order on Alternative Fuels will make the Federal government a "driving force behind efforts to increase the availability of both alternative fuel vehicles and fuel supplies." President Clinton signed the order today, which calls for Federal purchases of alternative fuel vehicles in numbers over the next 3 years at least 50% higher than those called for in the Energy Policy Act of 1992. President

Clinton also announced that Texas Land Commissioner Gary Mauro will head up the Federal Fleet Conversion Task Force to advise O'Leary on implementation of the Executive Order. "I am delighted that I will be working with Gary Mauro to make this happen," O'Leary said. "As Land Commissioner, Gary Mauro has helped make Texas a national leader in converting the state fleet to alternative fuels, and has been a tireless proponent of natural gas vehicles in speeches across the country." The task force is to issue a report within 90 days recommending a plan and schedule of implementation. "The Department of Energy and all of us in government must lead by example if the option of alternative fuels is to become a practical, affordable choice for fleet owners across the country," O'Leary said. "Increased use of domestically produced alternative fuels means reducing pollution while creating jobs. We believe that energy efficiency, protecting the environment, and a healthy economy are complementary goals."

O'Leary said that plans call for the Department of Energy to coordinate the agencies' 5-year purchase plans, help with funding for extra purchase or conversion costs, and work with GSA to encourage development of the fuel infrastructure needed to make fleet conversions practical. Under the order, the Department of Energy will also be working with states, local governments, and industry to coordinate vehicle purchases and encourage manufacturers and fuel suppliers to make alternative fuel vehicles and alternative fuels more widely available.

A Fact Sheet Brought to You by EcoGopher at the University of Virginia

This fact sheet was prepared with the assistance of the Worldwatch Institute. Lester Brown, Project Director of the Worldwatch Institute, is a member of Earth Day 1990's Board of Directors. This reading is available on the public domain EcoGopher and was downloaded from EcoGopher by the author.

How Do Cars Affect the Environment?

1. America's love affair with the automobile has a heavy impact on the environment. Burning gasoline emits pollutants into the air we breathe; chlorofluorocarbons (CFCs) from leaky car air conditioners deplete the ozone layer; oil and other automotive fluids contaminate water and soil; and large tracts of land are lost as they are covered with asphalt to make roads and parking lots. Despite the magnitude of these problems, more people are driving greater distances. The problem will only get worse unless changes are made in our transportation priorities. We desperately need better public trans-

portation, improved carpooling programs, increased interest in biking and walking, and higher gas mileage standards for automobiles.

2. Automobiles use approximately half of all the oil consumed in the United States. To keep up with this demand, oil companies are drilling in sensitive natural areas, such as in offshore waters and in the pristine wilderness of Alaska. With the Earth's known usable oil reserves expected to be depleted by the year 2040, oil is becoming harder to extract and the process is inflicting greater damage to the environment. As the US supply dwindles (it is expected to run out by 2020), more oil will be imported from foreign sources across great expanses of water, leading to increased oil spills. The recent Exxon Valdez oil spill in Alaskan waters clearly illustrated the scale of the risks involved. When oil is burned, large amounts of carbon dioxide, the major "greenhouse gas," are released into the air. Greenhouse gases trap heat from the sun in the Earth's lower atmosphere, causing temperatures to rise, a process known as global warming. Automobiles are responsible for about 20 percent of carbon dioxide emissions in the United States, with the average car releasing about five tons every year. Automobiles also emit about 40 percent of the nitrogen oxides that contribute to acid rain, as well as poisonous carbon monoxide and hydrocarbons that cause smog. 158 million Americans live in areas that violate the Clean Air Act standards.

3. Automobile air conditioners use CFCs (Freon) that, when discharged into the atmosphere, destroy the Earth's protective ozone layer that shields us from cancer-causing ultraviolet light. In 1985, a hole the size of the continental United States was discovered in the ozone layer over Antarctica. CFCs also are responsible for as much as 25 percent of the global warming trend. Although there are far fewer CFCs than carbon dioxide molecules in the atmosphere, each CFC molecule is up to 15,000 times more efficient at trapping heat. One charge of CFCs from an automobile air conditioner contributes as much to global warming as the carbon dioxide emitted from an average new car driven 20,000 miles.

4. More than 60,000 square miles of land have been paved in the lower 48 states to accommodate America's 135 million cars. This amounts to 2 percent of the total land surface—an area the size of Georgia. Close to half of the land area in most cities goes to providing roads, highways, and parking lots for automobiles, and two-thirds of Los Angeles is paved.

5. Transportation Facts
   FACT: Transportation consumes 63% of all oil used in the U.S.
   FACT: In 1989, imported oil accounted for $45 billion of our $101 billion annual trade deficit, more than 40% of the total.
   FACT: In 1989, the United States consumed 17.2 barrels of oil a day, 27% of the worldwide consumption.
   FACT: Motor vehicle transportation accounts for 22% of all energy use in the United States and half of all oil.
   FACT: More than 85% of all American workers commute to work by private automobiles.

FACT: Transportation is the only sector of the economy in which oil use grew from 1979 to 1989.

Energy Production

6. It is often difficult to grasp the importance of energy in our lives. On any given day, we may drive to work, turn on a heater, store food in a refrigerator, take a warm shower, watch TV, turn on lights, and cook dinner. All of these actions use energy. Americans use more energy per person than any other people on Earth, yet we also have a deep appreciation of nature. Unfortunately, our energy practices often harm the environment. Acid rain, global warming, oil spills, and nuclear waste are all directly related to the way each of us uses energy.

7. When fossil fuels (oil, coal, and gas) are burned to power vehicles and machines or to produce electricity, they release "greenhouse" gases (most notably carbon dioxide) and pollutants that cause acid rain and smog. Greenhouse gasses are changing the earth's climate, a process that scientists believe will lead to increased droughts and flooding, a rise in sea levels, and mass extinctions of plants and animals. Acid rain, also caused by fossil fuel use, is destroying rivers, lakes, and forests.

8. Nuclear energy produces between 15 and 20 percent of our electricity. But in the process of producing energy, nuclear power creates plutonium and other radioactive wastes that remain dangerous for tens-of-thousands of years.

Energy Efficiency

9. By using energy more efficiently we can reduce the negative impacts of energy production without sacrificing our standards of living. For example, there are now compact fluorescent light bulbs that screw into standard sockets and are easy on the eyes, but they use only a quarter as much energy as conventional incandescent bulbs. They cost more initially, but last about ten times as long, and save up to $40 apiece in energy costs over their lifetimes. For every incandescent bulb that is replaced with a compact fluorescent bulb, about half a ton of carbon dioxide is kept out of the atmosphere.

10. Other measures, such as insulating homes and buildings and insisting on higher gas mileage from our vehicles, have the potential to reduce our energy use significantly. In response to the oil shortage of 1973, the U.S. took measures to greatly improve its energy efficiency, and as a result was able to cut its oil use by 13 million barrels per day. Between 1973 and 1986 our economy grew 35 percent while energy use remained at the same level. Despite past improvements, the U.S. still uses twice as much energy as Japan per unit of economic output. If the U.S. reached Japanese levels of efficiency, we would save $220 billion annually.

Renewable Energy

11. Renewable energy resources, most notably solar, geothermal, and wind, are

abundant and cause little harm to the environment. Using renewable energy can be as simple as designing a building to face south to take advantage of heat from the sun.

12. Solar energy can be used for heating or to convert sunlight directly into electricity—a technology called photovoltaics. Photovoltaics are now commonly used to produce electricity in remote areas that lack power lines and for powering space satellites. Another form of solar energy, called solar thermal, produces heat and electricity by concentrating sunlight on a receiver containing fluid. The heated fluid runs through pipes that are submerged in water, creating steam to power an electric turbine. Improvements in solar energy technology over the past 15 years have greatly reduced its cost, and solar may soon be competitive with conventional energy sources, especially if environmental costs are included.

13. Geothermal energy uses natural steam from the earth to produce electricity. According to the Department of Energy, there could be more domestic energy potential in geothermal resources than in either oil or gas. Over 250 geothermal plants are in operation worldwide with a total and planned capacity of 13,000 megawatts. Natural steam resources provide California with almost 7 percent of its electricity needs. California Energy Company's Coso Geothermal Project currently produces 240 megawatts—enough electricity to meet the needs of 240,000 Southern California households.

14. In California, where most of the country's wind turbines are located, wind generates nearly 2 billion kilowatt hours of electricity per year—enough to meet the needs of a city the size of San Francisco. Every year, wind energy in California keeps 11 million pounds of air pollutants and 1.8 billion pounds of greenhouse gasses from passing into the atmosphere.

15. Renewable energy and energy efficiency are the only solutions to pollution caused by energy production. As energy consumers, each one of us can contribute to a healthier planet by using energy more wisely.

- Our currently used energy sources are resulting in many of our greatest environmental problems. These include: acid rain, global warming, air pollution, oil spills, radioactive waste, and more.
- Energy produced by the wind does not contribute to any of these problems and is renewable.
- The United States consumes one fourth of the world's energy each year. Experts say wind power could eventually produce 10 percent of this vast consumption.
- California's 17,000 wind turbines provide enough electricity to meet all the residential needs of a city the size of San Francisco.
- Since 1980 the cost of wind power in the United States has dropped quite considerably, from 25 cents per a kilowatt hour to about 7–9 cents a kilowatt hour.
- Sweden has begun to harness the strong ocean winds over the Baltic Sea with ocean-based windmills.

The Solution

16. Raising the fuel efficiency standards for automobiles will cut down on air pollution by requiring less gasoline to be burned per mile driven. There are already cars on the market that get 50 miles per gallon or more. Converting segments of our transportation system to cleaner burning fuels, such as compressed natural gas, methanol, and ethanol, may also improve air quality. However, methanol is a questionable fuel because when it is derived from coal it releases twice as much carbon dioxide as oil. Furthermore, alternative fuels do not address the problems of traffic congestion and highway expansion. The true solution to our transportation problems lies with improvements in public transportation and carpooling programs, and increased interest in biking and walking.

17. According to the American Public Transit Association, commuting on mass transit in place of driving cuts hydrocarbon emissions that produce smog by 90 percent, carbon monoxide emissions by more than 75 percent, and nitrogen oxide emissions by up to 75 percent. Despite these impressive figures, only one penny of the nine cents per gallon federal gasoline tax is used to improve mass transit.

18. *Railway Age Magazine* points out that a single highway lane can accommodate 2,250 people per hour in automobiles, 9,000 in buses, 15,000 on a light rail line, and 34,000 people on a heavy rail line. The newest French train is capable of traveling at a speed of more than 180 miles per hour while saving energy and providing a safe comfortable ride.

19. What You Can Do

    - Walk or bike for close errands.
    - Arrange for a carpool with your co-workers.
    - Use public transportation whenever possible.
    - If it's reasonable, ask your employer to allow you to work at home one or two days a week.
    - Encourage your employer to offer financial incentives in place of a parking permit.
    - Take a job close to your home or move closer to your place of work.
    - Enjoy local recreational activities rather than traveling long distances for entertainment.
    - Urge your local officials to improve and promote public transportation, carpooling programs, and bicycle lanes.
    - Write your elected officials and urge them to support legislation to raise the fuel efficiency standard for automobiles and to put funding towards public transportation rather than highway expansion.
    - If you are buying an automobile, consider a model that:

        —Gets good gas mileage (at least 35 miles per gallon).
        —Doesn't have an air conditioner.
        —Has radial tires with a high tread rating for longer use.

- For proper driving and maintenance:
  —If your car has an air conditioner, make sure the CFCs are recycled anytime it is serviced and before the car is scrapped.
  —Have your car smog checked and install pollution-control equipment if necessary.
  —Keep your car tuned up and the tires properly inflated.
  —Call ahead before shopping and consolidate errands.
  —Avoid quick acceleration and deceleration and keep your speed under 60.
  —Avoid "drive through" where your car engine idles for long periods.
  —Recycle used motor oil, transmission fluid, brake fluid, and antifreeze.
  —Turn in your old battery when you buy a new one.

Three-Tiered Study Guide

Part I. Literal Level—Reading Comprehension Skills—Accreting

Literal level comprehension is determining what the author(s) are saying, that is, what information their words convey. Students have difficulty reading at this level of comprehension. This may be because they do not understand the definitions of words; therefore, the information is unobtainable. Work on vocabulary development will properly prepare them for reading at this level. Guided practice in reading selections at the literal level will reinforce the vocabulary development skills. It also will develop a sense of how to identify essential information in the text (Herber, 1978).

Directions: Read the first statement with others in your group. Place a check on the numbered line if the statement contains information from the text (exact words or a paraphrase). You must be able to give evidence to support your opinion. If any person in the group has a problem with words in either the statements or the reading selection, be certain to help them develop an understanding of those words. React to all ten statements.

_____ 1. Burning gasoline emits pollutants into the air we breathe.
_____ 2. Two-thirds of Los Angeles is paved.
_____ 3. The Exxon Valdez oil spill provided work for many Native Americans.

_____ 4. Americans use about the same amount of energy per person as others on planet earth, yet we also have a deep appreciation of nature.

_____ 5. Nuclear energy produces between 15 and 20 percent of our electricity.

_____ 6. Renewable energy resources, most notably solar, geothermal, and wind, are abundant and cause little harm to the environment.

_____ 7. Geothermal energy uses natural chemical reactions in the earth to produce electricity.

_____ 8. Sweden has begun to harness the strong ocean winds over the Baltic Sea with a large series of dikes and cranes.

_____ 9. Use public transportation whenever possible.

_____10. Have your car smog checked and install pollution-control equipment if necessary.

Part II. Interpretive Level—Establishing relationships—Structuring

At the interpretive level of comprehension the readers determine what the author(s) mean by what they say. They develop intrinsic concepts from the relationships they perceive in the authors' information. The concepts are "intrinsic" because they are formulated from information presented in the information source (Herber).

Directions: Place a check on the numbered line before each statement which expresses an idea that can be reasonably supported with information from the reading selection. Be ready to discuss the supporting evidence with others in your group.

_____ 1. Public transportation, carpooling, biking, walking, and higher gas mileage standards for automobiles would help ease the energy crisis.

_____ 2. Within most of our lifetimes, planet Earth will run out of oil reserves.

_____ 3. Automobile air conditioners that use CFCs help to cool the ozone layer, thus protecting us from ultraviolet light.

_____ 4. Paving helps to prevent soils from eroding and washing into the sea.

_____ 5. Carbon dioxide is a "greenhouse" gas.

_____ 6. Photovoltaics are commonly used to produce electricity in remote areas and in space satellites.

_____ 7. California has more wind turbines than many other areas.

_____ 8. Burning natural gas (methanol and ethanol) may improve air quality.

_____ 9. Less than 10% of the federal gasoline tax is used to improve mass transit.

_____10. We should recycle motor oil, transmission fluid, brake fluid, and antifreeze.

Part III. Applied Level—Generalizing—Tuning

Prior knowledge and experience have a bearing on the relationships perceived in the information provided by the author(s). Hence, those factors influence the

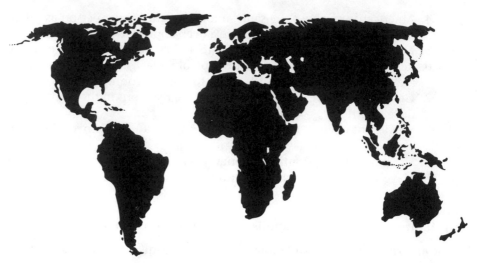

meanings you perceive in what you read. But in still another way prior knowledge and experience relate to what you read: that is, when you see a relationship between the ideas acquired from other sources and the ideas derived from the reading selection. Out of the perceived relationship, you evolve broad generalizations or principles which embrace both sets of ideas, but which represent something more than just the sum of the two. The applied level of comprehension is the process of taking what has been known, applying it to what has just been learned, and evolving ideas which encompass both but extend beyond them. These ideas can be called extrinsic concepts, since they are external to the text, even though they embrace ideas in the text (Herber, 1978).

Directions: Read through the statements. Think about the ideas and experiences that you have had which are similar in principle to what you found in the reading selection. Check each statement which you think is reasonable and which you can support by combining ideas contained in the reading selection with your own related ideas and experiences. Be ready to present evidence from both sources to support your decisions.

_____1. Everything must go someplace.
_____2. The oceans are nature's trash cans.
_____3. A stitch in time, saves nine (B. Franklin).
_____4. Plants and animals depend on each other; we say they are interdependent.
_____5. Humans are part of the natural environment.

Related Vocabulary Activities

1. Divide each word into syllables.
   automotive   fossil   megawatts   chlorofluorocarbons

2. Define each term.
   geothermal   solar   nuclear   pollutants

3. Write the plural of each word.
   automobile   gas   drought   activity

4. Write the singular of each word.
   rivers   barrels   megawatts   turbines

5. Write a rhyming word for each word.
   rely   bog   lithosphere   haste

6. Write a word that sounds the same but is spelled differently.
   too   waist   rein   knead

7. Below you will find sets of two words. In the first set the two words have a definite relationship. Under the first two words, there is a single word and then a blank. Next to the blank are three words; choose one of the three words and fill in the blank with the one that relates to the single word as the first two do to each other.

   a. people/carbon dioxide
      automobiles/_____ (oxygen, carbon monoxide, fluorine)

   b. shell/turtle
      ozone/ _____ (earth, gas, automobiles)

   c. solar/sun
      geothermal/ _____ (California, waste, earth)

8. Circle the word that is not related.
   acid rain   global warming   oil spills   recycle   radioactive waste

9. Solve this puzzle.

   a. E _ _ _ _ _ _ _ _ _ _
   b. N _ _ _ _ _ _ _   _ _ _ _ _
   c. E _ _ _ _ _ _ _ _
   d. R _ _ _ _ _ _ _ _ _
   e. G _ _ _ _ _ _ _ _
   f. Y _ _ _

   a. Nuclear energy produces 15 to 20% of our _____.
   b. Emission produced by automobile engines.
   c. When automobiles burn less gasoline, we say they are energy _____.
   d. Plutonium is considered _____ waste.
   e. Energy produced by natural steam.
   f. 365 days.

Related Science and Language Activities

1. Make a poster showing alternate energy sources.
2. Calculate the number of calories in a peanut (laboratory investigation).
3. Draw a cartoon about depicting a way to save energy.

4. Conduct a survey and determine ways that others in your class or group are saving energy.
5. Write a letter to your Congressperson or Senator asking them about their efforts to help save energy.
6. Gather information on the "greenhouse" effect and report your findings to others.
7. Survey your home and/or school and identify energy saving devices.
8. Determine the air quality in your neighborhood (laboratory investigation).
9. With a group of friends, brainstorm a design for a car to be used in the year 2100 A.D.

Finding Out

Title: Puffmobiles

Materials:

10 straws   4 macramé beads
25 straight pins   1 sheet 8½" × 11" paper

Procedure: Using the materials provided construct a "Puffmobile." A puffmobile is a wind propelled vehicle.

Rules: All materials must be affixed to the puffmobile. One straw must be reserved for the propulsion system.

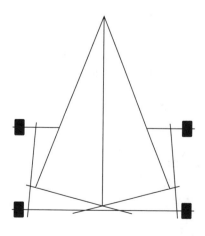

What have I learned about the energy crisis?

Target Objectives:

1. Am I able to define the term energy crisis? How likely am I to define the word energy?

Highly unlikely   Highly likely

2. Am I able to name 10 ways that gasoline powered automobiles directly and indirectly impact the environment? How many ways can I now name?

1	2	3	4	5	6	7	8	9	10

3. Am I able able to name three alternate energy sources? How many alternate energy sources am I able to name?

1	2	3	4	5	6	7	8	9	10

4. Am I able to construct a model of a wind powered vehicle? How likely am I to construct a model of a wind powered vehicle?

Highly unlikely   Highly likely

5. Am I able to identify solutions to the energy crisis? How likely am I to identify solutions to the energy crisis?

Highly unlikely   Highly likely

6. What new information have I learned about the energy crisis?

In using a TRICA technique, you begin the process by constructing the guide to accompany the reading material. Your students should be placed in cooperative groups of threes or fours. As a teacher, you should place stronger and weaker readers in each group. Cooperative groups should be constructed such that limited English proficient (LEP) students have the opportunity to interact with those who possess stronger English language skills. Begin the reading process by setting the task. Explain to your students that the textual passage they are about to read contains information about the current unit of study and that all students in the class should work together to understand what the author(s) is saying.

Literal Level

When using a three-tiered study guide, begin by instructing the students to read the statements that are written at the **literal level** in the study guide. Comprehension at the literal level, according to Herber, "is determining what the author(s) are saying, what information their words convey" (1978, p. 43). Tell the students that their job in reading is to find the specific passages of text in the article, book, or chapter that were mentioned in the study guide. Next, instruct the students to read the text passage together in groups. Allow your students to read aloud to each other. After reading aloud, ask the students to work cooperatively and find the specific place in the text in which the author(s) used the statements mentioned in the guide. Some of your students have difficulty reading at this level of comprehension because they do not understand the definitions of words; therefore, the information is temporarily unobtainable. Guided practice in reading selections at the literal level with others in their class will reinforce vocabulary development skills and assist these students in making sense of the textual information.

After your students have concluded their discussion of the literal level passages, allow for group reporting, that is, for reciprocal teaching. Have your students read aloud the literal level passages to the class and state whether they did or did not find the passage in the text. Have your students justify their answers. Ask your students clarifying questions, such as, "Where specifically did you find the textual passage or statement?" "Cite the page and paragraph." Allow your students to evaluate their responses and the responses of other groups in the classroom.

Interpretive Level

The second stage of the reading process involves developing skills at the interpretive level. According to Herber (1978, p. 45), when "reading at the **interpretive level** of comprehension the readers determine what the author(s) mean by what they say." It is at this level that your students develop **intrinsic** concepts from the relationships that they perceive in the authors' information or the textual passage. The concepts at this level are "intrinsic" because they are formulated from information presented in the information source. As with literal level learning, have your students begin by reading the statements in the study guide and then have the students work cooperatively in groups to address each statement. Your students should be guided by the question, "Is this what the author means?" As with literal level information, have your students read cooperatively and find instances of support for their statements in the textual material. Interactions between your students in their small groups should focus on formulating answers and justifying those answers based on the textual material. As you lead a full class discussion of the findings, you should focus not only on the content of the reading passage but also on the basic strategies of questioning, clarifying, and summarizing. Throughout this process, you should transfer the responsibility for comprehending the textual material to your students so that they "take charge" of their own learning.

Applied Level

Prior knowledge and experience have a bearing on the relationships perceived in the information provided by the author(s) and with the meaning that is constructed within the learner. According to Herber (1978, p. 47) "**applied level** knowledge involves the way that prior knowledge and experience relate to what the student has just read, that is, what the child sees in a relationship between the ideas acquired from other sources and the ideas derived from the reading selection." Out of the perceived relationships, children evolve broad generalizations or principles which embrace both sets of ideas, but which represent something more than just the sum of the two. The applied level of comprehension is the process of taking what has been known, applying it to what has just been learned, and evolving ideas which encompass both but extend beyond them. These ideas, according to Herber, can be called **extrinsic** concepts, since they are external to the text, even though they embrace ideas in the text.

When working at the applied level of reading, you should encourage children to read statements in the study guide and then ask them the question, "Does what you have just read and what you already know support this statement?" As you work at this level of the three-tiered study guide, focus on constructing meaning and linking new learning to what students already know. Reading at this level results in a conscious awareness of what is being learned, when it will be useful, and how to use it effectively in the future. At this level, your students should be applying the new knowledge that they have gained to what they already know.

Vocabulary Development in the Science Classroom

Vocabulary development may be operationally defined as being the ability of the child to sort out his or her experiences and concepts in relation to words and phrases in the context of what he or she is reading. For the vast majority of students, experience with building science concepts is much more critical than experience in pronouncing words. By the time students enter fourth grade, most have acquired the basic word-recognition skills which allow them to pronounce words they encounter in print (Vacca & Vacca, 1989).

Vocabulary development in the science classroom involves four hierarchical areas of responsibility for the teacher: (1) assisting students in developing new words for new concepts, (2) applying old words for new concepts, (3) acquiring new words for old concepts, and (4) using old words more broadly to describe old concepts already held in memory. The most time-consuming vocabulary development activity is assisting students in developing new concepts and attaching new labels or words to those concepts. For example, if you wish to have students develop a knowledge of the ecological concept of interdependence, you need to expose students to a variety of experiences which will allow them to develop a framework for themselves. Within this framework, students will be able to define operationally interdependence as meaning "depending on each other." Science vocabulary development is not simply a matter of using a glossary or a dictionary and looking up the "meaning" of a word; rather, it is a process of constructing meaning regarding objects and phenomena in the natural world. Reading activities should be part of an integrated thematic whole. Laboratory and/or "hands-on" activities which provide multiple modes of knowledge representation should be used in conjunction with reading activities. Writing and reporting activities should also be used to present students with a unified thematic approach to learning about the physical world.

After-Reading Activities

After-reading activities provide students assistance in developing background knowledge that they will need for subsequent learning. In addition, after-reading activities should provide the opportunity for students to integrate, consolidate, and synthesize new information with prior knowledge (Anders & Lloyd, 1989). Syllabification activities, developing analogies, concept mapping or word webbing, journal or diary writing, poetry writing, and so forth are activities which extend the reading activity and which assist students in developing competency in using the English language.

 CHAPTER SUMMARY

Reading is a vital part of science instruction. Children can construct knowledge of the physical world through their interactions with prose passages as well as through "hands-on" learning activities. In the multicultural classroom, interactions with other children during the reading process are vital as children talk about ideas and negotiate meaning with each other. Teachers may facilitate the learning of culturally diverse learners by providing (1) the task ("friendly" text passages), (2) the opportunities for social interactions in which children discuss those passages, and (3) the opportunity for group reporting as students work at the literal, interpretive, and applied levels of reading.

 TOPICS TO REVIEW

 REFLECTIVE PRACTICE

1. How is it possible for students to construct a knowledge of science from prose passages? Explain your answer.
2. What is meant by the concept that "reading is an interactive process"? Explain your answer.
3. Traditionally, reading instruction has frequently been conducted in homogeneous groups. How does that teaching strategy complement the reading strat-

egies proposed in this chapter? How does it conflict with the reading strategies proposed in this chapter?

4. In your opinion, what characteristics of text are important in terms of teaching culturally diverse students? Why?

5. The reading strategies discussed in this chapter are thematic reading strategies designed to foster the learning of culturally diverse students. Explain why thematic teaching might be useful for culturally diverse students? For all students?

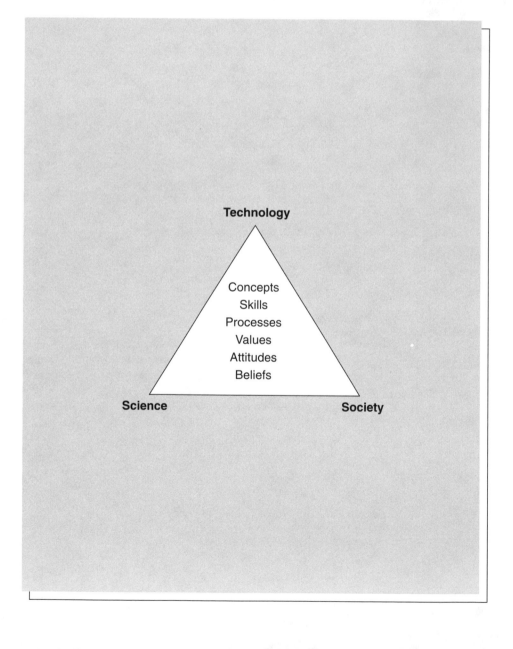

SCIENCE/TECHNOLOGY/ SOCIETY IN THE MULTICULTURAL CLASSROOM

 POINTS TO PONDER

1. How can students become engaged in taking action on social issues?
2. Why is the integration of science technology and society important?
3. How does STS education fulfill the need for "real world" applications of science?

REAL WORLD APPLICATIONS

"P*aper or plastic?" is the weekly refrain from the bag boy at my grocery store. Should I have my groceries encased in a plastic bag or a paper bag? Everyone else seems to have a rapid answer for this dilemma. I don't. Much to the annoyance of those in line behind me, I mentally go through a checklist to evaluate the pros and cons of each type of wrapping. If it is August, I normally take a paper wrapping, because I know my children will soon need paper covers for their school books. During the winter months, I opt for paper bags because I know that we will recycle them when we start our fireplace burning. The rest of the year, I anguish over this decision.*

    I know America's landfills are clogged with paper products and that paper is a greater source of pollution than plastics. I also know that I do not assume enough personal responsibility for recycling either product. If I were environmentally correct, I would carry my basket or cloth bags to the store and would not use either paper or plastic to carry my groceries home. Indeed, I have a stack of cloth bags in the trunk of my car, but I keep forgetting to carry them into the store. As is the case with many members of our society, I am aware of the issues involved with recycling our natural resources but do not take personal action frequently enough.

On recycling days, I separate my glass, aluminum, and paper at curbside, but I should not have all that waste in the first place. I know I should carry my vegetable scrapings out to the compost pile in the backyard, but I often forget and churn them up in the garbage disposal. While my husband and sons remember to recycle their cans and bottles, I sometimes forget and toss mine in the kitchen trash can. Instead of donating used clothing to an agency that can use it, I sometimes forget and toss out old garments. I remember to add grass clippings to our compost pile on the days we cut the lawn, but during the rest of the week I fall into bad habits. I am afraid that I add to the problem of solid waste management more often than I help. At various times in my life, I have been a water hog, a litter bug, and just plain socially irresponsible with regard to environmental issues. Building a social awareness of environmental issues, helping children to become responsible citizens in a democracy involves the integration of science and social living skills.

The American Association for the Advancement of Science began Project 2061 in 1985 when Halley's Comet was in the vicinity of the earth. At that time, there was a realization that children who were just starting school would live to see the return of the comet. One of the documents produced in conjunction with the work of Project 2061 dealt with the topic of scientific literacy for children and was entitled, *Science for All Americans*. According to this document, the goals of scientific literacy should include:

- Being familiar with the natural world and recognizing both its diversity and its unity;
- Understanding key concepts and principles of science;
- Being aware of some of the important ways in which science, mathematics, and technology depend upon one another;
- Knowing that science, mathematics, and technology are human enterprises and knowing what that implies about their strengths and limitations;
- Having the capacity to think scientifically; and
- Using scientific knowledge and ways of thinking about individual and social purposes (Rutherford, 1991).

Actualization of these goals will entail an integrated, thematic approach to teaching and learning: a science-technology-society (STS) world view. Indeed, at the elementary school level, STS is frequently thought of as the integration of social studies or social living with science. Science, technology, and society issues are frequently the same as social studies issues in that both speak to the relationship between humans and their environment.

What Is STS?

Science-technology-society (STS) may be defined as an integrated approach to teaching which seeks to (1) prepare students to use science for improving their own lives and for coping in an increasingly technological world, (2) teach students to deal responsibly with technology/society issues, (3) provide students with a fundamental knowledge of STS issues, and (4) give students a knowledge of career opportunities in STS related fields (Yager, 1990) (Figure 13.1). Wraga and Hlebowitsh (1991) have defined STS as being a topical curriculum that addresses a broad range of environmental, industrial, technological, social, and political problems. STS topics can include acid rain, air quality, deforestation, drugs, erosion, euthanasia, food preservatives or additives, fossil fuels, genetic engineering, greenhouse effect and global warming, hazardous waste, hunger, land usage, mineral resources, nuclear power, nuclear warfare, overpopulation, ozone layer, pesticide usage, and water quality/water usage.

Collette and Chiappetta have stated that individuals do not understand how science and technology influence society or, conversely, how much of an influence society exerts on science and technology (1989). Science according to these authors is a way of knowing that involves the pursuit of understanding the natural world. In addition, these authors define science as a way of thinking that promotes an attitude of objectivity, a search for evidence, and self-examination. Technology is defined as applied science. Technology is the translation of scientific knowledge into practical, everyday applications which benefit humankind. The Board of Directors of the National Science Teachers Association in January 1990 adopted the policy that it was vital that opportunities for all students to study real-life, personal, and societal science and technology problems be included in school curricula.

Science and technology rely on each other, and both have profound effects on society. Scientific knowledge has both positive and negative influences on

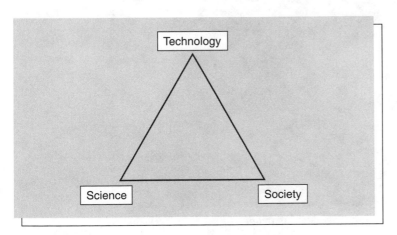

FIGURE 13.1   Science/Technology/Society Interaction

individuals within our society. The products of technology have the capacity to improve our daily lives. On the other hand, technology has the capacity to negatively impact our lives. New technologies are frequently accepted in human society because there is a demonstrated need for them. Society, therefore, passes judgments on the relative worth or merit of scientific discoveries and technological developments.

Ramsey, Hungerford, and Volk (1990) point out that science, technology, and society instruction involves a consideration of four levels of educational goals: (1) foundation (2) issue awareness, (3) investigation and evaluation, and (4) citizenship responsibility. At the foundation level, the goal of STS instruction

Science, technology, and society are interrelated in our lives. (© Frank Siteman)

is to provide learners with the knowledge needed to understand STS issues. This knowledge could include basic science content associated with the issues and the nature of science, technology, and society and the interrelationships among the three. At the second level, the issue awareness level, the goal of STS instruction is to foster the conceptual understanding of science-related social issues originating from the interactions of science, technology, and society. In addition, issues awareness focuses on developing students' expertise in investigation; evaluation; analysis of personal beliefs, attitudes, and values; decision making; and citizenship in action. The third level of educational goals associated with STS instruction, the investigation and evaluation level, provides for the development of the skills and knowledge necessary to permit students to inquire into social issues and generate and evaluate possible solutions to these problems. The fourth level of educational goals is concerned with the responsibilities of citizens in a democracy. Citizenship responsibility educational goals involve the development and application of those skills necessary for students to make informed decisions in a democracy. At this final level of educational goals for STS instruction, students are encouraged to take positive action to resolve science-related issues.

STS as Thematic Teaching

In writing of the need for science/technology/society instruction, Ramsey (1989) points out that all students will become citizens in a democracy. He also points out that students will be consumers of the products and services of science and technology. "All will assume and be responsible for the benefits and risks of scientific and technological decision-makers concerning matters of science and technology, either willfully via participation in democratic decision making or apathetically via the lack of such participation" (Ramsey, 1989, p. 40). STS education is distinguished from "traditional" environmental education in that STS focuses on the societal issues involved with science and technology. This connection with students' values, attitudes, and beliefs involves teachers in decisions about how best to address value formation with young children.

From a science education perspective, STS instruction focuses on issues that involve the interaction of people and the environment. Concepts such as interdependence, food chains, food webs, limiting factors, population growth, and resource management typically are incorporated into science, technology, and society instruction. In addition, STS instruction tends to develop a knowledge of science processes in students. From a social studies perspective, STS instruction focuses on the human experience, on the development of critical thinking, and on values education. Writing, reading, collecting and analyzing data, and reporting; competencies developed in language arts and reading and in mathematics classes are also incorporated into elementary schools' STS instruction. STS is thematic teaching in that it incorporates concepts, processes, and skills from many content area domains. Some examples of science, technology, and society issues are shown in Figure 13.2.

STS Issues

- Should scientists be permitted to exhume the bones of deceased Native Americans for scientific research?
- Should scientists be able to create and patent new organisms?
- Should laws be enacted to enforce mandatory water conservation?
- Should people be allowed to burn household paper waste on their own property?
- Is the burning of garbage in city incinerators a risk to public health?
- Should insect vectors (insects that feed on other insects) be imported into the United States to control insect pests?
- Should the use of herbicides (weed killers) be banned from farms?
- Should sports hunting of deers be allowed?
- Should animals be used in medical research? If not, why not? If so, should controls be used?
- What controls, if any, should be used on liquid waste poured into streams and rivers?
- What efforts should be made to preserve species on the endangered species list? Why?
- Are adequate efforts being made to preserve wetlands in your area? Why are wetlands important? Should they be protected? If so, how? If not, why not?

FIGURE 13.2   STS (Science, Technology, and Society) Issues

Values-Education Approaches.   Societal issues associated with STS instruction involve teachers and students in value identification, formation, and clarification. **Values education** encourages students to examine their personal points of view (which are based on their attitudes, beliefs, and values) and the viewpoints of others. Science, technology, and society issues involve students in becoming informed citizens in a democracy who will use their decision making abilities in a "real world" setting. Superka, Ahrens, Hedstrom, Ford, and Johnson (1976) have identified a continuum of values formation activities, ranging from inculcation to action learning (Figure 13.3).

Inculcation.   On this continuum, inculcation exists at one pole of the continuum. **Inculcation** may be defined as the instilling of values in students. This implies

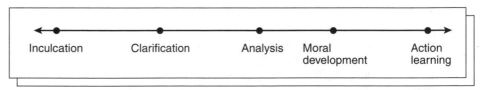

Inculcation   Clarification   Analysis   Moral   Action
                                                          development   learning

FIGURE 13.3   Values Education Continuum

that teachers identify a belief system, value that belief system, and attempt to impose the belief system on students. Inculcation may involve expository teaching and persuasive communication. In the extreme case, inculcation may be labeled propaganda. Often, inculcation is not an attempt to "warp" young minds, but rather is the result of a teacher being overly zealous about an environmental cause. Most teachers do not mean to "stand on a soap box" as they instruct students.

An example of inculcation may be seen in a story of a teacher who feels very strongly that the activities of tuna fishermen are interfering with welfare of dolphins. The teacher may lecture students about the problems of tuna fishing and how dolphins die when they are trapped for prolonged periods in fishing nets. This teacher may frequently refer to how fishermen are "killing" the dolphins and how this is a cruel and inhumane act. At every possible opportunity, the teacher speaks about the horrors of tuna fishing and not buying tuna from certain companies that engage in ecologically offensive fishing practices. If the teacher also assigns the students to draw a poster showing cruel fishermen killing "Flipper," we would say that this teacher is engaging in inculcation. The teacher is attempting to indoctrinate students with his/her personal environmental attitudes, values, and beliefs. Inculcation is an extreme attempt to influence deliberately children's values, attitudes, and beliefs.

Critics of inculcation frequently refer to it as the "hidden curriculum." In writing of the hidden curriculum, Welton and Mallan (1992) point out that the term refers to a multitude of things that schools and teachers convey to children that are not part of the formal school curriculum. Inculcation may involve relatively harmless values such as indoctrinating students to school rules: "line up when leaving the room," "take off your hat when entering the building," and "don't chew gum in rooms with carpeted surfaces." The hidden curriculum may also take on a more sinister meaning as teachers convey or confer attributes on students: "I need some strong boys to move the chairs" or "when your father goes to work . . . ." Welton and Mallan point out that some teaching materials, especially textbooks, try to emphasize only positive virtues, such as honesty or truthfulness, and downplay or exclude any mention of dishonesty or cheating. These authors assert that, while such approaches are well intentioned, even young children know that not everyone is honest or truthful. In terms of science education, values associated with protecting the natural environment are treated in the same manner when inculcation is used in the classroom.

Clarification.   Clarification is the second method or approach for addressing values education. **Clarification** is a method of providing students the opportunity to become aware of their personal beliefs and those of others through large group discussion techniques. Values clarification is an easy-to-use approach, which can be used to increase students awareness of science, technology, and society issues. This approach is often initiated through the use of a survey. Figure 13.4 is a survey, typical of those used in California during the last drought, which can be used to initiate discussions about water usage and the rights of individuals to use water resources.

Water Usage Survey

1. Are you a "water hog" (do you waste water)?
2. Are members of your family "water hogs"?
3. What efforts do you as a family make to conserve water?
4. What efforts is your community making to conserve water?
5. Do you think that people should be allowed to use water as they choose?
   • growing lawns?
   • growing gardens and fruit trees?
   • washing cars?
   • washing driveways?
   • filling swimming pools?
   • operating outdoor fountains?
6. Do you think there should be penalties for those who waste water?
7. How do you feel about laws that regulate the amount of water that each family can use per month?
8. How do you feel about laws that require homeowners and hotel businesses to buy low flow shower heads and low flush toilets?

FIGURE 13.4   Values Clarification Survey

After completing the survey, students share their findings with others in the class. Values clarification serves to inform students that there are many points of view on science-technology-society issues, that is, not everyone thinks or feels the same about all STS issues.

Brinckerhoff (1986) suggested the use of vignettes as a means of facilitating values clarification. When a vignette (Figure 13.5) is used, the teacher normally will allow the students the opportunity to read the vignette and react to it. Students reactions may be conducted during large group discussions or through the use of entries in written journals or diaries. The purpose of the vignette is to allow students to state their own values regarding a particular subject and then share them with others. Vignettes are meant to be springboards to discussions.

Opponents of values clarification point out that some values clarification activities have generated enough controversy that their use has been restricted or banned in some school systems. Some of the criticism of values clarification centers on a students' right to privacy. Many parents and school boards believe that students should not be required to state their beliefs publicly, that to do so is to violate a students' right to privacy. It is nearly impossible for students to reveal their beliefs about controversial topics without revealing personal information about themselves and their families. Values clarification has also been criticized for its failure to distinguish between moral or ethical values and amoral or esthetic values.

Analysis.   **Values analysis** goes beyond values clarification in that it stresses the gathering and organizing of factual information to ensure that students are bet-

Earthquake Problem

Scientists at a large California university are proposing to set off a series of minor earthquakes to preclude a large earthquake from occurring. The scientists have theorized that, if they remove stress along an earthquake fault, they might be able to prevent a large earthquake from occurring. The scientists at the university propose drilling a series of dry test wells on both sides of an active earthquake fault. The scientists will then pump water into the wells and "lubricate" the fault. It is the feeling of the scientists that this will allow minor slippage along the fault (resulting in minor earth tremors or small earthquakes). The minor earthquakes will cause some shaking and earth movement but should be far less severe than a major earthquake. Residents in the town near the fault object to the scientists' causing earthquakes. They fear that their homes and businesses will be damaged by a series of minor earthquakes. They want to obtain a court injunction to prevent the university from drilling the test wells. What is the point of view of the scientists? What is the viewpoint of the residents?

FIGURE 13.5   STS Vignette

ter informed about issues involving science, technology, and society. This third approach to values clarification involves students in library research, field studies, and determining other people's beliefs, attitudes, and values. The analytical approach encourages scientific inquiry on the part of students by encouraging students to separate facts from opinions.

Values analysis involves students in social moral issues associated with science, technology, and society topics, including (1) identifying the environmental question, (2) gathering information about the issue, (3) evaluating the data, (4) evaluating the worth or significance of the data, (5) proposing tentative solutions, and (6) determining acceptable solutions.

Suppose a company in a small town petitions the city council to allow it to treat its own industrial waste and discharge the treated effluent into a stream passing through the town. Students in the class have heard about the petition from their parents and are concerned that this might cause pollution and damage the stream. Students would begin by identifying the environmental question. Will treating and discharging waste pollute the stream? Next, the students need to gather data. What type of treatment will the company use for its industrial waste?

What is a standard way of treating waste products? As part of the process, students will need to identify salient variables and learn to separate facts from opinion. They will need to assess the company's plan according to what is known of "good" waste management plans and in relation to what is already being done in the community. The students will need to determine the impact of having a second sewage treatment plan in the community and the quality and quantity of the effluent to be produced by the company. Next, the students will need to compare plans of action. Will the company's plan be better than what is already being done? Are there other options available for waste treatment? Has the company considered all of the options? Finally, students will need to make a judgment: is the company's plan in the best interests of the community?

Students may determine that their city's former waste disposal procedures were inadequate and that the company's plan is better than past practice. They may also determine that the waste treatment might affect the town's water table and may pollute drinking water supplies. Analysis involves students in gathering and interpreting data. It engages students in real world problem solving, in generating alternative solution paths, and in judging between solution paths. An analytical approach to values clarification prepares students to be participating citizens in a democracy. It encourages students to use the science practices and procedures to gather data, evaluate data sources, form working hypotheses, and generate solutions to problems. Analysis involves students in an inquiry-approach, that is, in a problem solving approach, to issues involving science, technology, and society.

Critics of the analysis approach to values education point out that teachers need to be sensitive to the interest level of students who are not participating in the activity either because they are not interested in the topic or because they lack the verbal proficiency to participate. Typically, values analysis instruction relies heavily on teacher-directed questioning. Such instruction may be difficult for children who lack English language proficiency.

Moral Development.   The fourth type of values-education approaches identified by Superka, Ahrens, Hedstrom, Ford, and Johnson (1976) is defined as moral development. A **moral development** approach to education involves students in reasoning and thinking, but moral development focuses on personal moral values such as justice, equality, and fairness. Moral development is differentiated from analysis in that moral development focuses on the individual's reasoning and thinking, while analysis focuses on society's needs. Typically, the moral development approach to values education uses a vignette which represents a moral dilemma which causes students to examine their personal belief structures.

Kohlberg (1980) developed a five-stage model of moral development. At the lowest levels, students are concerned with external, concrete consequences for themselves. At the middle stages of Kohlberg's continuum, students are concerned with external social expectations. Finally, at the highest stages of moral development, students are concerned about "conscience," that is, about respect for the rights, life, and dignity of other persons. Kohlberg points out that most people do not achieve the final stage of moral development: a concern for the fundamental moral principles on which this nation was founded.

The use of moral dilemma vignettes causes students to choose between two alternatives, each of which is accompanied by a difficult consequence. Vignettes used in moral development may include readings, films, plays, and so forth. The moral reasoning level of students will influence how they respond to moral issues and social problems. A vignette appropriate for elementary school children is shown below:

> Your mother works for a large lumber company. Her company is currently
> clear cutting a large wooded area north of your town. As the lumber company
> has worked in the area, they have come upon nests of a new species of
> woodpecker. Lumbering in the forest has temporarily stopped while the plight
> of the woodpeckers is investigated. Scientists from a local university have
> stated that this is the only known habitat of the woodpecker and that
> removing more trees from the area will cause the extinction of the species. If
> the lumbering operations are stopped, your mother will lose her job. If the
> lumbering resumes, the woodpecker will become extinct. What do you feel
> should be done? Why?

In this vignette, the student is forced to think about his or her family's economical situation and also the plight of an endangered species. The student must choose between two equally viable alternatives. This vignette forces the student to think about personal moral values. This situation is very real in many communities as choices need to be made between people's jobs and the survival of endangered plant and animal species.

Critics of the moral development approach to values education point out that the moral reasoning approach has been questioned because of the inadequacy of Kohlberg's theory or because of the assumption that higher-stage reasoning is better than lower-stage reasoning. Some critics additionally point out that the development of moral reasoning is a slow process and requires a great deal of instruction before students actually move from one stage to another. Most instruction in school is "too shallow" to bring about significant changes in students' levels of moral reasoning.

Action Learning.   The final approach to values education is referred to as action learning. **Action learning** involves more than clarification, thinking, reasoning, and decision making; it involves students in taking personal action regarding science, technology, and society issues. Action learning extends learning beyond the walls of the classroom into the community. The North American Association for Environmental Education states that action learning stresses the need for active participation in solving environmental problems and preventing new ones (Tanner, 1987). Action learning helps students to become active in solving local environmental problems.

Action learning involves students in their communities. It empowers students to take action on local environmental issues. Suppose Mr. Johnson, a fourth grade teacher, wants to involve his students in learning about pollution in their local community. A small arroyo runs through the school grounds. On rainy days, the arroyo overflows onto the school grounds and for several days afterwards students need to remain inside during recess periods as the playground is flooded.

During the next rainstorm, the students notice that the old tires, metal cans, and scrap metal in the arroyo are damming the waters, causing the stream to flow onto the school grounds. When the arroyo dries out, Mr. Johnson and his students begin to remove the litter that was clogging the stream channel. They arrange with the school's trash removal service to cart away the old debris. The students volunteer to clean the arroyo during their recess periods. As the students clean the arroyo, they notice that some local businesses are using the arroyo as a landfill area. Mr. Johnson's students write letters to the city council asking if they can obtain city help in keeping the arroyo free from debris. The city arranges to have dumpsters installed for the merchants to use, thus eliminating the source of the litter. In this scenario, the students have learned that they can take action to improve the quality of their school grounds and that they can also influence others in the community to take part in efforts to improve the quality of the environment.

While values education approaches to STS issues range from inculcation to action learning, Rubba and Wiesenmayer point out that effective STS instruc-

STS issues exist in all American communities. (© Jim Pickerell)

tion empowers citizens with the knowledge, skills, and affective qualities needed to make responsible decisions and take action on science- and technology-related societal issues (Rubba & Wiesenmayer, 1991). Wraga and Hlebowitsh (1991) point out that STS education stresses the interaction of personal and social goals within a problem-focused framework. Finally, Mayer (1990) points out that future leaders and voters (today's students) must understand our interrelationships with peoples around the world and how our daily activities affect our planet and its resources.

STS Issues

Science, technology, and society instruction focuses on values formation. Within this context, the selection of appropriate issues is of vital importance. In writing of this concern for selecting appropriate STS issues, Rhoton (1990) points out that there must be a focus on the needs of students to understand and make decisions about STS issues that impact their lives. Some STS topics are more appropriate for older than for younger students.

A discussion of the implications of genetic engineering and surrogate mothers may be appropriate for high school students, but is probably not appropriate for elementary school students. If Rhoton's criterion is used, genetic engineering is probably not appropriate for young children since it is not readily understood by most elementary-aged children. Other topics, such as land management, water pollution, and recycling, are more likely to be of interest to younger children. "Good" STS issues are those which are understandable by younger children and are matters which directly impact the lives of children.

What Does the Research Say?

In writing of the impact of science, technology, and society instruction, Yager (1990) points out that STS instruction improves students' abilities in five areas: (1) connections and applications, (2) creativity, (3) attitudes, (4) science processes, and (5) content area knowledge. In the area of connections and applications of science knowledge, Yager points out that STS instruction assists students in relating classroom knowledge to their daily lives, that is, in connecting "classroom learning" to real world situations. Students involved in science, technology, and society instruction become involved in identifying and resolving social issues and they come to see science as a way of fulfilling their responsibilities as citizens (Yager, 1990). STS instruction provides students with a knowledge of the real world value and worth of technological developments and of the importance and relevance of science instruction.

In the area of creativity, STS instruction encourages students to ask more questions that reflect their own interests in science and technology. STS instruction encourages students to engage in inquiry learning by proposing possible solutions to real world problems. Science, technology, and science instruction assists students in identifying possible causes and effects of certain observations and actions.

STS instruction results in students seeing science as a way of dealing with problems. STS instruction encourages students to become curious about the real world and think about solutions to real world problems. In addition, STS instruction involves students in identifying local problems and resources to solve those problems. As students become personally involved in solving problems, their attitudes towards science improve and they come to view science as a way of dealing with problems. Finally, STS instruction helps students to become aware of their responsibilities as citizens as they attempt to resolve issues which they have personally identified in their local communities.

In terms of science processes, STS instruction assists students to view science processes as skills they can use to solve local problems. Students readily see the relationship between science processes and their own actions as they refine and develop their personal expertise. STS instruction encourages students to use science processes to solve real world problems and connect "school learning" to real world problems.

From the perspective of science content knowledge, an STS approach encourages students to view science knowledge as personally useful. Students who learn by experience readily retain information and are able to relate existing knowledge to new situations. Science, technology, and society instruction encourages students to view science content knowledge as more than a dead body of information to be stored in books and memorized. STS instruction encourages students to view science as an opportunity for students to enjoy what they are studying. An STS approach encourages students to see science knowledge as personally useful.

Researchers have asserted that STS instruction improves students' learning. In a study of the effectiveness of STS instruction, Pederson (1992) found that STS instruction, while not impacting students' learning of science concepts, does reduce students' anxiety towards learning science. Pederson concluded that, when students are placed in a situation in which they study issues relevant to them, share information cooperatively, present their perspective on the issue being studied, and cooperatively come to a group consensus on the issue, anxiety toward science is reduced (1992). He also points out that the goal of scientific literacy for all students is best met when students overcome their anxieties associated with the study of science.

CLASSROOM PRACTICE

As a teacher, one part of your "job" is to identify appropriate instructional activities for students. Science, technology, and society instruction is most effective when the topic is of local concern, that is, a subject that impacts the lives of all of your students and an issue on which your students can take personal action. Pizzini, Bell, and Shepardson (1988) developed a four-step method for developing science, technology, and society lessons called Search, Solve, Create, and Share. In this method, students seek out a local problem, use research meth-

ACTIVITIES

ods to gather information, create possible solution paths, and share their findings with others.

This section of the current chapter presents a series of activities which can be used to consider issues associated with land use. The activities are meant to be personalized or localized to the needs of your students. They may be used to encourage students to find a local problem they can solve using commonly available classroom resources. After finding a local problem involving land management issues (see Activity 13 for a template), students can establish a research agenda to investigate the problem and then seek solutions within the local community. Finally, students should be encouraged to share their findings with others. Prior to beginning the activities, collect three soil samples from your area (preferably sandy soil, loam, and clay). Also assemble topographic maps, land use maps, street maps, and so forth to assist students with the problem. This activity is designed to be flexible enough to be conducted in any geographical location.

PREPARATION FOR SOIL CONSULTATION PROJECT ACTIVITIES

Teacher Preparation: Prior to beginning the activity, locate three possible locations for the imaginary housing development in your geographic area. Provide students with maps showing the proposed locations. Also locate three buckets of soil samples (local samples) which are typical of the areas in question.

Problem: A national building company has proposed building a 300-unit housing project in your area. The company is attempting to decide among three locations. Adequate water resources have been found for the hosing development. In addition, it has already been determined that there are adequate roads and streets to reach the houses. A survey of local city, county, and state government agencies indicates that there will be adequate sewers, electrical services, and garbage removal for the area. The only remaining problem is soil analysis. Your group is to serve as a consulting team in helping the city council decide where to place the development. Keep a log of your investigations of the soil samples. If a soil testing kit is available, allow the students to investigate the physical and/or chemical properties of the soil. Prepare a report to the community (or your class) on your findings. As you write your final report, consider the following question: "Should houses be built on the best land (that is, the land which grows plants best)? Why or why not?"

ACTIVITY 13-1 ▪ SOILS AND PLANT GROWTH

Materials:

9 bean seeds

3 soil samples

3 containers for plants (paper cups, pots, etc.)

**A
C
T
I
V
I
T
I
E
S**

TABLE 13.1 Plant Growth Chart

Week number	Sandy Soil	Clay Soil	Loam
1			
2			
3			
4			

metric ruler   balance
graduated cylinder or measuring cup

Teacher Notes: This project requires approximately 4 weeks to complete.

Procedure: Fill each container with soil. Plant the bean seeds in each container (at a depth of about 1 centimeter). Water the plants every other day. Be sure to place the same amount of water in each cup (e.g., 20 milliliters every 2 days). Measure each plant's height each week and record the average height of the three plants on a plant growth chart (Table 13.1).

Follow-up: Have the students make a line graph showing the average plant growth in each soil.

ACTIVITY 13-2 ■ BIOMASS

Materials:

3 containers of plants   balance

Procedure: At the end of the 4 weeks of plant growth activities (Activity 13-3), have the students cut off the plants at soil level (where the plant touches the soil). Using a balance, have the students weigh all of the plants at one time, recording their findings (Table 13.2). This is the biomass or the weight of living

TABLE 13.2 Biomass Recording Sheet	
Soil Type	*Biomass (gm)*
Sandy	
Clay	
Loam	

plant material that has grown in 4 weeks in the soil sample. Biomass is the weight of living material.

Follow-up:

1. Which soil supported the greatest amount of biomass?
2. Why is biomass an important measure of a soil's vitality?

ACTIVITY 13-3 ■ THE LIVING SOIL

Materials:

3 soil samples (fresh, not dried out, samples)
3 ring stands and ring clamps

wire mesh (large enough to allow soil organisms to pass through yet small enough to hold soil in funnel)

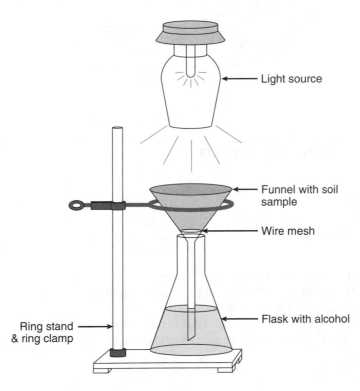

Light source

Funnel with soil sample

Wire mesh

Flask with alcohol

Ring stand & ring clamp

A
C
T
I
V
I
T
I
E
S

3 funnels   dissecting microscopes
3 flasks   eye droppers
alcohol   petri dishes
3 light sources

Procedure: Set up the apparatus as shown on the preceding page. Place about 50 grams of soil on top of a piece of wire mesh in the bottom of the funnel. Place the funnel such that the bottom is immersed in alcohol in the flask. Place a light source over the funnel. Allow the apparatus to set 1 or 2 days. Macro organisms in the soil will migrate from the soil into the alcohol (where they will be captured). Remove the organisms from the alcohol with an eye dropper, place them in a petri dish, and view them under the microscope. What organisms do you find in each soil sample? Draw and describe the organisms. Which soil has the most organisms? Which soil has the fewest organisms? From this activity, which soil is best for supporting living things?

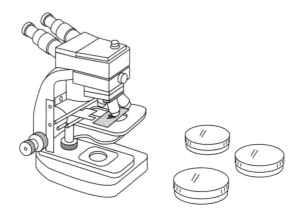

ACTIVITY 13-4 ■ HOLDING CAPACITY

Materials:

3 soil samples (dried out)   graduated beaker or graduated
3 ring stands and ring clamps   cylinder
3 pieces of filter paper   3 funnels
3 flasks   balance

Procedure: Weigh out 100 grams of each soil sample. Place each sample in a piece of filter paper in the holding capacity apparatus (shown on page 339). Pour 50 milliliters of water into each soil sample. Measure the amount of water that "runs off" the soil. The water that is retained by the soil is a measure of its holding capacity. Soils that hold more water have a greater holding capacity and

TABLE 13.3   Holding Capacity

Type of Soil	Amount of Runoff (in milliliters)	Amount of Water Retained in Soil (50 – runoff)	Percent of Water Retained ([Water held/50] × 100)
Sandy			
Clay			
Loam			

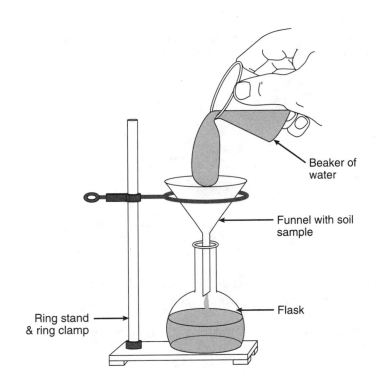

Beaker of water

Funnel with soil sample

Flask

Ring stand & ring clamp

capacity to provide water to plant roots (remember that if drainage is poor, plant roots may rot). Use the chart to record your data (Table 13.3).

ACTIVITY 13-5 ▪ SOIL COMPOSITION

Materials:

3 soil samples
3 jars with lids
balance

graduated cylinder
metric ruler

TABLE 13.4   Soil Composition

Soil Component	Sandy Soil	Clay Soil	Loam
Organic Matter			
Clay			
Silt			
Sand			
Gravel			

Procedure: Place 100 grams of each soil sample in a jar (mayonnaise jars work well). Add 200 milliliters of water. Cap the jar and shake vigorously. Allow the

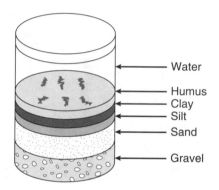

sample to sit overnight. The next day, measure and record the amount of gravel, sand, silt clay, and organic matter in each soil sample (Table 13.4). For older students, compute the percentage of each of these components. For younger students construct bar graphs comparing the amounts of each soil component.

ACTIVITY 13-6 ■ SOIL CONSULTATION PROJECT—OVERVIEW

Materials:

soil organisms chart (Table 13.5)   soil organisms food web (page 341)

Procedure: Construct five food chains using the information contained on the soil organisms chart and the soil organisms food web. Each food chain should begin with a producer. Producers are green plants that make the food. Producers are eaten by primary consumers or herbivores (plant eaters). Primary consumers are eaten by secondary consumers or carnivores (animal eaters) and/or omni-

TABLE 13.5   Forest Food Chains

Producers	Primary Consumer	Secondary Consumer	Decomposer
Oak	Termite	Centipedes	Bacteria
Maple	Beetle larvae	Beetles	Fungi
Grass	Mites	Ants	Earthworm
Algae	Proturan		Millipedes
	Thrips		
	Springtail		

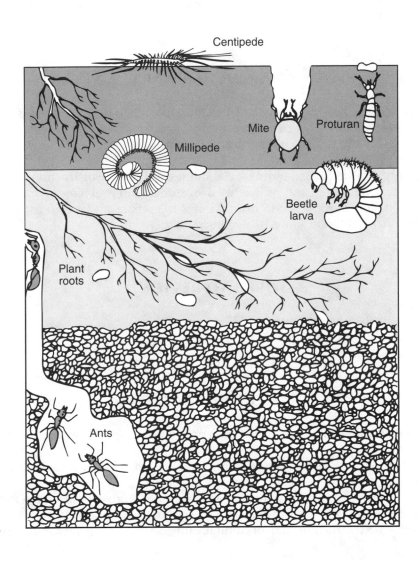

vores (animals that eat plants and animals). Decomposers (bacteria and fungi) feed on dead plant and animal materials. Sample food chain:

Oak tree ___ Termites ___ Beetle larva

ACTIVITY 13-7 ■ SOIL CONSERVATION PROJECT—SHARING

Presentation: Using a written report, an oral presentation, posters, and so forth, share your findings with others in your class. Based on what you have learned of soils, where would be the best location for a housing development in your neighborhood? Why?

 CHAPTER SUMMARY

Science, technology, and society is a thematic approach to teaching science which incorporates a knowledge of science, technological applications of science, and a concern for the societal implications of scientific endeavors. STS instruction incorporates values education. At the elementary school level, STS instruction is frequently regarded as combining social studies and science instruction. A study of science, technology, and society involves students in problem-solving in the real world. One purpose of STS instruction is to prepare students to participate as scientifically literate adults in a democratic society.

 TOPICS TO REVIEW

STS (science/technology/society), 323
values education approaches, 326

 REFLECTIVE PRACTICE

1. Based on your experience, which approach to values education might be best? Why?
2. Explain what is meant by the interrelatedness of science, technology, and society.
3. Based on your prior experience, what STS unit of study would you feel most comfortable teaching at the elementary school level? Why?
4. Why is STS instruction vital for culturally diverse learners? Justify your answer.

5. STS instruction is referred to as thematic instruction. How are science, social studies, language arts, reading, and mathematics incorporated into STS units?

6. Based on what you have read in this chapter and on your prior experience, why is STS instruction more valuable to culturally diverse learners than traditional science instruction? Justify your answer.

CHAPTER 14

What do they want to know?

What do they know?   What have they learned?

How will they find out?

GUIDING LEARNING IN THE MULTICULTURAL CLASSROOM

POINTS TO PONDER

1. What type of lesson planning best addresses the needs of culturally diverse learners?
2. How should you go about planning for learning?
3. How do all the parts and pieces about teaching and learning fit together?

WHENEVER YOU TEACH, TEACH WELL

f I had one admonition to give to teachers, it would be, whenver you teach, teach well. You never know when the product of your efforts will come into your life again. This realization hit me the night my first son was born. At around 5:00 am, I was lying on a stretcher in a hospital delivery room about to give birth. I had entered the hospital around midnight. After five hours of labor, I was ready for the great event. A nurse appeared at my bedside and announced that my doctor had been called away to perform an emergency delivery for a woman who had been in an automobile accident. She assured me that I need not worry, that all was progressing nicely, and that his resident would be with me momentarily.

I lay back on the stretcher as a labor pain moved from my back to my front. As I looked up, I saw a familiar face: "Carlton, what are you doing here?" I yelled. Carlton had been a student in the first Advanced Biology class that I ever taught. The last I had seen him was at his high school graduation ceremony. He smiled and announced that he was now a doctor and would be my attending physician. Suddenly, I remembered him and his work in class. I remembered that he could not distinguish between dorsal and ventral in biology class and that he had dissected his frog upside down. "Did you do well in medical school?" I inquired. I'll never know how well Carlton did in medical school because at that moment my regular doctor walked into the room. The experience did, however, teach me the value of teaching well. Planning is prerequisite to all good teaching. This chapter is designed to help you put into practice the topics that have been discussed throughout this book.

PUTTING THE PIECES TOGETHER

An effective program of science instruction for culturally diverse learners requires attention to scope and sequence documents, state frameworks, and local curricular guides. In addition, science instruction for culturally diverse learners should combine the elements of assessment, thematic teaching, experiential learning, and language acquisition, with a consideration of the needs of the individual learners mentioned previously in this text. In describing the characteristics of effective science instruction in the multicultural classroom, Atwater (1993) identifies classroom climate, creative curricula, multiple modes of communication, planned progress, and reflective teaching as some of the elements necessary for successful planning. Planning for culturally diverse students involves orchestrating elements in the learning environment to provide each child the opportunity to acquire knowledge of science concepts and processes.

The broad goal of producing a scientifically literate society carries implications for multiple levels of planning and implementation. In so far as possible, elementary science programs for culturally diverse learners should (1) provide a balanced curriculum of physical, earth, and life sciences; (2) show students that science is enjoyable; (3) reinforce conceptual understanding rather than rote learning; (4) present an articulated scope and sequence at the school level; (5) arrange classroom settings which encourage positive attitudes for learning science; (6) integrate science with other subject areas; and (7) use community resources (California Department of Education, 1990).

Balanced Curriculum

Just as a balanced diet is necessary for healthy bodies, a balanced science curriculum is necessary for the academic development of children. Each year, children should have experiences in physical, earth and space, and life sciences. Each of these disciplines lends itself to activities which involve students in "doing science." When science is taught, students should be encouraged to make connections between the disciplines of science. For example, energy is transferred during chemical reactions; it is also transferred during metabolism in living things and during earthquakes. The concept of energy transformation is a basic science theme that is found in physical, life, and earth and space sciences. Thematic teaching, that is, teaching which breaks down the divisions between sciences, encourages life-long learning and conceptual understanding in all children. A balanced curriculum, one in which all science disciplines are taught each and every year, provides for the varied science interests of young learners. Balanced science programs also consider the development of the affective and psychomotor domains as well as the cognitive domain.

Science Is Enjoyable

Too often science, especially when it has been taught to limited English proficient children, has been taught as a vocabulary activity: as a list of words and definitions to be committed to memory. When science is taught as a list of words, the joy of learning, the adventure of exploring the natural world, is frequently lost. Science is a way of doing: a way of exploring the physical world. When science is taught as a hands-on, laboratory-based, investigative activity, children become active in learning science. If science is an enjoyable experience, students will continue to learn after the instructional period ends. A desire to learn science begins with teachers who model a fascination with science and its dynamic presence in our daily lives (California Department of Education, 1990). Effective science instruction ought to encourage all students, particularly children from underrepresented groups, to take more science in the future.

Conceptual Understanding

When the science curriculum focuses on higher-order thinking skills and a problem-solving approach to learning, children tend to learn science more readily than when it is presented as low-level learning, replete with drill-and-practice activities. Conceptual understanding of science is strengthened when students relate what is being learned in school to what they have previously learned at home and in the community. The focus on open-ended questions which have multiple solution paths encourages students to use their existing knowledge to solve new problems. In the process, students expand their vocabularies and understanding of the natural world. Students should increase their conceptual understandings of science, and increase their knowledge of science processes.

Articulate Scope and Sequence

Teachers, in conjunction with parents and principals, should plan and sequence science instruction to meet the unique needs of children in the communities they serve. In other words, successful science programs are those tailored to meet the unique science education needs of the entire community. The process of articulating a curriculum involves identifying prior learnings as well as future learnings. Typically, district and/or building curricular committees divide units of instruction between grade levels. This ensures that students do not repeatedly study some topics while ignoring others. Working with colleagues, parents, and administrators provides teachers the opportunity to mesh their instructional program with the efforts of others in developing a unified instructional program.

Classroom Setting

Most science curricula today require the space and opportunity for hands-on learning activities. The physical environment of the classroom must be arranged such that small-group work is easily undertaken by students. Resources necessary for science learning should be provided within easy reach of all students. Laboratory equipment, computer software, library books, bulletin boards, learning centers, reference materials, and so forth must be readily available for student access. In addition, classroom setting considers the unique needs of culturally diverse learners. When students feel at ease in the classroom, learning is maximized. Part of effective planning is to consider the resources and classroom climate necessary to implement instruction.

Integrating Content. Science instruction does not occur in isolation. Effective science programs incorporate concepts, skills, processes, and affective appreciations from the domains of language and literature, mathematics, social studies, music, and art. Scientific literacy would receive a considerable boost if science were used as a vehicle to enhance reading, mathematics, and the arts.

Effective planning is the first step in effective instruction. (© Will Faller)

Integration of content from many disciplines leads to exemplary science teaching and learning. Math/science integration, Teaching Reading in the Content Area (TRICA), and Science/Technology/ Society (STS) are examples of thematic approaches to the teaching of science: approaches which integrate traditional disciplines.

Marshalling Resources.   No general would go into the field without knowledge of the objective and available resources and a plan to achieve the objective. Teaching requires a similar level of preparation in that teachers need to know their students, the community, and the objectives of instruction. In terms of culturally diverse learners, a knowledge of the community and the community's expectations is perhaps the most important advance preparation a teacher may undertake. Effective science curricula are those which capitalize on resources of the local community. These resources may include laboratory equipment; access to parks, fields, streams, and museums; and human resources. Effective science instruction involves components of career awareness as well as a conceptual understanding of science. In addition, access to resources frequently controls the depth and breadth of science instruction that is afforded students. Community support, including parental involvement, is necessary to ensure the vitality of science education programs.

Translating Curriculum into Practice

One "job" of the classroom teacher is to translate existing scope and sequence documents, frameworks, and curricular guides into classroom practice. Most school districts assign "units" of study or topics to particular grade levels. Typically, textbooks are purchased or adopted at the state or district level. Teachers function within these constraints when planning activities for children's science learnings.

Science units are normally organized around broad themes, questions, topics, or problems, and typically range in length from 2 weeks to several months in length. Normally, units contain broad unifying concepts as well as grade-level concepts and subconcepts. Four broad reflective questions should guide teachers in the planning, implementation, and assessment process: (1) What do they know? (2) What do I (we) want to know? (3) How will they find out? (4) What have they learned? Planning involves consideration of children's knowledge, interest and curiosity, awareness of available educational resources, and assessment of children's learning or understanding. One effective means of planning is through the use of a vee map (Roth & Bowen, 1993, Roth & Verechaka, 1993). This reflective teaching model encourages teachers to consider students' entry level knowledge and interests, the existing resources, and educational outcomes (Figure 14.1).

What Do They Know?   "What do they know?" is a question dealing with children's prior knowledge. Chapter 6 considered ways of assessing or measur-

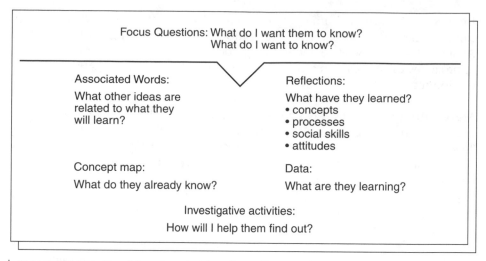

FIGURE 14.1   Vee Mapping (a plan for reflective teaching)

ing children's understandings of science. Before beginning any unit of study, teachers should assess children's knowledge in the cognitive, affective, and psychomotor domains. Concept mapping, word webbing, brainstorming, semantic mapping, journal writing, and pretesting are ways to "get a handle" on children's prior knowledge in the cognitive domain. Task tests can be used to assess children's motor skills. Attitude instruments and writing exercises can be used to assess children's attitudes.

"What do they know?" is a question that considers the conceptual knowledge children have acquired and the ways those ideas or notions are connected and related. In addition, assessment of children's knowledge also includes related or associated knowledge which children may hold and the way that knowledge is interrelated. Assessment of prior knowledge may include measurements on children's intellectual skills, cognitive strategies, verbal information, motor skills, and attitudes. Planning involves teachers in addressing the question, What do they know? at a yearly, unit, and daily level.

What Do I (We) Want to Know?   The question, "What do I (we) want to know?" may be answered at an individual, collective, or comparative level. At the individual level, each child may provide a blueprint for learning, that is, a list of questions that they individually want to have answered during a unit of study. At a collective level children (through talking with one another and by talking with others in the school, family, and community) should be encouraged to formulate a set of questions that they desire to answer as they discuss and study a particular topic. Finally, anticipation of future learning may be addressed at a comparative level by the teacher. How do my students compare with a standard set by my school district? By my state?

What do I (we) want to know? may be addressed in terms of long-range aims, goals, and target objectives, as well as by short-term or daily objectives. Aims are typically broad, long-range educational outcomes that are anticipated by school districts and/or states. One aim of science instruction is to produce a scientifically literate society. This aim of science teaching may require years to achieve. Goals, on the other hand, are typically narrower in scope and may be defined as statements of the outcomes of education (Gagné, Briggs, & Wager, 1988). The ability to read at grade level may be seen as a goal of education. Frequently, district curricular guides translate goals into grade level objectives.

The question, "What does my school district or state say that children ought to know about this topic or unit or concept?" involves a comparison of students' knowledge against a particular existing curricular standard. At this comparative level, teachers are actually identifying the educational needs of their students. An educational need may be defined as a discrepancy or gap between a desired state of affairs (goal) and the present state of affairs (Gagné, Briggs, & Wager, 1988).

Instructional objectives are the teachers' objectives for student learnings. Instructional objectives speak to the gap between what students know and what the district and/or state curriculum guide or framework suggests that they should know. In formulating instructional objectives, teachers typically include objectives that reflect students' concerns for new learning. Instructional objectives serve as guideposts or road maps for selecting activities that will attend to students educational needs. One instructional objective might be that students be able to measure the mass of an object using a pan balance. Another instructional objective might be that students be able to define operationally the terms "potential energy" and "kinetic energy." Unit planning is guided by instructional objectives, that is, teachers' expectations for student learning.

Teachers' instructional objectives eventually become **target objectives**. That is, instructional objectives are also instructional outcomes by which students monitor their progress in learning. A target objective may be thought of as an objective that both students and teachers share and that all work to achieve. Target objectives are guideposts for student learning. These objectives serve to inform students of the goals of instruction, that is, of what the students should achieve educationally. Suppose that a school district's elementary science curriculum calls for students to compare and contrast producers, consumers, and decomposers as an outcome from a unit of ecology studies. This goal may be translated into a series of target objectives for students consisting of questions such as, Am I able to define producers, consumers, and decomposers? Can I identify ways that producers, consumers, and decomposers are alike? Why they are different? How likely am I to do these things? Target objectives not only inform students and their teachers of what is to be learned, but also encourage students to reflect on their learning and on their need for additional learning. The relationship between instructional objectives and target objectives is shown in Figure 14.2.

In addition to guiding learning, target objectives serve as a basis for student

Instructional Objective:	By the end of the unit students will be able to operationally define the term erosion.
Target Objective:	• Am I able to define the term erosion?
Instructional Objective:	The students will be able to compare and contrast the characteristics of beetles and true "bugs".
Target Objective:	• Am I able to compare and contrast beetles and true "bugs"?
Instructional Objective:	The students will be able to construct a wet mount of a plant stem.
Target Objective:	• Am I able to construct a wet mount of a plant stem?
Instructional Objective:	The students will be able to measure linear distance using a meter stick.
Target Objective:	• Am I able to measure distances using a meter stick?

FIGURE 14.2 Relationship Between Instructional Objectives and Target Objectives

assessment. At the end of a particular unit of study, teachers may ask students if they have, in fact, mastered a particular set of target objectives. Target objectives become "test items" or assessment items for measuring students' knowledge.

How Will They Find Out?   "How will they find out?" is the third question guiding planning. From the perspective of the classroom teacher, this question encourages teachers to identify available educational resources and plan activities to initiate student investigations of the natural world. When planning instructional activities for students in the multicultural classroom, teachers need to consider the characteristics of the learners and the ways that children learn. In addition, teachers need to identify the mean(s) by which students will understand science concepts and processes.

The question How will they find out? engages the teacher in brainstorming. What materials, activities, and resources are available to me as I plan? What instructional strategies will I use? What conceptual knowledge will be included in this unit? What science processes will be highlighted during this unit of study? What accommodations will be made for children with special needs? Have I attended to the instructional needs of all students? Planning engages the teacher in identifying available resources to meet children's educational needs. When planning, teachers consider the nature of the learning situation; the type of learning outcome that is expected; the environment or climate for learning; the conditions under which children will receive instruction; and practical considerations such as cost, feasibility, and access to materials.

After activities, resources, and materials are identified, the teacher wrestles with the question of the instructional approaches to be used. Will this be a thematic unit or a stand alone unit? If the unit is a thematic unit, what subject or content areas will be included? What activities will be used to teach or illustrate the concept(s) in the unit? Are the materials and/or resources readily available? What materials and/or resources need to be gathered? Where will they be obtained?

Once the instructional activities have been selected, the next question is one of sequencing. Do some of the activities require prerequisite skills or knowledge? If so, which activities should be first, second, third, and so forth. How should the unit be structured? Suppose a teacher desires that students record data on mold growth as part of a unit of studies of fungi (Figure 14.3). The teacher should begin by examining this activity to determine what type(s) of prior knowledge are required. In this instance, the activity requires that students record data using a table, control variables, and make measurements of the size of colonies of fungi. If the students have not had previous experience using these science processes, these should be taught as the students work through the activity.

In addition, teachers should reflect on the total unit of study. Is there a variety of learning activities? Have the needs of all students been met? Does the unit include activities which will at some time or another appeal to every child? Are students encouraged to bring their "home learning" to school and combine it with new information to be presented in class? At this level, planning involves integrating parts to make a unified whole. Translating units into daily instruction involves teachers in identifying prerequisite concepts, skills, and processes and sequencing instruction such that students acquire a knowledge of science gradually.

What Have They Learned?   The final question in the planning process involves evaluation and reflection on what has been learned. "What have they learned?" is a question that teachers wrestle with on a daily basis, and not only on a unit or yearly basis. Students may be evaluated using teacher made or publisher made tests. They may also be evaluated by entries in journals, task tests, posters, and so forth.

Not only should teachers evaluate students' learning, they should also reflect on their own teaching. What things have I done well? What things might I do better? What types of learning activities "worked" well with this group of students? What types of learning activities might be improved on what I have already done? Planning involves teachers in planning and implementing instruction, as well as reflecting on what students have learned and on what might have been done.

Finally, as part of the reflection on planning, teachers should check to be sure that there is congruency and consistency among the objectives, the instruction, and the assessment. If your instructional objectives were to provide students with a knowledge of the characteristics of fungi and the conditions neces-

Mold Gardening

Activation Stage

Materials:	moldy bread, hand lens
Focus Question:	What is mold?
Procedure:	Allow the students to examine specimens of bread mold. Encourage the students to draw the mold and record some observations of the mold.
Summary Question:	What are the characteristics of mold?
	Describe your bread mold.

Actualization Stage

Materials:	plastic sandwich bags, pieces of bread, medicine droppers, water, metric ruler
Focus Question:	What conditions are needed to grow mold?
Procedure:	Allow the students to set up micro-environments to grow mold. Cut the bread into small pieces. Allow the students to place the pieces of mold in baggies (or allow the bread to sit out in the open).
Possible Growth Conditions (Independent variables):	Have the students suggest some ways that they can alter the bread to encourage the growth of mold.
	Placing the bread in the light, in dark, moisten the bread, dry out the bread, in a cold place, a warm place.
Checking for Growth (Dependent variable):	Each day, check each piece of bread and record the number and size of the mold colonies on the bread. Record the data on a table.

Growth Conditions	Number and Size of Colonies
Light, moist, warm	
Light, moist, cold	
Light, dry, warm	
Light, dry, cold	
Dark, moist, warm	
Dark, moist, cold	
Dark, dry, warm	
Dark, dry, cold	

Summary Question:	Which conditions best encourage the growth of mold?
	Which conditions are least favorable for mold?

FIGURE 14.3   Mold Gardening

Application Stage

Materials: plastic sandwich bags, food items
Focus Question: Where else can mold grow?
Procedure: Place materials in bags. Predict which ones will grow mold and which ones will not. Grow the mold under the most favorable conditions possible (Learned from prior experience in the previous activity).

Material	Prediction	Mold Growth?

Summary Questions: Based on your observations, what type(s) of materials support the growth of mold?

Why do you think mold grows on these materials?

What types of materials did not support the growth of mold?

Why do you think this occurs?

FIGURE 14.3   Mold Gardening (continued)

sary for fungal growth, you would evaluate your instruction to be sure that the activities met these objectives. Did I provide students the opportunity to learn the characteristics of fungi? Did I provide students the opportunity to learn about the conditions necessary to grow mold or fungi? Finally, did I measure students' learning in accordance with the objectives? If the objective was to identify the characteristics of fungi, did I design an assessment question which measured students' progress in mastering this objective? Did I measure students' knowledge of the conditions necessary for mold growth? Objectives, instruction, and assessment should match. In other words, teachers should teach according to the objectives and should find ways of measuring how well they were achieved.

CLASSROOM PRACTICE

Suppose you want to prepare a unit of instruction on sound for a second grade class. Your school district science curriculum guide requires that second graders in your district engage in a unit of study on sound. You might begin by admin-

Sharing is part of learning. (© Will Faller)

istering a pretest on sound or by asking your students to make a concept map or word web that shows what they know about sound. This not only provides information about students' notions of sound but also about their knowledge of associated or related concepts.

As you prepare to write a unit on sound, you would evaluate your students' knowledge of sound using the criteria that have been established by your school district. What does the district suggest that students know about sound? What do my students already know about sound? Once you have determined what your students already know about sound, you should also determine what they need to know. In addition, you should ask your students what they want to know about sound. What new information would they like to gain as the class studies sound? Planning begins by assessing your students' knowledge base and identifying discrepancies between what they already know and what they need to know (Figure 14.4).

The next step involves identifying resources. Which textbook chapters, tradebooks, or other readings will assist my students in constructing a knowledge of sound? What activities will I plan to help students add to their conceptual knowledge of sounds? What science processes will I emphasize as we study sound? What social skills will I encourage students to work on? How will I evaluate those skills? What attitudes will I stress during the unit?

In the unit plan shown below (Figure 14.5), a series of hands-on science activities may be integrated with TRICA (Teaching Reading in the Content Areas) activities, guest speakers, and cooperative tasks. The overall unit includes textual passages, videos, computer software programs, hands-on manipulative activities, guest speakers, and individual learning activities. Information on sound is presented to students in a variety of methods. The unit emphasizes not just

Focus Questions: What do I want them to know?
What do I want to know?

District objectives: Concept – Sound is a form of mechanical energy.
– Pitch is the highness or lowness of sound.
– Sound is caused by a vibration of matter.

Processes – Observing, recording data, predicting, using
cause and effect relationships

Students desiredlearnings: What causes sounds?
What kinds of sounds are there?
(Brainstorming session)   How can I make sounds?

Associated Words:

What other ideas are
related to what they
will learn?

- pitch
- music
- loudness
- vibration
- energy
- hearing

Concept map:

What do they already know?

- Word web for pre-assessment

Reflections:

What have they learned?
(Teacher reflections after the unit)

- concepts — assessed on posttest
- processes — assessed — journals
- social skills — checklist
- attitude — assessed on library day

Data:

What are they learning?

- Laboratory journal — record
  of activities and reflections
  on learnings
- Additions to word webs

Investigative activities:

How will I help them find out?

- Textbook readings on sound —
  three-tiered study guide
- Video on sound from library
- Beaker and tuning fork activity
- Ping pong ball and tuning for activity
- Bleach bottle banjo
- Meter stick activity
- Bottle flute
- Straw flute

- Shoebox activities on sounds
  (rubber bands, plastic
  instruments)
- Guest speaker — band director
- Reading corner — library books
- Poster on musical instruments
- Paper cup phone
- Computer disk on sound

FIGURE 14.4   Vee Map for Sound Unit

the acquisition of a conceptual knowledge of sound but also acquisition of science processes, attitudes, and social skills. Planning is a road map; the activities illustrated in the unit plan "schedule" (Figure 14.5) indicate approximate times. Most teachers recognize that activities sometimes go according to schedule and sometimes require adjustments in their timelines. Students' rate of acquisition of conceptual knowledge is frequently difficult to gauge in advance.

Students' conceptual knowledge of sound is evaluated through traditional posttesting, times for sharing learning, journal writing, and poster sessions. Ac-

Sound Unit Instructional Plan

	Monday	Tuesday	Wednesday	Thursday	Friday
Week 1	• Word webs on sound 14-1 • Brainstorming – What do we want to know about?	• Assess attitude during library period (books on sound checked out) 14-2	• Reading on sound • Introduce shoebox corner 14-3	• SCALed lesson – tuning fork and water 14-4 • Journal writing 14-5	• Video on sound • Mini-lecture on sound
Week 2	• SCALed lesson – Paper cup phone 14-6 • Add to word webs 14-1	• Finish sound readings – three tiered study guides	• Ping pong ball activity 14-7 • Sound vocabulary activities	• Meter stick activity 14-8 • Bleach bottle banjo 14-9	• Straw flute activity 14-10
Week 3	• Computer program on sound	• Reading study guide on sound	• Bottle flutes 14-11	• Guest speaker Band director	• Playing homemade instruments 14-12
Week 4	• Begin adopt an instrument activity – Jigsaw 14-13	• Complete jigsaw activity on sound • Use checklist to evaluate students group skills	• Post assessment on attitudes – library check • Sharing on musical instruments 14-14	• Make a poster – Share what you've learned about sound 14-15	• Post test sound

FIGURE 14.5 Sound Unit Instructional Plan

quisition of science processes is to be evaluated in this unit through an examination of students' laboratory journals. Attitudes towards sound are assessed through an unobtrusive observation of students' reading preferences during library periods. Finally, students' social skills are evaluated through an observational checklist. Evaluation is an ongoing process. Daily sharing of what students are learning and daily reflection on students' written work provide teachers with an understanding of the ways that students are constructing a knowledge of sound.

Following are activities associated with the sound unit.

ACTIVITY 14-1 ■ WORD WEBBING SOUND CONCEPTS

Type of Activity: Conceptual assessment: Pretest and Reflective Learning

Student Directions:

1. Draw a word web which shows your understanding of sound. Show all the words you can think of that are related to the concept of sound.
2. Draw lines to show the ways that the ideas are related. As you work through the unit, your teacher will ask you to look at your word web and add new ideas.

ACTIVITY 14-2 ■ ATTITUDES TOWARD SOUND

Type of Activity: Attitude assessment

Directions: Observe the students during their regular library period. As students leave the library, count the number of students who voluntarily select books on sound. The difference between the number of students who select a book prior to beginning a unit of study and those who select a book after study is a crude indicator of the change in interest toward the subject.

ACTIVITY 14-3 ■ SOUND SHOEBOX

Type of Activity: Self-directed learning activity.

Materials:

rubber bands (different sizes)   small box

Student Directions: Make a musical instrument by stretching the rubber bands across the top of a box. Pluck the rubber bands. Arrange the bands in order from the one that makes the lowest pitch to the one that makes the highest pitch.

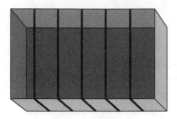

Record your observations:

1. Can you change the pitch of a rubber band? If so, how?
2. Does a thick rubber band make a sound different from a thin one? If so, how?
3. What happens when you pluck the rubber band quickly? Slowly?
4. What happens to the pitch when you stretch a rubber band? Let it sag?
5. How is a rubber band like a stringed instrument?

ACTIVITY 14-4 ▪ INVESTIGATING SOUND WAVES

Type of Activity: SCALed lesson (discrepant event)

Activation Stage:

Materials:

tuning fork   beaker of water

Focus Question: What happens when a tuning fork is placed in a container of water?

Procedure: Fill a container with water. Tap a tuning fork against the edge of a table or chair. Place the vibrating fork into the water. What happens?

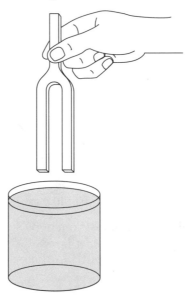

TABLE 14.1 Tuning Fork Variables	
Conditions	*Observations*
Beaker filled to top	
Beaker half full	
Beaker nearly empty	
Tuning fork added quickly	
Tuning fork added slowly	

Actualization Stage:

Materials:

tuning fork   beaker of water

Procedure: Change some of the variables and record what happens (Table 14.1).

Application Stage:

Focus Questions: Based on what you have observed, what would you say about sound? Explain your answer in your journal.

ACTIVITY 14-5 ■ JOURNAL WRITING

Type of Activity: Thematic language and science activity.

Materials:

outline of a vee map or a science journal

Directions:

1. As you work through the investigations of sound, keep a record of your investigations. Describe the materials and procedures you are using and keep a record of your findings.
2. As you do each activity explain what new information you are adding to your knowledge base about sound.

ACTIVITY 14-6 ■ PAPER CUP PHONE

Type of Activity: SCALed lesson

Activation Stage:

Materials:

paper cups, string

Procedure: Construct a paper cup phone like the one shown on page 362.

Actualization Stage:

1. What happens when you speak into the paper cup?
2. What happens when someone else speaks into the paper cup phone and you hold your cup to your ear?
3. What happens when the string is tight?
4. What happens when the string is loose?
5. How far can you stretch the phones apart and still have them work?
6. Does your phone work around corners? Why or why not?

Application Stage:

1. How is your paper cup phone like a real phone?
2. How is your paper cup phone different from a real phone?
3. How does a paper cup phone work? Explain your answer.

ACTIVITY 14-7 ■ PING PONG MAGIC

Type of Activity: SCALed lesson

Activation Stage:

Materials:

ping pong ball glued to a piece   tuning fork
   of thread

Procedure: Hold the ping pong ball (glued to a thread) very steady. Touch the ball with a vibrating tuning fork.

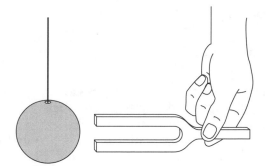

Actualization Stage:

Materials:

tuning fork   ping pong ball
ping pong ball on a string

Procedure:

1. Touch a vibrating tuning fork to a ping pong ball sitting on a table. What happens?
2. Touch a vibrating tuning fork to a ping ball suspended on a thread. What happens?
3. Do the two balls behave in the same manner. Why or why not?

Application Stage:

1. Explain why you think the suspended ping pong ball moves so much when it is touched by the vibrating tuning fork.
2. After this activity, how would you describe sound?

ACTIVITY 14-8 ■ MOVING METRIC RULER

Type of Activity: SCALed Learning

Activation Stage:

Materials:

metric ruler or meter stick

Focus Question: What happens when a meter stick is pressed down and released?

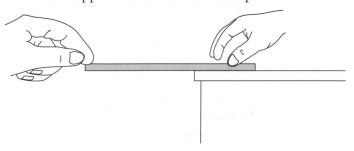

ACTIVITIES

Actualization Stage:

Materials:

metric ruler or meter stick

Focus Questions:

1. What happens to the meter stick when it is released?
2. What happens if you press harder on the meter stick?
3. What happens if you press lightly on the meter stick?
4. What happens if you move the vibrating meter stick onto the table?
5. What happens if you move the vibrating meter stick off the edge of the table?
6. As you hear the sound, can you see something happening to the meter stick? What?

Application Stage:

Focus Question:

1. Based on what you have observed, what do you think "causes" sound?

ACTIVITY 14-9 ■ BLEACH BOTTLE BANJO

Type of Activity: SCALed learning

Activation Stage:

Materials:

| empty bleach bottle (cleaned out | paper fasteners |
| with bottom removed) | rubber bands of varying thicknesses |

Procedure: Assemble the banjo as shown below. Can you play a tune on the banjo?

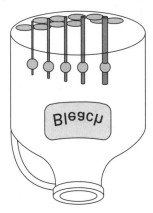

Actualization Stage:

1. Do the rubber bands make different sound? Why do you think this happens?
2. What is another name for the highness or lowness of sound?
3. What causes rubber bands to make different sounds?

4. What would happen if you had a thicker rubber band? A thinner band?

Application Stage:

1. How is your bleach bottle banjo like a real banjo or guitar?
2. How is your bleach bottle banjo different from a real banjo or guitar?

ACTIVITY 14-10 ▪ STRAW FLUTE

Type of Activity: SCALed Learning

Activation Stage:

Materials:

plastic straw   scissors

Procedure: Make a straw flute by cutting the straw as shown below.

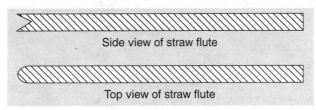

Side view of straw flute

Top view of straw flute

Press your teeth lightly in front of the cut portion of the straw and blow.

Focus Question: What happens?

Actualization Stage:

1. Can you make a high pitch sound with the flute? If so, how?
2. Can you make a low pitch sound with the flute? If so, how?
3. Could you do something to the flute so that you could make high and low sounds one after the other? What could you do?
4. Could you play a tune on the straw flute? Describe how you would do this.

Application Stage:

1. How is the straw flute like a real flute?
2. How is the straw flute different from a real flute?

ACTIVITY 14-11 ▪ BOTTLE FLUTE

Type of Activity: SCALed Lesson

Activation Stage:

Materials:

empty soda bottles   water

Procedure: Fill the bottles with different amounts of water. Blow across the top of each bottle.

Focus Question: What happens to the sound when different amounts of water are in the bottles?

Actualization Stage:

1. If sound is caused by a vibration of matter, what is vibrating in the bottles?
2. Which bottle makes the highest sound?
3. Which bottle makes the lowest sound?

Application Stage:

1. Is there some instrument in a band that works in the same way that a bottle flute works? If so, which one?
2. Why do you think different pitches of sound are produced?
3. From your experiences in working with different homemade instruments, what can you conclude about sound?

ACTIVITY 14-12 ▪ HOMEMADE INSTRUMENT ORCHESTRA

Type of Activity: Cooperative learning

Teacher Directions:

1. Tell the students that each group is to use their homemade instruments to play a simple tune. This might be follow-up to a guest speaker (such as a band director or an older student who plays a musical instrument).
2. As the students to arrange the pitches of the strings or sounds of their instruments in order from the lowest (1), to the highest (5 or 6 or 7 or 8).
3. Pass out music sheets (page 367) to the students. Allow them to select a conductor in each group and practice briefly playing a selection.

Mary Had a Little Lamb
(Music for soda bottle flute)

Mary had a   little   lamb,   little   lamb,   little   lamb
3 2   1   2 3   3   3   2 2   2   3 5   5

Mary had a   little   lamb,   its fleece   was   white as   snow.
3 2   1   2 3   3   3   2 2   2   3   2   1

ACTIVITY 14-13 ■ ADOPT AN INSTRUMENT

Type of Activity: Cooperative learning: Jigsaw

Materials (examples):

library books	markers
filmstrips	paints
videos on musical instruments	glue

Piano   Trumpet   Flute

Drums   Harp   Guitar

records   scissors
poster paper

Procedure:

1. Allow students to form cooperative or familiar working groups. Place pictures of musical instruments in a container and allow students to draw an instrument randomly.
2. Ask each group of students to become an expert on one musical instrument. Have the students research their instrument and prepare an oral presentation to tell the class about their instrument.

Note: Students may share with posters, songs, playing instruments, playing recordings of instruments, and so forth.

ACTIVITY 14-14 ▪ SOCIAL SKILLS CHECKLIST

Type of Activity: Student evaluation

Procedure: As students work in groups constructing a project to share what they have learned with others, circulate from group to group and evaluate students on their social interactions with others (Table 14.2).

ACTIVITY 14-15 ▪ SHARING WHAT YOU'VE LEARNED

Type of Activity: Authentic assessment

Materials:

Poster paper and art supplies (markers, glue, scissors)

TABLE 14.2   Social Interaction Checklist

Social Skills	Never	Sometimes	Often	Always
How often does the student listen when others speak?				
How often does the student contribute ideas to the group project?				
How often does the student share manipulative materials?				
How often does the student hand materials to others?				
How often does the student get materials for the group?				
How often does the student lead the discussion?				

Directions: Make a poster and write a report that describes what you have learned about sound as you worked through the activities in this unit of study.

 CHAPTER SUMMARY

Lesson planning involves teachers in "putting it all together" by developing a road map to guide students' learning. Reflective planning adresses the questions: What do they know? What should they know or want to know? How will they find out? and What have they learned? Lesson planning helps the teacher in assessing children's prior knowledge, involving children in planning for future learning, sequencing activities which may assist students to acquire new knowledge, and evaluating instruction and what has been learned.

 TOPICS TO REVIEW

 REFLECTIVE PRACTICE

1. In this chapter, planning is viewed as constructing a road map. Do you agree or disagree with this analogy? Why or why not?
2. In your opinion, what is the purpose of scope and sequence documents and district curricular guides? Explain your answer.
3. The author points out that planning is a guide and that teachers are rarely able to carry out unit plans as they were first written. Why do you think this happens?
4. In your opinion, why is it important that objectives, instruction, and assessment exhibit "congruency and consistency"?

SAFETY IN THE MULTICULTURAL SCIENCE CLASSROOM

INTRODUCTION

Safety in the science classroom is a concern for all students. A safe working environment for children includes a consideration of classroom management and planning, laboratory equipment, and safety awareness.

MANAGING AND PLANNING FOR SAFETY

If it can go wrong, it will go wrong. This motto should guide our planning for children. Young children especially lack the muscle coordination and hand-and-eye coordination of adults. Children will spill, drop, and break things. Relax.

- Prior to conducting an activity in the classroom, make sure that you have tried it yourself. Identify the "potholes" in the road of life, and try to find ways of avoiding these potholes in your activities.
- The activities in this book have all been field tested with real children in real classrooms. They were designed with a consideration for children's safety.
- Plan for disasters. Provide sponges, mops, and paper towels for activities involving liquids. Provide brooms and dust pans so that children can clean up after themselves.
- Make sure that proper safety equipment is available. If flames are used, be sure that you have a fire extinguisher on hand. If caustic chemicals are used, provide protective eye wear.
- Use flat topped tables or desks, or floor space for science activities. Tilted topped desks are difficult to use in the science classroom.
- Select plant specimens with care as some plants are poisonous.
- Plan carefully for students' interactions with animals.

LABORATORY SUPPLIES AND EQUIPMENT

- Whenever possible, use nonbreakable containers.
- Whenever possible use nontoxic chemicals. Children have a habit of tasting everything.
- Make sure that all equipment is in good working order prior to instruction.
- Test all electrical equipment prior to allowing children to use it.
- Dilute caustic chemicals to avoid injury.

SAFETY AWARENESS

- Be sure to cue children about potential hazards as part of preactivity orientation.
- Enforce the wearing of safety goggles whenever hazardous chemicals or flames are used in the classroom.
- Be consistent in enforcing safety regulations.
- Provide safety instructions in students' native languages if some students are not proficient in English.
- If working in a monolingual or bilingual classroom, provide safety posters in the child's native language.
- Involve children in planning a safe working environment.

CRITTERS IN THE SCIENCE CLASSROOM

INTRODUCTION

The presence of living organisms in the classroom enhances the quality of science instruction. Teachers need to provide adequate food and shelter for "critters" brought into the classroom. In certain areas of the country, school boards, animal protection agencies, and local statutes prevent the use of certain living organisms in classrooms. Common sense also dictates that certain organisms are not appropriate for use in science classrooms. For example, rattlesnakes would not be appropriate guests in a public school setting. Generally, the quality of instruction is vastly improved through the use of living specimens. This is a thumbnail guide to the care, feeding, and use of animals appropriate for most instructional settings.

ANTS

Ants make fascinating additions to any elementary science classroom. Stock for ant colonies can be obtained from scientific supply houses or from the natural world. If obtaining ants from the natural world, extract the queen from the anthill first. Also of note, colonies can be started without a queen, but all of the eggs laid by the workers will hatch into males.

While homemade ant housing constructed out of wide-mouthed jars is acceptable for most ants, ant houses available from commercial supply houses afford students a better opportunity to view the life history of the ant. Soil in the ant colony should be kept moist (by the insertion of a few drops of water each day). Suitable food for ants includes sugar granules, small pieces of vegetables (lettuce, carrots, potatoes), stale bread crumbs, dried fruits, and small pieces of raw ground meat.

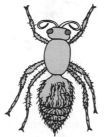

BUTTERFLIES

Lepidoptera specimens are easily raised in the classroom and provide hours of observational opportunities for children. The easiest way to begin raising butterflies is to obtain eggs or newly hatched larvae from the natural world. Summer and early fall are the best times of the year to obtain specimens.

Larvae should be kept in a clean, dry, well-ventilated container. Food should be changed once or twice a day. Droppings should be removed on a daily basis to prevent mold growth. If leaves are moistened prior to being placed in the container, the moisture needs of the insects will be met. Toward the end of the larval stage, the small sticks should be placed in the container to provide a place for pupation to occur.

After the period of pupation, the crystallizes will hatch into mature butterflies. At this time, the newly emerged butterflies will need several hours to "blow up" their wings. Blood is pumped through the wings and the wings harden before the butterflies take their maiden voyage.

CRAYFISH

Crayfish are readily raised in the classroom in standard aquariums. As with fish, the aquatic environment should be well aerated. Because crayfish are regarded as shellfish in some states, the season to collect specimens may be limited. After specimens are caught in a net, they should be placed in a moist environment for transportation to the classroom.

If an aquarium is used, the bottom should be covered with gravel. In addition, plastic flower pots or simulated rock caves should be placed in the bottom of the aquarium to serve as "houses" for the crayfish.

Crayfish are scavengers and, as such, eat a variety of fresh and/or frozen meats. Frozen or canned fish is a favorite food of crayfish.

FISH

Fish (especially guppies and goldfish) make wonderful additions to the elementary science classroom, and well oxygenated aquariums with gravel bottoms make wonderful habitats for these critters. As a rule of thumb, about 4 liters of water are needed for each small fish.

Appropriate water temperatures vary with the species housed in the aquarium. Goldfish typically prefer water that is 20 to 24°C. Some tropical species may require higher temperatures. Adult fish typically need to be fed on a daily basis. Commercially prepared fish foods are best for providing the nutritional needs of your fish.

MEALWORMS

Mealworms are the larval form of *Tenebrio* beetles. Commercial supply houses are the best source of stock to begin a beetle colony. Tenebrio larvae are comfortably accommodated in the classroom in plastic, glass, or enamel containers. Wheat middling or bran flakes are standard food for mealworms. The addition of carrot or apple slices into meal will supply beetles' moisture needs.

Spring time is the best season for beginning mealworm cultures. Once established, colonies can last many years so long as the food supply is periodically recharged. In addition to providing endless hours of observation, mealworms can serve as food for fish and crayfish being raised in the classroom.

SNAILS

Land snails make excellent pets for the classroom. They are easily maintained and provide students with a wealth of information about mollusks. Land snails are most easily collected during the early morning hours after a soaking rain. Typically, snails are found in dark damp places.

Snails require a very moist environment to survive. Glass containers, including discarded aquarium, make excellent snail housing. The bottom of the aquarium should be covered with soil. Rotted leaves, decaying tree branches, and moss provide appropriate fauna for the environment. A shallow container of water placed in a corner of the aquarium will supply the moisture needs of the snails. In addition, a glass cover on the top of the container will keep the humidity level high.

Decaying lettuce leaves and similar rotting vegetation provide an adequate food source for land snails.

FROGS

The life cycle of the frog is a source of fascination for young children. Frog eggs can be obtained from ponds and slow moving areas of streams in the early spring. Eggs should be placed in a shallow container. Roughly 1 liter of water is required for each 8 to 20 tadpoles. Water should be maintained at about 20°C.

Tadpoles may be fed dried yeast or small amounts of boiled lettuce. If the tadpoles become sluggish, or if the water becomes cloudy and foul smelling, you are overfeeding the tadpoles. Foul water should be changed. Typically, water should be changed every other day to maintain a clean and hygienic living environment for the tadpoles.

VERTEBRATES

Mice and gerbils make excellent classroom pets. Specimens should be purchased from a local pet store or a reputable supplier to avoid bringing diseased animals into the classroom. Due to a risk of Hantavirus infection, wild mice should never be used in the classroom. Animals should be housed in soundly constructed wire mesh cages.

The bottoms of cages should be covered with newspaper and cedar chips. Water bottles should be filled daily and animals should be provided with clean food on a daily basis. A feeding, cleaning, and watering schedule should be kept attached to each cage.

EQUIPMENT AND SUPPLIES FOR THE SCIENCE CLASSROOM

INTRODUCTION

Throughout the United States there are literally hundreds of corporations which supply equipment, supplies, and materials for science instruction. The listing provided on these pages is meant to introduce teachers to some of these companies, but the list is by no means inclusive. Updated lists of science education suppliers may be obtained annually from the National Science Teachers Association.

EQUIPMENT/SUPPLIES

AccuLab Products Group
200 California Ave. Suite 217
Palo Alto, CA 94306

SensorNet and "Plug & Go" interfacing materials

AIMS Education Foundation
P.O. Box 8120
Fresno, CA 93747

Supplier of AIMS labs

American Geological Institute
4220 King St.
Alexandria, VA 22302

Aquarium and Science Supply Co.
P.O. Box 29726
Elkins Park, PA 19117

Supplies for classroom animals

Arbor Scientific
P.O. Box 2750
Ann Arbor, MI 48106

General Lab Supplies

Brock Optical
P.O. Box 940831
Maitland, FL 32794

Labware

Carolina Biological Supply Co.
2700 York Rd.
Burlington, NC 27215

25,000 items for science teaching

Center for Multisensory Learning Lawrence Hall of Science University of California Berkeley, CA 94720	SAVI/SELPH Program
CHEMPAC E & L Instruments P.O. Box 1942 New Haven, CT 06509	Hardware, software and laboratory manuals
Connecticut Valley Biological 82 Valley Rd. P.O. Box 326 Southampton, MA 01073	General science supplies
Creative Publications 788 Palomar Ave. Sunnyvale, CA 94086	Elementary science supplies
Cuisenaire Company of America 12 Church St. New Rochelle, NY 10801	General science supplies
Dale Seymour Publications P.O. Box 10888 Palo Alto, CA 94303	Calculators and spatial visualization materials
Delta Education Inc. P.O. Box 915 Hudson, NM 03051	Supplies and lab equipment—SCIS, ESS, SAPA
Edmund Scientific Co. 101 E. Gloucester Pike Barrington, NJ 08007	General science supplies
Educational Rocks & Minerals P.O. Box 574 Florence, MA 01060	Rocks and minerals for ESS, SCIS, ISCS, & ESCP
EME P.O. Box 2805 Danbury, CT 06813	Videodiscs and CD-ROM technologies
Encyclopedia Britannica Educational Corp. 310 S. Michigan Ave., 6th Floor Chicago, IL 60604	Videodiscs and CD-ROM technologies
Estes Industries 1295 H St. Penrose, CO 81240	Rocket model kits
Fisher Scientific Educational Materials Division 4901 W. LeMoyne St. Chicago, IL 60651	General science supplies
Flinn Scientific 131 Flinn St. P.O. Box 219 Batavia, IL 60510	Chemistry supplies and laboratory chemicals

Forestry Suppliers Inc.
205 West Rankin St.
P.O. Box 8397
Jackson, MS 39284

General science supplies

Frey Scientific Co.
905 Hickory Ln.
Mansfield, OH 44905

General science supplies

Genesis
P.O. Box 2242
Mt. Vernon, WA 98273

Owl pellet kits

HEMCO Corporation
111 North Powell
Independence, MO 64056

Hoods and laboratory furniture

Hubbard Scientific
3101 Iris Ave., Suite 215
Boulder, CO 80301

General science supplies

Ken-A-Vision Mfg. Co., Inc.
5615 Raytown Rd.
Raytown, MO 64133

Microprojectors and microscopes

Lab-Aids, Inc.
249 Trade Zone Dr.
Ronkonkoma, NY 11779

Science modules

Lab Safety Supply, Inc.
401 S. Wright Rd.
P.O. Box 1368
Janesville, WI 53547

Safety equipment and supplies

LaMotte Company
P.O. Box 329
Chestertown, MD 21620

Test kits for water and soil

Learning Spectrum
1390 Westridge Dr.
Portola Valley, CA 94025

Science on a Shoestring kits

Learning Technologies, Inc.
59 Walden St.
Cambridge, MA 02140

Starlab portable planetarium

LEGO DACTA
555 Taylor Rd.
Box 1600
Enfield, CT 06083

Lego Technic I and II

Magnet Source
The Master Magnets, Inc.
607 S. Gilbert
Castle Rock, CO 80104

Magnets in kits

Meiji Techno America
500 W. Cummings Park, Suite 2350
Woburn, MA 01801

Microscopes

Merlan Scientific Ltd. 247 Armstrong Ave. Georgetown, Ontario Canada L7G 4X6	Computer interfaces
Midwest Products Co, Inc. School Division P.O. Box 564 Hobart, IN 46342	Kits for bridge building, airplanes, air balloons
Museum Products Company 84 Route 27 Mystic, CT 06355	Toys in Space, Repli Tracks
Nasco 901 Janesville Ave. Fort Atkinson, WI 53538	General science supplies
National Teaching Aids, Inc. 1845 Highland Ave. New Hyde Park, NY 11040	Models, Micro-slide viewers, Micromounts
Nebraska Scientific, a Division of Cyrgus Co., Inc. 3823 Leavenworth St. Omaha, NE 68105	Biological specimens
The NightStar Company 1334 Brommer St. Santa Cruz, CA 95062	Astronomy teaching tools
Norris Science Labs & Kits P.O. Box 61281 Las Vegas, NV 89160	Science labs and kits
Northwest Laboratories Inc. #20 - 225 Great Arrow Dr. Buffalo, NY 14207	General science supplies
Nurnberg Scientific Co. 6310 S.W. Virginia Ave. Portland, OR 97201	Microscopes and videomicroscopes
Ohaus Corporation 29 Hanover Rd. Florham Park, NJ 07932	Balances
Optical Data Corp. 30 Technology Dr. Warren, NJ 07059	Videodisc players and monitors
Parco Scientific Co. 316 Younstwon-Kingsville Rd. P.O. Box 189 Vienna, Oh 44473	Microscopes
PASCO Scientific 10101 Foothills Blvd. P.O. Box 619011 Roseville, CA 95661	Physics demonstration equipment

Sargent-Welch Scientific Co.
P.O. Box 1026
Skokie, IL 60076

General science supplies

Schoolmasters Science
745 State Circle
P.O. Box 1941
Ann Arbor, MI 48106

General science supplies

Science Inquiry Enterprises
14358 Village View Ln.
Chino Hills, CA 91709

Discrepant events

Science Kit and Boreal Laboratories
777 East Park Dr.
Tonawanda, NY 14150

General science supplies

Skulls Unlimited
P.O. Box 6741
Moore, OK 73153

Osteological specimens

Spectrum Educational Supplies
  Limited
125 Mary St.
Aurora, Ontario
Canada L4G 1G3

General science supplies

Swift Instruments, Inc.
P.O. Box 562
San Jose, CA 95106

Microscopes, telescopes, and optical
  instruments

Ward's Natural Science
  Establishments Inc.
5100 West Henrietta Rd.
P.O. Box 92192
Rochester, NY 14692

General science supplies

Young Naturalist Co.
614 East 5th St.
Newton, KS 67114

Kits for elementary science

COMPUTER SOFTWARE

AccuLab Products Group
200 California Ave., Suite 217
Palo Alto, CA 94306

Macintosh products

Addison-Wesley Publishing Co.
2725 Sand Hill Road
Menlo Park, CA 94025

Apple II, Macintosh, IBM

Apple Computer Inc.
20525 Mariani Ave.
Cupertino, CA 95014

Apple

Arbor Scientific
P.O. Box 2750
Ann Arbor, MI 48106

Apple II, IBM

Carolina Biological Supply Co. 2700 York Rd. Burlington, NC 27215	Apple, TRS-80, Macintosh, Commodore, IBM
Central Scientific Co. 11222 Melrose Ave. Franklin Park, IL 60131	Apple, Commodore, IBM
Children's Television Workshop Schools and Technology 1 Lincoln Plaza New York, NY 10023	Apple, Macintosh, Tandy, IBM, Commodore
CONDUIT The University of Iowa Oakdale Campus Iowa City, IA 52242	Apple, IBM
Connecticut Valley Biological Supply 82 Valley Rd., Box 326 Southampton, MA 01073	Apple, IBM
Cross Educational Software 504 E. Kentucky Ave P.O. Box 1536 Ruston, LA 71270	Apple, IBM, Commodore, Macintosh, Tandy
Daedalon Corporation P.O.Box 2028 Salem, MA 01970	Apple, Macintosh, Atari
EME P.O. Box 2805 Danbury, CT 06813	Apple, Macintosh, IBM
Fisher Scientific 4901 W. LeMoyne St. Chicago, IL 60651	Apple, IBM
Holt, Rinehart and Winston 1627 Woodland Ave. Austin, TX 78741	Apple, IBM
Houghton Mifflin Co. One Beacon St. Boston, MA 01208	Apple II
IBM Educational Systems P.O. Box 2150 - Ho6L1 Atlanta, GA 30301	IBM
Intellitool, Inc. P.O. Box 459 Batavia, IL 60510	Apple, IBM
Knowledge Revolution 497 Vermont St. San Francisco, CA 94107	Macintosh
LEGO DACTA 555 Taylor Rd., Box 1600 Enfield, CT 06083	Apple, MS-DOS

Macmillan School Publishers 4635 Hilton Corporation Dr. Columbus, Oh 43232	Apple II
Merlan Scientific Ltd. 247 Armstrong Ave. Georgetown, Ontario L7G 4XG Canada	Apple II, Commodore 64, PET, IBM
Milliken Publishing Co. 1100 Research Blvd. P.O. Box 21579 St. Louis, MO 63132	Apple II
Modern Talking Picture Service 5000 Park Street North St. Petersburg, FL 33709	Macintosh, Tandy, IBM
Nasco West, Inc. P.O. Box 3837 Modesto, CA 95352	Apple, TRS-80, Commodore, Atari, IBM
National Geograpic Society 17th & M Sts. NW Washington, DC 20036	Apple, IBM, Macintosh
Ohaus Scale Corporation 29 Hanover Rd. Florham Park, NJ 07932	Apple
Powell Laboratories Box 187 Gladstone, OR 97027	Apple, IBM, TRS-80, Macintosh, Commodore 64
Prentice Hall School Group 113 Sylvan Ave. Englewood Cliffs, NJ 07632	Apple, IBM, Macintosh
Sargent-Welch Scientific P.O. Box 1026 Skokie, IL 60076	Apple, TRS-80, IBM
Scholastic Software 730 Broadway New York, NY 10003	Apple, IBM, Macintosh
Science Kit and Boreal Labs 777 East Park Dr. Tonawanda, NY 14150	Apple, Macintosh, IBM, Commodore
Scott, Foresman and Co. 1900 E. Lake Ave Glenview, IL 60025	Apple, IBM
Silver Burdett & Ginn 250 James St., CN 1918 Morristown, NJ 07960	Apple, IBM
Sunburst Communications 1600 Green Hills Rd. P.O. Box 660002 Scotts Valley, CA 95067	Apple, Tandy, IBM

Tandy/Radio Shack   Tandy, MS-DOS
1600 One Tandy Center
Fort Worth, TX 76102

Texas Learning Technology Group   IBM, Sony
7703 N. Lamar
Austin, TX 78752

Vernier Software   Apple, IBM, Macintosh, Tandy
2920 S.W. 89th St.
Portland, OR 97225

Videodiscovery, Inc.   Apple, Macintosh, IBM
1515 Dexter Ave., N, Suite 400
Seattle, WA 98109

Wadsworth Publishing Co.   Apple, IBM, Macintosh
10 Davis Dr.
Belmont, CA 94002

Ward's Natural Science Est.   Apple, IBM, Macintosh
5100 W. Henrietta Rd.
P.O. Box 92912
Rochester, NY 14692

MEDIA AND VISUAL MATERIALS AND PRODUCTS

Acid Rain Foundation   Transparencies, pictures
1410 Varsity Dr.
Raleigh, NC 27606

Addison Wesley Publishing   Videodiscs, overheads, charts, maps
2725 Sand Hill Rd.
Menlo Park, CA 94025

American Chemical Society   Videotapes
1155 16th Street, NW
Washington, DC 20036

American Association of Physics   Films, videodiscs, slides, cassettes
  Teachers
5112 Berwyn Rd.
College Park, MD 20740

American Gas Association   Filmstrips
1515 Wilson Blvd.
Arlington, VA 22209

American Geophysical Union   Overhead
2000 Florida Ave., NW
Washington, DC 20009

American Institute of Physics
335 E. 45 St.
New York, NY 10017

American Nuclear Society   Films, cassettes, slides, videotapes,
555 N. Kensington Ave.   charts
LaGrange Park, IL 60525

American Water Works Assoc. 6666 W. Quincy Denver, CO 80235	Films, videotapes, charts, pictures
Astronomical Society of the Pacific 390 Ashton Ave. San Francisco, CA 94112	Videodiscs, cassettes, charts, pictures, games
Captioned Films/ Videos for the Deaf Modern Talking Picture Service 5000 Park St. N. St. Petersburg, FL 33709	Films, videotapes
Carolina Biological Supply 2700 York Rd. Burlington, NC 27215	Films, cassettes, videodiscs, games, dittos
Central Scientific Co. 11222 Melrose Ave Franklin Park, IL 60131	Films. cassettes, videodiscs, slides, dittos
Children's Television Workshop One Lincoln Plaza New York, NY 10023	Cassettes, games, dittos
Connecticut Valley Biological 82 Valley Road Southampton, MA 01073	Filmstrips, slides, overheads, charts, tapes
Coronet/MTI Film & Video 108 Wilmont Rd. Deerfield, IL 60015	Films, cassettes, videotapes
Cross Educational Software P.O. Box 1536 Ruston, LA 71270	Software
Delta Education P.O. Box 915 Hudson, NH 03051	Filmstrips, slides, overheads, charts
EME P.O. Box 2805 Danbury, CT 06813	Filmstrips, videodiscs, slides, overheads
Encyclopedia Britannica Corp. 310 S. Michigan Ave., 6th Floor Chicago, IL 60604	Films, videodiscs, cassettes
Entomological Society of America 9301 Annapolis Rd. Lanham, MD 20706	Slides
Foundation for Biomedical Research 818 Connecticut Ave., NW Suite 303 Washington, DC 20006	Videotapes, charts
Jeppesen Sanderson 55 Inverness Dr, E. Englewood, CO 80112	Filmstrips, overheads, charts, dittos

MECC   Filmstrips, software
6160 Summit Drive North
Minneapolis, MN 55430

MMI Corporation   Films, videodiscs, slides, overheads
2950 Wyman Pkwy.
Baltimore, MD 21211

Modern Talking Picture Service   Films, videos, overheads, software
5000 Park St. N.
St. Petersburg, FL 33709

Nasco   General media supplies
901 Janesville Ave.
Fort Atkinson, WI 53538

National Association of Conservation   Videotapes
   Dist.
408 E. Main St.
League City, TX 77574

National 4-H Council   Slides
7100 Connecticut Ave.
Chevy Chase, MD 20815

National Geographic Society   Films, videos, charts, software
17th & M Sts. NW
Washington, DC 20036

National Wildlife Federation   Films, videodiscs, overheads, charts
1400 Sixteenth St. NW
Washington, DC 20036

PBS Video   Videotapes
1320 Braddock Place
Alexandria, VA 22314

TOPS Learning Systems   Media modules
10970 S. Mulino Rd.
Canby, OR 97013

GLOSSARY

Accommodation   Something supplied for convenience or to satisfy a need; to take in new information; to accept new knowledge; to become aware of new learning

Accretion   First step in taking in new knowledge according to Norman's theory of learning; to cause to adhere or to become attached

Activation Stage   First step in SCALing; activation of prior knowledge or recall of prior knowledge

Actualization Stage   Second step in SCALing; appending new knowledge of science concepts to existing mental structures; conceptualizing new knowledge

Adaptation Level   Third and final level of psychomotor skills; adapting or modifying existing knowledge to new uses

Additive Model   A way of accommodating diversity by appending the names of culturally diverse individuals and white females to existing information--normally in footnotes or endnotes

Advance Organizer   Derived from work of Ausubel: an activity, word, or symbol which prepares a student for new learning

Adversative Pattern   Text organization pattern expressing antithesis, opposition, or adverse conditions

Affective domain   The part of human knowledge that deals with human feelings and emotions; values, attitudes, and beliefs

Analogies   Inferences formed when two or more things agree with one another in some respect: similarities, correspondence in function, correspondence between the members of pairs or sets of linguistic forms that serve as a basis for creation of another form

Analysis   Fourth level of Bloom's taxonomy, involves breaking knowledge into its component parts; questioning that examines complexity in terms of elements and functions

Androcentric   Man-centered as opposed to woman-centered; also having to do with one individual rather than a group of individuals

Application   Third level of Bloom's taxonomy: involves breaking knowledge into its component parts and questioning that examines complexity in terms of elements and functions

Application Stage   Third stage of SCALing: to apply new learning or conceptualizations

Applied Level   Practical application of new knowledge; to use a "real world" application of knowledge

Articulation   To utter distinctly, to be able to speak, to discuss, to present one's viewpoint

Assessment   The act or instance of assessing or measuring; appraisal; to make a determination of size or value or importance

Assimilation   To take in; to incorporate, as in to append new knowledge to existing knowledge structures

Attribution Pattern   Text organization pattern; to list the characteristics or attributes of an object, concept, or event in a textual passage

Attribution Theory   To assign characteristics to mental processes

Attrition Rate   Drop out rate, reduction in size

Authentic Assessment Tools   Portfolios, task tests, pictorial tests, journal writing activities, concept maps, word webs, and semantic maps used to assess cognitive knowledge

Automaticity   To perform automatically, without conscious thought

Axiological   The study of nature, types, and criteria of values and value judgements, especially in ethics

Behavioral Psychology   Branch of psychology based on theories of stimulus and response learning; includes programmed instruction and training modules

Bidialectic   A dialect of English, e.g., Appalachian English, street English

Bilingual/Bicultural   Possessing two or more languages and/or cultures

Camaraderie Skills   Social skills involved with group dynamics

Career Awareness   Awareness of adult work experiences, opportunities for employment

Cataphora   Linking textual passages which involves linking to a future or predicted referent

Characteristics of Science   Scientific knowledge is amoral, creative, developmental, parsimonious, testable, and unified

Chunking   Treating increments of knowledge as a single unit

Classifying   Science process: to arrange in groups by some common attribute, to assign to a category

Cluster Skills   Social skills involved in group work

Coach   Function of the teacher in the classroom which involves training intensively by instruction, demonstration, and practice

Cognitive Disequilibrium   State of temporary mental confusion which results when new knowledge does not fit with existing mental structures

Cognitive Dissonance   State of temporary mental reflection, confusion about information; psychological conflict

Cognitive Domain   Knowledge that deals with elements of perception, process of knowing including both awareness and judgement

Cognitive Psychology   Branch of psychology which deals with learning, based on medical models of brain function and human perception of environmental stimuli

Cohesion   The mutual attraction by which the elements of a body are held together or joined

Communicating   Science process, involves disseminating information to others via written and spoken words and through the use of language

Comprehension   Second level of Bloom's taxonomy, involves understanding

Computer-Assisted Instruction   Electronic means of communicating information, typically drill-and-practice software or tutorials

Concept Application Phase   Learning to classify stimuli according to an appropriate principle; applying newly gained conceptual knowledge to a new situation

Concept Invention Phase   Part of learning cycle in which students construct a mental representation for a concept

Concept Map   Visual organizer which shows declarative knowledge a student holds and how it is organized

Conceptual Density   The number of concepts introduced during a textual passage

Concrete Concept   Second level of Gagné's taxonomy of cognitive knowledge

Confirmatory Feedback   A knowledge of results in which the child is appraised of the "correctness" of the answer

Confluent Education   Educational philosophy which incorporates social action into educational foundations

Congruency   The quality or state of agreeing or corresponding

Connectionism   The theory that all mental process can be described as the operation of inherited or acquired bonds between stimulus and response

Consistency   Agreement or logical coherence among things or parts; compatibility or agreement among successive acts, ideas or events; the condition of holding together; firmness; the degree of firmness or agreement

Constructivism   A child-centered view of learning which holds that each child constructs a knowledge of science by himself or herself

Controlling Variables   Science process, controlling the conditions which cause an event to occur

Convergent Questions   Questions having a single correct answer

Cooperative Learning   Arrangement in which students work in mixed-ability groups and are rewarded on the basis of the success of the group

Corrective Feedback   A knowledge of results in which the child is appraised of the "correctness" of the answer and, in the case of incorrect responses, the correct response

Criterion-Referenced Tests   Testing in which scores are compared to a set performance standard

Cultural Deficit Models   Explanations for the lack of culturally diverse individuals in careers which presume that children lack academic skills

Cultural Pluralism   The acceptance of multiple cultures as equally valid

Culturally Diverse Students   A reference to "minority" students

Culturally Familiar Elaborations   Examples of phenomena which are familiar in one culture but which may not be common to all cultures

Culturally Transforming   Social reconstructionist view of history which includes culturally diverse individuals, group discoveries, and oral traditions

Curandera   A midwife and herbal healer in the Hispanic community; practitioner of traditional herbal medicine

Declarative Knowledge   Knowledge that can be stated

Defined Concept   Third level of Gagne's taxonomy of cognitive knowledge

Demonstrations   The act of making evident or proving; an illustration or explanation as of a theory or product; by exemplification or practical application

Dependent Variable   Responding variable; variable measured to determine changes as a result of changes in the independent variable

Discrepant Event   Unexpected natural phenomena which causes cognitive dissonance in the observer

Discrimination First level of Gagné's taxonomy of cognitive knowledge

Divergent Questions Questions have no single correct answer

Domains of Learning Fields of action or thought

Educational Technology Instructional systems design approach to curriculum development

Elaborations Adding and extending meaning by connecting new information to existing knowledge

Epistemological The division of philosophy that investigates the nature and origin of knowledge

Eurocentric A European-centered viewpoint; European-centered as opposed to Eastern- or Native American-centered practices

Evaluation Sixth level of Bloom's taxonomy; involves judging the quality of answers

Evaluator One who makes decisions about student performance and about appropriate teaching strategies

Events of Instruction Gagné's theory of learning that relates phase of instruction to stages of information processing

Expediter One who speeds up the progress of; helps; assists; facilitates

Experimenting Science process: involves identifying and controlling variables

Explanatory Feedback A knowledge of results in which the child is appraised of the accuracy of his or her answer, the "correct" answer, and the reasons for that response

Explication Critical exposition and interpretation, as with literary texts; method of literary criticism in which a detailed reading and analysis of a given text in each of its linguistic, compositional, and expressive parts is undertaken

Exploration Phase Beginning phase of learning cycle during which students manipulate materials and ideas; the act of exploring

Expository Teaching Teacher as lecturer model of teaching

Extraneous Variable Introduced or coming from without; not belonging or proper to a thing; external

Extrinsic External rewards; coming from without

Familia Groups Extended family group that could include members of the immediate family, neighbors, cousins, and so forth

Feeling Tone Motivation factor dependent upon the physical atmosphere of the classroom

Formal Debate A formal contest in which the affirmative and negative sides of a proposition are advocated by opposing speakers

Formative Evaluation Ungraded testing used before or during instruction to aid in planning and diagnosis

Formulating Hypothesis Science process: a scientific guess

Fotonovela A highly visualized textual material similar to a comic book but dealing with an academic topic; also called a photonovel

Generative Cognitive Strategies Embedded learning strategies which enhance learning; using rules to generate surface forms from underlying abstract forms; proverbial; intuitive rules

Geocentric Perspective Earth-centered curriculum used in many Native American science programs

Graphing Packages   Computerized software which generates a graphic representation of knowledge

Gustatory   Of or pertaining to the sense of taste

Hierarchy of Needs   Maslow's model of levels of human needs from physiological requirements to self-actualization

Holistic Learning   Total learning; combining all curriculum areas; used commonly in Native American schools

Home Culture   A child's belief system, based on country of origin, cultural background, or ethnic group

Home Language   Language of the child's home or culture

Home Learning   Values, attitudes, and beliefs derived from a child's home or home culture

Humanistic Psychology   Branch of psychological thought that stresses the uniqueness of the human condition

Hydroponic   Cultivation of plants in water containing dissolved inorganic nutrients rather than soil

Icons   A picture or symbol used to present a concept or idea

Identifying Variables   Science process identifying causal conditions or effects of the condition

Independent Variable   Variable which is changed or manipulated

Inferring   Science process drawing an inference from data

Instructional Maps   Embedded graphic device which reports students' location in a software package

Instructional Systems Design   Systematic design of curriculum based on principles of learning from authors such as Gagné

Instrument Interfacing   Connecting devices to computers to record data in real time

Intellectual Exceptionality   Reference to special needs children; need may range from handicapping condition to intellectually gifted and talented

Intellectual Skills   Skills involved with learning, verbal ability

Interest   Motivational factor that is based on a child's internal curiosity

Internalizing   To incorporate through learning, socialization, or identification

Intrinsic   Internally motivated

Investigating   Science process that involves finding out about the physical world

Journal Writing Activity   Assessment of students' knowledge which shows students' knowledge base and awareness of learning

Kinesthetic   Sensation of movement or strain in muscles, tendons, and joints; muscle sense

Kinetic Energy   Energy due to motion

Knowledge   First level of Bloom's taxonomy

Knowledge of Results   Feedback or knowledge of the correctness of an answer

Learning   Process through which experience causes permanent change in knowledge or behavior

Learning Disability   Educators employ the term as an umbrella concept to refer to children and adolescents who encounter difficulty with school-related material although they appear to have normal intelligence

Lecturer   A member of the faculty of a college or university who is usually qualified without rank or tenure

Level of Concern   Motivation factor in learning dependent upon a student's level of anxiety

Likert Instrument   A variation of the graphic rating scale; used for attitude evaluation; numerically scored on a 5- to 7-point scale

Long-Term Memory   Permanent store of knowledge

Manipulative Materials   Realia or real world objects used in concept formation

Mathemagenic Models   Computer software which is linear in nature and is an electronic drill-and-practice application

Measuring   Science process through which standard units of mass, volume, temperature, length, and so on are assigned to given quantities

Mediated Conversations   Meanings derived from social discourse

Mediator   One who mediates; especially a person who serves as an intermediary to reconcile differences

Metacognition   Knowledge about our own thinking processes

Metaphysical   Based on speculative or abstract reasoning

Modes of Learning   Deriving information from written words, spoken words, realia, icons, or other visual representations

Motivation   Internal state that arouses, directs, and maintains behavior

Multicultural Models   Curriculum models and materials which assume that one culture is to be valued as much as another

Multimedia   Including or involving the use of several media of communication, entertainment, or expression

Navigator   One who explores; a crew member who plots the course of a ship or aircraft or, in a classroom, the course of learning

Need   Something required or wanted; a requisite

Negotiated Doing   Deriving meaning from interacting in a social group that usually includes the use of manipulative materials

Negotiated Meaning   Meaning derived from social discourse

Networking   A supportive system of sharing information and services among individuals and groups having a common interest

Neurobiology   The branch of biology concerned with the anatomy and physiology of the nervous system

Neuropsychology   The study of the functioning of the human mind

Norm-referenced Tests   Testing in which scores are compared with the average performance of others

Objectivism   Any of several doctrines holding that all reality is objective and external to the mind and that knowledge is reliably based on observed objects and events

Observing   Science process according to which the senses are used to gain information about the natural world

Olfactory   Of or contributing to the sense of smell

Operant Conditioning Learning in which voluntary behavior is strengthened or weakened by consequences or antecedents; learning in which a response continues to be made because it is reinforced

Operational Definition A working definition; specifying a variable by expressing the activities or operations required to measure it

Operational Question A question which can be answered by manipulating materials or conducting an investigation

Operationally Defining Science process: formulating a working definition or a definition based on usage

Organizational Strategies Strategies for organizing information

Organizing To pull or put together into an orderly, functional, structured whole

Peer Tutoring Individual or small group tutoring by students of the same approximate age level

Perception Level First level of psychomotor skills

Physical Exceptionality Handicapping condition involving the use of sight, limbs, and so on

Physiological Needs Food, clothing, and shelter: basic survival needs

Pictorial Tests Testing which uses pictures or icons in questioning

Pipeline Theory An explanation derived to explain the lack of minority children and females in science careers

Portfolio Container of documents which shows proficiency or mastery of subject material

Potential Energy Stored energy; energy due to position

Predicting Science process that involves foretelling future occurrences

Procedural Knowledge Knowledge that can be done

Psychometric The measurement of psychological variables such as intelligence, aptitude, and emotional disturbance

Psychomotor Domain Physical ability objectives

Realia Objects such as coins, tools, and so on used by a teacher to illustrate everyday living

Realism Inclination toward literal truth and pragmatism

Receiving Perceiving information

Rehearsal Strategies Repeating words, terms, or phrases over and over until they are encoded into long-term memory

Research Team Approach Cooperative learning strategy according to which a group of students researches part of a topic

Response Observable reaction to a stimulus

Retrieval Process of searching for and finding information in long-term memory

Review Sessions Practicing declarative knowledge, usually in preparation for a test or other measure of long-term memory

Role Models Adults whom children voluntarily emulate

Rule Using Fourth level of Gagné's taxonomy of cognitive knowledge

Scaffolding Layers of meaning conveyed through photos or drawings, low level reading material, and higher level reading material

SCALE Science Concept and Language Experience

Schema Mental structures that are basic structures for organizing information

Schooling   Instruction or training given at school, especially a program of formal education

Science Anxiety   Apprehension about the study of science

Scientific Method   A systematic way of investigating the physical world

Selective Perception   The focusing of attention on certain aspects of experience while ignoring irrelevant or distracting sensations

Self-Directed Learning   Independent or individual self-initiated learning

Self-Referenced Tests   Reference made to one's self or one's own experience

Semantic Differential Scale   A technique for measuring the connotative meaning of concepts by having an individual rate each concept on a series of graduated scales, with each scale defined by a pair of polar adjectives such as good-bad or strong-weak.

Semantic Network   The study of meanings

Sensory Stimuli   Stimuli which are received by skin, eyes, ears, nose, or tongue

Set Level   Second level of psychomotor skills

Short-Term Memory   Working memory; holding a limited amount of information briefly

Simulations   The representation of the behavior or characteristics of one system through the use of another system

Smoothness   Norman's theory of learning; stage that describes expert performance

Social Interactions   Working, talking together in groups

Social Learning Theory   Theory that learning social traits occurs through imitation of and identification with other people

Social-Emotional Exceptionality   Handicapping condition that interferes with one's ability to engage in social interactions

Sociocultural Context   Of or pertaining to the combination or interaction of social and cultural elements

Socratic Method   The use of questions to develop a latent idea

Stage Setting Behaviors   Social behaviors which precede academic work, such as pencil sharpening, calling to friends, and so on; noted by Wilma Longstreet among African-American students

Stage Theory   The particular set of schemata that are in a relative state of equilibrium; a phase of intellectual development

Status   Motivation factor in learning dependent upon a child's social status due to country-of-origin, socioeconomic status, and so forth

Status Characteristics   The position of one individual in relation to another

Stimulus   Event that activates behavior

Structural Knowledge   Sometimes referred to as problem solving, higher order thinking skills; incorporates declarative and procedural knowledge

Structuring   To construct, give form, or arrange

Success   The achievement of something desired, planned, or attempted

Summative Evaluation   Testing that follows instruction and assesses achievement

Superordinate Figure   A significant other or role model in a child's life

Synthesis   Fifth level of Bloom's taxonomy

Tactile   Perceptible to the sense of touch

Talk Story   Phenomena of group construction of a story observed by Kevin Au among Hawaiian American children

Target Students   Students with whom the teacher interacts more than others

Task Skills   Social skills that involve task performance in a group setting

Task Tests   Piagetian-based assessments of students' science process knowledge

Teaching   The work or occupation of teachers; a precept or doctrine

Tuning   Final step in Norman's schema formation process

Unassimilated   To be incompletely integrated culturally or linguistically into mainstream culture

Unobtrusive Measure   Assessment without the conscious knowledge of the observed

Using Numbers   Science process involving manipulation and use of numbers

Using Space/Time Relationships   Science process involving use of relationships pertaining to time, distance, and so on

Valuing   To determine or estimate the worth or value of; appraise

Visual   Serving, resulting from or pertaining to the sense of sight

Wait Time   Time allowed for student to process a teacher's question or response

BIBLIOGRAPHY

Abraham, M. R., & Renner, J.W. (1986). The sequence of learning cycle activities in high school chemistry. *Journal of Research in Science Teaching, 23*(2), 121–143.

Abruscato, J. (1988). *Teaching children science.* Englewood Cliffs, NJ: Prentice Hall.

Adams, D. W. (1990). Fundamental considerations: The deep meaning of Native American schooling, 1880–1900. *Harvard Educational Review, 58*(1), 1–28

Al-Daffa, A. A., & Stroyls, J. J. (1984). *Studies in the exact sciences in medieval Islam.* Dhahran, Saudi Arabia: University of Petroleum and Minerals.

Alic, M. (1986). *Hypatia's heritage: A history of women in science from antiquity to the nineteenth century.* London: Women's Press Ltd.

Allen, J. A. (1987). The gunpowder river project: Experiential education in a large public school system. *Journal of Experiential Education, 19*(3), 11–15.

Allen, W. H. (1960). Audio-visual communication. In C. W. Harris (Ed.). *Encyclopedia of educational research* (pp. 115–137). New York: Macmillan.

Allen, W. H. (1975). Intellectual abilities and instructional media design. *AV Communication Review, (23)*(2), 139–167.

American Association for the Advancement of Science (1990). *The liberal art of science: Agenda for action.* Washington, DC: American Association for the Advancement of Science.

American Association of University Women (1992). *The AAUW report: How schools shortchange girls.* Washington, DC: American Association of University Women Educational Foundation.

American Chemical Society (1988). *ChemCon: Chemistry in the Community.* Dubuque, IA: Kendall/Hunt.

American Psychological Association Task Force on Psychology in Education (August, 1992). *Learner-centered psychological Principles: Guidelines for school redesign and reform.* Washington, DC: American Psychological Association.

Anders, P. L., & Lloyd, C.V. (1989). The significance of prior knowledge in the learning of new content-specific instruction. In D. Lapp, J. Flood, & N. Farnan (Eds.). *Content area reading and learning: Instructional strategies* (pp. 258–271). Englewood Cliffs, NJ: Prentice Hall.

Anderson, C. (1962). *Technology in American education: 1650–1900* (Report No. OE-34018). Washington, DC: Office of Education, U.S. Department of Health, Education, and Welfare.

Anderson, K. (1989). Urban coalition encourages minority youth to "Say YES" to math and science. *Black Issues in Higher Education, 5*(2), 6–8.

Anderson, O.R. (1992). Some interrelationships between constructivist models of learning and current neurobiological theory, with implications for science education. *Journal of Research in Science Teaching, 29*(10), 1037–1058.

Anderson, T.H., & Armbruster, B.B. (1986). *The value of taking notes during lectures. Technical report no. 374.* Cambridge, MA: Bolt, Beranek & Newman.

Arnold, L.B. (1984). *Four lives in science: Women's education in the nineteenth century.* New York: Schocken.

Asimov, I. (1964). *Asimov's biographical encyclopedia of science and technology: The living stories of more than 1000 great scientists from the age of Greece to the space age chronologically arranged.* Garden City, NY: Doubleday.

Assetto, A.R., & Dowden, E. (1988). Getting a grip on interfacing. *The Science Teacher, 55*(6): 65–67.

Atkinson, J.W. (1964). *An introduction to motivation.* Princeton, NJ: Van Nostrand.

Atwater, M.M. (1993). Multicultural science education: Assumptions and alternative views. *The Science Teacher, 60*(3), 32-37.

Atwood, V.A., & Wilen, W.W. (1991). Wait time and effective social studies instruction: What can research in science education tell us? *Social Education, 55*(3), 179–181.

Au, K.H. (1980). Participation structures in a reading lesson with Hawaiian children: Analysis of a culturally appropriate instructional event. *Anthropology and Education Quarterly,11*(2), 91–115.

Au, K.H., & Jordan, C. (1977). *A multidisciplinary approach to research in education: The Kamehameha early education program.* Paper presented to the American Anthropological Association, Houston.

Ausubel, D.P. (1963). *The Psychology of Meaningful Verbal Learning.* New York: Grune & Stratten.

Ausubel, D.P., Novak, J.D., & Hanesian, H. (1978). *Educational psychology: A cognitive view.* New York: Werbel and Peck.

Banchoff, T. F. (1990). Dimension. In L.A. Steen (Ed). *On the shoulders of giants* (pp. 11–59) Washington, DC: National Academy Press.

Bandura, A. (1977). *Social learning theory.* Englewood Cliffs, NJ: Prentice Hall.

Bandura, A. (1962). Social learning through imitation. In N.R. Jones (Ed.), *Nebraska symposium on motivation.* Lincoln, NB: University of Nebraska Press.

Barba, R.H. (1987). In pursuit of the yeast beast. *The Science Teacher, 54*(7): 30–32.

Barba, R., & Cardinale, L. (1991). Are females invisible students: An investigation of teacher-student questioning interactions. *School Science and Mathematics, 91*(7), 306–310.

Barba, R.H., & Rubba, P.A. (1992). A comparison of preservice and in-service earth and space science teachers' general mental abilities, content knowledge, and problem-solving skills. *Journal of Research in Science Teaching, 29*(10), 1037–1058.

Barman, C.R. (1989). The learning cycle: Making it work. *Science Scope,12*(5), 28–31.

Barnes, L.W., & Barnes, M.B. (1991). Assessment, practically speaking. *Science and Children, 28*(6), 14–15.

Beane, D.A.B. (1990). "Say YES to a youngster's future": A model for home, school, and community partnership. *Journal of Negro Education, 59*(3), 360–374.

Bennett, W.J. (1986). *First lessons: A report on elementary education in America.* Washington, DC: U.S. Government Printing Office.

Benson, F.C. (1986). *From straw into gold.* Santa Rosa, CA: Occasional Publications of the Jesse Peter Memorial Museum.

Berlin, D.F. SMILES. *School Science and Mathematics, 90*(3), 254–257.

Berryman, S. (1983). *Who will do science?* New York: Rockefeller Foundation.

Biehler, R.F,. & Snowman, J. (1986). *Psychology applied to teaching.* 5th ed. Boston, MA: Houghton Mifflin.

Bierer, L.K., Lien, V.F., & Silberstein, E.P. (1987). *Heath life science.* Lexington, MA: D.C. Heath & Co.

Blakely, R.J. (1979). *To serve the public interest: Educational broadcasting in the United States*. Syracuse, NY: Syracuse University Press.

Blaschke, C.L., & Sweeney, J. (1977). Implementing effective educational technology: Some reflections. *Educational Technology, 17*(1): 13–18.

Bloom, B.S. (1971). Affective consequences of school achievement. In J.H. Block (Ed.), *Mastery learning: Theory and practice*. New York: Holt, Rinehart and Winston.

Bloom, B.S. (1956). *Taxonomy of educational objectives. Handbook I. Cognitive domain*. New York: David McKay.

Bomeli, C.L. (1991). Mathematics and meteorology: Perfect partners. *School Science and Mathematics, 91*(1), 31–33.

Bracey, G.W. (1984). *Issues and problems in devising a research agenda for special education and technology*. Paper presented at Special Education Technology Research and Development Symposium. Washington, DC: Department of Education.

Bracey, G.W. (1982). What the research shows. *Electronic Learning*. Nov/Dec: 51–54.

Breslich, E.R. (1936). Integration of secondary school mathematics and science. *School Science and Mathematics, 36*(1), 58–67.

Brinckerhoff, R.E. (1986). *Values in school science: Some practical materials and suggestions*. Exeter, NJ: Philips Exeter Academy.

Brown, A.L., & Palincsar, A.S. (1989). Guided cooperative learning and individual knowledge acquisition. In L.B. Resnick (Ed.), *Knowing, learning, and instruction: Essays in honor of Robert Glaser* (pp. 393–451). Hillsdale, NJ: Erlbaum.

Brown, R., Fournier, J.F., & Moyer, R.H. (1977). A cross-cultural study of Piagetian concrete reasoning and science concepts among rural fifth grade Mexican and Anglo-American students. *Journal of Research in Science Teaching, 14*, 329–334.

Brunig, I.L. (1983). An information processing approach to a theory of instruction. *Educational Communications and Technology Journal, 31*: 91–101.

Burbridge, L.C. (1991). *The interaction of race, gender and socioeconomic status in education outcomes*. Wellesley, MA: Center for Research on Women.

Burns, P.C., Roe, B.D., & Ross, E.P. (1984). *Teaching reading in today's elementary schools*. Boston: Houghton Mifflin.

California State Board of Education. (1990). *Science Framework for California Public Schools Kindergarten Through Grade Twelve*. Sacramento, CA: California Department of Education.

Carin, A.A. (1993). *Teaching science through discovery*. New York: Macmillan.

Carnegie Commission of Educational Television (1967). *Public television: A program for action*. New York: Harper & Row.

Carrier, C.A. (1983). Notetaking research: Implications for the classroom. *Journal of Instructional Development, 6*(3), 19–26.

Carter, D.J., & Wilson, R. (1991). *Tenth annual status report: Minorities in higher education*. Washington, DC: American Council on Education, Office of Minorities in Higher Education.

Chambliss, M.J., & Calfee, R.C. (1989). Designing science textbooks to enhance student understanding. *Educational Psychologist, 24*, 307–322.

Cheng, L.R.L. (1992). *Language difference vs. language disorders: An ESL/EFL perspective*. Paper presented at the jointly sponsored ESL Symposium (San Diego State University & National Kaohsiung Normal University, R.O.C.). San Diego, California.

Chittenden, E.A. (1970). Piaget and elementary science. *Science and Children, 8*(4), 9-15.

Chu, G.C., & Schramm, W. (1967). *Learning from television: What the research says*. Washington: National Association of Educational Broadcasters.

Cicourel, A.V. (1974). *Cognitive sociology*. New York: Free Press.

Clark, M. (1986). Predictors of scientific majors for black and white college students. *Adolescence, 21*, 205–213.

Clarkson, P. C. (1991). *Bilingualism and mathematics learning.* Geelong, Victoria, Australia: Deakin University Press.

Clawson, T., Firment, C., & Trower, T. (1981). Test anxiety: Another origin for racial bias in standardized testing. *Measurement and Evaluation in Guidance, 13*, 210–215.

Cobern, W.W. (1991). *Contextual constructivism: The impact of culture on the learning and teaching of science.* Paper presented at the Annual Meeting of the National Association for Research in Science Teaching (Lake Geneva, WI, April 7–10).

Cohen, E.G., DeAvila, E.A., Navarette, C., & Lotan, R. (1988). *Finding out/Descubrimiento implementation module.* Stanford, CA: Program for Complex Instruction.

Cohen, E.G., Intili, J.K., & Robbins, S.H. (1979). Task and authority: A sociological view of classroom management. Paper published in *Seventy-eighth Yearbook of the National Society for the Study of Education.* Chicago, IL: The Society.

Cohen, E.G., & Lotan, R.A. (1990). *Beyond the workshop: Conditions for first year implementation.* Paper presented at International Association for the Study of Cooperation in Education. Baltimore, MD, July.

Cohen, E.G. & Lotan, R.A. (1991). *Producing equal-status interaction in the heterogeneous classroom.* Stanford, CA: Program for Complex Instruction.

Cohen, E.G., Lotan, R., & Catanzarite, L. (1990). Treating status problems in the cooperative classroom. In S. Sharan (Ed.), *Cooperative learning: Theory and research* (pp. 203–229). New York: Praeger.

Cohen, E.G., Lotan, R.A., & Leechor, C. (1989). Can classrooms learn? *Sociology of Education, 62*(4), 75–94.

Cohen, M. (1984). Exemplary computer use in education. *Sigcue Bulletin, Computer Uses in Education, 18*(1), 16–19.

Cohen, P.A. (April, 1981). *Educational outcomes of tutoring: A research synthesis.* Paper presented at the Annual Meeting of the American Educational Research Association. Los Angeles, CA.

Cohen, V.B. (1983). *A learner-based evaluation of microcomputer software.* Paper presented at the annual meeting of the American Educational Research Association, Montreal, Canada.

Cole, M., & Griffin, P. (1987). *Improving science and mathematics education for minorities and women: Contextual factors in education.* Madison, WI: Wisconsin Center for Education Research.

Collette, A.T., & Chiappetta, E.L. (1989). *Science instruction in the middle and secondary schools.* Columbus, OH: Merrill.

Collins, A. (1992). Portfolios: Questions for design. *Science Scope, 15*(6), 25–27.

Combs, A.W., & Avila, D.L. (1985). *Helping relationships* (3rd. ed.). Boston: Allyn & Bacon.

Comes-Diaz, L. (1984). Content themes in group treatment with Puerto Rican women. *Social Work with Groups, 7*(3), 75–84.

Comfort, K.B. (1992). Missouri's process skills approach. *Science Scope, 15*(6), 56–57.

Connery, M.A. (April, 1990). *An interpretive study of target students and classroom interactions.* Paper presented at the Annual Meeting of the National Association for Research in Science Teaching. Atlanta, GA.

Contreras, A., & Lee, O. (1990). Differential treatment of students by middle school science teachers: Unintended cultural bias. *Science Education, 74*(3), 433–444.

Conway, J.K. (1968). Information presentation, information processing, and the sign vehicle. *AV Communication Review, 16*(4), 403–414.

Cortes, C.E. (1986). The education of language minority students: A contextual interaction model. In C.F. Leyba (Ed.), *Beyond language: Social and cultural factors in schooling language minority children* (pp. 3–33). Los Angeles, CA: Evaluation, Dissemination, and Assessment Center California State University, Los Angeles.

Costantino, G., Malgady, R.G., & Rogler, L.H. (1988). Folk hero modeling therapy for Puerto Rican adolescents. *Journal of Adolescence, 11*(2), 155–165.

Covington, M.V. (1984). The self-worth theory of achievement motivation: Findings and implications. *Elementary School Journal, 85,* 5–20.

Crandall, V.C. (1969). Sex differences in expectancy of intellectual and academic reinforcement. In C.P. Smith (Ed.), *Achievement related motives in children.* New York: Russell Sage Foundation.

Cronnel, B. (1981). *Dialect and writing: A review.* Los Alamitos, CA: Southwest Regional Laboratory for Educational Research and Development.

Culp, L., & Malone, V. (1992). Peer scores for group work. *Science Scope, 15*(6), 35–36.

Cummins, J. (1979). Linguistic interdependence and the educational development of bilingual children. *Bilingual education paper series. No. 2.* Los Angeles: National Dissemination and Assessment Center.

Cunningham, J.W., Cunningham, P.M., & Arthur, S.V. (1981). *Middle & secondary school reading.* New York: Longman.

Czerniak, C., & Chiarelott, L. (1985). Science anxiety among elementary school students: Equity issues. *Journal of Educational Equity and Leadership, 5,* 291–308.

Daintith, J., Mitchell, S., & Tootill, E. (1981). *A biographical encyclopedia of scientists.* New York: Facts on File.

Dale, E. (1946). *Audio-visual methods in teaching.* New York: Dryden.

Dansereau, D.F., Collins, K.W., McDonald, B.A., Holley, C.D., Garland, J., Diekhoff, G., & Evans, S.H. (1979). Development and evaluation of a learning strategy training program. *Journal of Educational Psychology, 71:* 64–73.

Dantonio, M., & Beisenherz, P.C. (1991). Don't just demonstrate—Motivate! *The Science Teacher, 57*(2), 27–28.

Day, W.F., & Beach, B.R. (1950). *A survey of the research literature comparing the visual and auditory presentation of information.* Air Force Technical Report 5921, Contract No. W-33-039-AC-21269. Charlottesville: University of Virginia.

DeAvila, E.A., Duncan, S.E., & Navarrete, C. (1987). *Finding out/Descubrimiento.* Northvale, NJ: Santillana.

Debus, A.G. (1968). *World who's who in science: A biographical dictionary of notable scientists from antiquity to the present.* Chicago: Marquis.

Definition and Terminology Committee of the Association for Educational Communications and Technology (1972). The field of educational technology: A statement of definition. *Audiovisual Instruction, 17*(8): 36–43.

DelGiorno, B.J. (1960). *The research team approach (ReTAL): A structure for openness.* Fairfield, CT: Fairfield Public Schools.

Dembo, M.H. (1988). *Applying educational psychology in the classroom* (3rd ed.). New York: Longman.

Dence, M. (1980). Toward defining the role of CAI: A review. *Educational Technology, 20*(11): 50–54.

Denenberg, S.A. (1988). Semantic network designs for courseware. In D.H. Jonassen (Ed.), *Instructional designs for microcomputer courseware.* Hillsdale, NJ: Lawrence Erlbaum.

Dick, W. & Carey, L. (1985). *The systematic design of instruction.* Glenview, IL: Scott, Foresman.

Dinkheller, A., Gaffney, J., & Vockell, E. (1989). *The computer in the mathematics curriculum.* Santa Cruz, CA: Mitchell.

Docking, R.A. (1978). *Anxiety, achievement, and cognitive incongruence.* Unpublished manuscript, Murdoch University, Murdoch, Western Australia.

Doran, R.L., & Hejaily, N. (1992). Hands-on evaluation: A how-to guide. *Science Scope, 15*(6), 9–11.

Dowd, F. (1990). Geography is children's literature, math, science, art and a whole world of activities. *Journal of Geography, 89*(2), 68–73.

Doyle, J. J. (1980). The order of attainment of eight projective groupings: An analysis of Piaget's spatial model. *Journal of Research in Science Teaching, 17*(1), 55–58.

Driver, R. (1989). The construction of scientific knowledge in school classrooms. In R. Millar (Ed.). *Doing science: Images of science in science education* (pp. 83–106). New York: Falmer Press.

Driver, R., & Bell, B. (1986). Students' thinking and the learning of science: A constructivist view. *School Science Review, 67*, 443–456.

Driver, R., Guesne, E., & Tiberghien, A. (1985). Children's ideas and the learning of science. In R. Driver, E. Guesne, & A. Tiberghien (Eds.), *Children's ideas in science* (pp. 1–9). Philadelphia, PA: Milton Keynes.

Driver, R., & Oldham, V. (1986). A constructivist approach to curriculum development in science. *Studies in Science Education, 13*, 105–122.

Duckworth, E. (1987). *"The having of wonderful ideas" and other essays on teaching and learning.* New York: Teachers College Press.

Dufresne, R.J., Gerace, W.J., Hardiman, P.T., & Mestre, J.P. (1992). Constraining novices to perform expertlike problem analyses: Effects on schema acquisition. *The Journal of the Learning Sciences, 2*(3), 307–331.

Dunne, J.J. (1984). *Gaming approaches in educational software: An analysis of their use and effectiveness.* (ERIC Document ED 253 207).

Dwyer, F.M. (1978). *Strategies for improving visual learning.* State College, PA: Learning Services.

Edwards, D. & Mercer, N. (1987). *Common learning.* London: Methuen.

Ehindero, O.J. (1980). The influence of two languages of instruction on students' levels of cognitive development and achievement in science. *Journal of Research in Science Teaching, 17*(4), 283–288.

Elementary Grades Task Force (1992). *It's elementary! Elementary grades task force report.* Sacramento, CA: California Department of Education.

Elliott, D. (1987). Scientific illiteracy in elementary school science textbook programmes. *Journal of Curriculum Studies, 19*(1), 73–76.

Entwistle, N. & Duckworth, D. (1977). Choice of science courses in secondary school: Trends and explanation. *Studies in Science Education, 4*, 63–82.

Erickson, F. (1984). School literacy, reasoning, and civility: An anthropologist's perspective. *Review of Educational Research, 54*(4), 525–546.

Esler, W.K. & Esler, M.K. (1993). *Teaching elementary science.* Belmont, CA: Wadsworth.

Fiber, H.R. (1987). The influence of microcomputer-based problem-solving activities on the attitudes of general mathematics students toward microcomputers. Dissertation, The Pennsylvania State University. *Dissertation Abstracts International.* 48/05A:1102.

Fields, S. (1988). Cooperative learning: A strategy for all students. *Science Scope, 12*(3), 12–14.

Finn, J.D. (1972). The emerging technology of education. In R.J. McBeath (Ed.), *Extending education through technology: Selected writings by James D. Finn.* Washington, DC: Association for Educational Communications and Technology.

Filep, R., & Schramm, W. (1970). *A study of the impact of research on utilization of media for educational purposes sponsored by NDEA Title VII 1958–1968. Final Report: Overview.* El Segundo, CA: Institute for Educational Development.

Flora, C.B. (1980). Women in Latin American fotonovelas: From Cinderella to Mata Hari. *Women's Studies International Quarterly, 3*, 95–104.

Foley, M.U. (1984). Personal computers in high school general mathematics: Effects on achievement, attitude, and attendance. Dissertation, University of Maryland. *Dissertation Abstracts International*, 46/07A: 1859.

Forgan, H.W. & Mangrum, C.T. (1989). *Teaching content area reading strategies*. Columbus, OH: Merrill.

Fradd, S. & Hallman, C.L. (1983). Implication of psychological and educational assessment and instruction of culturally and linguistically different students. *Learning Disability Quarterly, 6*(4), 468–478.

Freire, P. (1970). Cultural action and conscientization. *Harvard Educational Review, 40*(3), 452–477.

Friend, H. (1985). The effect of science and mathematics integration on selected seventh grade students' attitudes toward and achievement in science. *School Science and Mathematics, 85*(6), 453–461.

Fry, E. (1982). *Writeability*. Paper presented at the Annual Meeting of the International Reading Association, Chicago, IL.

Gaffney, K.E. (1992). Multiple assessment for multiple learning styles. *Science Scope, 15*(6), 54–55.

Gagné, R.M. (1987). *Instructional technology: Foundations*. Hillsdale, NJ: Lawrence Erlbaum.

Gagné, R.M., Briggs, L.J., & Wager, W.W. (1988). *Principles of instructional design* (3rd. ed.). New York: Holt, Rinehart & Winston.

Gallagher, J.J., & Tobin, K. (1987). Teacher management and student engagement in high school science. *Science Education, 71*(4), 535–555.

Garcia, G.E., & Pearson, P.D. (1990). *Modifying Reading Instruction to Maximize Its Effectiveness for All Students*. Technical Report No.489. Center for the Study of Reading, Illinois University, Urbana. Cambridge, MA: Bolt, Beranek & Newman.

Gascoigne, R.M. (1984). *A historical catalogue of scientists and scientific books: From the earliest times to the close of the nineteenth century*. New York: Garland.

Gay, G. (1988). Designing relevant curricula for diverse students. *Education and Urban Society, 20*(4), 327–340.

Gega, P.C. (1986). *Science in elementary education* (5th ed.). New York: John Wiley & Sons.

Gesshel-Green, H.A. (1987). The effect of interactive microcomputer graphics on student achievement and retention in second year algebra in an academic high school. Dissertation, Temple University. *Dissertation Abstracts International*, 48/02A: 326.

Gibb, H.H. (1989). A model program for gifted girls in science. *Journal for the Education of the Gifted, 12*(2), 142–155.

Gibson, J.J. (1947). *Motion picture testing and research*. Army Air Forces Psychology Program Research Report No. 7. Washington: U.S. Government Printing Office.

Gilbert, S.E., & Gay, G. (1985). Improving the success in school of poor Black children. *Phi Delta Kappan, 10*, 133–137.

Gonzales, N.A. (1989, Dec.). *Searching for insight by viewing mathematics through the eyes of Hispanic students*. Paper presented at the Mathematics Science Education Board, "Making Mathematics Work for Minorities" Region VI Workshop, San Antonio, TX.

Gooding, C.T., Kephart, M.M., Swift, P.R., Swift, J.N., & Schell, R.E. (April, 1990). *A comparative analysis of target and nontarget students*. Paper presented at the Annual Meeting of the National Association for Research in Science Teaching. Atlanta, GA.

Goodman, K. (1970). Behind the eye: What happens to reading. In *Reading process and program* (pp. 25–26). Urbana, IL: National Council of Teachers of English.

Gornick, V. (1983). *Women in science: Portraits from a world in transition*. New York: Simon & Schuster.

Granger, C.R. (1986). *Restructuring introductory biology according to the learning cycle instructional strategy*. Washington, DC: Fund for the Improvement of Postsecondary Education.

Greenberg, P.J. (1932). Competition in children: An experimental study. *American Journal of Psychology, 44*, 221–248.

Greeno, J.G. (1989). Some conjectures about number sense. In J.T. Sowder & B.P. Schappelle (Eds.), *Establishing Foundations for Research on Number Sense and Related Topics: Report of A Conference* (pp. 43–56). (Tech. Rep. of National Science Foundation, Grant No. MDR-8751373). San Diego: San Diego State University, Center for Research in Mathematics and Science Education.

Gumpert, G. (1967). Closed-circuit television in training and education. In A.E. Koenig & R.D. Hill (Eds.), *The farther vision: Educational television today*. Madison, WI: University of Wisconsin Press.

Hadfield, O.D., Martin, J.V., & Wooden, S. (1992). Mathematics anxiety and learning style of the Navajo middle school student. *School Science and Mathematics, 92*(4), 171–176.

Halpern, D.F., Hansen, C., & Riefer, D. (1990). Analogies as an aid to understanding and memory. *Journal of Educational Psychology, 82*(2),298–305.

Hamm, M., & Adams, D. (1991). Portfolio assessment: It's not just for artists anymore. *The Science Teacher, 58*(5), 18–21.

Hannafin, M.J. (1985). Keeping interactive video in perspective. In E. Miller (Ed.), *Educational media and technology yearbook 1985*. Littleton, CO: Libraries Unlimited.

Harding, S. (1991). *Whose Science? Whose Knowledge? Thinking from Women's Lives*. Ithaca, NY: Cornell University Press.

Harlen, W. (1985). Girls and primary-school science education. *Prospects: Quarterly Review of Education, 15*, 553–564.

Harris, G.A. (1985). Consideration in assessing English language performance of Native American children. *Topics in Language Disorders, 5*(4), 42–52.

Hart, D. (1977). Enlarging the American dream. *American Education, 13*(4), 10-17.

Haughton, E., & Loeb, A.L. (1965). Symmetry: The case history of a program. *Journal of Research in Science Teaching, 2*, 132–145.

Healy, J.M. (1990). *Endangered minds: Children's learning in today's culture*. New York: Simon and Schuster.

Heid, M.K. (1988). Resequencing skills and concepts in applied calculus using the computer as a tool. *Journal for Research in Mathematics Education, 19*(1): 3–25.

Herber, H.L. (1978). *Teaching reading in content areas*. Englewood Cliffs, NJ: Prentice Hall.

Herron, J.D. (1952). Piaget for chemists: Explaining what "good" students cannot understand. *Journal of Chemical Education, 53*(3), 145–150.

Herzenberg, C.L. (1986). *Women scientists from antiquity to the present: An index*. West Cornwall, CT: Locust Hill Press.

Hezel, R.T. (1980). Public broadcasting: Can it teach? *Journal of Communication, 30*: 173–178.

Hill, J.H., & Browner, C. (1982). Gender ambiguity and class stereotyping in the Mexican fotonovela. *Studies in Latin American Popular Culture, 1*, 43–64.

Hill, K.T. & Wigfield, A. (1984). Test Anxiety: A Major Educational Problem and What Can Be Done About It. *Elementary School Journal, 85*, 105–126.

Hill, O.W., Pettus, C., & Hedin, B.A. (1990). Three studies of factors affecting the attitudes of blacks and females toward the pursuit of science and science-related careers. *Journal of Research in Science Teaching, 27*(4), 289–314.

Hochel, S.S. (1983). *A position paper on teaching the acquisition of the mainstream dialect in kindergarten and elementary school*. Paper presented at the Annual Meeting of the Speech Communication Association (Washington, DC, Nov. 10–13).

Hockberg, J. (1962). Psychophysics of pictorial perception. *AV Communications Review, 10*: 22–54.

Holford, D.G., & Kempa, R.F. (1970). The effectiveness of stereoscopic viewing in the learning of spatial relationships in structural chemistry. *Journal of Research in Science Teaching, 7*, 265–270.

Horn, M. (1983). Recent Mexican scholarship on comics. *Studies in Latin American Popular Cuiture, 2*, 208–212.

Howard, A.V. (1951). *Chamber's Dictionary of Scientists.* London: Chambers.

Humphreys, B., Johnson, R.T., & Johnson, D.W. (1982). Effects of cooperative, competitive, and individualistic learning on students' achievement in science class. *Journal of Research in Science Teaching, 19*(5), 351–356.

Hunter, M. (1982). *Mastery teaching.* El Segundo, CA: TIP.

Hvitfeldt, C. (1986). Traditional culture, perceptual style, and learning: The classroom behavior of Hmong adults. *Adult Education Quarterly, 36*(2), 65–77.

Hykle, J.A. (1992). *The Effect of Laboratory Versus Lecture Science Teaching Methods: A Meta-analysis.* Paper presented at the Annual Meeting of the National Association for Research in Science Teaching (Boston, March 22).

Jacobson, W.J., & Bergman, A.B. (1987). *Science for Children: A Book for Teachers* (2nd ed.). Englewood Cliffs, NJ: Prentice-Hall.

Jacques Cattell Press (1986). *American men and women of science: Physical and biological sciences* (16th ed.). New York: R.R. Bowker.

Johnson, D.W. & Johnson, R.T. (1987). *A meta-analysis of cooperative, competitive, and invidivualistic goal structures.* Hillsdale, NJ: Erlbaum.

Johnson, D.W., & Johnson, R.T. (1994). *Learning together and alone: Cooperation, competition, and individualization.* Englewood Cliffs, NJ: Prentice-Hall.

Johnson, R.T., & Johnson, D.W. (1987). How can we put cooperative learning into practice? *The Science Teacher, 54*(6), 46–50.

Johnson, R.T., Johnson, D.W., Scott, L.E., & Ramolae, B.A. (1985). Effects of single-sex and mixed-sex cooperative interaction on science achievement and attitudes and cross-handicap and cross-sex relationships. *Journal of Research in Science Teaching, 22*(3), 207–220.

Jonassen, D.H. (1988). *Instructional designs for microcomputer courseware.* Hillsdale, NJ: Lawrence Erlbaum.

Kagan, S., Zahn, G.L., Widaman, K.F., Schwarzwald, J., & Tyrrell, G. (1985). Classroom structural bias: Impact of cooperative and competitive classroom structures on cooperative and competitive individuals and groups. In R. Slavin, S. Sharan, S. Kagan, R. Hertz-Lazarowitz, C. Webb & R. Schmuck (Eds.), *Learning to cooperate, cooperating to learn* (pp. 277–312). New York: Plenum Press.

Kahle, J.B. (1985). Minority women: Conquering both sexism and racism. In J.B. Kahle (Ed.), *Women in science*, pp. 102-123. Philadelphia, PA: Falmer.

Kahle, J.B. (ed.) (1985). *Women in Science: A Report from the Field.* Philadelphia: Falmer.

Kanis, I.B. (1991). Ninth grade lab skills: An assessment. *The Science Teacher, 58*(1), 29–33.

Karlin, M., Coffman, T.L., & Walter, G. (1969). On the fading social stereotypes: Studies in three generations of college students. *Journal of Personality and Social Psychology, 13*,1–16.

Karplus, R. (1974). *Science curriculum improvement study: Teacher's handbook.* Berkeley, CA: Lawrence Hall of Science.

Karplus, R., et. al. (1977). *Science teaching and the development of reasoning.* Berkeley, CA: Lawrence Hall of Science.

Kass-Simon, G., & Farnes, P. (1990) *Women of Science: Righting the Record.* Bloomington, IN: Indiana University Press.

Keig, P.F. (1992). *Construction of conceptual understanding in the multicultural science class-*

room. Paper presented at "Multicultural Classrooms—A Constructivist Viewpoint," Symposium conducted at San Diego State University, May 20–21, San Diego, CA.

Kessler, C., & Quinn, M.E. (1980). Bilingualism and science problem-solving ability. *Bilingual Education Paper Series, 4*, 1–30.

Kitano, M.K. (1991). A multicultural educational perspective on serving the culturally diverse gifted. *Journal for the Education of the Gifted, 15*(1), 4–19.

Knight, G.P. & Kagan, S. (1977). Acculturation of prosocial and competitive behaviors among second- and third-generation Mexican-American children. *Journal of Cross-Cultural Psychology, 8*, 273–284.

Kohlberg, L. (1980). High school democracy and education for a just society. In R.D. Mosher (Ed.), *Moral education: A first generation of research and development*. New York: Praeger.

Kolesnik, W.B. (1978). *Motivation: Understanding and influencing human behavior*. Boston, MA: Allyn & Bacon.

Koopmans, M. (1987). Formal school and task familiarity. *Cognition, 27*,109–110.

Koran, J.J., Koran, M.L., & Baker, S. (1980). Differential response cueing and feedback in the acquisition of an inductively presented biological concept. *Journal of Research in Science Teaching, 17*(2), 166–172.

Koran, M.L. (1972). Varying instructional methods to fit trainee characteristics. *AV Communications Review 20*: 135–146.

Kracjik, J.S., Simmons, P.E., & Lunetta, V.N. (1988). A research strategy for the dynamic study of students' concepts and problem-solving strategies using science software. *Journal of Research in Science Teaching, 25*(2): 147–155.

Kracjik, J.S., Simmons, P.E., & Lunetta, V.N. (1986). Improving research on computers in science learning. *Journal of Research in Science Teaching, 23*(5): 465–470.

Kren, S.R., & Huntsberger, J.P. (1977). Should science be used to teach mathematical skills? *Journal of Research in Science Teaching, 14*(6), 557–561.

Krendl, K.A., & Lieberman, D.A. (1988). Computers and learning: A review of recent research. *Journal of Educational Computing Research, 4*(4): 367–389.

Kulik, J.A., Bangert, R.L., & Williams, G.W. (1980). Effects of computer based teaching on secondary school students. *Journal of Educational Psychology, 75*(1): 19–26.

Kurtz, R., & James, R. K (1975). Implementation of an integrated program of science: A process approach and nuffield mathematics. *School Science and Mathematics, 75*(3), 258–266.

Lapp, D. & Flood, J. (1992). *Teaching reading to every child*. New York: Macmillan.

Lapp, D., Flood, J. & Farnan, N. (1989). *Content area reading and learning*. Englewood Cliffs, NJ: Prentice-Hall.

Lawson, A.E. (1975). Developing formal thought through biology teaching. *The American Biology Teacher, 37*(7), 411–420.

Lawson, A.E., Abraham, M.R., & Renner, J.W. (1989). A theory of instruction. *Monographs of the National Association for Research in Science Teaching*, Number 1. New York: John Wiley & Sons.

Lawson, A.E., & Renner, J.W. (1975). Piagetian theory and biology teaching. *The American Biology Teacher, 37*(6), 336–343.

Lazarus, B.D. (1991). Guided notes, review, and achievement of secondary students with learning disabilities in mainstream content courses. *Education and Treatment of Children, 14*(2), 112–127.

le Boterf, G. (1984). The challenge of mass education in Nicaragua. *Quaternaire Education, 65/68*, 247–266.

Lee, V.E. (1988). Identifying potential scientists and engineers: An analysis of the high school-college transition, In *Elementary and secondary education for science and engineering, grade school to grad school*, Office of Technology Assessment, U.S. Congress.

Lefkowith, E.F. (1955). *The validity of pictorial tests and their interaction with audio-visual teaching methods.* Technical Report, SDC-269-7-49. Port Washington, NY: Special Devices Center, Office of Naval Research.

Lefley, H.P. (1990). Rehabilitation in mental illness: Insights from other cultures. *Psychosocial Rehabilitation Journal, 14*(1), 5–11.

Lehman, J.R., & McDonald, J.L. (1988). Teachers' Perceptions of the Integration of Mathematics and Science. *School Science and Mathematics, 88*(8), 642–649.

Lesh, R., Landau, M., & Hamilton, E. (1983). Conceptual models and problem-solving research. In R. Lesh & M. Landau (Eds.), *Acquisition of Mathematics Concepts and Processes* (pp. 263–342). New York: Academic Press.

Levie, W.H., & Dickie, K.E. (1973). The analysis and application of media. In Travers, R.M.W. (Ed.), *Second handbook of research on teaching.* Chicago: Rand McNally.

Levie, W.H., & Levie, D. (1975). Pictorial memory processes. *AV Communication Review, 23*(1), 81–96.

Levine, M.A., & Hanes, M.L. (1976). *Dialect Usage as a Factor in Developmental Language Performance of Primary Grade School Children.* ERIC Document.

Lewis, A.C. (1990). Getting unstuck: Curriculum as a tool of reform. *Phi Delta Kappan, 71*(7), 534–538.

Liftig, I.F., Liftig, B., & Eaker, K. (1992). Making assessment work: What teachers should know before they try it. *Science Scope, 15*(6),4–8.

Lipson, A. (1984). *The Concentration Choice Study, 1978–1983.* Boston: Henry A. Murray Research Center.

Lockard, J., Abrams, P.D., & Many, W.A. (1987). *Microcomputers for Educators.* Boston, MA: Little & Brown.

Longstreet, W. (1978). *Aspects of ethnicity.* New York: Teachers College Press.

Lorsbach, A., & Tobin, K. (1992). Constructivism as a referent for science teaching. *NARST News, 34*(3), 9–11.

Lucas, T., Henze, R., & Donato, R. (1990). Promoting the success of Latino language-minority students: An exploratory study of six high schools. *Harvard Educational Review, 60*(3), 315–340.

Lucker, G., Rosenfield, D., Sikes, J., & Aronson, E. (1976). Performance in the interdependent classroom: A field study. *Journal of Education Psychology, 68*, 588–596.

Lunetta, V.N. (1972). The design and evaluation of a series of computer simulated experiments for use in high school physics. Dissertation, University of Connecticut. *Dissertation Abstracts International,* 33:2785A.

Maehr, M. (1978). Sociocultural origins of achievement motivation. In D. Bar-Tal & L. Saxe (Eds.), *Social psychology of education: Theory and practice.* Washington, DC: Hemisphere.

Manoleas, P., & Carrillo, E. (1991). A culturally syntonic approach to the field education of Latino students. *Journal of Social Work Education, 27*(2), 135–144.

Marek E.A., & Methven, S.B. (1991). Effects of the learning cycle upon student and classroom teacher performance. *Journal of Research in Science Teaching, 28*(1), 41–53.

Marrett, C.B. (1981). *Minority females in high school mathematics and science* (NIE report on the Program on Student Diversity and School Processes). Madison, WI: Wisconsin Center for Education Research.

Marshall, N. (1989). The students: Who are they and how do I reach them? In D. Lapp, J. Flood, & N. Farnan (Eds.), *Content area reading and learning: Instructional strategies.* (pp. 59–72). Englewood Cliffs, NJ: Prentice Hall.

Martinez, D. I., & Martinez, J.V. (1982). *Aspects of American Hispanic and Indian Involvement in Biomedical Research.* Bethesda, MD: Society for Advancement of Chicanos and Native Americans in Science.

Maslow, A. (1962). *Toward a psychology of being.* New York: Van Nostrand.

Mason, C.L., Kahle, J.B., & Gardner, A.L. (1991). Draw-a-scientist test: Future implications. *School Science and Mathematics, 91*(5), 193–198.

Maurer, J.F. (1981). *Concise Dictionary of Scientific Biography*. New York: Charles Scribner's Sons.

Mayer, V.J. (1990). Teaching from a global point of view. *The Science Teacher, 57*(1), 47-51.

McBride, J.W., & Silverman, F.L. (1991). Integrating elementary/middle school science and mathematics. *School Science and Mathematics, 91*(7), 285–292.

McBridge, J.W., & Silverman, F.L. (1991). Integrating elementary/middle school science and mathematics. *School Science and Mathematics, 91*(7), 285–292.

McClelland, D.C. (1965). Toward a theory of motive acquisiton. *American Psychologist, 20*, 321–333.

McCormack, A.J., & Yager, R.E. (1989). A new taxonomy of science education. *The Science Teacher, 56*(2), 47–48.

McGarry, T.P. (1986). Integrating learning for young children. *Educational Leadership, 44*(3), 64-66.

McGinnis, J.R. (1992, March). *Science teacher decision-making in multicultural classrooms*. Paper presented at the Annual Meeting of the National Association for Research in Science Teaching, Boston, MA.

McGraw-Hill (1966). *McGraw-Hill modern men of science*, vol. 1. New York: McGraw-Hill.

McGraw-Hill (1966). *McGraw-Hill modern men of science*, vol. 2. New York: McGraw-Hill.

McGraw-Hill (1980). *McGraw-Hill modern scientists and engineers*. New York: McGraw-Hill.

McNeil, J.D. (1985). *Curriculum: A Comprehensive Introduction*. Boston: Little, Brown & Co.

Mechling, K.R., & Oliver, D.L. (1983). *Handbook I. Science Teaches Basic Skills*. Washington, DC: National Science Teachers Association.

Melnik, A. (1968). Questions: An instructional-diagnostic tool. *Journal of Reading, 11*, 509.

Merrill, M.D. (1988). Applying component display theory to the design of courseware. In D.H. Jonassen (Ed.), *Instructional Designs for Microcomputer Courseware*. Hillsdale, NJ: Lawrence Erlbaum.

Merrill Publishing Co. (1987). *Focus on Physical Science*. Columbus, OH: Merrill Publishing Co.

Milson, J.L., & Ball, S.E. (1986). Enhancement of learning through integrated science and mathematics. *School Science and Mathematics, 86*(6), 489–493.

Montagu, A. (1965). *The human revolution*. New York: World Publishing.

Moran, J.B., & Boulter, W. (1992). Step by step scoring. *Science Scope, 15*(6), 46–47.

Mucha, L. (1987). *Attitudinal and achievement effects of mathematics homework games on second grade students and their parents*. (ERIC Document Reproduction Service No. ED 283698).

Mulkey, L.M., & Ellis, R.S. (1990). Social stratification and science education: A longitudinal analysis, 1981-1986, of minorities' integration into the scientific talent pool. *Journal of Research in Science Teaching, 27*(3), 205–217.

Mullis, I.V.S. & Jenkins, L.B. (1988). *The science report card elements of risk and recovery: Trends and achievement based on the 1986 national assessment*. Princeton, NJ: Educational Testing Service.

Nachmias, R., & Linn, M.C. (1987). Evaluations of science laboratory data: The role of computer-presented information. *Journal of Research in Science Teaching, 24*(5): 491–506.

Naisbitt, J. (1982). *Megatrends: Ten new directions transforming our lives*. New York: Warner Books.

National Research Council (1990). *Everybody counts: A report to the nation on the future of mathematics education*. Washington, DC: National Academy Press.

National Science Board Commission on Precollege Education in Mathematics, Science and Technology. (1983). *Educating Americans for the 21st century*. Washington, DC: National Science Foundation.

National Science Foundation. (1987). *The science and engineering pipeline*. PRA Report 67-2, 3.

National Science Teachers Association Board of Directors (1991). *An NSTA Position Statement: Multicultural Science Education*. Washington, DC: National Science Teachers Association.

Nijhof W., & Kommers, P. (1985). Cooperation in relation to cognitive controversy. In R. Slavin, S. Sharan, S. Kagan, R. Hertz-Lazarowitz, C. Webb, & R. Schmuck (Eds.), *Learning to cooperate, cooperating to learn* (pp. 126–133). New York: Plenum Press.

Norman, D., Gentner, S., & Stevens, A.L. (1976). Comments on learning schemata and memory representation. In D. Klahr (Ed.), *Cognition and instruction*. Hillsdale, NJ: Lawrence Erlbaum.

Nott, L., Reeve, C., & Reeve, R. (1992). Scoring rubrics: An assessment option. *Science Scope, 15*(6), 44–45.

Novak, J. (1991). Clarify with concept maps: A tool for students and teachers alike. *The Science Teacher, 58*(7), 45–49.

Odubunmi, O. & Balogun, T.A. (1991). The effect of laboratory and lecture teaching methods on cognitive achievement in integrated science. *Journal of Research in Science Teaching, 28*(3), 213–224.

Ogbu, J.U. (1992). Understanding cultural diversity and learning. *Educational Researcher, 21*(8), 5–14.

Okebukola, P.A. (1986). The influence of preferred learning styles on cooperative learning in science. *Science Education, 70*(5), 509–517.

Okebukola, P.A. (1985). The relative effectiveness of cooperative and competitive interaction techniques in strengthening students' performance in science classes. *Science Education, 69*(4), 501–509.

Okebukola, P.A., & Ogunniyi, M.B. (1984). Cooperative, competitive, and individualistic science laboratory interaction patterns—effects of students' achievement and acquisition of practical skills. *Journal of Research in Science Teaching, 21*(9), 875–884.

Okebukola, P.A., & Ogunniyi, M.B. (1986). Effects of teachers' verbal exposition on students' level of class participation and achievement in biology. *Science Education, 70*(1), 45–51.

Olion, L., & Gillis-Olion, M. (1984). Assessing culturally diverse exceptional children. *Early Child Development and Care, 15*, 203–232.

Olsen, J.R., & Bass, V.B. (1982). The application of performance technology in the military 1960–1980. *Performance and Instruction, 21*(6): 32–36.

Olson, D.R. (1986). The cognitive consequences of literacy. *Canadian Psychology, 27*(2),109–121.

Olson, D.R., & Torrance, N. (1987). Language, literacy, and mental states. *Discourse Processes,10*, 157–167.

Oram, R.F. (1986). *Biology living systems*. Columbus, OH: Merrill.

Ornstein, A.C., & Hunkins, F.P. (1988). *Curriculum: Foundations, principles,and issues*. Englewood Cliffs, NJ: Prentice Hall.

Ornstein-Galicia, J.L., & Penfield, J. (1981). A problem-solving model for integrating science and language in bilingual/bicultural education. *Bilingual Education Paper Series, 5*, 1–22.

Ortiz, A.A., & Maldonado-Colon, E. (1986). Recognizing learning disabilities in bilingual children: How to lessen inappropriate referrals of language minority students to special education. *Journal of Reading, Writing, and Learning Disabilities International, 2*(1), 43–56.

Ortiz, F.I. (1988). Hispanic-American children's experiences in classrooms: A comparison between Hispanic and Non-Hispanic children. In L. Weis. (Ed.), *Class, race, and gender in American education* (pp. 63-85). New York: SUNY Press.

Ostlund, K.L. (1992). Sizing up social skills. *Science Scope, 15*(6), 31–33.

Pallrand, G.J., & Seeber, F. (1984). Spatial ability and achievement in introductory physics. *Journal of Research in Science Teaching, 15*, 507–516.

Pang, V.O. (1988). Ethnic prejudice: Still alive and hurtful. *Harvard Educational Review, 58*(3), 375–379.

Parakh, J.S. (1967). *A study of relationships among teacher behavior, pupil behavior, and pupil characteristics in high school biology classes: Final report.* Bellinghan: Western Washington State University.

Patchen, M. (1982). *Black-White contact in schools: Its social and academic effects.* West LaFayette, IN: Purdue University Press.

Pearson, W., & Bechtel, H.K. (1989). *Blacks, science, and American education.* New Brunswick, NJ: Rutgers University Press.

Pedersen, J.E. (1992). The effects of a cooperative controvery, presented as an STS issue,on achievement and anxiety in secondary science. *School Science and Mathematics, 92*(7), 374–380.

Piaget, J. (1964). Cognitive development in children: Development and learning. *Journal of Research in Science Teaching, 2*, 176–186.

Pitman, M.A. (1989). *Culture acquisition: A holistic approach to human learning.* New York: Praeger.

Pizzini, E.L., Bell, S.A., & Shepardson, D.S. (1990). Rethinking thinking in the science classroom. *The Science Teacher, 55*(9), 22–25.

Pogge, A.F., & Lunetta, V.N. (1987) Spreadsheets answer "What If. . . ?" *The Science Teacher, 54*(8): 46–49.

Pollard, R.J. (1992). *Using instructional strategies for conceptual change.* Paper presented at the National Association of Research in Science Teaching. Boston, MA, March 20–25.

Premack, D. (1965). Reinforcement theory. In D. Levine (Ed.), *Nebraska Symposium on Motivation.* Lincoln, NB: University of Nebraska Press.

Purser, R., & Renner, J. (1983). Results of two tenth-grade biology teaching procedures. *Science Education, 67*(1), 85–98.

Raizen, S.A. (1991). The state of science education. In S.K. Majumdar, L.M. Rosenfeld, P.A. Rubba, E.W. Miller & R.F. Schmalz (Eds.), *Science education in the United States: Issues, crises and priorities* (pp. 25–45). Phillipsburg, NJ: The Pennsylvania Academy of Science.

Rakow, S.J. (1992). Assessment: A driving force. *Science Scope, 15*(6), 3.

Ramirez, M. & Castaneda, A. (1974). *Cognitive strategy research: Educational applications.* New York: Springer-Verlag.

Ramsey, J. (1989). A curriculum framework for community-based STS issue instruction. *Education and Urban Society, 22*(1), 40–53.

Ramsey, J.M., Hungerford, H.R., & Volk, T.L. (1990). Analyzing the Issues of STS. *The Science Teacher, 57*(3), 60–63.

Reed, M. (1991). Videodiscs help American Indians learn English and study heritage. *T.H.E. (Technological Horizons in Education) Journal, 19*(3), 96–97.

Reed, S.K. (1988). *Cognitive theory and applications.* Pacific Grove, CA: Brooks/Cole.

Renner, J.W., & Lawson, A.E. (1973). Promoting intellectual development through science teaching. *The Physics Teacher, 6*, 273–276.

Resnick, L.B. (1987). *Education and learning to think.* Washington, DC: National Academy Press.

Rhodes, R.W. (1988). Holistic teaching/learning for Native-American students. *Journal of American-Indian Education, 27*(2), 21–29.

Rhoton, J. (1990). An investigation of science-technology-society education perceptions of secondary science teachers in Tennessee. *School Science and Mathematics, 90*(5), 383–395.

Rigney, J. (1978). Learning strategies: A theoretical perspective. In H.F. O'Neil (Ed.), *Learning strategies*. New York: Academic Press.

Riley, J.P. (1986). The effects of teachers' wait-time and knowledge comprehension questioning on science achievement. *Journal of Research in Science Teaching, 23*(4), 335–342.

Roblyer, M.D. (1985). *Measuring the impact of computers in instruction: A non-technical review of research for educators.* Washington, DC: Association for Educational Data Systems.

Rodriguez, I., & Bethel, L.J. (1983). An inquiry approach to science/language teaching. *Journal of Research in Science Teaching, 20,* 291–296.

Roehler, L.R., & Duffy, G.G. (1989). The content area teacher's instructional role: A cognitive mediational view. In D. Lapp, J. Flood & N. Farnan (Eds.). *Content area reading and learning: Instructional strategies* (pp. 115–122). Englewood Cliffs, NJ: Prentice Hall.

Rogers, C.R. (1983). *Freedom to learn for the 80's.* Columbus, OH: Merrill.

Ronan, C.A. (1982). *Science: Its history and development among the world's cultures.* New York: Hamlyn Publishing.

Roschelle, J. (1992). Learning by collaborating: Convergent conceptual change. *The Journal of the Learning Sciences, 2*(3), 235–276.

Rosenthal, D.B. (1990). Warming up to STS. *The Science Teacher, 54*(9), 28–32.

Roth, W.M. (1992). Bridging the gap between school and real life: Toward an integration of science, mathematics, and technology in the context of authentic practice. *School Science and Mathematics, 92*(6), 307–317.

Roth, W.M. (1990). *Collaboration and constructivism in the science classroom.* Paper presented at the Annual Meeting of the American Educational Research Association (Boston, MA, April 16–20).

Roth, W.M. (1992). Dynamic evaluation. *Science Scope, 15*(6), 37–40.

Roth, W.M. & Bowen, M. (1993). The unfolding vee. *Science Scope, 16*(5), 28–32.

Roth, W.M., & Verechaka, G. (1993). Plotting a course with vee maps. *Science and Children, 30*(4), 24–27.

Rowe, M.B. (1974). Wait-time and rewards as instructional variables, their influence on language, logic, and fate control: Part I, Wait-time. *Journal of Research in Science Teaching, 11*(2), 81–91.

Rowe, M.B. (1974). Relation of wait-time and rewards to the development of language, logic, and fate control. Part II, Rewards. *Journal of Research in Science Teaching, 11*(4): 291.

Rowe, M.B. (1983). What can science educators teach chemists about teaching chemistry? A symposium: Getting chemistry off the killer course list. *Journal of Chemical Education, 60*(11), 954–956.

Rubba, P.A., & Anderson, H. (1978). Development of an instrument to assess secondary students' understanding of the nature of scientific knowledge. *Science Education, 62*(4), 449–458.

Rubba, P.A., & Wiesenmayer, R.L. (1991). Integrating STS into school science. In S.K. Majumdar, L.M. Rosenfeld, P.A. Rubba, E.W. Miller, & R.F. Schmalz (Eds.). *Science education in the United States: Issues, crises and priorities.* Easton, PA: The Pennsylvania Academy of Science.

Rubin, R.L., & Norman, J.T. (1989). *A comparison of the effect of a systematic modeling approach and the learning cycle approach on the achievement of integrated science process skills of urban middle school students.* Paper presented at the Annual Meetings of the National Association for Research in Science Teaching (San Francisco, March 30–April 1).

Rumelhart, D.E., & Ortony, A. (1977). The representation of knowledge in memory. In R.C. Anderson, R.J. Spiro, & W.E. Montague (Eds.), *Schooling and the acquisition of knowledge*. Hillsdale, NJ: Lawrence Erlbaum.

Rutherford, F.J. (1991). Project 2061: An agenda for achieving national scientific literacy. In S.K. Majumdar, L.M. Rosenfeld, P.A. Rubba, E.W. Miller, & R.F. Schmalz (Eds.). *Science Education in the United States: Issues, crises and priorities*. Easton, PA: The Pennsylvania Academy of Science.

Rutherford, F.J., & Ahlgren, A. (1988). Rethinking the science curriculum. In R.S. Brandt (Ed.) *Content of the curriculum: 1988 ASCD yearbook of the association for supervision and curriculum development*. New York: Jarboe.

Sadker, M.P., & Sadker, D.M. (1979). *Beyond pictures and pronouns: Sexism in teacher education textbooks*. Washington, DC: Women's Educational Equity Act Program of US Department of Health, Education, and Welfare.

Saettler, P. (1968). *A history of instructional technology*. New York: McGraw-Hill.

Sammons, V.O. (1990). *Blacks in science and medicine*. New York: Hemisphere.

Saunders, W.L. (1992). The constructivist perspective: Implications and teaching strategies for science. *School Science and Mathematics, 92*(3), 136–141.

Saville-Troike, M. (1978). *A Guide to Culture in the Classroom*. Rosslyn, VA: National Clearinghouse for Bilingual Education.

Scarnati, J.T., & Weller, C.J. (1992). The write stuff. *Science and Children, 29*(4), 28–29.

Schallert, D.L., & Rose, N.L. (1989). The role of reading in content area instruction. In D. Lapp, J. Flood, & N. Farnan (Eds.), *Content area reading and learning: Instructional strategies* (pp. 25-35). Englewood Cliffs, NJ: Prentice Hall.

Scharmann, L.C., & McLellan, H. (1992). Enhancing science-technology-society (STS) instruction: An examination of teacher goal orientations. *School Science and Mathematics, 92*(5), 249–252.

Schick, F.L., & Schick, R. (1991). *Statistical handbook on US Hispanics*. Phoenix, AZ: Oryx Press.

Schimmel, B.J. (1986). *A meta-analysis of feedback to learners in computerized and programmed instruction*. Paper presented at the annual meeting of the American Educational Research Association, Montreal (ERIC Document 233 708).

Schimmel, B.J. (1988). Providing meaningful feedback in courseware. In D.H. Jonassen (Ed.), *Instructional designs for microcomputer courseware* (pp. 183–195). Hillsdale, NJ: Lawrence Erlbaum.

Schlenker, R.M. (1983). The molar concept: A Piagetian-oriented learning cycle. *Journal of College Science Teaching, 12*(6), 431–434.

Sevenair, J.P., & Carmichael, J.W. (1988). A high school chemistry prep course designed to increase the number of Black Americans in science-related careers. *Journal of College Science Teaching, 18*(1), 51–54.

Severin, W. (1967). Another look at cue summation. *AV Communication Review, 15*(3), 233–245.

Seymour, L.A., Padberg, L.F., Bingman, R.M., & Koutrieck, P.G. (1974). A successful inquiry methodology. *The American Biology Teacher, 36*(9), 348–353.

Shade, B.J. (1982). Afro-American cognitive style: A variable in school success. *Review of Educational Research, 52*, 219–244.

Shann, M.H. (1977). Evaluation of an interdisciplinary, problem solving curriculum in elementary science and mathematics, *Science Education, 61*(4), 491–502.

Shapiro, K.R. (1975). An overview of problems encountered in aptitude treatment interaction (ATI) research for instruction. *AV Communications Review 23*: 227–241.

Shapiro, S.B. (1972). Developing models by 'unpacking' confluent education, Occasional Paper No. 12, *Development and research in confluent education*. Santa Barbara, CA: University of California.

Sharan, S. (1985). Cooperative learning and the multiethnic classroom. In R. Slavin, S. Sharan, S. Kagan, R. Hertz-Lazarowitz, C. Webb, & R. Schmuck (Eds.), *Learning to cooperate, cooperating to learn* (pp. 255–276). New York: Plenum Press.

Shick, J. (1990). Textbook tests. *The Science Teacher, 57*(6), 33–39.

Showalter, V. (1974). Program objectives and scientific literacy. *Prism II, 2*(4), 1–3,6–8.

Shrigley, R.L. (1974). The attitude of preservice teachers toward science. *School Science and Mathematics, 74*, 243–250.

Sieber, J., O'Neil, H., & Tobias, S. (1977). *Anxiety, learning, and instruction.* Hillsdale, NJ: Lawrence Erlbaum.

Silberman, R.G., & Zipp, A.P. (1986). The science and magic of chemistry: A learning cycle laboratory on oxidation-reduction. *Journal of Chemical Education, 63*(12), 1098.

Simpson, E.J. (1972). *The classification of educational objectives: Psychomotor domain.* Urbana, IL: University of Illinois Press.

Singer, H., & Donlan, D. (1990). *Reading and learning from text.* Hillsdale, NJ: Lawrence Erlbaum.

Singer, H., & Simonsen, S. (1989). Comprehension and instruction in learning from a text. In D. Lapp, J. Flood, & N. Farnan (Eds.), *Content area reading and learning: Instructional strategies.* (pp. 25–35). Englewood Cliffs, NJ: Prentice Hall.

Slavin, R.E. (1982). *Cooperative learning: Student teams.* Washington, DC: National Educational Association.

Sleeter, C.E., & Grant, C.A. (1987). An analysis of multicultural education in the United States. *Harvard Educational Review, 57*(4), 421–444.

Slesnick, I.L., Balzer, L., McCormack, A.J., Newton, D.E., & Rasmussen, F.A. (1985). *Scott Foresman biology.* Glenview, IL: Scott Foresman.

Sless, D. (1983). Visual literacy: A failed opportunity. *ECTJ, 32*(4), 224-228.

Sloyer, C., & Smith, L.H. (1986). Applied mathematics via student-centered computer graphics. *The Journal of Computers in Mathematics and Science Teaching,* Spring: 17–20.

Smith, T.R., & Smith, S.W. (1992). *It's elementary! Elementary grades task force report.* Sacramento, CA: California Department of Education.

Smith, W.S. (1983). Science careers in the classroom. *Science and Children, 20*(5), 19–29.

Smith, W.S., Frazier, N.I., Ward, S., & Webb, W. (1983). Early adolescent girls' and boys' learning of a spatial visualization skill—Replications. *Science Education, 67*(2), 239–243.

Solomon, J. (1989). The social construction of school science. In R. Millar (Ed.), *Doing science: Images of science in science education* (pp. 126-136). New York: Falmer Press.

Sosa, A.S. (1986). *Valued youth partnership program: Dropout prevention through cross-age tutoring.* San Antonio, TX: Intercultural Development Research Association.

Souviney, R.J. (1981). *Teaching and learning mathematics in the community schools of Papua New Guinea,* Indigenous Mathematics Project Working Paper, No. 20, Department of Education, PNG.

Sowder, J.T. (1991, Aug.). *Considerations for research on computation: Borrowing from others.* Paper presented at the Gwinganna Computation Conference, Gold Coast, Australia.

Spitler, H. R. (1989). *The syntonic principle, its relation to health and ocular problems.* Eaton, OH: College of Syntonic Optometry.

Spring, D. (1950). Awareness of racial differences of preschool children in Hawaii. *Genetic Psychology Monographs, 41*, 214–270.

Stahl, R.J. (1992, Mar.). *Using the information-constructivist (IC) perspective to guide curricular and instructional decisions toward attaining desired student outcomes of science education.* Paper presented at the Annual Meeting of the National Association for Research in Science Teaching, Boston, MA.

Stahl, R.J., Hunt, B.S., & Matiya, J.C. (1980). Humanism and behaviorism: Is there really a difference?, *Educational Leadership, 38*(3), 230–231.

Stasson, M.F., Kameda, T., Parks, C.D., Zimmerman, S.K., & David, J.H. (1991). Effects of assigned group consensus requirement on group problem solving and group members' learning. *Social Psychology Quarterly, 54*(1), 25–35.

Staver, J.R. (1991). Why is science basic in elementary school? In S.K. Majumdar, L.M. Rosenfeld, P.A. Rubba, E.W. Miller, & R.F. Schmalz (Eds.),*Science education in the United States: Issues, crises and priorities,* pp. 117–126. Easton, PA: The Pennsylvania Academy of Sciences.

Steen, E.B. (1971). *Dictionary of biology.* New York: Barnes & Noble.

Steen, L.A. (1990). *On the shoulders of giants: New approaches to numeracy.* Washington, DC: National Academy Press.

Stewart, D.A., & Benson, G. (1988). Dual cultural negligence: The education of Black deaf children. *Journal of Multicultural Counseling and Development, 16*(3), 98–109.

Superka, D.P., Ahrens, C., Hedstrom, J., Ford, L.J., & Johnson, P.L. (1976). *Values education sourcebook.* Boulder, CO: Social Science Education Consortium.

Suzuki, B.H. (1984). Curriculum transformation for multicultural education. *Education and Urban Society, 16*(3), 294–322.

Tanner, T. (1987). Environmental education for citizen action. *Science through science, technology and society reporter.* University Park, PA: The Pennsylvania State University.

Tanner, L.N., & Lindgren, H.C. (1971). *Classroom teaching and learning: A mental health approach.* New York: Holt, Rinehart and Winston.

Taton, R. (Ed.) (1963). *History of science: Ancient and medieval science from the beginnings to 1450.* New York: Basic Books.

Taylor, R.P. (1980). *The computer in the school: Tutor, tool, tutee.* New York: Teachers College Press.

Temple, R.K.G. (1986). *China: Land of discovery.* Wellingborough, UK: Patrick Stephens.

Thompson, C.L., & Shrigley, R.L. (1986). What research says: Revising the Science Attitude Scale. *School Science and Mathematics, 86*(4), 331–343.

Thurgood, D.H., & Weinman, J.M. (1991). *Summary report 1990: Doctorate recipients from United States universities.* Washington, DC: National Academy Press.

Tippins, D.J., & Dana, N.F. (1992). Culturally relevant alternative assessment. *Science Scope, 15*(6), 50–53.

Tobias, S. (1980). *Paths to programs for intervention: Math anxiety, math avoidance, and reentry mathematics.* Washington, DC: Institute for the Study of Anxiety in Learning.

Tobias, S. (1990). *They're not dumb, they're different: Stalking the second tier.* Tucson, AZ: Research Corporation—A Foundation for the Advancement of Science.

Tobin, K.G. (1984). Effects of extended wait-time on discourse characteristics and achievement in middle school grades. *Journal of Research in Science Teaching, 21*(8), 779.

Tobin, K.G. (1989). Learning in science classrooms. In *Curriculum development for the year 2000* (pp. 25–38). Colorado Springs, CO: BSCS.

Tobin, K.G. (1990). Research on science laboratory activities: In pursuit of better questions and answers to improve learning. *School Science and Mathematics, 90*(5), 403–418.

Tobin, K.G., & Capie, W. (1981). *Wait-time and learning in science.* Paper presented at the annual meeting of the Association for Educators of Teachers of Science, Washington, DC.

Tobin, K.G., & Gallagher, J.J. (1987). The role of target students in the science classroom. *Journal of Research in Science Teaching, 24*(1), 61–75.

Tobin, K., Tippins, D., & Hook, K. (1992, March). *Critical reform of the science curriculum: A journey from objectivism to constructivism.* Paper presented at the annual meeting of the National Association for Research in Science Teaching, Boston, MA.

"Total Enrollment in Institutions of Higher Education, by Race or Ethnicity of Student and by State and Territory: Fall 1988." In *Digest of Educational Statistics*, 1990. Washington, DC: National Center for Educational Statistics. p. 201

Towell, R. (1991). Innovation and feedback in a self-access learning project in modern languages. *British Journal of Educational Technology, 22*(2), 119–128.

Tyler, F.B., Dhawan, N., & Sinha, Y. (1989). Cultural contributions to constructing locus-of-control attributions. *Genetic, Social, and General Psychology Monographs, 115*(2), 207–220.

Useem, E.L. (1990, April). *Social class and ability group placement in mathematics in the transition to seventh grade: The role of parental involvement.* Paper presented at the Annual Meeting of the American Educational Research Association, Boston, MA.

Vacca, R.T., & Vacca, J.L. (1989). *Content area reading.* Glenview, IL: Scott Foresman.

Valle, R. (1986). Cross-cultural competence in minority communities: A curriculum implementation strategy. In M.R. Miranda & H.H.L. Kitano (Eds.)., *Mental health research and practice in minority communities: Development of culturally sensitive training programs* (pp. 29–49). Rockville, MD: National Institute of Mental Health.

Valle, R. (1989). Cultural and ethnic issues in Alzheimer's disease family research. In E. Light & B.D. Lebowitz (Eds.), *Alzheimer's disease treatment and family stress: Directions for research* (pp. 122–153). Rockville, MD: National Institute of Mental Health.

Valle, R. (1978). The development of a polycultural social policy curriculum from the Latino perspective. In D.G. Norton (Ed.), *The dual perspective: Inclusion of ethnic minority content in the social work curriculum* (pp. 58–79). New York: Council on Social Work Education.

Valle, R. (1990). The Latino/Hispanic family and the elderly: Approaches to cross-cultural curriculum design in the health professions. In U.S. Department of Health & Human Services (Ed.), *Minority aging: Essential curricula content for selected health and allied health professions* (pp. 433–452). Washington, DC: U.S. Department of Health & Human Services.

Van Otten, G.A., & Tsutsui, S. (1983). Geocentrism and Indian education. *Journal of American-Indian Education, 22*(2), 23–27.

Van Sertima, I.V. (1986). Blacks in science: Ancient and modern. New Brunswick, CT: *Journal of African Civilizations.*

VanTassel-Baska, J., Patton, J., & Prillaman, D. (1989). Disadvantaged gifted learners at risk for educational attention. *Focus on Exceptional Children, 22*(3), 1–15.

Vargas, E.M., & Alvarez, H.J. (1992). Mapping out students' abilities. *Science Scope, 15*(6), 41–43.

Verhoeven, L.T. (1987). Literacy in a second language context: Teaching immigrant children to read. *Educational Review, 39*(3), 245–261.

Vockell, E., & Schwartz, E. (1988). *The computer in the classroom.* Santa Cruz, CA: Mitchell.

Voss, B.E. (1980). Objectives for middle school science. *School Science and Mathematics, 80*(7), 573–576.

Vygotsky, L.S. (1978). *Mind in society: The Development of Higher Psychological Processes* (M. Cole, V. John-Steiner, S. Scribner, E. Souberman, Eds.). Cambridge, MA: Harvard University Press.

Wadsworth, B.J. (1978). *Piaget for the Classroom Teacher.* New York: Longman.

Wallace, J. (1986). *Social Interaction within Second Year Groups Doing Practical Science,* Unpublished master's thesis, University of Oxford, England.

Ware, N., & Steckler, N. (1983). Choosing a science major: The experience of women and men. *Women's Studies Quarterly, 11*(2), 8–15.

Watson, S.B. (1991). Cooperative learning and group educational modules: Effects on cognitive achievement of high school biology students. *Journal of Research in Science Teaching, 28*(2), 141–146.

Watts, S. (1986). Science education for a multicultural society. In R.K. Arora & C.G. Duncan (Eds.), *Multicultural education: Towards good practice* (pp. 135-160). London: Routledge & Kegan Paul.

Weatherford, J. (1988). *Indian Givers: How the Indians of the Americas Transformed the World.* New York: Fawcett Columbine.

Weiner, B. (1980). The role of affect in rational (attributional) approaches to human motivation. *Educational Researcher, 9,* 4–11.

Weisner, T.S., Gallimore, R., & Jordan, C. (1988). Unpackaging cultural effects on classroom learning: Native Hawaiian peer assistance and child-generated activity. *Anthropology and Education Quarterly, 19*(4), 327–353.

Weiss, I.S. (1987). *Report of the 1985-86 National Survey of Science and Mathematics Education.* National Science Foundation. SPE-8317070. Washington, DC: U.S. Government Printing Office.

Welton, D.A., & Mallan, J. T. (1992). *Children and Their World: Strategies for Teaching Social Studies.* Boston: Houghton Mifflin.

Wertsch, J.V., & Toma, C. (1991). *Discourse and Learning in the Classroom: A Sociocultural Approach.* Presentation made at the University of Georgia Visiting Lecturer Series on Constructivism in Education, April 2, Athens, Georgia.

Wheatley, G.H. (1991). Constructivist perspectives on science and mathematics learning. *Science Education, 75*(1), 9–21.

Williams, H., Fast, J., Berestiansky, J., Turner, C.W., & Debreuil, L.(1979). Designing science lessons to promote cognitive growth. *The Science Teacher, 46,* 26–29.

Williams, T.I. (1982). *A Biographical Dictionary of Scientists.* (3rd ed.). New York: John Wiley.

Winner, A.A., & Holloway, R.E. (1983). Technology integration for a new curriculum. *Journal of Computers in Mathematics and Science Teaching, 2*(4), 30–35.

Wittrock, M.C. (1978). The cognitive movement in instruction. *Educational Psychologist,* 15:15–29.

Woerner, J.J., Rivers, R.H., & Vockell, E.L. (1991). *The computer in the science curriculum.* Santa Cruz, CA: Mitchell.

Wolfinger, D.M. (1984). *Teaching science in the elementary school: Content, process, and attitude.* Boston: Little, Brown and Co.

Woodward, J., & Noell, J. (1991). Science instruction at the secondary level: Implications for students with learning disabilities. *Journal of Learning Disabilities, 24*(5), 277–284.

Woolfolk, A.E. (1993). *Educational Psychology* (5th ed.). Boston, MA: Allyn and Bacon.

Wraga, W.G., & Hlebowitsh, P.S. (1991). STS education and the curriculum field. *School Science and Mathematics, 91*(2), 54–59.

Wright, E.L. (1981). Fifteen simple discrepant events that teach science principles and concepts. *School Science and Mathematics, 81*(7), 575–580.

Yager, R.E. (1987). Assess all five domains of science. *The Science Teacher, 54*(7), 33–37.

Yager, R.E. (1990). STS: Thinking over the years. *The Science Teacher, 57*(3), 52–55.

Yost, E. (1943). *American Women of Science.* Philadelphia: J.B. Lippincott.

Young, S.L. (1990). IDEAS. *Arithmetic Teacher, 38*(2), 24–34.

Zakaluk, B.L., Samuels, S.J. (Eds.). (1988). *Readability: Its past, present, and future.* Newark, DE: International Reading Association.

INDEX